# IBM-PC 8088 MACRO
## Assembler Programming

# IBM-PC 8088 MACRO Assembler Programming

### Dan Rollins
**Software Consultant**

**Macmillan Publishing Company**
New York
**Collier Macmillan Publishers**
London

Macmillan Publishing Company
866 Third Avenue, New York, New York 10022

Collier Macmillan Canada, Inc.

*IBM, IBM Personal Computer, PC-DOS,* and *IBM MACRO Assembler*
are trademarks of International Business Machines Corporation.
*Microsoft* and *MS-DOS* are trademarks of Microsoft Corporation.
*Motorola* is a trademark of Motorola, Inc.
*Intel* and *iAPX* are trademarks of the Intel Corporation.

Library of Congress Cataloging in Publication Data


Rollins, Dan.
    IBM-PC  8088 MACRO Assembler programming.

    Includes index.
    1. IBM Personal Computer--Programming.   2. Intel
8088 (Microprocessor)--Programming.   3. Assembler
language (Computer program language)   I. Title.
II. Title: IBM-PC  8088 MACRO Assembler programming.
QA76.8.I2594R64      1985        001.64'2        84-19461
ISBN 0-02-403210-7


Printing:   2 3 4 5 6 7 8         Year: 5 6 7 8 9 0 1 2

ISBN  0-02-403210-7

This book is dedicated to
Jane,
who makes it all worthwhile.

# Preface

IBM's stamp of approval on both the 8088 microprocessor and the MS-DOS operating system indicates that these products are both state-of-the-art and upwardly compatible with future technologies. The 8088 microprocessor and MS-DOS (and their descendants) are sure to be around for a while. Learning about these tools now will prove to be advantageous in the future.

Assembly language is an excellent second language for several reasons. It is by far the fastest, most flexible, and most compact of all programming languages. It shows how and why higher-level languages operate. It gives access to features of a machine that are inaccessible with other languages.

Assembly language is the most basic computer language. Paradoxically, it is also the most complex computer language. This book attempts to unravel the mysteries of assembly language programming on the IBM PC. Even programmers familiar with other assembly languages find themselves perplexed by a host of entirely new concepts associated with the 8088—the segmented memory scheme, doubly indexed memory variables, enhanced arithmetic operations, and string manipulation. This book covers these areas in detail, taking up where the IBM manuals and other books leave off. It is meant to be both a tutorial work and a complete desk reference for 8088 assembly language programming.

The book addresses the most common needs of the IBM-PC assembly language programmer, placing emphasis on interfacing with high-level languages, modular and structured program design, and the use of assembly language in graphics and other screen-oriented applications. One of the difficulties of learning assembly language is the shortage of example listings. This book contains more than 30 program listings. Also, an appendix contains program *templates*—outlines of the most often needed types of programs.

For programmers who are just starting to use assembly language, Chapter 1 provides an introduction to the fundamental premises of this low-level language, including numbering systems and binary operations.

Chapter 2 defines the pieces of the 8088 assembly language puzzle. It discusses the registers and status flags, as well as the powerful addressing modes of the 8088 microprocessor.

Chapter 3 introduces the 8088 instruction set. It is divided into six groups for easier digestion. Each instruction is mentioned in the book. The most frequently used and the most complex instructions are covered in detail, with many examples of their use in various algorithms.

Chapter 4 discusses the tools of the assembly language programmer—the assembler, the linker, and the debugging utility. We write a first program and change it, step by step, from source code into an executable program. The rest of the chapter describes the pseudo-ops that give the IBM-PC MACRO Assembler its power and flexibility.

Chapter 5 is devoted to the services provided by PC-DOS and the IBM-PC's Basic Input and Output System (BIOS). This chapter shows how to use these tools in order to control the video screen and to read and write disk files. The advanced concepts of background processes and DOS 2.00 I/O redirection and device drivers are explained. Example programs are used to show how to use these services in real applications. We begin building a "toolbox" of assembly language subroutines to simplify future programming tasks.

Chapter 6 provides an in-depth look at one of the most powerful features of the MACRO Assembler—its macro capability. Starting with some simple tools, we build up to a complete macro library that simplifies and speeds up program development.

One of the most important reasons for learning assembly language is to enhance and extend the functions available in high-level languages. Chapter 7 crosses the bridge between assembly language and the high-level languages BASIC and Pascal. It explains the standard interfaces between all of the Microsoft languages, focusing on the interface for interpretive and compiled BASIC and IBM Pascal.

Chapters 8 and 9 provide a comprehensive explanation on how to use assembly language to access the video screen. Chapter 8 discusses how to access the screen, addressing the features and problems associated with each of the display modes. Special emphasis is placed on graphics; the example programs for this chapter include line, circle, and shape-drawing subroutines. Chapter 9 describes the hardware that drives the video display and explains how to initialize and use the undocumented 16-color, low-resolution graphics mode available on the IBM PC.

The appendices include a summary of the 8088 instruction set, a hex to decimal and decimal to hex conversion table, a decimal/ASCII/hex/binary cross-reference chart, a set of templates to use as outlines for developing programs, and a one-stop summary of the PC-DOS and ROM-BIOS interrupt service routines.

Although this book assumes no previous assembly language experience, at least a general knowledge of programming, ideally in BASIC, is a must. The text moves quickly into advanced assembly language concepts. Because of the scope of the subject matter, there are times when reference is made to a programming concept or tool that has not yet been introduced. The author has made every effort to minimize these forward references. However, you'll get the most out of this text by reading it *iteratively*. In the first reading, you will absorb the fundamental concepts. In subsequent readings, the more advanced topics will become clear. For instance, parts of Chapters 3 and 4 explain quirks of 8088 programming that are not necessary to know when you are starting out. You may choose to skim through parts of these chapters and refer back to them later.

Some texts spend so much time in the preliminary discussion that there is no coverage of advanced programming practices. These books are often inadequate for reference purposes. Other books contain so little introductory and tutorial material that they are useful only for reference, after you have learned assembly language. In this book, the author covers a middle ground. Chapters that seem to contain too much information may seem overwhelming at first, but they will become a valuable reference as you begin writing serious application programs.

## SUPPLEMENTARY REFERENCES

In order to get the most out of this book, you should have an IBM PC, an IBM XT, or a PC-compatible computer. You should have the IBM MACRO Assembler and the Disk Operating System software and documentation. Additionally, the Technical Reference Manual, though not required, is very useful; it provides the detailed technical information that is needed to write hardware-specific applications.

The Intel Corporation publishes several books that provide technical information about the 8086/8088 microprocessor. In particular, the *8086 Family User's Manual and Numeric Supplement* and the *iAPX 88 Book* are excellent references. Although it's not specifically about the IBM—PC MACRO assembler, *An Introduction to ASM86* is a useful second source of general information about programming the 8088.

## ACKNOWLEDGMENTS

I wish to express my gratitude to a number of persons who have helped me prepare this book and bring it to publication. First, I'd like to thank my wife, Jane, who is a terrific copy-editor. After reading the manuscript several times, she has involuntarily learned assembly language. My thanks go to several authors who got me started in programming: David A Lein, William Barden, Jr., Nat Wadsworth, and Christopher L. Morgan. Thanks also to Michael Suchoff, Harmon Washington, and the anonymous professionals who took time out to review and critique the manuscript. Their suggestions have been invaluable.

## PROGRAM DISKETTE

The numerous programs that are listed in this book are available on diskette. The diskette contains a library of macros, routines that speed up screen access in BASIC, a library of graphics utilities, and the programming templates from Appendix C. The price is $40.00, including shipping and handling. The address is:

> Unique Software
> Dept. B
> P.O. Box 12147
> La Crescenta, CA 91214.

D. R.

# Contents

## Appendices

# Figures

# Listings

# Tables

# Chapter 1

# Introduction to Assembly Language

## 1.1 WHY ASSEMBLY LANGUAGE?

You've mastered BASIC or Pascal. You understand variables and program logic and can compose the code to solve the majority of programming problems. Why, then, should you spend the time and effort to learn a new programming language? Maybe it's because you're tired of speaking through an interpreter when you talk to your machine. Perhaps you would like to *understand* this alien being with which you communicate every time you sit at the keyboard.

Everything that your computer does is done in machine language. The statements and functions of every higher-level language, such as BASIC or Pascal, are ultimately executed at a level understandable to the machine. In the IBM PC, this level is the collection of opcodes that make up the 8088 microprocessor instruction set.

Language interpreters examine source code and execute predefined subroutines of 8088 code. Because they must repeatedly reevaluate expressions and test for error conditions, interpreters tend to execute very slowly.

Compilers read in source code and churn out a sequence of opcodes that the machine will execute directly. They have the advantage of speed over interpreters, but compiled programs can grow very large very quickly. The compiler must be able to execute a wide variety of commands, so there is usually a certain amount of code overhead required for even the smallest compiled program. A compiled BASIC program takes at least 30K bytes of your machine's memory and disk storage to print one character on the video display. An assembly language program that does the same thing can be written in as few as 10 bytes of instructions.

While the 8088 instruction set is one of the most sophisticated and versatile available, it is composed wholly of a few arithmetic instructions, some I/O (input/output) functions, and the ability to alter its point of execution. Compared to BASIC, the language of the 8088 is as primitive as baby talk.

For example, if a high-level language had the statement

```
BUILD A FENCE
```

then coding the same statement in low-level assembly language would look something like

```
1    GET A SHOVEL

2    DIG A HOLE

3    GET A POST

4    PUT THE POST IN THE HOLE

5    GET SOME BOARDS

6    GET SOME NAILS

7    GET A HAMMER . . .
```

and so on. The machine has no idea what BUILD A FENCE means, but it does know the simpler commands. The machine is never aware that the fence is being built. It simply performs each step, one at a time. You, the programmer, needn't be bothered with the details of the individual steps; you're concerned only with the big picture.

But what if you wanted to build a chain link fence? If the designer of the high-level language were aware of this need, the command might be

```
BUILD A FENCE(CHAINLINK)
```

To make the language really useful, a statement syntax would evolve:

```
BUILD A FENCE(MATERIAL,COLOR,HEIGHT)
```

Now we're seeing the overhead involved in high-level languages. Before any fence construction takes place, the language translator needs to examine the command and determine which set of low-level instructions is to be performed. It must determine that CHAINLINK is a known material and check to see if the height is within a certain range. And the low-level instructions would end up executing more slowly. Extra instructions would be needed to replace step 3 in the preceding example:

```
2    DIG A HOLE

3.0  GO TO THE ENGINEER

3.1  ASK HOW HIGH THE FENCE SHOULD BE

3.2  ASK WHAT MATERIAL TO USE

3.3  GO TO THE SHED

3.4  GET A POST OF THE CORRECT HEIGHT AND MATERIAL

3.5  BRING IT BACK TO THE HOLE

4    PUT THE POST IN THE HOLE
```

Thus, if the only fence you ever build is 4 feet high, made of wood, and painted white, the high-level language is taking extra steps. If you recoded the function in the low-level language and left out the bells and whistles, it would run dramatically faster.

In BASIC, this sort of inefficiency happens constantly. For instance, every time you use the PRINT command, BASIC has to determine whether you are printing a number (and the precision thereof) or a string (and if it's a literal in the program or defined in string memory—and if so, where). It must see if you want the formatting capabilities of the USING modifier, and if the characters go to a file, the printer, or the screen.

When characters go to the screen, BASIC must check the mode (graphics or text) and the width (40 or 80 columns) of the screen. It checks to see if the entire string will fit on the current line and if it should scroll the screen because it's at the last line. It must look up the color or blink attribute of each character. BASIC goes through a check for the monochrome or color card as every character is printed, even if your IBM computer has never been within 50 feet of a color card.

Word processing and arcade-type games are examples of applications that fall apart under this sort of inefficiency. Imagine space nasties crawling across your screen at a snail's pace! Word processors that are written in BASIC must use machine language subroutines to get the text on the screen if they are to be competitive.

In addition to a dramatic speedup and more concise code, assembly language offers other advantages to the discerning programmer. Unless you know how to code in assembly, your IBM PC will be forever limited to doing only those functions that IBM and Microsoft have provided. If a student wants to wipe out the bad results on a computer-given test, he or she need only press CTRL-ALT-DEL. IBM has provided no way to disable the system reset, but a tiny program in assembly language will do this easily.

Programs that work intimately with the machine's hardware must be written in assembly language. The Basic Input and Output System (BIOS) that is the foundation of all communication with your IBM computer is written in 8088 mnemonics. Programs designed to interface with the BIOS must also be written at this level; random access memory (RAM) disk programs, print spoolers, and high-speed data acquisition equipment drivers are examples.

Software developers who were in on the ground floor of the 8080 and Z80 explosion know that one advantage of working at the machine code level is being able to interface with a computer's operating system. In the 1970s, programmers with the ability to interface with the Control Program for Microprocessors (CP/M) disk operating system (DOS) were (and still are) highly in demand. The new generation of 16-bit computers is likely to revolve around MS-DOS, Microsoft's generic name for the PC-DOS that controls your IBM PC. The only way to communicate with MS-DOS is with assembly language.

Finally, assembly language programming is *fun!* Sure, the complexity of assembly language virtually ensures some frustration along the way. This just makes it more of a challenge. Putting together a program is like solving an intricate jigsaw puzzle. When you open the box and spill the pieces onto the table, they are a chaotic jumble of cardboard. You'll become familiar with the categories of the shapes of the pieces, and your eyes will begin to discern subtle differences in the colors. As patterns emerge, you'll piece together subassemblies. When you link them all into a finished whole, you will have created a thing of beauty. When you've written and executed an assembly language program, you've spoken directly to the soul of your IBM computer. And that is an awesome feat.

### A Toolbox Approach

As with a cabinet maker or machinist, your skill as a programmer depends on your knowledge of the materials with which you work and your experience with the tools of your trade. Assembly language "materials" are crude—like a rough-hewn block of wood or an uncut ingot of steel—but the tools available to work those opcodes and data into a finished program are sophisticated and versatile.

The IBM Macro Assembler, LINK, and DEBUG are the tools of the assembly language programmer. Learning how to wield those tools skillfully can be a painful and difficult process. But programming skill grows exponentially with experience. And the tough parts *do* get easier.

Just as every journeyman machinist was once an apprentice, every experienced assembly language programmer has struggled with the basic concepts of bits and bytes, registers and stacks, opcodes and pseudo-ops. These are the fundamental materials of which assembly language programs are built. Before learning the intricacies of the vertical turret lathe, a machinist becomes familiar with the bolt and the wrench and learns the properties of aluminum and steel.

Experienced machinists often find that they can perform their job more quickly by first making up a set of *jigs*—special tools that hold their work piece in place. This is an example of creating a tool in order to use another tool more easily. Experienced programmers take this "make a tool to use a tool" concept to its highest degree of sophistication. Given the machine language instruction set as the fundamental building blocks, a programmer will forge a set of low-level subroutines. These subroutines become the building blocks of more sophisticated routines. These routines, in turn, make up the foundation of even more complex functions and procedures. As each new subroutine is forged, it is placed into a library, or toolbox, where it is available for creating more tools. The powerful tools created by this process make programs easier to write, debug, and maintain.

## 1.2 DATA TYPES AND NUMBERING CONVENTIONS

Before you are ready to dive into the complexities of the Macro Assembler, you will need to have firm background knowledge of the properties of the materials with which you will be working.

The foundation of assembly language programming is the set of operations that the machine can perform and the data on which it operates. You can instruct the 8088 to transfer data within memory or to external devices. It can add, subtract, multiply, and divide numeric data. It can compare two values and make decisions based on the results of the comparison.

The limited nature of the machine language instruction set is both a curse and a blessing. The curse is that each opcode does very little by itself. The opcodes must be strung together in complex patterns in order to accomplish even the simplest programming tasks. The blessing is that there are few commands to memorize, their syntax is uniform, and they combine easily with great flexibility.

The data that the 8088 processes are similarly simple yet flexible. The basic unit of value or truth is the *bit*, or *binary* dig*it*. A bit is a simple switch that indicates ON or OFF, TRUE or FALSE, 1 or 0. At the lowest level, everything that the central processing unit (CPU) does depends on the state of certain bits. It is possible to look at the computer's memory as a single long string of 1s and 0s.

Although most programming involves larger groups of bits such as bytes or words, there are many cases in which you must reference individual bits in assembly language. The IBM-PC's high-resolution graphics screen is a string of over 128,000 bits. Each bit that is set to a 1 is displayed as a lit dot; dark dots indicate where a bit has been reset to a 0. Bit values are also used as hardware status "flags" in the ROM-BIOS. For example, it is possible to determine if the keyboard is in CapsLock state by examining a single bit.

### Binary and Hexadecimal

The binary numbering system is an integral part of low-level programming. Some of the instructions that the CPU executes are meaningful only when viewed in the context of the binary system. But binary is far too clumsy for day-to-day use. The decimal numbering system is the most familiar, but is far removed from the data that a computer understands. A compromise system, the base-16 hexadecimal (hex) numbering system, has evolved as the most convenient one for assembly language programming. This is largely because conversions are easily done between hexadecimal and binary.

A group of four bits is often referred to as a *nibble*. A nibble can hold values ranging from 0 to 15. In the base-16 numbering system, each of these possible values has been given a unique symbol:

| decimal | binary | hexadecimal |
|---------|--------|-------------|
| 0 | 0000 | 0 |
| 1 | 0001 | 1 |
| 2 | 0010 | 2 |
| 3 | 0011 | 3 |
| 4 | 0100 | 4 |
| 5 | 0101 | 5 |
| 6 | 0110 | 6 |
| 7 | 0111 | 7 |
| 8 | 1000 | 8 |

| 9 | 1001 | 9 |
| 10 | 1010 | A |
| 11 | 1011 | B |
| 12 | 1100 | C |
| 13 | 1101 | D |
| 14 | 1110 | E |
| 15 | 1111 | F |

## Bytes

A byte is a group of two nibbles or eight bits. When we refer to the individual bits of a byte, we number them 0-7, starting from the rightmost, least significant bit:

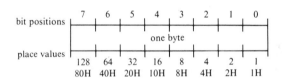

A byte contains values ranging from 0 to 255 (decimal) and 00 to FF (hex). If you add 1 to a byte that is already equal to 255, it will cycle around to 0. Bytes are represented in hex notation as a pair of nibbles suffixed with the letter *H*. The first (high-order) nibble is the number of 16s (like the 10s digit in a decimal number). The second (low-order) nibble is the units digit.

Conversion of a hexadecimal byte to a binary representation consists of breaking the byte into nibbles and writing the 1s and 0s that make up each nibble:

```
2FH          byte (hex notation)

2   F        nibbles (hex digits)

0010 1111    bits (binary digits)
```

Converting decimal to hexadecimal (and vice versa) is a more complicated problem. The charts in Appendix D will help you make an exact conversion if you need one. Fortunately, there is seldom any need to do so. Just as you don't ordinarily need to convert centigrade to Fahrenheit (when it's 35 degrees centigrade outside, it's *hot*), you can often get by with just knowing the general magnitude of a hexadecimal number. For instance, 1000H is just over 4,000, and FFFFH is about 64,000.

## THINGS TO DO

1.  Without doing a formal conversion, determine whether the binary number 01010001 is odd or even.

2. Memorize this silly mnemonic for hex to decimal conversion: "D is an unlucky grade." In other words, the hex digit *D* is equal to 13 in decimal. Knowing that the hex numbers 0-9 are the same as their decimal counterparts, and remembering that *F* is equal to 15, this mnemonic helps to extrapolate the values of all the hex "letter digits."

## Adding and Subtracting in Hexadecimal

Adding two hexadecimal numbers may seem complicated at first, but it is really as easy as adding two decimal numbers. The only difference is that while two decimal digits generate a carry when they add up to 10 or more, hex numbers don't generate a carry until their sum is 16 (decimal) or more. For example:

```
  3H
+ 8H

  BH        (11 in decimal)

  9H
+ 9H

 12H        (18 in decimal; i.e., one 16 and two 1s)
```

Likewise, when you subtract hexadecimal numbers, just remember that a borrow from the higher-order digit adds 16 to the current subtrahend digit.

```
 22H
-  3H

 1FH
```

## THINGS TO DO

1. Try adding and subtracting some hexadecimal numbers without first converting them to decimal. Get a feel for borrowing 16 when you subtract. Remember to wait until you get a digit value of at least 16 before carrying in addition.

## ASCII Characters

Bytes are very handy units of information. Besides being numerical entities, bytes are used to represent alphabetic and numeric characters. The American Standard Code for Information Interchange (ASCII) is an arbitrary assignment of a numeric value to each letter, digit, and special character. The ASCII set also includes control codes that have been given special meanings, such as "carriage return" and "top of page." Appendix D has a complete list of ASCII codes.

A series of ASCII characters that have been strung together is called a *string*. If your first language is BASIC, you are going to be rudely awakened to the fact that the assembly language equivalent of a BASIC string is much harder to work with. Strings are just groups of adjacent characters. For example, the string "Hi there" is represented by these 9 ASCII bytes:

```
   H   i           t   h   e   r   e   !
  48H 69H        20H 74H 68H 65H 72H 65H 21H
```

Keeping track of string data in assembly language involves knowing a string's length and the memory address of its first character. There are no LEFT$, RIGHT$, or MID$ functions in assembly language, and strings can't really be added together, as BASIC might lead you to believe. You will need to get used to doing extra work when you input, manipulate, and display strings of characters.

## Words

When we must represent numbers that are larger than FFH, we juxtapose two bytes and form a *word*. The word is an important bit grouping. The IBM-PC is a 16-bit computer, and it operates most efficiently on 16-bit values. Integer variables are stored and manipulated as words. The memory locations of string data and integer variables are kept track of by 16-bit address *pointers*.

The two bytes that make up a word can be thought of as a base-256 numbering system. The first digit (0-255) holds the units place; the next digit holds the 256s place. Just as a two-digit decimal number can define values from 0 to 99, two-byte word contains values ranging from 0 to FFFFH, that is, FFH times the base (256) plus FFH. This value is a good one to remember. In decimal, it's 65,535—one less than 64K.

Note: *K-byte* is an artificial term that may be confusing because it combines binary and decimal. A single K-byte is actually 1,024 in decimal (it's the multiple of 2 that comes closest to 1,000), so 64K is really 64*1,024 or 65,536 (decimal).

The two bytes that represent a word are stored in memory in reverse order. The least significant byte (LSB) comes first, and the most significant byte (MSB) is stored at the next higher address in memory.

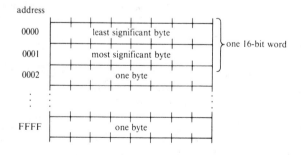

Even though you write a word in hexadecimal as, say, 1234H, it will be stored in memory as 34H followed by 12H. This makes a lot of sense to the computer, but it is a trifle confusing to humans at first. You can think of this as a "back*words*" representation, or you can just remember that the higher-valued byte is stored in the higher address. You will confront this reversal only when you are examining memory with a machine language monitor such as DEBUG. When you specify a 16-bit value to the assembler, the switch will be made automatically.

While working with words, it is best to think of them as 16-bit entities rather than as two 8-bit bytes. Here's a diagram of a word represented as a single 16-bit value.

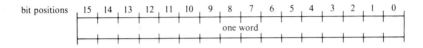

## THINGS TO DO

1.  The IBM-PC color/graphics card contains 16K of storage. What is the highest address in video card memory?

2.  The byte at address 0011H has a value of 03H, and the byte at address 0012H is 4FH. What is the value of the *word* at 0011H?

3.  What value should you subtract from the ASCII character 3 to make it a binary 3?

## Doublewords

A 32-bit value is represented by two adjacent words. This bit grouping is sensibly called a *doubleword* (it might have been called a *phrase* or, worse, a *mouthful*). Because the 8088 is capable of accessing over 1 million bytes of memory, a 16-bit value is not large enough to point to all of these addresses. Intel's strategy for accessing the unreachable memory addresses involves combining two 16-bit words in a memory segmentation scheme. For this reason, we will sometimes be working with 32-bit doublewords as pointers to data within memory. Also, arithmetic operations sometimes need the elbow room supplied by 32-bit operands.

When a doubleword is stored in memory, the least significant word is stored first, followed by the most significant word. Thus, a 32-bit (two-word) operand is stored as a series of four bytes starting with the LSB and ending with the MSB.

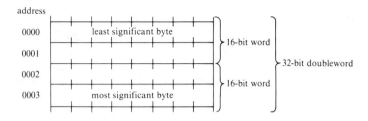

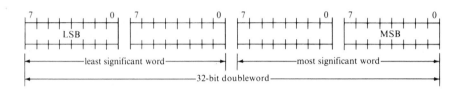

## Odd-Sized Bit Fields

Here's a final note on bit fields: While we normally see values broken into bytes, words, or doublewords, occasionally programmers try to pack a lot of information into a small area. One example is seen in the way that PC-DOS keeps track of the time/date stamp of a disk file. Since there are only 12 months in a year, Microsoft thought it foolish to reserve an entire byte to store the month reference. Likewise, the day can only be a number from 1 to 31, which will easily fit into five bits. Microsoft chose to compress the month, day, and year references into a two-byte bit field in this format:

```
                ———————— byte ————————    ———————— byte ————————
 position:  15 14 13 12 11 10  9  8  7  6  5  4  3  2  1  0
 name:       y  y  y  y  y  y  y  m  m  m  m  d  d  d  d  d
                ——————— field ———————  ——— field ———  ——— field ———

 yyyyyyy     7-bit year field ranges from 0 to 127 (0-119 valid)
 mmmm        4-bit month field ranges from 0 to 15 (1-12 valid)
 ddddd       5-bit day field ranges from 0 to 32 (1-31 valid)
```

The value of the year field is added to 1980 to yield a year from 1980 to 2099.

Another example of an odd-sized bit field is seen in midresolution graphics. The graphics hardware will display only four colors when in midresolution mode. To keep this information compact, each byte of display memory is viewed as a set of four 2-bit fields. Two bits can hold values from 0 to 3, just enough to indicate which of the four colors to display.

**THINGS TO DO**

1.  Write the 16-bit binary encoding of the date December 25, 1985.

2.  Decode 025EH to see if it represents a valid date.

**Signed Numbers**

A special numbering convention is used to keep track of negative values. This is the *two's complement convention*. It takes advantage of the limitations of computer memory. When a word of memory has been assigned a value of 1, adding FFFFH will cause the word to become 0. That's as if FFFFH had the value of -1. It follows that adding any value that is greater than 7FFFH to a value that is less than 8000H will exhibit a response identical to that of subtraction. When we are using the two's complement convention, we say that the high bit (bit 15) of a 16-bit word is the *sign* bit. If this bit is 1, then the number is above 7FFFH, so it is negative.

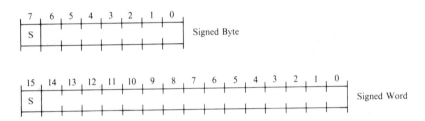

Two's complement numbers are often called *integers*. The terms *integer addition* and *integer multiplication* refer to operations that assume that the highest bit is being used to indicate the sign of the number. Since there are only 15 bits to hold the absolute value, it can only indicate numbers from 0 to 7FFFH (32,767 decimal). It appears that 0000H and 8000H should both represent the same value (0 and -0), but 8000H is treated as the most negative number, so 16-bit integers can range from -8000H (-32,768) to +7FFFH (+32,767).

To form a negative signed number, start with its positive counterpart, break it down into binary, reverse all 1s to 0s and all 0s to 1s, and then add 1 to the result. For example, to form -30ABH:

```
     3      0      A      B       break into nibbles
     0011   0000   1010   1011    convert to bits

     1100   1111   0101   0100    toggle all bits (1s become
                                  0s, 0s become 1s)

  +  0000   0000   0000   0001    add 1

     1100   1111   0101   0101    = AF55H (note sign bit = 1)
```

```
        1100   1111   0101   0101
   +    0011   0000   1010   1011        verify by adding back 30ABH
   1    0000   0000   0000   0000
```

Notice that adding 30ABH to AF55H actually results in a sum of 10000H, but because a word operand will hold only the lowest 16 bits, the highest bit is dropped into the bit bucket and the sum is saved as 0000H. So adding the two's complement to the original number is identical to subtracting it from itself, or adding it to its negative counterpart.

The same convention can be used for representing signed bytes. When the highest bit of a byte is a 1, it can be assumed to be a negative number. Signed bytes range in value from -80H (-128) to +7FH (+127).

A process called *sign extension* sometimes allows us to use an 8-bit byte to represent a 16-bit number. We simply take the highest bit of the LSB and replicate it through all of bits of the MSB.

```
              00000001B   =     +01H
   00000000   00000001B   =   +0001H (sign extended)

              11010011B   =    -53H
   11111111   11010011B   =   -0053H (sign extended)
```

**THINGS TO DO**

1. The radio announcer at station KHEX in Alaska announces that today's temperature is FFE0H. How cold is it?

2. The forecast says that the temperature will rise 15H degrees by afternoon. How warm will it get?

3. Determine the two-digit hex equivalent of negative 17 (-17) decimal.

## 8088 Segment Addresses

The 8088 is capable of accessing over 1,000,000 bytes (a megabyte) of memory (i.e., addresses 0 through FFFFFH). This is one of its chief advantages over earlier eight-bit CPUs. But the 8088 is a 16-bit machine, and 16 bits can hold values only up to 64K. To store values in addresses above 65,536, it was necessary to work out a sophisticated memory addressing scheme that involves memory *segments*.

FFFFFH is one less than $2^{20}$, so we need to address memory locations that may be as large as a 20-bit number. The designers of the 8088 could have created a couple of 4-bit segment pointers and allowed us to access any of 16 64K-byte segments. Or they might have come up with a three-byte addressing scheme for pointing to memory (3 bytes can represent a number up $2^{24}$, so this would actually be adequate for addressing 16 megabytes).

Instead, they chose a more complex but very flexible system. They chose to use 16-bit segment pointers that can point to any of 65,536 16-byte *paragraphs*. A paragraph is just the arbitrary name given to a 16-byte unit of memory.

| address<br>(hex) | | |
|---|---|---|
| 00000 | paragraph 0 (bytes 0-15) | |
| 00010 | paragraph 1 (bytes 16-31) | 1 paragraph |
| 000F0 | paragraph 15 (bytes 240-255) | |
| 00100 | paragraph 16 (bytes 256-271) | 1 page |
| 00FF0 | paragraph 255 (bytes 4080-4095) | |
| 01000 | paragraph 256 (bytes 4096-4111) | |
| 0FFF0 | paragraph 4095 (bytes 65520-65535) | |
| 10000 | paragraph 4096 (bytes 65536-65551) | 1 segment |
| 1FFF0 | paragraph 8191 (bytes 131056-131071) | |
| 20000 | paragraph 8192 (bytes 131072-131087) | |
| FFFF0 | paragraph 65535 (bytes 1048560-1048575) | 1 Megabyte |

The opcodes and data in memory are always referenced as being at a 16-bit address that is an offset from the start of a memory paragraph. Any address within 64K of the segment pointer is thus available for program code and data. The advantage is that once the starting paragraph is set, memory locations can be referred to by 16-bit pointers, and indexing into memory can be performed with 16-bit arithmetic instructions.

The great majority of programs need less than 64K of memory, so the limitation of 16-bit addressing is rarely encountered. When more than 64K of memory must be accessed, it is easy to set up a different memory paragraph as the base of operations. Finally, memory segmentation provides an upward path for microprocessors to access more than the 8088's one-megabyte maximum. For instance, the chip designers could increase the value of a paragraph. If paragraphs were 256 bytes long, a CPU would have an addressing range of 16 megabytes, and software written for such a CPU would still be compatible with the 8088. The advanced 80286 microprocessor takes a different tack; it uses the segment pointers to reference a look-up table that contains pointers to the true physical addresses. Coupled with sophisticated operating system software, this table allows the CPU to access a gigabyte of *virtual memory* because memory segments are not tied to any physical address space. But that's a subject for another book.

## The MegaRoom Hotel

The concept of segmentation might best be explained by analogy. Imagine a desk clerk at the MegaRoom Hotel. The clerk's job is to keep track of room keys and messages for each of the hotel's more than one million guests. Behind the reception desk is a tall array of pigeonholes that correspond to each of the rooms in the hotel. The hotel has 16 rooms to a floor on each of over 65,000 floors.

Now the clerk, who used to play professional basketball, is tall enough to reach the shelf for the 4,096th floor, a total of 65,536 rooms. When he receives a message for the gentleman in room 65,537, he gets out his trusty stepladder and climbs up one rung. This gives him access to rooms up to 65,551. He can no longer reach down to the bottom shelf without overbalancing and crashing to the floor, so he has a range from 16 to 65,551. He can still place messages in any of 65,536 pigeonholes, but the bottom shelf is out of his reach.

The large law firm of Brown, Irwin, Olsen, and Smith (BIOS, Inc.) has reserved all of the rooms on floors 640 through 1000. When Ms. Brown asks the clerk to get her messages, she prefers not to rattle off her 6-digit room number. She simply indicates BIOS, suite 31. The clerk quickly climbs up to the 640th rung of the ladder and then reaches for the 31st box above that level.

The 8088 segment pointers (segment registers) are like the stepladder the clerk uses to access the different shelves of pigeonholes (or paragraphs of memory addresses). His 4,096-shelf reach is analogous to one 64K memory segment. The number of the rung he stands on is the value of a segment register.

Just as the clerk must climb the rungs of his ladder to reach the upper floors of the hotel, so must we use segment registers to access portions of the IBM-PC's memory. Segments may overlap; that is, many of the pigeonholes that can be reached from the first rung of the ladder are also within reach from the floor or from the second rung.

A notation convention has developed to keep track of addresses in this memory segmentation scheme. The format is:

```
ssss:oooo
```

where ssss is the segment number and oooo is an offset within that segment. Addresses named in this manner are always represented in hexadecimal. Examples:

```
0000:30AB      30ABH from the absolute start of memory
F600:0007      a high memory address (in ROM BASIC)
0040:0000      first byte of the BIOS data segment
0000:0400      another way to specify the same address
```

The latter two examples illustrate how segments may overlap. Address 0000:0400 is the same memory location as 0040:0000 (room 400H in the MegaRoom hotel is on floor 40H). In fact, there are 1000H (4,096) different ways to refer to any address! This system may cause some confusion, but the result is a great deal of flexibility in the IBM's memory management. It means that with only a few changes to segment references, programs can be loaded and executed at any memory paragraph. It doesn't matter whether DEBUG, for example, is loaded at 03AB:0000 or 0732:0000; its execution will be unchanged.

**20-Bit Address Calculation**

Normally, you will not need to know the 20-bit address of any byte. A segment and offset are a perfectly good reference. But it is easy to calculate the absolute 20-bit address of any byte in memory: Multiply the segment reference by 16 and add the offset reference. Just as multiplication by 10 is accomplished in the decimal system by shifting all the numbers to the left and appending a 0 to the right, you can multiply a hexadecimal number by 16 by tacking a 0 nibble onto the right side of the number.

```
 1234:5678  segment:offset format

    12340   segment * 10H (shift left by 4 bits)
+    5678   add offset

    17988   20-bit absolute memory location
```

**THINGS TO DO**

1. How many rungs must the clerk of the MegaRoom Hotel climb in order to place a message in the slot for room 34F21H?

2. Determine how many bytes (in hex) lie between address 8765:4321 and address 9ABC:DEF0. Hint: Convert each of these *segment:offset* addresses to an equivalent five-digit hexadecimal number before subtracting.

3. Just as bytes and words "wrap around" to 0 after reaching FFH and FFFFH, so do *segment:offset* addresses. Determine the five-digit hex address of the byte located at FFFF:1234.

## 1.3 Binary Operations

When you reach the heart of any microprocessor, you'll find that at the lowest level, it doesn't even add or subtract. (There are "adder circuits" in the 8088, but these are just low-level tools that ultimately rely on bit-by-bit comparisons). The only thing a computer truly does is compare the value of two bits. Depending on the outcome of the comparison, a result flag is set. There can be three possible combinations:

* Both bits are 0, so the result flag is a 0.
* Exactly one of the bits is a 1, so the result flag is a 1.
* Both bits are 1, so an "overflow" occurred and the result flag is a 0.

Although the CPU has only the fundamental tools of comparing two bits and storing the result, it has been designed to use these tools in more sophisticated operations. Specifically, it is able to perform a series of comparisons, storing a series of results as it goes.

Consider how a CPU adds two binary numbers: It compares the LSB of the first operand with the LSB of the second operand. It stores the resulting bit in its internal storage area and sets a temporary carry flag if an overflow occurred. After the result of the first comparison has been stored, the next two bits are examined. The result of this comparison is then *compared against the carry flag*, and then that result is stored. This process is continued throughout the two operands. The resulting series of bits is nothing more than a complex comparison, but we humans like to think of it as the arithmetic sum of the operands.

The point here is that the CPU's specialty is binary comparisons. The CPU is "wired" for the sequences of comparisons that we call addition, subtraction, multiplication, and division. Along with these complex comparisons, the assembly language programmer has access to the more primitive "logical," or bit manipulation, operations. These operations are most meaningful when you can think of the operands as groups of true/false flags rather than as numeric quantities. Bit manipulation operations include AND, OR, XOR, SHIFT, ROTATE, and COMPLEMENT (CPL).

The logical AND operation compares two bits, saying, "If this bit AND that bit are both 1, then the resulting bit is a 1."

```
      1 0 1 0 1 0 1 0
AND   0 0 0 0 1 1 1 1

      0 0 0 0 1 0 1 0
```

The AND operation is usually used in an operation called *masking*. Masking is used to isolate a bit or group of bits by resetting all of the irrelevant bits to 0s. Masking is useful for resetting selected bits and for testing whether an operand has certain bits set. In the preceding example, the second operand has only the lowest four bits set. With that as the mask, the AND operation will preserve only the bits in the lower half of the first operand.

The OR operation also does just what it says. "If this bit is a 1 OR that bit is a 1, then the resulting bit is a 1."

```
      1 0 1 0 1 0 1 0
OR    0 0 0 0 1 1 1 1

      1 0 1 0 1 1 1 1
```

This operation is used to turn on (set to 1) certain bits of an operand. Wherever there is a 0 in the second operand, the result reflects an exact duplicate of the first operand. Wherever the second operand contained a 1, the result bit has also become a 1.

XOR (eXclusive OR) is a more abstruse operation. As each bit is compared, the result is a 1 only when the bits are different. XOR says, "If this bit is a 1 and that bit is a 0 *or* if this bit is a 0 and that bit is a 1, then the result is a 1."

```
      1 0 1 0 1 0 1 0
XOR   0 0 0 0 1 1 1 1

      1 0 1 0 0 1 0 1
```

The XOR operation can be used to toggle a group of bits within an operand. Notice in the preceding example that each of the lower four bits has been changed from its original state in the first operand into the opposite state in the result. The upper four bits have remained the same.

CPL, SHIFT, and ROTATE operate on a single operand rather than the two operands used in AND, OR, and XOR. CPL inverts (toggles) the state of each bit in the operand. It says, "If this bit is a 1, then change it to a 0; otherwise make it a 1."

```
CPL   0 0 0 0 1 1 1 1

      1 1 1 1 0 0 0 0
```

Shifts and rotations alter the bit pattern of their operand in a special way. The original pattern is replaced by an identical pattern that has been *moved by one bit position*. A shift left (SHL) moves the value of each bit to the neighboring position to the left. The vacated rightmost bit is set to 0, and the leftmost bit is shifted into the bit bucket (lost). For each bit in the operand it says, "If the bit to the right is a 1, then the result bit becomes a 1; otherwise the result becomes a 0":

```
SHL   0 0 0 0 1 1 1 1

      0 0 0 1 1 1 1 0
```

Similarly, a shift right (SHR) moves the bit pattern to the right, discarding the rightmost bit and shifting a 0 into the leftmost position:

```
SHR   0 0 0 0 1 1 1 1

      0 0 0 0 0 1 1 1
```

Shifts are used to move bit patterns to certain positions in a byte or word. A graphic shape can be moved by one dot by shifting its bits. Special bit patterns (such as the 16-bit value that PC-DOS uses to represent a date) can be manipulated with shifts and masks to isolate the individual bit fields in order to treat them as numeric data.

You can use shift operations to do multiplication or division by 2. For example, 40H shifted to the left becomes 80H. The bit pattern of number 5, when shifted to the right, becomes 2, that is, the integer result of 5/2. The remainder of such a division (the bit that is "lost" during a shift operation) can be found in the CPU's carry flag.

Bit rotations are the CPU's way of playing musical chairs. They work like the shifts, but the bit that is normally "lost" is copied into the opposite end of the operand. Here's a rotation to the left:

```
ROL   1 1 1 1 0 0 0 0

      1 1 1 0 0 0 0 1
```

and a rotation to the right:

```
ROR   1 1 1 1 0 0 0 0

      0 1 1 1 1 0 0 0
```

Notice that if a byte is rotated (in either direction) eight times, it will return to its original value. This operation is useful for checking the bits of an operand one by one in a selected sequence.

**THINGS TO DO**

1.  What binary mask could be used to convert a lowercase ASCII value (a-z) to an uppercase value (A-Z)? Consult Appendix D for help.

2.  Calculate X in the following two equations. Convert to binary if necessary.

    ```
    X = (43H AND F5H) OR 0FH.

    X = (3F7AH XOR 562FH) XOR 562FH.
    ```

    Did you find the shortcuts?

# Chapter 2

# Organization of the 8088

## 2.1 HISTORY OF THE 8088

The 8088 is a very close relative of the 8086, which was introduced by Intel in 1978. It was billed as the precocious offspring of the 8085 microprocessor, and is therefore a descendant of the 8008 and the 8080. It is based on the same general principles as the earlier chips, but it was designed to work with 16-bit numbers (the 8085 has a limited set of 16-bit operations, but they basically work with two 8-bit numbers). The chip was also upgraded to handle operations similar to those implemented in Zilog's Z-80 microprocessor.

The 8086 works with equal ease on 8-bit or 16-bit values, but it is designed to work with a *16-bit bus*, that is, hardware that stores and retrieves 16 bits of memory at a time. Intel thoughtfully included the ability to link *coprocessors* to the chip so that any limitations of the 8086 can be overcome by external processing devices. For instance, the 8087 *math chip* effectively expands the instruction set of the 8088 to provide it with 80-bit floating point arithmetic operations. Another coprocessor, the 82730, is sometimes called the *word processing chip* because it handles such things as character font definition, window scrolling, and light pen input, all without bothering the 8086 central processor.

The 8086 is far more than a 16-bit upgrade of the 8085. It has enhanced arithmetic operations, including multiplication and division commands, and it has the ability to access a much larger amount of memory. Special string-handling instructions have been included, making the 8086 the processor of choice for writing in high-level languages that process strings of characters and work with arrays of numbers.

Soon after the introduction of the 8086, Intel brought out the 8088. This chip is software compatible with the 8086, but it works with tried-and-true 8-bit bus hardware. Programs that run on the 8086 will work without change on the 8088. The main difference is that the 8088 fetches 16 bits from memory with two 8-bit fetches. This action is invisible to the programmer, so any books that describe assembly language programming on the 8086 are also about the 8088. The terms *iA PX 86* and *iA PX 88* are alternative ways to refer to systems built around the 8086 and 8088 microprocessors. This book will refer to the 8086/8088 microprocessor chip as being the CPU, or simply the 8088.

When IBM annointed the 8088 by including it as the "brain" of their first entry in the personal computer market, the rest of the industry took notice. The Intel 16-bit chips offer an upward path toward the 32-bit processing that has long been the domain of mainframe computers.

## 2.2 COMPONENTS OF THE CPU

The 8088 architecture can be summarized as being a register-oriented micro-processor with 14 registers. Four are general-purpose registers; four are used as pointers to access information within specific areas of memory; four are used to define (or point to) the start of these memory areas or *segments*; one register is used to keep track of the position of the instruction being executed; and the final register is a set of flags that reflect the status of the CPU while it's running.

All computers execute programs in *cycles*. They fetch an instruction from memory, decode it to decide what to do, and then execute the instruction. The execution may require as many as two transfers of data to or from memory. Older processors performed these steps in sequence; after an instruction was executed, the processor was tied up with the fetch of the next instruction. Every transfer to or from memory stole time from the processor's appointed task of decoding and executing instructions. The designers of the 8088 saw a way to improve dramatically upon this situation by dividing the CPU's work into separate tasks.

The 8088 CPU is physically divided into two main elements, the Execution Unit (EU) and the Bus Interface Unit (BIU). The EU decodes and executes each instruction, and the BIU handles all of the data transfers to and from memory. The beauty of this system is that both units are working simultaneously. The EU is never tied up with the slow process of fetching an instruction or storing and retrieving data. It can devote all of its attention to the details of decoding and executing an instruction. At the same time that the EU is figuring out what to do about an instruction, the BIU is handling the most recent request for a memory read or write. In its free time, the BIU fetches the next instructions to be executed. It assembles a *queue* (pronounced like *cue*) of instructions, so that the EU is very seldom idle.

This system of queuing instructions is analogous to the situation of a chess player who sees a forced checkmate in three moves. Let's say that the BIU is playing the black pieces and sees what appears to be a way to checkmate white (the EU). Black feels that no matter what white does, black will have an instant reply. White will take time "decoding" the move and forming a reply, but when the move is finally made, black is ready with another move. Thus, the game will go twice as fast because only one of the players is taking any time to think.

The exception occurs when white makes a brilliant move that black accidentally overlooked. In that case, black will need to sit back and do some thinking before making a move. This is analogous to the situation in which the last instruction decoded by the EU is a jump (GOTO) instruction. The instruction queue will contain opcodes that are not supposed to be executed, so the EU will need to pause while the BIU refills the queue, starting from the new location.

All this instruction queuing and execution is invisible to the programmer. Conceptually, an instruction is simply executed. If it requires two memory accesses, then so be it; the instruction is executed just the same. The fact that a jump instruction takes longer is simply a fact about that jump instruction—something of interest, but nothing to worry about. Now, if you decide to *design* a microprocessor, you might want to create a more intelligent BIU that will look ahead and queue up two separate branches of instructions whenever it encounters a jump. You might also decide to name your CPU chip something other than a string of numbers—that's so *impersonal.*

## Memory Access

The 8088 can access 1,048,576 bytes of memory and 65,536 input/output ports. It has built-in stack operations and sophisticated interrupt handling capabilities.

The 1 megabyte (1,024K bytes) of memory is addressed through the system of segments and offsets discussed in Chapter 1. Certain parts of this memory are reserved for special uses by the CPU. The very highest 16 bytes (addresses FFFF:0000 to FFFF:000F) are reserved as the power-up instruction area. In other words, when the 8088 starts up, it first executes the instruction beginning at FFFF:0000. In the IBM PC, these addresses are designated as read-only memory (ROM) and contain an instruction to jump to the power-on diagnostic test procedures in the ROM-BIOS.

## Interrupts

The lowest 1,024 bytes of the 8088's addressing space are reserved for a table of *interrupt vectors.* An interrupt vector is an address that points to a special kind of subroutine called an *interrupt handler.* Unlike normal subroutines, these interrupt handlers may be invoked by the system's hardware as well as the software.

In olden days, whenever a computer needed to interact with external devices such as a keyboard or printer, it had to wait until the device was ready. For instance, in order to see if a key had been pressed, it periodically needed to check the status of the keyboard. Imagine what would happen if your telephone was not equipped with a ringer. You wouldn't be able to tell if someone was calling you unless you picked up the phone and listened for a voice. You would find it hard to get any work done because you would be spending so much time picking up and putting down the receiver.

At some point, an engineer had the inspiration to give external devices "ringers" and the computer "ears." When the keyboard is ready with a key, it simply rings its bell. The computer stops what it is doing and "picks up the phone" to handle the call.

The 8088 is equipped with the ears needed for this interruption processing. When a device interrupts, it specifies an *interrupt type.* The CPU goes to the interrupt vector table and finds the location of the subroutine that will handle that type of interrupt. It saves its current status, including the address of the routine it was executing, and then executes the interrupt handling subroutine. When that task is finished, the CPU takes up where it left off in the interrupted program.

The 1,024 bytes of the interrupt vector table define the four-byte addresses of 256 interrupt types. Of these, the 8088 reserves five for its own exception processing and other special purposes. These *internal interrupts* include an execution route taken in the event of a division error (division by 0, or a division where the result won't fit in the destination operand); a pointer to a single-step subroutine for use by debugging programs; a nonmaskable (never disabled) interrupt to handle very high-priority requests (such as when the power supply is accidentally lost); a routine to handle the special "breakpoint" instruction used by debugging programs; and an interrupt that can be taken when an arithmetic operation has a result that won't fit in its intended destination.

The other 251 interrupt types can be used by any hardware device or software program. For the most part, these interrupts go unused, but some are used by the ROM-BIOS and PC-DOS to perform often needed input/output functions. The functions of these interrupt types are described in Appendix B and will be discussed and used in examples throughout this book.

## The Stack

The 8088 has built-in tools to maintain a *stack*—a holding area for temporary values. Using the stack is like writing a phone number on a bit of scratch paper. If you think you might need that number later, you will record it permanently in your address book. You can throw out the paper, or you can hand it to your secretary, who will do something with it.

That's what a stack is used for. The way it works can best be explained by a different analogy. Think of a stack of dirty plates and imagine yourself washing them after a big Thanksgiving dinner. You can wash only one plate at a time; you always remove and wash the top plate from the stack. As the big eaters and late diners finish, they bring their plates into the kitchen and place them on top of the stack. No matter whose plate is on top (they're all alike), you always remove the top plate.

The stack of dirty plates is a LIFO (last-in-first-out) structure. When a new plate is added to the stack, you must process (wash) it before you can get back to where you were before it was placed there. If you can make the intuitive leap between dirty dishes and data, you will understand how the 8088 stack works. The CPU keeps placing data on top of the stack and then removing it from the top. In this way, its most recent "note to itself" is the one that gets processed first.

When a subroutine or interrupt is invoked, the CPU needs to remember where it left off. It must save the current address so that it can return to it after the subroutine is finished. The CALL and INT instructions automatically save the return address in a stack. If the called routine calls another routine, then that address must also be saved. The RET and IRET opcodes retrieve the address data that was most recently put on the stack and use it as the new starting point. After an address has been retrieved, the bytes that were used to store it are free to be used again and again.

In addition to saving addresses, the stack is very handy for keeping track of data values that you don't need to save permanently. There are only four general registers in the 8088 CPU, and you will find many occasions to use one of them without letting the CPU forget its current value. The PUSH and POP instructions allow you to save and restore a register on demand. When you must save the values in several registers, you must be sure to POP them in the sequence in the opposite order in which you PUSHed them. The 8088 is equipped with special tools that make working with stacked data easier than it was with previous processors.

**THINGS TO DO**

1.   What is the difference between programs that run on the 8086 and those that run on the 8088?

2.   What would happen if the stack segment was set to be in ROM?

## 2.3 REGISTERS

Like most modern microprocessors, the 8088 architecture is based on groups of *registers*. A register is a holding device that the processor uses for calculations and as pointers to data in memory.

Like variables in BASIC, registers are the principal media for calculations. Unlike BASIC variables, there is a very limited number of registers, so they are primarily used for holding operands and intermediate results. The 8088 has four sets of registers for holding and operating on data. Three of these sets may be directly manipulated by the program. These are the *general* registers, the *pointer* and *index* registers, and the *segment* registers. The fourth set, the *instruction pointer (IP) and flags*, is manipulated indirectly. The IP register always contains the memory address of the opcode that is about to be executed. It is altered by the jump and call instructions, allowing programs to execute nonsequential and iterative code. The flags are affected by arithmetic and logical operations. The CPU flags are decision makers of assembly language programming. An "if . . . then" construct always involves testing the state of one or more of the flags and branching to or around parts of the 8088 code.

Figure 2.1 diagrams the register sets. Note that the general registers AX, BX, CX, and DX are 16-bit registers but are subdivided into high and low halves. Either half may be accessed as an 8-bit register. A 16-bit register may contain values ranging from 0 to 65,535 (0-FFFFH; a word). An 8-bit register may hold values ranging from 0 to 255 (0-FFH; a byte). If you ever add 1 to a register that already contains its maximum, the result is 0.

```
ØFFH + 1 = Ø (8-bit register)

ØFFFFH + 1 = Ø (16-bit register)
```

**Figure 2.1**
**8088 Registers**

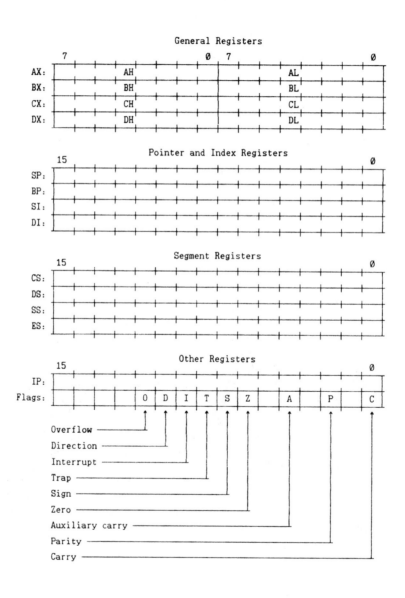

## General Registers

The four general registers are used in much the same way as variables in a BASIC program. You can transfer values to or from them and perform arithmetic operations with them. Besides being general purpose, each of these registers has additional special-purpose functions. The names of these registers reflect their special uses.

1. AX  is often used as an "accumulator" because certain arithmetic operations automatically leave their results in this register (it therefore "accumulates" results). Some operations take fewer bytes of storage when AX (or AL) is one of the operands.

2. BX  can be used as a "base register." When we are working with arrays or tables of data, it is often useful to point BX to the address of the base of the table. There are special (fast) ways to access data that are in a table pointed to by BX.

3. CX  is a "counter." Some operations can be automatically repeated many times. These operations use CX as a counter to keep track of which interation is being performed and for testing when the operation is finished.

4. DX  is a "data register" for certain arithmetic operations—namely, 16-bit multiplication and division. Multiplying two 16-bit values can result in a product that is 32 bits long (FFFFFFFFH or 4,294,967,295). When two 16-bit values are multiplied, the 32-bit result ends up in two registers: DX and AX. DX will hold the most significant word, and AX will contain the least significant word. Similarly, DX is used to hold the high 16 bits of any 32-bit dividend. DX is also used as a port pointer in some types of I/O operations.

The special uses of these general registers are tricky, and perhaps hard to remember. Some people consider them to be a flaw in the 8088's design (by comparison, in the Motorola 68000 microprocessor, any general-purpose register can be used in a special-purpose operation). Figure 2.2 lists the specialties of each of the 8088's general registers. Study it well. Knowing these idiosyncrasies saves hours of frustration. For instance, if you remember that the value of DX is changed by 16-bit multiplication, you won't place any critical value in that register before performing the multiplication.

## Pointer and Index Registers

The pointer and index registers are specifically designed to implement the 8088's advanced memory addressing modes. While they can be used in arithmetic operations like the general registers, they must always be treated as 16-bit operands.

These registers are most useful for pointing to data in memory. Whenever a program uses sequences of data, as in a look-up table or array, these registers make it easier to access those data. In particular, strings of characters are much simpler to process when you don't need to know the address of each character. You just start out by loading the pointer register with the address of the start of the string, fetch and process the character at that address, and then add 1 to (increment) the pointer register. When you repeat this process, the register points to the next character, so that you can continue this operation until the pointer reaches the end of the string.

**Figure 2.2**
**Register Specialties**

| | |
|---|---|
| AL: | Source operand for: AAA; AAD; AAS; DAA; DAS; CBW; OUT; SCASB; STOSB; XLAT; 8-bit MUL, IMUL; 8-bit OUT |
| | Destination for: AAA; AAD; AAS; DAA; DAS; IN; LODSB; XLAT; 8-bit IN; quotient of 8-bit DIV, IDIV |
| AH: | Source operand for: SAHF |
| | Destination for: LAHF; CBW; remainder of 8-bit DIV, IDIV |
| AX: | Source operand for: CWD; OUT; SCASW; STOSW; 8-bit DIV, IDIV; low word of 16-bit MUL, IMUL; 16-bit OUT |
| | Destination for: AAM; AAD; CBW; LODSW; 16-bit DIV, IDIV; 8-bit MUL, IMUL; 16-bit IN quotient of 16-bit MUL, IMUL |
| | Some variations of the following operations execute fastest or take fewest opcode bytes when AX or AL is one of the operands: ADC; ADD; AND; CMP; MOV; OR; SBB; SUB; TEST; XCHG; XOR |
| BX: | Used as base register to form effective address of memory operands. With DS, points to look-up table used in XLAT. |
| CL: | Used as counter for repeating forms of: RCL; RCR; ROL; ROR; SAL; SAR |
| CX: | Tested for zero in JCXZ. Used as counter in LOOP; LOOPNE; LOOPE; REP; REPNE; REPE |
| DX: | Source operand for: high word of 16-bit DIV, IDIV |
| | Destination for: CWD; remainder of 16-bit DIV, IDIV |
| | When the address of an input or output port is greater than FFH, DX must be used as an indirect pointer for IN and OUT. |
| SI: | Points to source string for, and is automatically altered by: CMPS; LODS; MOVS |
| | Used as index register to form effective address of memory operands. Default segment is DS when used as memory pointer. |
| DI: | Points to destination string for, and is automatically altered by: CMPS; MOVS; SCAS; STOS |
| | Used as index register to form effective address of memory operands. Default segment is DS when used as memory pointer. String operations use ES:[DI] as destination memory operand. |
| SP: | Points to the current top of the stack. Affected by: CALL; INT; INTO; IRET; POP; POPF; PUSH; PUSHF; RET Always points to addresses within stack segment (SS register). |
| BP: | Used as base register to form effective address of memory operands that are in the stack segment. Default segment is SS. |
| DS: | Default segment for all effective addresses except when BP is used. Points to source segment of all string operations. Affected by LDS. |
| ES: | Points to destination segment of all string operations. Affected by LES. |
| SS: | Segment for all stack operations. Default segment for all addresses that use BP as part of the effective addresss calculation. |

Sequentially accessing characters of a string or elements in a table is a fundamental part of assembly language programming. The 8088 supports a set of specialized instructions, using the pointer registers to simplify this process.

SI   is the *source index*. When you transfer strings of data from one address to another, you point SI to the address where the string currently resides; it indexes the source data. Some operations will automatically increment or decrement SI. It is normally used in forming an effective address that is an offset within the data segment (DS) register.

DI   is the *destination index*, the counterpart of SI. String move operations expect DI to point to the new address for the string—the string's destination. When used as a simple index (in a nonstring operation), DI points within DS. But for all string operations (MOVS, STOS, CMPS, and SCAS), the DI register describes an offset within the extra segment (ES) register.

A stack is a data structure that is used to keep track of temporary data and addresses quickly and efficiently. The following registers are used in conjunction with the 8088's stack:

SP   is the *stack pointer*. It automatically keeps track of the current top of the stack, that is, the next available address in the stack structure. It is manipulated with the PUSH, POP, CALL, and RET opcodes and may be initialized with a MOV opcode. Once it is initialized, you usually don't need to bother with it. It always points to an address in the stack segment (SS) register.

BP   is the *base pointer*. It is useful for accessing data that are on the stack (usually parameters that are being passed to a subroutine). When an effective address is formed using BP as the base register, the data are assumed to be in SS unless a segment override is specified.

## Segment Registers

As discussed in Chapter 1, accessing a full megabyte of memory with 16-bit pointers requires a segmented memory scheme. The 8088's segment registers are the basis upon which it operates. Whenever the 8088 calculates an effective address in order to access memory, it does so in the context of a memory paragraph (16-byte boundary) specified by one of the segment registers.

It is quite useful to be able to break your program into distinct code and data areas by using separate segments for each. Most 8088 programs define separate segments (physical chunks of memory, each beginning on a different paragraph address) for the code, data, and stack areas. The EXE files produced by IBM-PC compilers and the assembler all use this method. Some programmers prefer to simplify their code by initializing all the segment registers to the same value. PC-DOS external commands (.COM programs) use this option.

The segment registers are a different breed of register. You can't ask the CPU to do any arithmetic operations with a segment register as an operand. Also, there is no way to place a value directly into a segment register. You usually move the value into a general register and then transfer it to the segment register.

As with the other registers, the names of the segment registers have been chosen to reflect their main function.

CS   is the start of the *code segment*. Each opcode that the CPU fetches and executes is contained in the current code segment. Programs may be broken into several different code segments. You might want to place your main program in one segment and all its subroutines in another.

DS   is the *data segment* register. All program variables and arrays usually reside there. Effective addresses are assumed to point within this segment unless a segment override is specified or BP is part of the effective address calculation. String operations assume that the source address of the string is somewhere in the data segment.

ES   is the *extra segment* register. Whenever you need a segment register that points to neither the stack, data, nor code segments (as when accessing video memory), the ES register is handy to have around. This register has a very important specialty. It is assumed to point to the destination segment for all string operations.

SS   defines a program's *stack segment*. All data pointed to by SP (stack pointer) or BP (base pointer) are in this segment. Since the stack grows downward (the more data PUSHed onto the stack, the closer SP gets to 0), SP is usually initialized by a program (or by PC-DOS) to point to the end of the stack segment.

## Instruction Pointer and Flags Registers

In addition to the general and indexing registers, the 8088 has two special-purpose registers that don't fit into any other categories. These registers are not manipulated in the same way as the rest of the registers. Each is affected in predictable ways by the execution of certain specialized opcodes.

IP   is the *instruction pointer*, but unlike the other pointer registers, it is never used to point to data. The CPU uses it to keep track of the address of the opcode that it is currently executing. Commands such as JMP, CALL, and RET affect IP by replacing its contents with a new address.

FLAGS  is a 16-bit register that contains bit values that describe the result of arithmetic and logical operations. Every decision that your program makes is based on the condition of these flags. When we say that a flag is SET or true, that means it has a value of 1; when RESET, cleared, or false, it is a 0.

## 2.4 8088 FLAGS

The importance of understanding the CPU flags cannot be stressed enough. The only way to make a decision in an assembly language program is to do an arithmetic or bit logic operation, test the resulting state of one or more flags, and then, depending upon the result, force execution to the desired branch of the program.

Each flag is actually a single bit of memory, but the flags are rarely considered as having numeric value. They always represent one of the logical values TRUE or FALSE. The exception to this rule is the carry flag, which conceptually holds a numeric 1 or 0 bit during shift and rotate instructions. These concepts are discussed in greater detail in Chapter 3.

The CPU flags can be subdivided into two groups. Some are *control flags* that are set by the program in order to affect the way the CPU operates. Others are *status flags* that are automatically altered by the CPU to reflect the status of the results of arithmetic and logical operations. Each CPU flag has its own name and role. The following discussion describes each flag and gives the two-letter abbreviation that DEBUG uses when it displays the value of the flags.

### Processor Control Flags

DF    is the *direction flag* (UP = 0, DN = 1). The string operations (MOVS, CMPS, SCAS, LODS, and STOS) automatically adjust the string pointer registers (SI and/or DI) after operating on the data. This flag determines the direction of that adjustment. When DF = UP, the registers are incremented; otherwise, the operation goes backward from higher to lower addresses.

IF    is the *interrupt flag* (DI = 0, EI = 1). It determines whether maskable external interrupts are enabled or disabled. When IF is DI (disabled), the CPU will take no notice of hardware interrupts (such as the keyboard or timer interrupts). This means that the CPU will pay full attention to your code; it won't pause to perform "background" tasks. This flag should be cleared when timing considerations are crucial or during the execution of a hardware interrupt service routine. Note: Interrupt type 2 (the nonmaskable interrupt) and all software interrupts are always recognized.

TF    is the *trap flag* (not displayed by DEBUG). When TF = 1, the CPU is in a special "debugging" state. After each instruction is executed, a type 1 interrupt is forced. This allows a debugging program to single-step through a program (even a ROM program). DEBUG sets this flag.

### Arithmetic and Logical Result Flags

Perhaps the trickiest part of assembler programming is learning how to direct the flow of your program (i.e., to make decisions). The only way to do this is to test the status flags and route execution to different parts of your program. The flags are altered by every arithmetic and logic instruction. You route execution by using *conditional jumps*, which test for certain flags and flag combinations and then branch accordingly. The conditional jumps and techniques for making decisions are discussed in Chapter 3.

CF   is the *carry flag* (NC = 0, CY = 1). Whenever the result of an unsigned integer addition is too large to fit into the specified sum register (or memory location) or when an unsigned integer subtraction requires a borrow, then CF is set to 1. Some additions and subtractions take this into account, and the carry or borrow is "remembered" in the next operation. Some of the logic operations use CF as a 9th or 17th bit.

ZF   is the *zero flag* (NZ = 0, ZR = 1). It indicates if an operation ended with a result of 0. Programs constantly reference this flag, especially to determine if the last interation of a loop is completed. Note: Don't get confused by the numeric (0 or 1) state of this flag. Just consider the logical (false or true) value.

SF   is the *sign flag* (PL = 0, NG = 1). It echoes the highest bit of the result of an arithmetic operation. When the two's complement convention is being used, SF indicates whether the result of an operation is positive or negative.

OF   is the *overflow flag* (NV = 0, OV = 1). It indicates whether the result of an operation was too large to fit into the destination operand. This flag allows a program to make sure that no significant digits were lost during an operation. It is used in conjunction with other flags (SF and ZF) to test a result's relationship with 0. Also, OF and CF are both reset when a multiplication operation returns a result that fits entirely in the lower half of the accumulator.

PF   is the *parity flag* (PO = 0, PE = 1). It represents a 1-bit "checksum" of all the 1 bits in the result of an operation. If there is an even number of 1s in the result (0, 2, 4, etc.), PF = PE (called *even parity*). Conversely, if there is an odd number of 1s, PF = PO (*odd parity*). This flag is very seldom referenced except in telecommunications software.

AF   is the *auxiliary carry flag* (NA = 0, AC = 1). It indicates a carry out to, or a borrow from, the high nibble of an operand in an eight-bit arithmetic operation. Its use is internal to the CPU and has no significance to the programmer.

**THINGS TO DO**

1.  Without looking at Figure 2.1, name each of the CPU registers and identify a function that is a specialty of that register.

2.  Which status flag indicates whether a subtraction resulted in a negative value?

3.  What control flag must be set in order for the IBM-PC to recognize a CTRL-ALT-DEL keyboard reset?

## 2.5 ADDRESSING MODES

One of the advanced features of the 8088 is its wealth of memory *addressing modes*. In earlier processors, programmers have had few options for accessing the computer's memory. Using the Z80, for example, a program can say, "Copy the byte (or word) at address *xxxx* into a register" (*xxxx* being a 16-bit absolute address). Or it can say, "Load a register with *xxxx*, and then retrieve the byte (or word) at the address pointed to by that register." This is the simplest form of indirect addressing (i.e., accessing the data at the address named by a register).

The pointer and index registers offer whole new categories of convenience to the 8088 programmer. We can set a register to point to the base of a table and then say, "Retrieve the data that are *xxxx* bytes above the address named by that register." We can also use a second register to specify the offset from the base: "Retrieve the data that are at the address formed by adding these two registers." Finally, we can manipulate data that are offset from a base plus an index plus a constant.

In other words, when we access memory, we specify an *effective address* that can consist of a combination of up to three of the following:

* The variable address held in a base register (BX or BP).
* The variable address held in an index register (SI or DI).
* A constant offset (16-bit value).

What's more, any such effective address is calculated as an offset from an associated segment register. And we have the capability of overriding the normal segment register with the segment register of our choice.

All of this flexibility indicates that it is conceptually quite easy to keep track of a program and its data. We can segregate the opcodes of a program from its data and differentiate easily between different groups of data. For instance, a word processing program is likely to keep its program variables in one segment and the user's text in another.

The 8088 makes integer variables a breeze to handle. Lists of data and character strings are easy to visualize and manipulate. Two-dimensional arrays can be accessed in assembly language in much the same way that they are in BASIC and other high-level languages. For example,

```
MOV AL,DATA_TABLE[BX+SI]
```

says, "BX is the address of a row of data and SI is a column number. Place into AL the byte from the indicated row and column of the table that starts at the address of DATA_TABLE." Note the similarity with the BASIC statement:

```
LET AX = DATATABLE(BX,SI)
```

This comparison between BASIC array addressing and assembly language table addressing is not truly accurate; the BASIC statement doesn't need to have BX adjusted to the offset of the current row of the array. In BASIC, you point to the next higher row by adding 1 to the row index. In assembly language, you point to the next higher row by adding the *length of a row* to the row index. Figure 2.3 diagrams this type of indirect memory access.

**Figure 2.3**
**Effective Address Calculation Diagram**

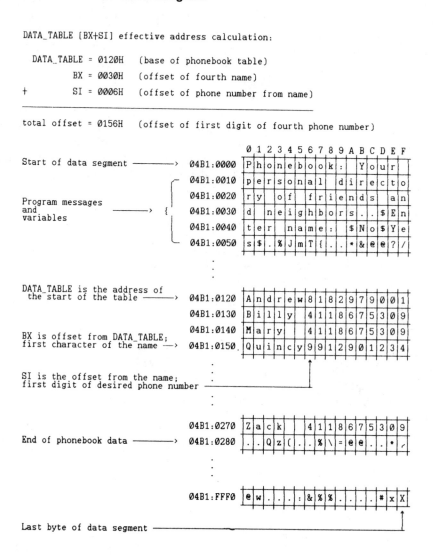

```
DATA_TABLE [BX+SI] effective address calculation:

    DATA_TABLE = 0120H   (base of phonebook table)
           BX = 0030H    (offset of fourth name)
 +         SI = 0006H    (offset of phone number from name)
 ─────────────────────────────────────────────────────────────
 total offset = 0156H    (offset of first digit of fourth phone number)
```

Figure 2.4 presents several examples of the 8088 addressing modes. The important thing to observe is how the components of the effective address are combined to form an offset within the indicated segment. The values of each of the components are simply added together. If one of the components is a signed number (above 7FFFH), then the addition works like a subtraction. A variable address such as MY_ARRAY is just another component, added in like the rest.

**Figure 2.4**
**Addressing Mode Examples**

Assume that these Effective Address components have these values:

```
DS <————— 0432H
ES <————— B800H

BX <————— 0001H
DI <————— 0003H
SI <————— FFFFH (i.e., -1)

MY_ARRAY <— 0006H
```

| Address segment:offset | Example destination,source | Addressing mode | Offset Calculation |
|---|---|---|---|
| | MOV  AL,BL | register | none |
| | MOV  AL,1 | immediate | none |
| 0432:0000 | | | |
| 0432:0001 | <— MOV  AL,[BX] | base-relative | 1 |
| 0432:0002 | | | |
| 0432:0003 | <— MOV  AL,[DI] | indexed | 3 |
| 0432:0004 | <— MOV  AL,[BX+DI] | base-relative indexed | 1 + 3 |
| 0432:0005 | <— MOV  AL,MY_ARRAY[SI] | indexed direct | 6 - 1 |
| 0432:0006 | <— MOV  AL,MY_ARRAY | direct | 6 |
| 0432:0007 | <— MOV  AL,MY_ARRAY[BX] | base-relative direct | 6 + 1 |
| 0432:0008 | <— MOV  AL,MY_ARRAY[DI-1] | indexed direct | 6 + 3 - 1 |
| 0432:0009 | <— MOV  AL,MY_ARRAY[DI] | indexed direct | 6 + 3 |
| 0432:000A | <— MOV  AL,MY_ARRAY[BX+DI] | base-relative indexed direct | 6 + 1 + 3 |
| B800:0000 | | | |
| B800:0001 | <— MOV  AL,ES:[BX] | base-relative with segment override | 1 |
| B800:0002 | | | |
| B800:0003 | <— STOSB | string addressing (DI offset implied) | 3 |

Here's a quick look at each of the addressing modes. The name of the mode is not particularly important to remember. Just pay attention to which combinations of components can be used.

*Register addressing* is the simplest addressing mode. It means that both the source and destination operands are registers—no external memory is accessed; for example,

```
MOV AX,BX
```

*Immediate addressing* takes the source operand from the bytes *immediately* following the opcode. That value can be manipulated arithmetically or just transferred directly to a register or memory location; for example,

```
MOV AX,1234H
```

*Direct addressing* also contains an operand that follows the opcode in memory. But unlike immediate addressing, the value specifies an offset address where the data are located. This is the addressing mode most often used to initialize and modify a program's scalar (nonarray) variables; for example,

```
MOV AX,MY_VARIABLE
```

*Indexed addressing* uses the value held by either SI or DI as the offset address of the memory operand; for example,

```
MOV AX,[SI]
```

Similar to indexed addressing is *base-relative addressing*, in which the operand address is specified by either BX or BP; for example,

```
MOV AX,[BX]
```

*String addressing* is a special mode used only with the 8088's powerful string operations. The effective address of the string operands is not calculated in the same manner as with other operations. These instructions always assume that the SI register contains the complete offset of the source string (SI is the *source* index) and that the DI register contains the offset of the destination string (DI is the *destination* index). It's important to note that the DS segment register is implied as the segment of the source operand and that ES segment register must point to the segment of the destination memory operand (of course, ES and DS may have the same value, so that both the source and destination operands are in the same memory segment); for example,

```
MOVSW
```

The real flexibility of 8088 addressing results from the available combinations of addressing modes. When you use BX or BP with a direct offset, you are using *base-relative direct addressing*. Using either SI or DI with a direct offset is called *indexed direct addressing*. Using either BX or BP with either SI or DI is an example of *base-relative indexed addressing*. And you can use all three together (i.e., either BP or BX with either SI or DI and a direct offset). This is conveniently called *base-relative indexed direct addressing*. Any effective address can refer to a byte or a word memory operand, depending on the opcode.

All effective addresses are actually offsets from the address pointed to by a certain default segment register. Except for some forms of string addressing, you can always select another segment register with a segment override. However, that means that you are always limited to accessing memory that is pointed to by a segment register. For example, you can never say, "Give me the value at 0040:0018." You must first point a segment register to 0040H and then fetch the data that are at address 0018H. You may find this irritating at first, but it's a limitation that you'll need to learn to live with.

Table 2.1 shows all the valid variations and combinations of these addressing modes. If you memorize those combinations, you will never make the mistake of trying, for example, to point AX at a variable or attempting to make CX a component of an effective address (AX and CX are neither base registers nor index registers). The table also shows which segment register is normally used as the base of operations for each of the addressing modes. Memorize this or keep it close at hand. Your program must always keep track of the segment registers, and you must be sure that when you access a memory variable, the expected segment register is being used. You can always reinitialize a segment register or use a segment register override to access data outside of the current default segment.

The rightmost column of Table 2.1 shows the number of clock cycles that the CPU takes to perform the effective address calculation. That might not mean too much at this point, but when you begin to write programs that must execute at the fastest possible pace, you will want to select the addressing mode that uses the fewest possible clock cycles.

**Table 2.1**
**8088 Addressing Mode Summary**

| Addressing Mode | Operand Format | Default Segment | Address calculation clock cycles |
|---|---|---|---|
| Register | reg8 or reg16 | — | — |
| Immediate | data8 or data16 | DS | — |
| Direct | [disp] or label | DS | 6 |
| Indexed | [DI] | DS | 5 |
|  | [SI] | DS | 5 |
| Base-relative | [BX] | DS | 5 |
|  | [BP] | SS | 5 |
| Indexed Direct | [SI+disp] | DS | 9 |
|  | [DI+disp] | DS | 9 |
| Base-relative Direct | [BX+disp] | DS | 9 |
|  | [BP+disp] | SS | 9 |
| Base-relative Indexed | [BX+SI] | DS | 7 |
|  | [BP+DI] | SS | 7 |
|  | [BP+SI] | SS | 8 |
|  | [BX+DI] | DS | 8 |
| Base-relative Indexed Direct | [BX+SI+disp] | DS | 11 |
|  | [BP+DI+disp] | SS | 11 |
|  | [BP+SI+disp] | SS | 12 |
|  | [BX+DI+disp] | DS | 12 |
| String (source) | [SI] | DS | — |
| String (destination) | [DI] | ES | — |

Notes: disp is either a 16-bit signed value or an 8-bit sign-extended value.
Add 2 clock cycles when segment override is used.

## What Mode When?

With all these ways of accessing memory, you may find yourself in the pleasant predicament of trying to select from among several that appear to be functionally identical. There is no hard-and-fast rule to help you decide; any two programmers will invariably have three conflicting opinions. But experience will teach you that certain of the addressing modes are tailor-made for certain tasks, making them easier to program, faster-running, or more concise.

Direct addressing is the most common mode. You use it whenever you know in advance exactly where something will be in memory. For instance, you know where each program variable is because you personally defined them all in the source code. The assembler does the work of keeping track of the storage address of simple variables; you access them just by using their symbolic name. There is little reason to use a base or index register to point to a variable when you can more easily access that variable by name.

Since string addressing must use SI and DI as the source and destination of string operations, it makes sense to use these registers whenever you need pointers into strings of text — even if you will not be using the special string operations. In the same vein, if you have any block of data that you consider to be a "source" of information, you should try to use SI to point to it; likewise, use DI to point to areas that are to receive or become the destination for data of any type, even if BX appears to work as well. Thus, you will find that the indexed addressing mode is very common because of its compatibility with string addressing.

Base-relative addressing using BP gets very little exercise. Since this mode defaults to data in the stack segment, it is hardly ever used except to access subroutine parameters that have been pushed onto the stack. This subject is mentioned in Chapter 3 and covered in detail in Chapter 7.

Base-relative addressing through the BX register can be used for many of the same purposes as indexed addressing. That is, you can often choose BX as your source of destination memory pointer as easily as SI or DI. You may tend to avoid this mode because the BX register has capabilities that SI and DI do not; it can be treated as two separate 8-bit registers.

Base-relative indexed addressing using either BX+SI or BX+DI is very handy when you need to access two-dimensional tables. In fact, there is little reason to use it for any other task. For instance, when you have read a file of mailing list entries into memory, it is convenient to point BX to a particular record (name, company, address, and zip code) and use SI or DI to access the individual fields within that record.

The complex base-relative indexed direct addressing is used for the same purpose —in applications that work with two- or three-dimensional arrays. You generally specify a value such as MY_TABLE as the start of the table, and then access records with BX and access subrecords or fields with SI or DI.

Your final selection of an addressing mode is usually based on whether or not you've painted yourself into a corner with regard to registers. For instance, if you are already using BX as a counter, then you're likely to use SI or DI for indirect memory access. You will also find that library procedures, either your own or those provided by PC-DOS and the ROM-BIOS, tend to use certain registers for certain purposes. For example, the ROM-BIOS routine that prints a character requires that BX be used to indicate a video page. If BX is tied up with this function, you will probably prefer to avoid base-relative addressing in the code near the call to that service. As you gain experience, you will learn to arrange your code so that it blends smoothly with the parameters of the routines it calls, especially those powerful ROM-BIOS and PC-DOS function calls.

## THINGS TO DO

1.  What is the only situation in which the ES segment register *must* be used?

2.  A segment value is always part of an effective address calculation. Name three other elements that may be used to access a memory location.

3.  Determine which of the following are not legal memory operands:

```
       [SI+1234]
   ES:[DX]
       [DI+BP+1]
       [SI+DI+BP]
   CS:[BP+2]
```

## The Addressing Mode Byte

This section discusses how the CPU decodes and executes opcodes. The process is interesting, but not essential to learning how to write 8088 assembly language. Skip this section if you are not interested in these low-level processes.

As the CPU reads the object code created by the assembler, it splits each opcode into several components. Each opcode in the 8088 instruction set is composed of one or two bytes, followed by as many as four bytes of address displacement and/or immediate data. A few selected opcodes require only one opcode byte, but for the most part, opcodes are two bytes long; the first byte indicates the operation, and the second byte indicates the addressing mode.

This addressing mode byte is a set of three bit fields that is decoded by the CPU to determine where to find the operands of an opcode. For example, when data are transferred between two registers, the addressing mode byte names the two registers. When the value at an address in memory is added to a register, it names the register and names the components that will be used to create the effective address of the memory operand. The direction (which operand is the source and which is the destination) and the size (byte or word) of the operation are defined by the opcode itself, rather than the addressing mode byte.

The fields of the addressing mode byte are in a notation that is easy for a CPU to decode but somewhat cryptic to the average person. Although you may never need to break an addressing mode byte into its components, it is instructive to see what the CPU goes through every time it executes a multibyte opcode. Table 2.2 decodes the components of the addressing mode byte for your perusal. The three fields are:

MOD (mode): 2-bit field determines if the operand is a register or in memory. Determines how to decode R/M.

R/M (register or memory): A 3-bit field names either the register operand or the components of the effective address of a memory operand, depending on the value of the MOD field.

REG (register): A 3-bit field names the register operand. This field can take on other meanings with certain opcodes. For example, in one type of MOV, it indicates that an immediate byte is specified as the source operand.

**Table 2.2**
**Addressing Mode Byte**

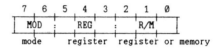

| REG | register 8-bit | register 16-bit |
|-----|-------|--------|
| 000 | AL | AX |
| 001 | CL | CX |
| 010 | DL | DX |
| 011 | BL | BX |
| 100 | AH | SP |
| 101 | CH | BP |
| 110 | DH | SI |
| 111 | BH | DI |

| R/M | MOD = 00 | MOD = 01 | MOD = 10 | MOD = 11 8-bit | MOD = 11 16-bit |
|-----|----------|----------|----------|-------|--------|
| 000 | DS:[BX+SI] | DS:[BX+SI+disp8] | DS:[BX+SI+disp16] | AL | AX |
| 001 | DS:[BX+DI] | DS:[BX+DI+disp8] | DS:[BX+DI+disp16] | CL | CX |
| 010 | SS:[BP+SI] | SS:[BP+SI+disp8] | SS:[BP+SI+disp16] | DL | DX |
| 011 | SS:[BP+DI] | SS:[BP+DI+disp8] | SS:[BP+DI+disp16] | BL | BX |
| 100 | DS:[SI] | DS:[SI+disp8] | DS:[SI+disp16] | AH | SP |
| 101 | DS:[DI] | DS:[DI+disp8] | DS:[DI+disp16] | CH | BP |
| 110 | DS:[disp16] | SS:[BP+disp8] | SS:[BP+disp16] | DH | SI |
| 111 | DS:[BX] | DS:[BX+disp8] | DS:[BX+disp16] | BH | DI |

Note:  disp8 is an 8-bit signed value ranging from +127 to −128.
       disp16 is a 16-bit signed value ranging from +32,767 to −32,768.

Table 2.3 shows the possible ways that an opcode may be stored in memory. Some opcodes are self-contained, even to the extent that the affected register is named in the opcode. Others require an addressing mode byte, and some require that one or two bytes of immediate data follow the opcode. When the addressing mode indicates that a displacement must be used as a component of the effective address, then the one or two bytes of that displacement will follow directly after the addressing mode byte.

**Table 2.3**
**Object Code Formats**

| Format | Example |
|---|---|
| [ opcode ] | PUSH AX |
| [ opcode ] [ data8 ] | ADD AL,3 |
| [ opcode ] [ data16 ] | ADD AX,303H |
| [ opcode ] [ disp8 ] | JNE TAG |
| [ opcode ] [ disp16 ] | JMP NEAR_TAG |
| [ opcode ] [ addr16 : segment ] | CALL FAR_PROC |
| [ opcode ] [ mode ] [ data16 ] | ADD BX,303H |
| [ opcode ] [ mode ] | ADD AL,BL |
| [ opcode ] [ mode ] [ data8 ] | ADD BL,3 |
| [ opcode ] [ mode ] [ disp8 ] | ADD CX,[DI+3] |
| [ opcode ] [ mode ] [ disp8 ] [ data8 ] | ADD [BX+2],0FH |
| [ opcode ] [ mode ] [ disp8 ] [ data16 ] | ADD [BX+2],1234H |
| [ opcode ] [ mode ] [ disp16 ] [ data8 ] | ADD MY_VAR,3 |
| [ opcode ] [ mode ] [ disp16 ] [ data16 ] | ADD MY_VAR,1234H |

This situation is complicated by the 8088's ability to use sign-extended offsets and data. In some cases, the assembler must make a decision about the types of operands because two or more different opcode/offset/data combinations will perform identical functions. For example, there are four different ways to add 3 to the word that is one byte above the address pointed to by SI. The following assembler line uses the WORD PTR operator (discussed in Chapter 4) to indicate that the operation will be on a 16-bit value:

```
ADD WORD PTR [SI+1],3   ;WORD PTR specifies a 16-bit operand
```

Even though a 16-bit operation is specified, the assembler could generate any of these combinations, all of which perform identical actions:

```
83 44 01 03                 ADD        WORD PTR,[SI+1],+3

83 84 01 00 03              ADD        WORD PTR,[SI+0001],+3

81 44 01 03 00              ADD        WORD PTR,[SI+1],0003

81 84 01 00 03 00           ADD        WORD PTR,[SI+0001],0003
```

In this case, there are two different opcodes and two different addressing mode bytes. The 81H opcode adds an 8-bit sign-extended immediate operand, and 83H specifies that the source operand is a 16-bit immediate word. The two different addressing mode bytes of 44H and 84H indicate that the destination operand is at either an 8-bit sign-extended offset or a 16-bit offset, respectively. The assembler will generate the shortest sequence of bytes wherever possible. It sometimes generates a 16-bit offset for an operand that would apparently fit into an 8-bit value. This happens so that the relocating linker (discussed in Chapter 4) can adjust the address when the code or data is loaded at a different memory location.

Obviously, the process of encoding these opcodes is very tedious. If you needed to keep track of the bytes that force the CPU to execute each option of each opcode, you would probably never do any real programming.

## But Don't Worry

The names of these addressing modes and the bit patterns of the addressing mode byte are most useful when you run out of things to say at a cocktail party. As you write assembly language, you never actually specify the addressing mode you want to use; the assembler does that for you. All you need to know is the combinations of registers and displacements that can be used to access program variables.

## THINGS TO DO

1. Figure out why a DEBUG disassembly (with the U command) might show a sequence of these mnemonics:

   ```
   ADD  [BX+SI],AL
   ```

2. Looking at Table 2.2, see if you can determine why Intel selected the combination R/M = 110 and MOD = 00 to specify the direct addressing mode.

# Chapter 3

# 8088 Instruction Set

## 3.1 INSTRUCTING THE CPU

The opcodes that the 8088 executes are just numbers stored in its memory. All but a very few of the 256 possible values of a byte have special meaning to the CPU. Exactly what an opcode instructs the 8088 to do often depends on the addressing mode byte and any address or immediate data bytes that follow it in memory. Each opcode can be broken down into the bit fields that the machine actually decodes, but unless you intend to rewrite the Macro Assembler, there is very little need to know which bit pattern does what. Instead, you should think of the instruction set as just another computer language.

Every computer language translates words and phrases from a format that is meaningful to humans into a format that the machine can work with. Assembly language is a low-level language because its commands and statements have a one-to-one correspondence to the operations that are performed by the computer. The 8088's repertory of operations is small; it has a vocabulary of fewer than 100 different statements, many of which are small variations of similar statements. Learning assembly language is a matter of memorizing the name and function of each operation, learning the options of each operation, and learning how to specify those options in your source text. As with all computer languages, the source code of assembly language is a series of text lines containing commands specified in a rigidly defined syntax.

### Assembly Syntax

The syntax of assembly language is simplicity itself. Each sentence is in the following format:

```
[label[:]]  mnemonic  [operand[,operand]]  [;comment]
```

Lines of source text may be up to 132 characters long, but there is rarely any need for a line longer than the 80 characters displayed on a line of the video monitor. Even a 40-character line is long enough to specify most assembly language commands.

An assembler source code line may be completely blank — to separate visibly sections of a program. Most lines will include one or more of the previously mentioned fields, and if the line is to generate any object code or instruct the assembler in how to assemble your code, it must contain a word in the mnemonic field. Each of the fields must be separated by at least one blank space or a tab. Exactly how many spaces separate the fields is not important, but the fields must always be in the indicated order. Here's an example of a source code line that contains all four fields:

```
TOP_OF_PAGE:   MOV  CX,66     ;initialize the line counter
```

**The Label Field**

The label is optional. If present, it is a name by which you may refer to the line in other lines. Labels are used to name a procedure, a subroutine, or any line of code to which execution may branch during execution. Labels are also used to name the addresses of memory variables and macros. A label can be composed of up to 31 characters chosen from among the following:

* Alphabetic letters A through Z (lowercase is the same as uppercase)
* the digits 0 through 9
* the special characters ? _ . @ $

The label can start with any of these characters except a digit. The period (.) has special meaning for certain variable names, so its use should be avoided, but it may be used as the first character of a label. The names of the registers and assembler reserved words (such as assembler mnemonics) cannot be used as labels.

The special characters can be used to make your labels more readable by separating words. When a label starts with a special character, it tends to be highly visible. Some programmers adopt the convention of naming certain types of procedures or variables with a special character. For instance, you could use the dollar sign ($) as the first character of general-purpose library procedure names. The programmers of IBM PC Pascal have *ended* each of their library procedure names with *QQ*. Naming conventions such as these can be a great aid in deciphering someone else's (or your own!) cryptic source code.

When a label ends with a colon (:), it indicates that the line is the first part of a set of instructions—usually the destination of a near jump. In this book, most labels that end with a colon are set on a separate line. This tends to make branching points stand out in the listing, and it allows a label to be long without displacing the mnemonic and operand fields of the line.

You have a great deal of flexibility in naming the branches of your program, so you *could* use labels such as these:

```
BRANCH_TAKEN_WHEN_THE_USER_ANSWERS_YES:
```

However well this documents your program, you are not likely to want to do that much typing. Also, many program branches are difficult to name, either because their function is so abstract or because there are other labels in the program that begin similar functions. Some programmers solve this problem by appending a number to the end of each label in a procedure:

```
READ_INPUT PROC NEAR
          .
          .
RI_1:
          .
          .
RI_2:
          .
          .
READ_INPUT ENDP
```

This technique tends to avoid "collision" or duplication of label names, but taken to the extreme, it can leave code as undocumented as the line numbers in a BASIC program. Some programmers use a modification of this technique to achieve the best of both worlds. Simple detours in the program logic to handle a single decision are best named with simple numbered names. Special branches, including the tops of major loops and procedure exits, should be given names that have more meaning. For instance, the READ_INPUT procedure is likely to contain labels named RI_NEXT_ CHARACTER and RI_EXIT.

## The Mnemonic Field

A mnemonic (the first *m* is silent) is a way to remember something. Mnemonics are "keys" that you can use to "open up" your memory to fuller definitions. For example, your shopping list might have the mnemonic "2 CHIX" to remind you to pick up a couple of whole fryers at the meat counter.

Assembly language mnemonics are little keys to help you remember what each opcode does. These mnemonics are cryptic, but they do contain clues to the functions they represent. As in learning any foreign language, it is helpful to use these "words" in "phrases" and to *speak them aloud*. Once you have associated a word with a phrase several times, it has become integrated into your vocabulary.

The mnemonic is either an opcode name or an assembler directive (also called a *pseudo-op*). These are the most basic tools in your assembly language toolbox. You will need to become well acquainted with the 8088 mnemonics—to be aware of their strong points and weaknesses. Section 2 of this chapter discusses the opcode mnemonics that go into this field. Chapter 4 covers the pseudo-ops and other elements that can be used in a line of assembly language source code.

One thing you need to know about a mnemonic is how many operands it requires. Some mnemonics stand alone; either they operate on implied operands, or their action is entirely internal to the CPU. If an opcode has a number of options or makes any access to registers or memory, then it will have at least one operand.

### The Operand Field

The operand field defines the addressing mode of an operation. In other words, it indicates where the CPU will find the operands that an opcode affects. This field may contain zero, one, or two operands, depending on the opcode. Most arithmetic and logic operations have two operands, and all transfers between registers and between register and memory must explicitly name both of the operands. When an opcode needs two operands, they must be separated by a comma. The first operand is invariably the *destination*, and the second is the *source*.

Reading this foreign language has a little twist that might take some getting used to. The operands may seem backward at first. For instance,

```
MOV   AX,BX
```

should be read aloud as:

"Move to register AX the value in register BX."

There is nothing new in this format. You will recognize similarities in

```
LET AX = BX
```

"I bought my IBM PC with petty cash."

"We moved to LA from NY."

"I'll walk to ETERNITY from HERE." (Oh, well...)

Unlike mnemonics, which are always a single word that must match an assembler keyword (or a macro name), operands are often written as *expressions*. That is, you can let the assembler do arithmetic operations and type conversions on an operand. This can be as simple as saving yourself a moment with a calculator, such as:

```
MOV   AX,1234H+20
```

or more complex, such as:

```
MOV   BYTE PTR CS:[SI][MY_TABLE+4],(TYPE MY_VAR) * 5 + '0'
```

In either case, there are still two operands. In the latter case, a complex addressing expression is used as the destination (memory) operand, and an arithmetic expression is used as the source (immediate) operand. The assembler operators are covered in Chapter 4.

### The Comment Field

The comment field gives programmers an easy way to describe what the code is doing. The comment must be preceded by a semicolon (;) and is ignored by the assembler (i.e., it does not generate any machine language). If the first character in a line is a semicolon, the entire line is ignored.

Because assembler code by itself is so obscure, a piece of code that you write today may be all but meaningless tomorrow ("Now, just what was I doing *here?*"). A major programming task that takes weeks or months to code will be all but impossible to debug unless it is fully documented with comments. Serious programmers write programs as a series of modules. If your modules are well documented, they can be used and reused in many different applications.

Be creative with your comments! You can make the flow of your program much clearer if you make certain things stand out in your listing:

```
;    =-=-=-=-=-=-=-=-=-=-=-=-=-=-=-=-=-=-=-=-=-=-=
;    = CLEAR_STORE                                =
;    = This procedure zeros all of the elements   =
;    = in the screen storage array.               =
;    =-=-=-=-=-=-=-=-=-=-=-=-=-=-=-=-=-=-=-=-=-=-=
;-- CX,DX (the X,Y coordinate) is ready, now plot the dot --
;  ** program only gets here when page counter is over 66 **
         RET   ;<<<<<------- PROGRAM EXIT ---------<<<<<
RI_3:          ;branch here when user answers yes
```

## THINGS TO DO

1. Identify the fields of each of the following lines of source code:

```
         MOV   AX,BX
EXIT:    RET
         CALL  CLEAR_SCREEN ;clear the 80-column screen
;--- start of main loop ----
         MOV   WORD PTR CS:PAGE_COUNTER,5
```

2. Is it correct to leave a blank line in your source code?

3. Must the fields of assembly language source code be lined up in columns? What is the penalty if they aren't?

## 3.2 THE INSTRUCTION SET

The 8088 has the capability of adding, subtracting, multiplying, dividing, and comparing two values. It can transfer data from place to place, and it can receive data from and send data to external devices. Most important, the order in which it executes these functions can be altered.

There are six groups of opcodes in the 8088 instruction set. They are

1. Data transfer.

2. Arithmetic.

3. Bit manipulation.

4. Program sequence control.

5. String manipulation.

6. CPU control.

There are several good reference books that discuss each of the 8088 opcodes in detail, diagramming their actions and listing their bit patterns. In this book, we will concentrate on the opcode groups, pausing to examine special features of the opcodes that merit special attention. As we encounter an unusual or particularly powerful opcode, we will take the time to demonstrate its usage. A complete alphabetical list of the opcode mnemonics is found in Appendix A.

### 3.2.1 Data Transfer Instructions

The 8088 is blessed with a wealth of data transfer instructions, but they are all variations on a theme—taking 8 or 16 bits from one place and copying it to another. Table 3.1 lists the various transfer instructions.

### The MOV Instruction

MOV is the general-purpose instruction that is used to transfer data between registers and memory. The assembler syntax is

```
MOV   destination,source
```

Here *destination* is one of

* A register.

* A location in memory.

And *source* is one of

* The value in a register.

* A value at an address (a memory operand).

* A value specifice in the opcode (an *immediate* value).

The source operand is copied into the destination; that is, the destination operand is overwritten by the new value, and the source remains unchanged. The CPU flags are not affected by the MOV commands.

**Table 3.1**
**Data Transfer Instructions**

| Mnemonic | | Format | O | D | I | T | S | Z | A | P | C |
|---|---|---|---|---|---|---|---|---|---|---|---|
| | | | CPU flags affected | | | | | | | | |

| Mnemonic | | Format | O | D | I | T | S | Z | A | P | C |
|---|---|---|---|---|---|---|---|---|---|---|---|
| | | ——— GENERAL DATA TRANSFER ——— | | | | | | | | | |
| MOV | MOV | destination,source | | | | | | | | | |
| PUSH | PUSH | source | | | | | | | | | |
| POP | POP | destination | | | | | | | | | |
| XCHG | XCHG | register,reg/mem | | | | | | | | | |
| XLAT | XLAT | [translation_table] | | | | | | | | | |
| | | ——— TRANSFER FLAGS ——— | | | | | | | | | |
| PUSHF | PUSHF | | | | | | | | | | |
| POPF | POPF | | * | * | * | * | * | * | * | * | * |
| LAHF | LAHF | | | | | | | | | | |
| SAHF | SAHF | | | | | | * | * | * | * | * |
| | | ——— TRANSFER ADDRESS ——— | | | | | | | | | |
| LDS | LDS | destination,mem32 | | | | | | | | | |
| LES | LES | destination,mem32 | | | | | | | | | |
| LEA | LEA | destination,memory | | | | | | | | | |
| | | ——— INPUT/OUTPUT ——— | | | | | | | | | |
| IN | IN<br>IN | accumulator,port8<br>accumulator, DX | | | | | | | | | |
| OUT | OUT<br>OUT | port8,accumulator<br>DX,accumulator | | | | | | | | | |

Note: * means that the flag is altered by the operation.

The MOV operation itself is very simple. The complication is that there are a large number of ways in which you can specify a memory operand. All memory operands are at an effective address that consists of the 20-bit value formed by combining a segment register value with an offset value. The offset part of the effective address is a 16-bit value that is

* Explicitly named in the opcode.

* Pointed to by a base register (BX or BP).

* Pointed to by an index register (SI or DI).

* Formed by adding a combination of any or all of the preceding.

The entire effective address is always a memory address that is offset from a segment register. All memory operands are associated with a default segment register (usually DS), but you can specify that an alternate segment register be used in the effective address calculation.

Here are a few examples of the MOV command:

```
MOV AX,BX           ;value in a register is copied into
                    ;another

MOV AX,30ABH        ;immediate value copied into register

MOV AX,MY_VARIABLE  ;memory operand into register

MOV MY_VARIABLE,AX  ;register into memory operand

MOV AX,[BX]         ;base-relative memory word operand to
                    ;register

MOV AX,ES:[SI]      ;register to indexed memory in extra
                    ;segment

MOV [BX+SI],AX      ;register to memory at base+index
                    ;address

MOV AX,[BX+SI+5]    ;value at base+index+offset into
                    ;register

MOV CS:[BX+DI],AX   ;segment override for CS segment
```

There are so many options that you're better off learning what moves you *can't make*. You can MOV any valid memory operand or any register to any other one *except*

* A memory operand to another memory operand.

* A 16-bit operand to an 8-bit destination.

* An 8-bit operand to a 16-bit destination.

* An immediate value to a segment register.

* Any value (register, memory, or immediate value) to the CS or IP registers.

To complicate matters, the assembler allows several different ways to identify the same address. If the label MY_TABLE is the start of a list of bytes and you want to retrieve a byte from that list, here are several of the ways you can do so:

```
MOV  AL,MY_TABLE        ;get the first byte in
                        ;the table

MOV  AL,[MY_TABLE+3]    ;get the fourth byte
                        ;(+00 is the first)

MOV  AL,MY_TABLE[3]     ; same as above
```

```
MOV   AL,[DI,+MY_TABLE]              ;byte indexed by DI
MOV   AL,[DI] MY_TABLE [3]           ;indexed by DI plus 3
MOV   AL,MY_TABLE.FIELD_1 [DI+BX+3]  ;special structure
                                     ;reference
```

If a base or index register is part of the effective address, then it must be enclosed in brackers ([]). However, any other effective address components can be written in any order, inside or outside the brackets. You can use this method to your advantage to make your code more readable. However, the examples in this book will always show the registers and any explicit offsets of a memory operand as being inside of the brackets.

Note: When you read a memory reference aloud, read the brackets ([]) as "the contents of." For example, MOV AX,[BX+3] is read as: "Move the contents of BX plus three to AX."

Programmers who have had experience with other microprocessors may find certain of the IBM-PC Macro Assembler notations somewhat peculiar. Many assemblers assume that when you specify a label as an operand, you mean the *address* of the label. The Macro Assembler, on the other hand, generates code to retrieve the *value* at the label's address. In other words, the "contents of" part of the variable name reference is implied. If you want to MOV an address value into a register, you must use the OFFSET operator:

```
MOV   SI,OFFSET MY_TABLE
```

The OFFSET operator is discussed in Chapter 4.

**Other Transfers**

XCHG (eXCHanGe) allows you to swap the values in two operands. At least one of the operands must be a register, but segment registers cannot be exchanged with anything. Obviously, the order in which you specify the operands makes no difference to the assembler; each operand is both a "source" and a "destination." For example:

```
XCHG    [DI],AL    ;temp<-- AL. AL <-- [DI], [DI] <-- temp
```

XLAT (transLATe) is an unusually high-level command to find at the machine language level. It automatically looks up a value in a table. The syntax is:

```
XLAT   [translation_table]
```

The BX register is a pointer to a look-up table, and the AL register is used as both a table index and a destination operand. The byte that is AL bytes from the start of the table pointed to by DS:BX is copied into AL. In BASIC, you might write:

```
AL = TABLE(AL) '** where BX identifies the start of the table
```

The TRANSLATION_TABLE operand may be omitted; the assembler just uses it to check your code to find if the table has been defined in the data segment (and to provide a segment override if needed). However, it must be included if you need to use an explicit segment override:

```
MOV    AL,CODE

MOV    BX,OFFSET TRANS_TABLE

XLAT   DS:TRANS_TABLE ;must use unless ES = DS
```

Regardless of whether or not the TRANSLATION_TABLE operand is specified, the assembler does *not* initialize BX. It is the responsibility of the programmer to make sure that BX has been pointed to the start of the translation table.

For instance, if you need to translate an ASCII character to an EBCDIC (another convention for storing characters), XLAT will simplify the process. Just point BX to the start of a table of EBCDIC characters and load AL with the ASCII code to be looked up. Executing the XLAT command causes AL immediately to hold the matching EBCDIC character.

Here's another example. Suppose you have a binary nibble, 0-15, in the AL register, and you want to translate it to a hex digit between 0 and *F*. There are several quick ways to do this through a series of calculations, but the XLAT command offers a unique alternative. The following is a subroutine that performs the translation. In this case, the TRANSLATION_TABLE is in the code segment.

```
MOV      BX,OFFSET NIB_TABLE

XLAT     CS:NIB_TABLE

RET

.

.

.
```

```
NIB_TABLE DB '0123456789ABCDEF'
```

LAHF (Load AH from the Flags) and SAHF (Store AH to the Flags) provide a means to duplicate the 8-bit flags register of the 8080 and Z-80 CPUs. These commands require no parameters in the operand field.

LAHF and SAHF will hardly ever come up in your own code, but you may see these opcodes when you disassemble someone else's code. If so, you can be pretty sure that the program is a conversion of a program from an 8080 or Z80 CPU.

SAHF has a useful function when used in programs that employ the 8087 NDP. Several of the "condition" bits in the 8087's Status Word line up directly with the 8088's flags. In particular, the Carry and Zero flags just happen to be in the right place. So, after doing a floating-point comparison with the 8087, it is possible to store the Status word to memory, put the high byte into AH, and store that value to the Flags register. After doing that, the conditional jump opcodes work as if the comparison had been done on the 8088:

```
FCOM    ST(3)          ;compare ST to ST(3) . . . 8087 registers

FSTSW   STATUS         ;place result flags into memory

FWAIT                  ;synchronize coprocessors

MOV     AX,STATUS

SAHF                   ;give 8087 flags to 8088

JAE     NOT_BELOW  ;test and go . . . as if CMP ST,ST(3)

.

.

.

NOT_BELOW:
```

## Stack Data Transfers

The PUSH and POP opcodes store and retrieve 16 bits of data from the stack. These instructions have only one operand. These commands are actually indexed MOV instructions that always use the SP register as a pointer to the memory operand. The POP opcode fetches data from the address pointed to by SS:[SP] and then adds 2 to SP to prepare for the next POP. PUSH works in a complementary fashion. It first subtracts 2 from SP and then places data into the address at SS:[SP].

The general format is:

```
PUSH    source
```

and

```
POP     destination
```

where source and destination are always 16-bit register or memory operands, including all segment registers. The only exception is that there is no POP CS opcode.

Figure 3.1 illustrates what takes place when the PUSH and POP opcodes are executed. The most important thing to remember is that if you PUSH an operand, you must be sure to POP it at some later point to avoid uncontrolled growth of the stack (the stack could grow so large that it begins to write information over a program's opcodes, destroying the program). If you push two or more values on the stack, be sure to POP them back off in the reverse order.

The 8088's PUSH and POP opcodes allow you not only to save and retrieve registers, but to move stack data into and out of your memory variables:

```
PUSH    MY_VARIABLE

POP     MY_TABLE[DI]
```

The preceding examples amount to a memory-to-memory transfer of the value of MY_VARIABLE to an address in MY_TABLE. This transfer can be used to avoid destroying the value of one of your precious registers with a MOV operation.

**Figure 3.1**
**PUSH and POP Operations**

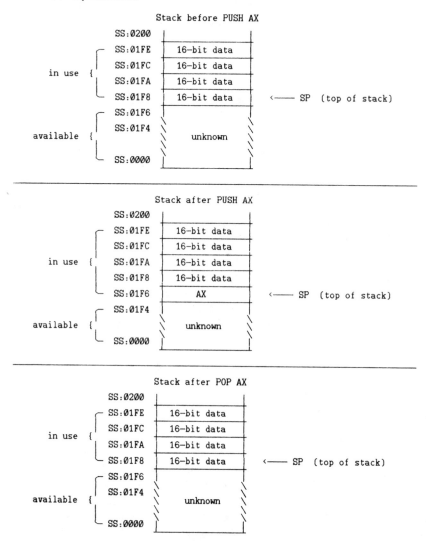

You can also PUSH and POP the segment registers. Thus, one way to copy the CS register into DS is:

```
PUSH  CS

POP   DS
```

PUSHF and POPF transfer the flags register to and from the stack. These are the only operations that can be used to store and retrieve the state of the flags. It is not possible to move them directly to another register. The PUSHF and POPF opcodes require no operands.

## Object-Address Transfers

The object-address transfer instructions are used to keep track of addresses of variables and strings in memory.

LEA (Load Effective Address) calculates an offset value from the addressing mode information of a memory operand. It *does not* transfer any data to or from memory, but it requires a memory reference as its source operand. For example,

```
LEA  BX,[BX+SI+20H]  ;set up new table base
```

is identical to

```
ADD  BX,SI
ADD  BX,20H
```

The LEA instruction seems to have little value because it is no faster than manually adding up the components of the effective address. However, it might be used to clear up the logic of a muddy piece of table indexing code. If you ever find yourself saying "Ok, I'm pointing at the right place, but just where *is* it?", you might consider using LEA.

LEA may also be used as an alternate way to retrieve the *offset* of a memory operand. For instance, the following two examples perform the identical operation of moving the address of the start of MY_TABLE into the DI register in preparation for processing that table.

```
MOV  DI,OFFSET MY_TABLE  ;generates three bytes of code

LEA  DI,MY_TABLE         ;generates four bytes of code
```

The 8088 provides a rudimentary means of retrieving 32-bit operands from memory in a single instruction. All memory addresses require both segment and offset components to define fully their location. In most smaller programs, the segment in which an object resides will always be known. But when a program uses many objects (i.e., strings of data or blocks of information) that may be scattered through more than 64K of memory, it is necessary to keep track of both a segment and an offset for each object. The LDS and LES opcodes are used to retrieve both a segment and an offset value of such an object.

The LDS (Load pointer into DS) retrieves a 32-bit doubleword from memory and places the low-order 16 bits in a destination register and the high-order 16 bits in the DS register. For example, if IN_BUF_PTR is a doubleword variable that contains both a segment and an offset value for your program's input buffer, then

```
LDS  SI,IN_BUF_PTR  ;prepare to process the input buffer
```

will set up DS with a segment value and SI with an offset value in preparation for processing the string of characters that are in the input buffer. This takes the place of the two step sequence

```
MOV   SI,IN_BUF_PTR      ;fetch the offset into SI

MOV   DS,IN_BUF_PTR+2  ; and the segment address into DS
```

LES (Load pointer into ES) is identical to LDS except that it transfers the high-order 16 bits to the ES register. This instruction is most often used when you must initialize a destination pointer for a string operation (the ES register must always point to the destination segment of string operations). For example:

```
LES   DI,STRING_TABLE[BX]  ;prepare to fill the string
```

## Input/Output Transfers

The 8088 supports 65,536 I/O (input/output) ports. There are IN and OUT commands for receiving or sending 8-bit data through any port. The 16-bit IN and OUT opcodes send or receive two bytes through adjacent ports (the LSB comes from the lower port address, and the MSB comes from the port address just above it). AL (or AX) is always the destination or source for these opcodes. When the port number is between 0 and FFH, it may be specified as an immediate data byte. For example:

```
IN   AL,123  ;read data at port 123 into AL

IN   AX,123  ;read AL from port 123 and AH from port 124

OUT  123,AL  ;output AL to port 123

OUT  123,AX  ;output AL to port 123 and AH to port 124
```

When the port that must be accessed is at a port address greater than FFH, or whenever you write code that must select from among several port addresses, you must use DX as an *indirect port pointer*. Consider the following for examples:

- Accessing port 3B0H:

```
MOV  DX,3B0H

IN   AL,DX
```

- Accessing a port selected from among several:

```
MOV  SI,OFFSET PORT_TABLE   ;point to a table

ADD  SI,4                    ;select second 2-byte entry

MOV  DX,[SI]                 ;fetch the port number

OUT  AL,DX                   ;send AL out the selected port
```

**THINGS TO DO**

1.  What is wrong with each of these opcodes?

    ```
    MOV    MY_VARIABLE,[DI]

    MOV    DS,DATA_SEG

    MOV    AL,SI

    XCHG   DS,BX

    MOV    IP,DI

    OUT    AL,3B5H

    LEA    BYTE_VAR,SI
    ```

2.  Can you figure out why the assembler will not accept the POP CS opcode?

3.  Which two registers are affected by the LES   BX,CS:[DI] opcode?

### 3.2.2 Arithmetic Operations

Older microprocessors were only able to add and subtract, and a certain "accumulator" register was needed as one of the operands. The 8088 has extended these basic arithmetic operations to include multiplication and division (see Table 3.2). Addition and subtraction are not limited to leaving a result in an accumulator. Any two registers or a register and a variable in memory may be used as operands, and either may be selected as the destination.

### Addition, Subtraction, and Comparison

As with the MOV instructions, the first operand specifies the destination.

```
ADD   AX,BX      ;16-bit register addition: AX = AX + BX

ADD   BL,CL      ; 8-bit register addition: BL = BL + CL

SUB   AX,9       ;16-bit subtraction: AX = AX - 9

SUB   MY_VAR,DX  ;memory operand = memory operand - DX
```

After the CPU performs the operation, it sets the flags to describe the result. For example, if the result is zero, then ZF (zero flag) is set to true. If you subtract a large number from a smaller number, CF (carry flag) is set to indicate that a borrow was needed to complete the operation.

CMP (CoMPare) is used to compare two values in order to make decisions in your program. It works just like a subtraction, except that the result is thrown away; only the flags are kept to describe the result. This operation is very important because all decisions of an assembly language program are based on flag settings—tested by the

**Table 3.2**
**Arithmetic Instructions**

| Mnemonic | | Format | O | D | I | T | S | Z | A | P | C |
|---|---|---|---|---|---|---|---|---|---|---|---|
| | | | | | | | CPU flags affected | | | | |
| ADDITION | | | | | | | | | | | |
| ADD | ADD | destination,source | * | | | | * | * | * | * | * |
| ADC | ADC | destination,source | * | | | | * | * | * | * | * |
| INC | INC | destination | * | | | | * | * | * | * | |
| AAA | AAA | | ? | | | | ? | ? | * | ? | * |
| DAA | DAA | | ? | | | | * | * | * | * | * |
| SUBTRACTION | | | | | | | | | | | |
| SUB | SUB | destination,source | * | | | | * | * | * | * | * |
| SBB | SBB | destination,source | * | | | | * | * | * | * | * |
| DEC | DEC | destination | * | | | | * | * | * | * | |
| NEG | NEG | destination | * | | | | * | * | * | | * |
| CMP | CMP | destination,source | * | | | | * | * | * | * | * |
| AAS | AAS | | ? | | | | ? | ? | * | ? | * |
| DAS | DAS | | ? | | | | * | * | * | * | * |
| MULTIPLICATION | | | | | | | | | | | |
| MUL | MUL | source | * | | | | ? | ? | ? | ? | * |
| IMUL | IMUL | source | * | | | | ? | ? | ? | ? | * |
| AAM | AAM | | ? | | | | * | * | ? | * | ? |
| DIVISION | | | | | | | | | | | |
| DIV | DIV | source | ? | | | | ? | ? | ? | ? | ? |
| IDIV | IDIV | source | ? | | | | ? | ? | ? | ? | ? |
| AAD | AAD | | ? | | | | * | * | ? | * | ? |
| CBW | CBW | | | | | | | | | | |
| CWD | CWD | | | | | | | | | | |

Note: * means that the flag is altered by the operation.

? means that the state of flag is undefined after the operation.

various conditional jump commands. The names of the conditional jump commands make the most sense when they directly follow a compare instruction. This subject is handled in more detail in the section "Conditional Jumps: Making Decisions."

Decisions are easiest to understand when you read the statements aloud.

```
          CMP   AL,1     ;"Compare register AL to 1, then . . ."

          JNE   NOT_1    ;"Jump to the label NOT_1 if they are

                         ;Not Equal"

          . . .          ;  --   process commands for when AL = 1

NOT_1:    . . .          ;continuation for when AL <> 1
```

ADC (ADd with Carry) and SBB (SuBtract with Borrow) are special forms of addition and subtraction that make it easier to perform multiple-precision arithmetic. In decimal addition, when the digits in the 1s column add up to more than 9, then you simply carry a 1 to the 10s column. Similarly, when you add two binary numbers and the result won't fit in the destination, the carry flag is automatically set to record the fact. If you are working with large numbers, 32-bit operands for instance, you can use ADC to carry that extra 1 over to the next addition:

```
MOV   AX,OP1_LOW_WORD   ;get low 16 bits of 32-bit operand

ADD   AX,OP2_LOW_WORD   ;if result is > 0FFFFH then set carry

MOV   RESULT_LOW,AX     ;store lower 16 bits of the result

MOV   AX,OP1_HI_WORD    ;get upper 16 bits of 32-bit operand

ADC   AX,OP2_HI_WORD    ;remember the carry in this addition

MOV   RESULT_HI,AX      ;store the upper 16 bits of the result
```

In effect, the ADC adds the two operands and then adds the value of the carry flag (0 or 1) to the destination operand.

Likewise, SBB can be used to remember that an earlier subtraction required a borrow. After the subtraction, the value of the carry flag is subtracted from the destination operand.

```
MOV   AX,OP1_LOW_WORD   ;get low 16 bits of 32-bit operand

SUB   AX,OP2_LOW_WORD   ;if result is < 0 then set carry

MOV   RESULT_LOW,AX     ;store lower 16 bits of the result

MOV   AX,OP1_HI_WORD    ;get upper 16 bits of 32-bit operand

SBB   AX,OP2_HI_WORD    ;remember the carry in this
                        ;subtraction

MOV   RESULT_HI,AX      ;store the upper 16 bits of the result
```

The high-speed INC (INCrement) and DEC (DECrement) commands add 1 to and subtract 1 from their single operand. These are helpful in keeping track of the iterations of a program loop. The flags are set just as they are in addition and subtraction, except that the carry flag is not affected. Thus, you can test whether the loop counter has become 0 or -1 and branch accordingly:

```
              MOV     BX,5      ;set up the loop counter
     AGAIN:

              .
              .(the body of the loop)

              .

              DEC     BX        ;BX = BX - 1
              JNE     AGAIN     ;loop back unless BX has become 0
or

              DEC     BX

              JL      AGAIN ;loop back if BX has become Less than 0
```

As with all arithmetic instructions, you can directly INC or DEC a memory operand specified with any of the addressing modes. Because these commands do not indicate the operand's size (8 or 16 bits), you may need to use a WORD PTR or BYTE PTR operator in the address expression:

```
     INC   WORD PTR MY_VARIABLE   ;16-bit increment

     DEC   BYTE PTR ES:[SI+DI]    ;8-bit decrement in ES
```

The BYTE PTR and WORD PTR operators are covered in Chapter 4.

The NEG (NEGate) opcode is a fast way to reverse the sign of an operand. It simply subtracts its single operand from 0:

```
     NEG   AX              ;AX = 0 - AX

     NEG   WORD PTR [DI]   ;[DI] = 0 - [DI]
```

## Multiplication and Division

The 8088 supports two types of multiplication and division and two sizes for their operands. MUL and DIV work with unsigned operands. IMUL (Integer MULtiply) and IDIV (Integer DIVide) work with signed numbers. Either operation can be on 8-bit or 16-bit operands.

Figure 3.2 illustrates an important limitation of these commands. Unlike addition and subtraction, which will leave their result in any register or memory location, these are accumulator-specific commands (i.e., the destination of the result is always an accumulator register). The accumulator for division is AX or AL, and the accumulator for multiplication is the 32-bit register pair DX:AX or the 16-bit register AX.

**Figure 3.2**
**Multiplication and Division**

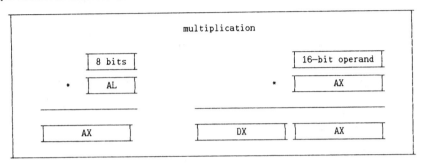

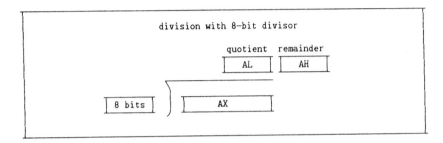

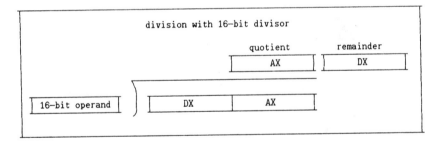

Thus, the destination is implied, not stated in the opcode mnemonic. The multiplicand or dividend is also an implied accumulator. The options are few, so we'll list examples of all of them:

```
DIV  BL  ;8-bit,  AL = int(AX / BL),    AH = remainder
DIV  BX  ;16-bit, AX = int(DX:AX / BX), DX = remainder

MUL  BL  ;8-bit,  AX = AL * BL
MUL  BX  ;16-bit, DX:AX = AX * BX
```

The source operand (divisor or multiplier) cannot be an immediate value. It may be a memory operand, but its size must be known. So the destination may need to be specified with an operand size override:

```
MUL   BYTE PTR [SI]   ;AX = AL * 8-bit memory operand

DIV   WORD PTR [SI]   ;DX:AX = AX / 16-bit memory operand

MUL   MY_VAR          ;destination depends on size of MY_VAR
```

After the multiplication or division, the CPU flags are mostly undefined, so you can't tell as much about a result as you can with the simpler arithmetic operations. After division, all of the flags are undefined. After multiplication, both CF and OF are reset when the significant digits of the result fit entirely in the lower half of the destination register (AL for the byte source and AX for the word source). In other words, if, after an 8-bit MUL, either CF or OF is 0, then AH is 0; after a 16-bit MUL, DX is 0.

Incidentally, the 8088 will happily divide a number by zero, but when it's finished, it recognizes the error and forces an INT 0. This is actually a special case of what is called *division overflow*. INT 0 is always forced whenever the quotient is too large to fit in the destination accumulator. For example:

```
MOV   BL,10

MOV   AX,65000

DIV   BL
```

will cause a division overflow because the result of 65,000/10 is 6,500, which won't fit in the implied accumulator (AL).

IMUL (Integer MULtiply) and IDIV (Integer DIVide) allow you to multiply and divide signed integers. These instructions keep track of the signs of the operands and the result. They are slightly slower than the unsigned versions. As with MUL, after an IMUL, only the CF and OF result flags are meaningful. When CF and OF are set, the upper half of the result will be a sign extension of the lower half; that is, all the significant digits of the result will be found in AL (AX for a 16-bit source operand).

### Preparing the Dividend

A final word on division: When you do any division, you must be certain that the high byte (or word) of the accumulator operand is correctly initialized. For example, even though you are only dividing two 8-bit numbers and you know that the result will fit in AL, the CPU will use the AH register in the operation. So you must be certain that it doesn't contain a value that will invalidate the result. CBW (Convert Byte to Word) and CWD (Convert Word to Doubleword) are designed to prepare the accumulator for division.

CBW takes the sign bit (bit 7) of the AL register and replicates it through the AH register:

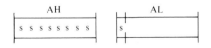

CWD takes the sign bit (bit 15) of the AX register and replicates it through the DX register:

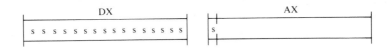

To make sure that the quotient is accurate, always do the following:

```
CBW         ;sign-extend AL into AH (prepare AX)

IDIV  BL  ;do the 8-bit division
```

and

```
CWD         ;sign-extend AX into DX (prepare DX:AX)

IDIV  BX  ;do the 16-bit division.
```

## Binary-Coded Decimal Arithmetic

Spreadsheet and other number-oriented applications are hard pressed to do their work purely on binary values. The problem is caused by an inherent loss of precision when fractional numbers are represented in binary. These applications often choose to use *binary-coded decimal (BCD)* values to represent numeric quantities accurately. BCD arithmetic is very accurate because there is no limit to the size of the operands and the decimal point can be repositioned easily. The same algorithms you were taught in elementary school for pencil-and-paper arithmetic apply to BCD arithmetic. By contrast, the 8088 has no inherent ability to work with floating-point numbers (numbers that include fractions), and there are certain size limitations for every type of operation.

The BCD system is based on the fact that each of the decimal digits 0 through 9 can be held conveniently in a single 4-bit nibble. One format, called *packed BCD*, uses the two nibbles of a byte to represent two decimal digits. *Unpacked BCD* ignores the upper half of a byte and uses the lower nibble to hold a decimal digit.

BCD arithmetic involves conversion overhead before and after each operation. Packed BCD requires that two digits be packed into a series of bytes before the operation and then unpacked into a displayable ASCII representation after the operation. Unpacked BCD is simpler because the ASCII digits '0' through '9' *start out* in the correct format. For example, the low nibble of the ASCII character '5' is a binary 5.

The 8088 provides instructions to aid in doing arithmetic operations on BCD values. Specifically, the opcodes DAA and DAS aid in packed BCD arithmetic, and the opcodes AAA, AAS, AAM, and AAD are used in doing unpacked BCD operations. They all require that nothing be in the operand field of the source line because their source and destination are both the implied register AX. Let's see why these adjustments are needed and how to use the tools provided in the instruction set.

A string of ASCII characters has little meaning to the 8088, but the lowest four bits of the digits '0' through '9' just happen to be the binary equivalents of these digits. So, if we shave off the upper four bits and operate with only the low nibble, we can obtain valid binary sums, differences, products, and quotients. For example,

```
ASCII   Hex    Binary
  '5' = 35H = 0011 0101
+ '1' = 31H = 0011 0001
        x6H = xxxx 0110 (ignore high nibble)
  '6' = 36H = 0011 0110 (set high nibble to 3 to convert
                          back to ASCII)
```

The same logic applies to subtraction, multiplication, and division: You can use the low nibble of an ASCII digit as if it were a binary value. However, things are not quite that simple. For instance, here's what happens when the two nibbles of an ASCII addition add up to more than '9':

```
ASCII   Hex    Binary
  '6' = 36H = 0011 0110
+ '8' = 38H = 0011 1000
        xEH = xxxx 1110
  '>' = 3EH = 0011 1110 (3EH is not an ASCII digit)
```

In this case, the result of the addition was in error; it doesn't reflect a valid unpacked BCD digit. What we really wanted here were the two ASCII digits '1' and '4'.

The AAA (Adjust for ASCII Addition) opcode corrects the result of this operation so that it represents two nibbles that can be converted to ASCII. The operand must be in the AL register before AAA is executed. This fragment of code illustrates the preceding example:

```
MOV  AL,'6'   ;ASCII '6' is 36H

ADD  AL,'8'   ;AL is now 6EH  (36H + 38H = 6EH)

AAA           ;AH is now 1 and AL is 4
```

After the AAA, the meaningless (in terms of ASCII decimal digits) value 6EH has been converted to the two bytes 1 and 4. One further step, adding 30H to each of these bytes, will result in the two ASCII digits '1' and '4.'

In effect, AAA replaces the sequence:

```
CMP  AL,9

JBE  BCD_OK   ;if Below or Equal, no problem, so skip

              ; else, make low nibble valid
```

```
        ADD   AL,6    ; 0AH = 10H, 0BH = 11H, etc.

        INC   AH      ; and show the carry in AH

BCD_OK:

        AND   AL,0FH;clear high nibble (10H = 0, 11H = 1, etc.)

                      ;AH and AL are ready to be converted

                      ;to ASCII
```

AAS (Adjust for ASCII Subtraction) makes a similar adjustment for subtractions of unpacked BCD values. It is used in an identical manner: After subtracting two ASCII digits, use AAS to correct the result, and then OR a 30H to the accumulator to obtain an ASCII representation of the difference. If the subtraction required a borrow, the carry flag will be set and may be used in subsequent subtractions via the SBB operation.

AAM and AAD are tools used to correct the errors that occur when unpacked BCD characters are multiplied and divided. AAM (Adjust for ASCII Multiplication) is used after two unpacked BCD values have been multiplied. Unlike AAA and AAS, this instruction will *not* disregard the upper nibble of an ASCII digit. So, before the multiplication, you must be certain that both operands are binary numbers between 0 and 9 (not 30H and 39H). The logical AND instruction can be used to "mask off" the unwanted bits. For example:

```
MOV   BL,'7'   ;multiplier = 37H

AND   BL,0FH   ;             = 07H (mask off high nibble)

MOV   AL,'8'   ;multiplicand = 38H

AND   AL,0FH   ;             = 08H (mask off high nibble)

MUL   BL       ;product in AX = 0039H = 56 decimal

AAM            ;AH = 5, AL = 6 (ready for conversion to ASCII)
```

The AAM opcode divides the product by 10, leaving the integer result in AL and the remainder in AH. In fact, you could obtain a result identical to that shown in the previous example by replacing the AAM with

```
MOV   BL,10

CBW            ;make sure that AH = 0

DIV   BL
```

It is interesting to note that the AAM opcode is in two bytes and that the second byte is a 0AH (10 decimal). Although Intel will make no such claim, this second byte is actually an *immediate divisor* of an undocumented division operation. The only difference between AAM and DIV BL (When BL is 10) is that AAM does not use AH as part of the operand, and it performs the division somewhat more quickly. As a division by 10, the AAM instruction can be used as a shortcut for conversion of binary values to ASCII decimal digits.

AAD (Adjust for ASCII Division) corrects for the errors in unpacked BCD division. As with AAM, the division must be on operands that have a high nibble of 0. Unlike AAM, you must use this opcode *before* dividing the ASCII operands.

```
MOV   BL,'7'      ;divisor in BL = 37H
AND   BL,0FH      ;mask off high nibble (BL = 07H)

MOV   AH,'4'
MOV   AL,'2'      ;dividend in AX = 3432H
AND   AX,0F0FH    ;mask off high nibbles (AX = 0402H)

AAD               ;prepare for division
                  ;AX is now 002AH = 42 decimal
DIV   BL          ;42/7 quotient in AX; AH = 0 and AL = 6, so
                  ; AL is ready for conversion back to ASCII
```

After the division, the integer portion of the quotient will be in the AL register and the remainder will be in AH.

As with the AAM opcode, it is no accident that the second byte of the AAD opcode is a 10. The AAD instruction actually multiplies AH by 10, adds the result to AL, and sets the AH register to 0.

The DAA and DAS instructions adjust for errors in adding and subtracting packed BCD operands. There is no simple adjustment for packed BCD multiplication and division. However, you could unpack the two digits in a BCD byte, perform the operation on each digit, and then repack the two resulting bytes.

## THINGS TO DO

1. Name three ways to subtract 1 from the AX register.

2. Determine why this instruction won't work:

   ```
   MUL   25
   ```

3. How will this instruction affect the AX register?

   ```
   ADC   AX,0
   ```

4. (*) Assume that you have retrieved the value of the real-time clock from PC-DOS and that the current minute (0-59) is the binary value in the AL register. Find a way to convert this value into two ASCII digits with the 10s place in AL and the 1s place in AH. This can be accomplished in as few as two instructions.

### 3.2.3 Bit Manipulation Instructions

Bit manipulation instructions are used to alter the bit pattern of an operand. This makes it easy to keep track of bit flags such as those that indicate the various keyboard shift states. These opcodes are also very useful in directly manipulating the colors displayed in the graphics mode. Table 3.3 lists the 8088's bit manipulation instructions.

**Table 3.3**
**Bit Manipulation Instructions**

| Mnemonic | Format | | O | D | I | T | S | Z | A | P | C |
|---|---|---|---|---|---|---|---|---|---|---|---|
| | | | CPU flags affected | | | | | | | | |
| ——— LOGIC ——— | | | | | | | | | | | |
| AND | AND | destination,source | 0 | | | | * | * | ? | * | 0 |
| OR | OR | destination,source | 0 | | | | * | * | ? | * | 0 |
| NOT | NOT | destination | | | | | | | | | |
| TEST | TEST | destination,source | 0 | | | | * | * | ? | * | 0 |
| XOR | XOR | destination,source | 0 | | | | * | * | ? | * | 0 |
| ——— SHIFTS ——— | | | | | | | | | | | |
| SAL/SHL | SAL | destination,1 | * | | | | * | * | ? | * | * |
| | SAL | destination,CL | * | | | | * | * | ? | * | * |
| SAR | SAR | destination,1 | * | | | | * | * | ? | * | * |
| | SAR | destination,CL | * | | | | * | * | ? | * | * |
| SHR | SHR | destination,1 | * | | | | * | * | ? | * | * |
| | SHR | destination,CL | * | | | | * | * | ? | * | * |
| ——— ROTATIONS ——— | | | | | | | | | | | |
| ROL | ROL | destination,1 | * | | | | | | | | * |
| | ROL | destination,CL | * | | | | | | | | * |
| ROR | ROR | destination,1 | * | | | | | | | | * |
| | ROR | destination,CL | * | | | | | | | | * |
| RCL | RCL | destination,1 | * | | | | | | | | * |
| | RCL | destination,CL | * | | | | | | | | * |
| RCR | RCR | destination,1 | * | | | | | | | | * |
| | RCR | destination,CL | * | | | | | | | | * |

Note: * or 0 means that the flag is altered by the operation.

? means that the state of flag is undefined after the operation.

### Logic Operations

The AND, TEST, OR, and XOR opcodes are logical arithmetic instructions. They each require two operands:

```
AND     destination,source

TEST    destination,source

OR      destination,source

XOR     destination,source
```

These operations alter the CPU flags as expected by any operation; that is, if the result is 0, then ZF = ZR; if the result is negative (the high bit is set), then SF = PL. These opcodes have a notable effect on the CF, the carry flag. No matter what the result of the operation, CF is always reset to 0 (NC).

You should be familiar with the AND and OR operations from the discussion in Chapter 1. When you AND two operands, the result will contain a 1 in each position that was a 1 in *both* operands. AND is often used to mask off or filter out certain bits in an operand. For example, we can force an ASCII alphabetic character into uppercase by making certain that bit 5 is a 0.

```
MOV AL, 'y'       ;AL starts lowercase:  01111001 = 79H = 'y'

AND AL,11011111B ;mask has bit five=0   11011111 = DFH

                  ;AL ends as UPPERCASE: 01011001 = 'Y'
```

TEST is a variation of AND in which the result is not saved; only the flags are affected. This is a useful function because no operand is destroyed. For example, you can determine if either of the shift keys is being pressed without using up one of the precious registers to hold a temporary value.

```
TEST  KBD_FLAG, 00000011B  ;either low bit on?

JZ    NO_SHIFT             ;if not, branch around shift code
```

Just remember that if any 1 bits match, the (discarded) result is Not Zero. Thus, a JZ will be taken only when there is no match, and a JNZ will be taken when any bits match up.

The result of an OR is a byte or word that contains a 1 in each bit position that was a 1 in *either* operand. You could use this function to force the IBM-PC keyboard into CapsLock state, as in:

```
OR   KBD_FLAG, 01000000B ;make sure bit six is true.
```

XOR (eXclusive OR) compares each of the bits of both operands. When both bits are different, the result bit is set to 1. When both bits are the same, the result bit is set to 0. You can use this instruction to toggle specific bit fields in an operand. When you XOR a register with itself, it becomes 0. So this is one way to set a register to 0.

A not so obvious use of XOR is seen in graphics applications. XORing one operand with another operand twice in succession will result in the original value. If you XOR the bytes of a graphics shape with screen bytes twice in succession, the shape will appear and then disappear. By doing this operation in cycles and changing the position of the shape on the screen after each cycle, you can make the shape appear to move around on the screen without affecting the background. This rudimentary principle of animation is discussed in Chapter 8.

### Shift Instructions

The logic instructions contain a group of opcodes that rearrange an operand's bit pattern. They move the bit pattern left or right by one or more positions. These operations are best understood as though they work on sets of true/false flags; however, some of the logic instructions can be used to do blazing-fast multiplications and divisions.

Figure 3.3 diagrams the actions of the shift and rotation opcodes. These instructions will work on 8-bit or 16-bit register or memory operands. The assembler syntax is:

```
SHL   destination,1

SHR   destination,1

SAR   destination,1
```

### Figure 3.3
### Shift and Rotate Operations

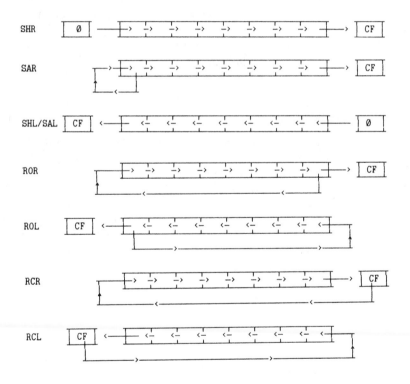

The second operand is always 1 in these operations. A special feature of the 8088 allows this operation to be repeated a variable number of times. This unusual feature is in the section "Repeated Shifts and Rotations." For the most part, the single-shift operations are by far the most often used.

The SHR (SHift logical Right) opcode moves the bits in its operand to the right by one position. The rightmost bit is copied into the carry flag, and 0 is placed into the vacated leftmost bit. If we shifted a decimal number to the right, it would cause the value to be divided by 10, but since these operations are binary, a right shift forces a division by 2.

```
        00010100 = 12H = 18 (before the shift)

-->     00001010 = 09H = 9 (after right shift)
```

SAR (Shift Arithmetic Right) is a seven-bit variation of the same operation. This opcode comes in quite handy for shift division of signed numbers. The shift works the same as SHR except that bit 7, the sign bit, remains untouched.

```
        10111110 = BDH = -66 (two's complement convention)

-->     10011111 = 9FH = -33
```

In a shift division by 2, the remainder can only be 0 or 1. You can find out what that remainder is by testing the carry flag. If CF = NC, then the division has no remainder; if CF = CY, then there is a remainder of 1.

Similarly, SHL (SHift logical Left) and SAL (Shift Arithmetic Left) multiply an operand by 2. There is no distinction between these two commands. The reason is this: If a signed number is positive, all of the leading bits are 0s. If a signed number is negative, all the leading bits are 1s. So it doesn't matter if the sign bit is preserved or not.

## High-Speed Multiplication and Division

The shift instructions are very important because of the speed you can gain by using them. If you use DIV to divide a number by 2, the machine takes at least 80 clock cycles —one of the slowest operations. The same division using SHR takes only two clock cycles—the fastest operation performed by the CPU! The time advantage is so great that you may sometimes go out of your way to use it.

Because of the IBM-PC's screen layout, graphics programs often multiply by 80 in order to find the address of the graphic screen row. IMUL takes up to 98 cycles; MUL takes as many as 77 cycles. The following sequence whittled the time down to 17 cycles:

```
SHL AX,1    ;times 2

SHL AX,1    ;times 4

SHL AX,1    ;times 8

SHL AX,1    ;times 16

MOV BX,AX   ;save partial value

SHL AX,1    ;times 32

SHL AX,1    ;times 64

ADD AX,BX   ;(AX*16 + AX*64) = AX*80
```

This example shows that there are infinite puzzles within puzzles. Finding the fastest way to accomplish a goal is just another level of intrigue.

## Rotation Instructions

There are four bit-rotation instructions. They are valid for both 8-bit and 16-bit destination operands:

```
ROR   destination,1

ROL   destination,1

RCR   destination,1

RCL   destination,1
```

A rotation is the computer's way of playing musical chairs. When we ROR (ROtate Right) an operand, every bit is shifted to the right but the rightmost bit (bit 0) is not lost. It is rotated into the leftmost position (bit 7 or bit 15). ROL (ROtate Left) does the same thing in the other direction.

RCR (Rotate through Carry Right) and RCL (Rotate through Carry Left) perform 9-bit rotations. CF, the carry flag, is used as an extension of the operand. For instance, in RCR the operand is shifted right, the carry flag is copied into the "vacated" bit 7 (bit 15 in word operands), and the "lost" bit 0 is copied into the carry flag.

## Repeated Shifts and Rotations

Finally, all the shift and rotate opcodes may be performed a variable number of times. If you don't know in advance how many times to shift the operand, your program can calculate a shift count and place it in the CL register. Then use CL as the second operand in the instruction.

```
MOV   CL,SHIFT_COUNT    ;get the count that was calculated

SHL   AX,CL            ;shift it that many times
```

One thing to note here is that CL is *not decremented* during the operation. It starts and ends with the same value.

A series of single shifts will execute faster than the same number of iterations of a multiple shift operation. You will use this operation only when you can't tell in advance how many shifts are required. For example, the ROM-BIOS uses a variable shift when it positions graphics bits because the code must handle both one-bit (high-resolution) and two-bit (low-resolution) pixel displays.

## THINGS TO DO

1. One graphics function needed by most arcade-type games is to determine if two moving shapes have collided. What opcode could be used to find out if the bits of a shape were in any way "touching" anything except a blank area of the screen?

2. Use shifts and rotations to write a sequence of instructions that will quickly and accurately divide a signed 32-bit number in DX:AX by 4, leaving the result in DX:AX and the remainder (0 to 3) in BL.

### 3.2.4 Program Sequence Control

Beyond performing a sequence of arithmetic and logic operations, the CPU must be able to alter its point of execution. In particular, the CPU must be able to branch to different parts of a program, depending on the results of previous computations. Table 3.4 lists the 8088's sequence control commands.

At some point in the history of computers, someone invented the idea of subroutines or *procedures* that could be invoked from any point in a program. These procedures make it possible to reuse a series of machine language steps without needing to have them in the direct line of execution.

As the CPU executes each opcode, the IP (instruction pointer) register is bumped to point to the next opcode. If a program needs to execute any but that opcode—for example, when the program must loop back to a previous instruction to do something again—the IP register must be pointed to the new address. Conceptually, this operation is just a transfer of address data to IP. There is no instruction to

```
MOV  IP,TARGET                        ;(nonexistent opcode)
```

But there *is* a large set of instructions that alter the IP register. These are the JMP and CALL commands.

The JMP command is almost, but not quite, a transfer of data to IP. It is really an addition of an immediate value to IP. This means that when you code

```
JMP   TARGET
       .
       .
       .
TARGET:
```

the distance (number of opcode bytes) between the JMP command and the target label is added to the IP register. The operation is a signed addition, so that adding a negative value will force execution to a point earlier in the program.

The designers of the 8088 chose this method because it makes jumps *self-relative*. That is, the actual address for execution to resume can change dynamically; only the distance between the jump and the landing pad needs to be known. Thus, a program may be moved to different memory addresses and still function correctly. This property makes it easier to write code that can be placed in a library and used repeatedly in different applications.

The segmented nature of the 8088 memory structure demands that this concept be extended to include jumps between different segments of code. So jumps come in two basic flavors: intrasegment and intersegment. Intrasegment jumps simply change the IP register, as we've been discussing. One variation of the intrasegment jump, called a *SHORT jump*, adds a sign-extended byte to IP, giving it a range of -128 to +127. The

**Table 3.4**
**Program Sequence Control Instructions**

| Mnemonic | Format | | CPU flags affected | | | | | | | | |
|---|---|---|---|---|---|---|---|---|---|---|---|
| | | | O | D | I | T | S | Z | A | P | C |
| ——————— UNCONDITIONAL ——————— | | | | | | | | | | | |
| CALL | CALL | *target* | | | | | | | | | |
| RET | RET | [*stack_displacement*] | | | | | | | | | |
| JMP | JMP | *target* | | | | | | | | | |
| ——————— CONDITIONAL ——————— | | | | | | | | | | | |
| JA/JNBE | JA | *short_target* | | | | | | | | | |
| JAE/JNB | JAE | *short_target* | | | | | | | | | |
| JB/JNAE | JB | *short_target* | | | | | | | | | |
| JBE/JNA | JBE | *short_target* | | | | | | | | | |
| JC | JC | *short_target* | | | | | | | | | |
| JE/JZ | JE | *short_target* | | | | | | | | | |
| JG/JNLE | JG | *short_target* | | | | | | | | | |
| JGE/JNL | JGE | *short_target* | | | | | | | | | |
| JL/JNGE | JL | *short_target* | | | | | | | | | |
| JLE/JNG | JLE | *short_target* | | | | | | | | | |
| JNC | JNC | *short_target* | | | | | | | | | |
| JBE/JNA | JBE | *short_target* | | | | | | | | | |
| JNE/JNZ | JNE | *short_target* | | | | | | | | | |
| JNO | JNO | *short_target* | | | | | | | | | |
| JNS | JNS | *short_target* | | | | | | | | | |
| JNP/JPO | JNP | *short_target* | | | | | | | | | |
| JO | JO | *short_target* | | | | | | | | | |
| JP/JPE | JP | *short_target* | | | | | | | | | |
| JS | JS | *short_target* | | | | | | | | | |
| JCXZ | JCXZ | *short_target* | | | | | | | | | |
| ——————— ITERATION CONTROL ——————— | | | | | | | | | | | |
| LOOP | LOOP | *short_target* | | | | | | | | | |
| LOOPE/LOOPZ | LOOPE | *short_target* | | | | | | | | | |
| LOOPNE/LOOPNZ | LOOPNE | *short_target* | | | | | | | | | |
| ——————— INTERRUPTS ——————— | | | | | | | | | | | |
| INT | INT | *type* | | | | * | * | | | | |
| INTO | INTO | | | | | * | * | | | | |
| IRET | IRET | | * | * | * | * | * | * | * | * | * |

Note: * means that the flag is altered by the operation.

other version, called a *NEAR jump*, adds a 16-bit signed value to IP, so that it can transfer control to any point within the current code segment.

Intersegment (or FAR) jumps, on the other hand, must be able to transfer control to a new code segment. Thus, the CS register must also be changed. This variety is an absolute jump (i.e., a transfer of address data to IP and CS rather than a signed addition). Therefore, intersegment jumps are not self-relative. A program that contains these kinds of jumps must go through a relocation process before it can be executed.

With both types of jumps available, you can program the CPU to transfer control to any part of the current code segment or to any part of any code segment anywhere in the 8088's megabyte of memory.

## Procedures: Calling and Returning

Invoking a subroutine is just a temporary transfer of control to a certain part of a program. The CPU performs a CALL to a procedure by saving the value of IP and then pointing it to the address of the procedure. Execution continues from that point. After a procedure has finished performing its function, control must be transferred back to the calling program. The RET instruction simply restores the address that was saved by the CALL instruction back into IP.

The return address within the calling program needs to be saved only temporarily. As soon as the RET instruction uses those data to get back to the point after the call, the address is valueless. As discussed in Chapter 2, the stack is used expressly for temporarily saving data. It is the ideal structure for saving the return address. In fact, a CALL is nothing more than

```
        PUSH OFFSET RET_ADDR   ; (nonexistent opcode)

        JMP TARGET

   RET_ADDR:
```

and a RET is simply:

```
        POP     IP              ; (nonexistent opcode)
```

As with jumps, calls can be either intrasegment or intersegment. The NEAR (intrasegment) variety is self-relative; FAR (intersegment) calls are to absolute addresses. A FAR call must save the value of the CS register as well as that of IP. Thus, in order to restore both values, there must be a special intersegment or FAR return instruction. A FAR call and return sequence is conceptually:

```
     PUSH   CS                 ;place four bytes of address
     PUSH   OFFSET RET_ADDR     ;data on the stack
                                ; (nonexistent opcode)
     JMP    FAR_TARGET          ;move new values into IP
                                ;and CS
```

```
RET_ADDR:

        .

        .

        .

FAR_TARGET                      ;(in a different segment)

        .

        .

        .

        POP     IP              ;these two actions take
        POP     CS              ;place simultaneously
                                ;(nonexistent opcodes)
```

The Macro Assembler includes no RETF (RETurn Far) mnemonic. Instead, it keeps track of the *type* of each procedure. Any RET that is found in the body of a FAR procedure is considered a FAR return. When you write a procedure, you must specify its type in the procedure declaration:

```
FAR_PROC PROC  FAR

        .

        .

        .

        RET     ; this is a FAR (intersegment) return
FAR_PROC ENDP

NEAR_PROC PROC  NEAR     ;or simply PROC (NEAR is the default)

        .

        .

        .

        RET     ; this is a NEAR (intrasegment) return
NEAR_PROC ENDP
```

**Procedures with Parameters**

The 8088 supports a special type of return instruction in the format:

```
RET     STACK_ADJUSTMENT
```

This is either a near or far RET as defined by the type of procedure that contains it. It is special because the STACK_ADJUSTMENT value will be used to change the value of SP just before execution is passed back to the caller. The effect is that the stack is cleared of any parameters that were placed there prior to the call.

Most procedures process one or more input values. It is often easiest to supply these values in registers, according to a protocol established by the calling program. This system becomes unwieldy when there are more than one or two parameters to pass. It breaks down completely when there are many parameters of varying types. An alternative method is to PUSH a series of parameters onto the stack before calling a procedure. That way, the procedure can examine those parameters at its leisure, without worrying about keeping track of specific registers.

The BP register is designed expressly for accessing those parameters because its default segment is the stack segment. The designers of the 8088 also saw the need to be able to rid the stack of the parameters after the procedure is finished, so they developed this special form of the RET instruction. The assembler source line

```
RET     4
```

restores the IP register to its value before the call and then makes a separate adjustment to SP, setting it to the position before two parameters were pushed onto the stack. We will examine this instruction in more detail in Chapter 7 when we discuss how BASIC and Pascal pass values to assembly language routines.

## Indirect Jumps and Calls: N-Way Branching

The 8088 CPU contains provisions for selecting a procedure from among the entries in a table. You can call or jump to a procedure that has the value of its address stored in a register or a memory variable—an indirect jump. For example,

```
JMP     AX
```

is identical to the nonexistent instruction

```
MOV     IP,AX
```

This gives you the capability of looking up an address in a table, loading that value into a register, and jumping to or calling that address.

```
MOV  SI,OFFSET JUMP_TABLE
MOV  AX,[SI+10]              ;select the fifth 2-byte vector
JMP  AX
```

Indirect jumps such as this are sometimes referred to as *computed gotos* because the program can select the branch to take according to the result of previous calculations (the BASIC statement ON X GOTO . . . . is analogous). You can even skip a step and directly jump to or call the address specified as a memory operand:

```
JMP   SAVED_ADDR

JMP   [BX+DI]

JMP   PROC_TABLE[DI]
```

In the last example, the word at the effective address of DS:PROC_TABLE+DI is transferred into the IP register. Notice that all indirect jumps and calls are transfers and not self-relative additions, as with the direct intrasegment jumps.

FAR jumps and calls can be to addresses stored in memory, but the memory variable must be four bytes long—a doubleword variable. You will learn how to define storage for variables of different sizes when we discuss the assembler pseudo-ops in Chapter 4, but for now, just be aware that the DD pseudo-op creates and initializes storage for a doubleword:

```
ADDR_SAVE DD MY_FAR_PROC  ;initialize to a 4-byte address

      .

      .

      .


      CALL    ADDR_SAVE;generate a far call to address pointed

                    ;to by the memory location ADDR_SAVE
```

This technique is useful when you call procedures that are part of your own program, but sometimes you may want to call or jump to an absolute address in ROM. For instance, when you interface an assembly language routine with interpretive BASIC, you may want to access the BASIC floating point conversion routines. The normal way of doing this operation is to declare a ROM segment and use the ORG pseudo-op to declare an offset in that segment as the starting point of a FAR procedure:

```
ROM_SEG SEGMENT AT 0F600H

      ORG      3          ;start of ROM floating point

                          ;conversion routine

FRCINT LABEL    FAR

ROM_SEG ENDS


MY_CODE  SEGMENT

      .

      .


      CALL     FRCINT   ;generate a FAR call to 0F600:0003

      .

      .


MY_CODE  ENDS
```

The SEGMENT, ORG, and LABEL pseudo-ops are discussed in Chapter 4.

For advanced students: There's an alternative method of calling an absolute FAR address. The machine language bytes that compose a direct intersegment call are 9AH xxxx yyyy, where xxxx is a 16-bit offset and yyyy is a 16-bit segment address. It is possible to create a "synthetic opcode" by defining bytes within the code segment as if they had been generated by the assembler. In the previous example, when the assembler encounters the call to FRCINT, it actually generates the bytes 9A 03 00 00 F6. You can do the same thing with this sequence:

```
DB  9AH    ;define storage for a direct call opcode

DW  0003H  ; and storage for 2-byte offset

DW  0F600H ; and storage for 2-byte segment
```

Change the first byte into a 0AEH, and you will generate a synthetic direct far JMP. Note: Normally, the DB and DW pseudo-ops are used to define messages and storage for variables in the data area of your program. Using them to create opcodes to be executed by the CPU can be dangerous unless you are experienced with this technique.

## Interrupts: Transferring Control by Proxy

An INT (INTerrupt) is a short way to make a FAR call, with the added benefit that it will save the status of the CPU flags. Soon after someone realized the value of calling subroutines, someone else thought it would be a good idea to be able to call certain often-used subroutines with a special shorthand convention. "Why not," our anonymous genius asked, "put the addresses of the often-called routines all in one list and then be able to request one of those routines?"

The argument was sound; most modern processors have just such a capability. The 6809 SWI (SoftWare Interrupt) is a shorthand call; there are three of them. The Z80 shorthand call is an RST (or sometimes TRP), and it provides for eight of them. With the 8088, this function is referred to as an INT (INTerrupt). The 8088 pulled out all the stops; it handles 256 different interrupts.

At the very basement of the IBM-PC's RAM, there is a list of 256 intersegment jump vectors (locations of interrupt procedures). Each of these vectors is four bytes long—specifying both a segment and an offset. Thus, the first 1K (1,024 bytes) of an 8088's memory is reserved for this interrupt vector table, and is never used for storing a program.

The interrupt routines are invoked (called) from a program by specifying which of the 256 routines you want to use. The format is:

```
INT   type
```

where *type* is a number from 0 to FFH. This instruction performs a set of several actions. It pushes the flags register on the stack, sets TF to false (disabling single-step mode), sets IF to DI (disabling hardware interrupts), pushes CS and then IP onto the stack, and loads CS and IP with the low-memory interrupt vector table element specified by *type*.

The function calls that are in the ROM-BIOS are conveniently pointed to by interrupt vectors. These software interrupts make programming much simpler because with a single command we can invoke the sophisticated routines that the folks at IBM and Microsoft have provided. For example, INT 10H is a package of routines that simplify the work of displaying characters and graphics on the screen. All of the PC-DOS service routines used in handling disk files and other DOS-related functions are available by specifying a function number in the AH register and then invoking an INT 21H. Appendix B contains a listing of these functions, and we will examine them in detail as they are used in example programs in this book.

## An IBM Mistake

One reason the ROM-BIOS and PC-DOS service routines are set up as interrupt handlers is that this arrangement makes it easy to correct mistakes in those routines or add additional services. A program that uses a PC-DOS service need not know exactly where the opcodes of that service reside—only that a certain INT will invoke the service.

The earliest IBM PCs had an error in the printer control code in the ROM-BIOS. The printer character handling routine includes logic to look for a time-out error in case the printer is offline or disconnected. That's a good idea, but the BIOS programmers did not realize how long the IBM printer would take to get to the top of a new page. Thousands of IBM-PC owners were getting "printer time out error" messages when the printer was not at fault.

The problem was in the IBM-PC firmware (i.e., the ROM-BIOS), but because of the flexibility of the interrupt system, IBM did not need to rush out new ROM chips to every owner. Instead, they just came out with a new version of PC-DOS (first, version 1.05, then version 1.10) that changed the printer interrupt vector to point to a new piece of code that didn't contain the "time-out error" error. Another celebrated error in the way BASIC performs double-precision arithmetic was corrected in a similar manner.

You can use this changing of an interrupt vector to great advantage in your own programs. For example, it is possible to write a keyboard interrupt handler that can filter out the CTRL-ALT-DEL combination so that no malicious passerby can wipe out your beautiful graphics display or unsaved data. You can extend the video interrupt so that it will work with the mysterious low-resolution graphics that are mentioned in the IBM-PC *Technical Reference Manual*. In other words, it is possible to customize the firmware routines to handle the special requirements of your system.

## Background Interrupts

The real value of an interrupt becomes clear when you realize that an external device may specify, via hardware interrupt lines, which of the 256 procedures to call and when to call it. When an external interrupt takes place, the CPU stops what it's doing, saves its place, and processes the interrupt (i.e., executes the specified subroutine). The interrupt service routine will perform the action requested by the external device and then transfer control back to the interrupted program. The interrupted program is never aware that anything has happened. It simply chugs away at its appointed task. It will run somewhat more slowly than an uninterrupted program, but most of the time the CPU is simply waiting around for poky humans to input data.

A person running a word processor, for example, may never realize that between two keystrokes, the CPU has executed dozens of interrupt service routines. This idea of interrupts that are invisible to a human operator is often referred to as *foreground/background processing*. The word processing program is running in the foreground (easily visible), and the hardware interrupt takes place in the background (behind the scenes).

One special interrupt is connected to the IBM-PC's real-time clock. Whatever routine is pointed to by interrupt vector 1CH will be executed 18.5 times per second. You can write your own routine to handle a background task and install it into the system. Just replace the four bytes starting at address 0000:0070 with the offset and segment of your interrupt handler. PC-DOS even provides a FIX_IN_MEMORY service (see Appendix B) that allows you to make sure that your interrupt handling program will remain safe from all other programs. This powerful feature is a high point of the IBM-PC's design.

## Breakpoint Interrupt

Although it is generated by the assembler using the normal syntax, the INT 3 command is actually a 1-byte instruction (CCH). DEBUG and other machine language tracing and monitoring programs use this command to set breakpoints in a program. You use breakpoint in your code to stop execution when a certain instruction is reached. It is actually a call to the command mode of DEBUG. This allows you to examine the registers, flags, and memory variables to help in locating errors in your code.

The 1-byte INT 3 breakpoint is preferred over a 2-byte INT or a 5-byte intersegment call because it may be placed anywhere in a program without disturbing the subsequent code. For example, if you placed a 2-byte INT at a 1-byte RET instruction, the byte following the RET (probably the first byte of the next procedure) would be overwritten. If that byte were ever executed, the results would be, euphemistically speaking, unpredictable.

## Returning from an Interrupt

Any interrupt service routine, whether for a hardware or a software interrupt, must terminate with an IRET instruction. As mentioned previously, an INT is much like a call for a FAR procedure, except that the CPU flags register is saved on the stack along with the 4-byte return address. The IRET instruction makes sure that those flags are restored before returning to the interrupted program. Aside from the horrifying possibility of uncontrolled growth of the stack, the flags register must be POPped because the very act of invoking an interrupt alters both the TF and IF flags.

## Conditional Jumps: Making Decisions

All decisions that you make in assembly language boil down to this: You either execute a piece of the program, or you skip it by jumping to a different branch. The 8088 offers a complete assortment of conditional jumps so that you can make these choices.

All of these jumps depend on the state of various combinations of the CPU flags after an arithmetic or logic instruction has been executed. But you usually don't need to know exactly which flags are set or cleared. Instead, concentrate on how to ask a question and what to do with the answer.

A decision is made in two stages. First, you perform an arithmetic function; then you direct execution according to the result. Our first example is a simple loop counter. Let's say we want to perform a subroutine eight times. In BASIC, we might say

```
10 AL = 8                   'counter starts at 8
20   GOSUB 1000             '  perform the repeated action
30   AL = AL - 1            '  adjust the counter
40 IF AL > 0 THEN GOTO 20   'make the decision
50                          ' if not, fall through to next
                              line
```

The steps of an 8088 program are similar. Instead of line numbers, we are allowed to use expressive, self-documenting labels, and we can use the DEC function to adjust the counter quickly.

```
        MOV   AL,8           ;initialize the counter
AGAIN:                       ;label for the top of the loop
        CALL MY_SUBROUTINE   ; indicate action to be repeated
        DEC   AL             ;   AL = AL-1 (question: "Is
                             ;AL = 0?")
        JNZ   AGAIN          ;if AL is Not Zero, repeat the loop
                             ;. . . else exit loop
```

In this example, we used the arithmetic function DEC to ask the question (set the flags). The first seven times through the loop, ZF (the zero flag) will be cleared to NZ by the DEC opcode. Because the state of ZF is NZ, the JNZ (Jump if Not Zero) will send control back to the label AGAIN. But on the eighth time through the loop, when AL is 1, the DEC opcode will bring it down to 0 and at the same time set ZF to a ZR condition. In that case, the JNZ conditional jump will *not* be taken because the condition is not met (ZF isn't NZ); execution falls through the bottom of the loop to the subsequent instructions.

With a couple of changes in the code, we can specify that the loop counter increases from 1 to 8 instead of decreasing from 8 to 1.

```
        MOV   AL,1           ;initialize the starting value
AGAIN:                       ;label for the top of the loop
        CALL MY_SUBROUTINE   ;   action to repeat
```

```
INC   AL              ;  AL = AL+1
CMP   AL,8            ;  question: "What is AL's
                     ;  relationship to 8?"
JBE   AGAIN          ;when Below or Equal, repeat the loop
                     ;...else exist the loop and continue
```

The arithmetic CMP (CoMPare) function was used to ask the question this time. The jump decision was based on whether the value of AL had grown to over 8. Conditional jump opcode mnemonics are most meaningful when used with this CMP operation. Reading the previous example aloud might help: "Compare AL to 8, then jump if it is below or equal."

When the code includes a conditional jump based on some other arithmetic operation (DEC, SUB, etc.), it might help you to think of the conditional branch opcode as if it included its own "CMP with 0."

```
DEC   AX
JE    AGAIN   ; "compare AX with 0, and jump if it's equal"
```

Conditional jumps come in two types, and you must be aware of the difference. The mnemonic you use in your program depends on whether you are working with signed or unsigned numbers. Remember, the value FFFFH can be thought of as being either signed or unsigned. If it is unsigned, its value is 65,535. But if you are treating it as a signed number, its value is -1. Therefore, you must be very careful about how you ask the question. Someone at Intel arbitrarily came up with the following convention:

* Unsigned numbers can be *Above, Below,* or *Equal.*
* Signed numbers can be *Greater, Less,* or *Equal.*

After comparing two unsigned numbers, use the conditional jumps:

JA    (Jump if Above)
JAE   (Jump if Below or Equal)
JB    (Jump if Below)
JBE   (Jump if Above or Equal)
JE    (Jump if Equal)

After you compare two signed numbers, use the conditional jumps:

JG    (Jump if Greater)
JGE   (Jump if Greater or Equal)
JL    (Jump if Less)
JLE   (Jump if Less or Equal)
JE    (Jump if Equal)

To crystallize the distinction, here's a problem I had when I was starting out: I needed to use a variety of time delays to add skill levels to a game program. The code I used looked like this:

```
        SUB   AX,AX              ;initially 0
DELAY:                           ;label for the top of the delay loop
        INC   AX                 ;bump counter
        CMP   AX,DELAY_COUNT     ;see if finished
        JL    DELAY              ; if not, delay some more
        RET                      ; if so, go back to caller
```

When the value of my variable DELAY_COUNT was small (as in the higher skill levels), there was no problem. But the slowest game speed required a delay of 50,000 counts. Can you figure out why the game actually ran faster at the slowest level than at the fastest one?

Answer: A 2-byte value of 50,000 represents an *unsigned* value—it is more than 32,767. But the JL opcode should be used only with *signed* numbers. The program "thought" that 50,000 was -15,535. Therefore, on the very first trip through the loop, when DELAY_COUNT was -15,535 and AX was 1, the condition was not satisfied (AX was not less than DELAY_COUNT), so execution dropped through to the RET opcode. There was no delay at all! When I recoded the JL to a JB, the delay routine worked smoothly.

There is an assortment of other conditional jumps that you should be aware of. These don't make as much sense as the "above/below" and "greater/less" conditional jumps when used after a CMP instruction. They test the state of specific CPU flags.

JC and JNC test the state of CF (carry flag). Note: Same as JB and JAE.
JP and JPO test the state of PF (parity flag).
JO and JNO test the state of OF (overflow flag).
JS and JNS test the state of SF (sign flag).

The MACRO Assembler will recognize alternate forms of many of the conditional jumps. For example, JNLE (Jump if Not Less or Equal) is the same as JG (Jump if Greater). This duplication of mnemonics can tend to help you document the type of decision that is being made.

## The Problem with Conditional Jumps

Finally, all of the conditional jumps are SHORT jumps. The destination label must be within -128 to +127 bytes of the jump command. If your decision is to jump to a distant label, you must *jump around the jump*. For instance, in a large program requiring many user inputs, you might write a routine that prints "ERROR: function aborted." If that routine is in a distant part of the program (more than 128 bytes away), you can't get there with a conditional jump. The code to test if an input value is between 0 and 15 might look like this:

```
        CMP    AX,15

        JBE  NO_ERROR      ;if AX <= 15 and AX => 0, then no error

        JMP  ERROR_ABORT   ;else, jump to the distant error

                              handler

NO_ERROR:
```

### Jump When CX Is Zero

JCXZ *target* is a conditional jump opcode that does not depend on the state of the flags. It is based entirely upon whether or not the CX register contains 0. When CX is 0, execution is forced to the *target* label (a SHORT jump). But if CX is not 0, then execution falls through to the subsequent instructions. The JCXZ instruction comes in handy when used in conjunction with some repeated string operations. An example usage of this instruction is shown in the "String Manipulation Instructions" section of this chapter.

### Loop Instructions

LOOP is a particularly handy opcode for keeping track of the iterations of a program loop. This instruction takes care of the loop counter as well as the conditional jump. The CX register is assumed to be the loop counter in this operation, and it is assumed that you want it to grow smaller. The action is similar to that of the BASIC FOR . . . NEXT loop.

```
10 FOR CX = 8 TO 1 STEP -1

20    GOSUB 1000

30 NEXT CX
```

The 8088 assembly language equivalent is:

```
        MOV    CX,8

AGAIN:

        CALL   MY_SUBROUTINE

        LOOP   AGAIN
```

Every time the LOOP opcode is executed, the CX register is decremented; if the result was not 0, the branch is taken to the indicated label. You must be careful that CX doesn't start at 0 unless you want the loop to be executed 65,536 times! Note that unlike the normal DEC CX instruction, LOOP does not set the zero flag when CX becomes zero.

LOOPZ (also called LOOPE) and LOOPNZ (or LOOPNE) are variations of the LOOP command. They perform the same way; the CX register is decremented, and if

CX has not become 0, control is transferred to the target label. The difference is that these jumps also check the state of ZF (the zero flag) before deciding to jump. LOOPZ forces the jump only when CX is not 0 and ZF is ZR. LOOPNZ forces the jump only when CX is not 0 and ZF is NZ.

These commands give you the ability to base a decision on either of two criteria: "Have the maximum number of loop iterations been completed *or* has ZF changed to the desired state?" An example should clarify this issue.

Suppose you have written a simple text-formatting program that is capable of printing a variable number of lines on a page. You want to skip to the top of a new page whenever that number of lines is reached *or* you encounter an ASCII 12 top-of-form character in the text. The following program fragment illustrates how the LOOPNZ opcode could be used to aid in making this decision.

```
            MOV     SI,OFFSET TEXT_BUFFER   ;point to start of text
NEXT_PAGE:
            MOV     CX,PAGE_LEN             ;set counter to
                                            ; maximum lines per page

NEXT_LINE:
            CALL    PRINT_LINE              ;print to just past a
                                            ; CRLF, update SI

            CMP     BYTE PTR [SI],12        ;test for top-of-form
                                            ; character in text

            LOOPNZ NEXT_LINE                ; if not top-of-form
                                            ; and not max line, loop
                                            ; back

            CALL    TOP_OF_FORM             ;force printer to top
                                            ; of form

            JMP     NEXT_PAGE               ;restart process on
                                            ; next page
```

## THINGS TO DO

1. Write a series of comparisons and jumps that determine if AL contains an ASCII value between '0' and '9'.

2. Why should you never use a JB or JA conditional jump based on the result of a DEC or INC instruction?

3. The keyboard I/O handler in the ROM-BIOS (INT 16H) returns ZF to indicate whether or not a key has been pressed. Knowing that the IRET instruction automatically restores the flags before returning to the caller, can you figure out how INT 16H passes ZF as a return parameter?

### 3.2.5 String Manipulation Instructions

Perhaps the most powerful innovation of the 8088 is its ability to initialize, transfer, and compare character strings. Consider the steps that go into copying a series of characters from one place to another:

1. Initialize a pointer to the source (address of the first character).
2. Initialize a pointer to the destination address.
3. Set a counter register to the number of characters to move.
4. Get a source byte into a register.
5. Put this byte into the address pointed to by the destination register.
6. Point to the next source byte.
7. Point to the next destination address.
8. Decrement the counter register.
9. If the counter is not 0, go to step 4.

Although we still must do the initialization steps 1 through 3, the 8088 string commands allow us to compress step 4 through 9 into a single line of assembler code.

All of the string commands are based on *string primitive* operations. These are opcodes that automatically transfer or compare two operands and then adjust the pointers to prepare for the next action. The pointer registers are SI and DI. SI points to the source and DI points to the destination.

Note: SI is assumed to be pointing within the data segment (defined by the DS segment register), and DI to be pointing within the extra segment (named by the ES segment register) in all string operations.

Table 3.5 shows the formats for each of the 8088's string commands. Their functions are described here:

MOVS (MOVe String) copies the source memory operand, DS:[SI], to the destination memory operand, ES:[DI], and then adjusts both SI and DI.

CMPS (CoMPare String) compares the source memory operand, DS:[SI], against the destination memory operand, ES:[DI], and adjusts both SI and DI.

SCAS (SCAn String) compares an accumulator register (AL or AX) against the destination memory operand, ES:[DI], and adjusts DI.

LODS (LOaD String) copies the source memory operand, DS:[SI], into an accumulator register (AL or AX) and adjusts SI.

STOS (STOre String) copies an accumulator register (AL or AX) into the destination memory operand, ES:[DI], and adjusts DI.

**Table 3.5**
**String Manipulation Instructions**

| Mnemonic | | Format | CPU flags affected | | | | | | | | |
|---|---|---|---|---|---|---|---|---|---|---|---|
| | | | O | D | I | T | S | Z | A | P | C |
| | | ─── MOVE STRING ─── | | | | | | | | | |
| MOVS | MOVS | dest_string,source_string | | | | | | | | | |
| MOVSB | MOVSB | | | | | | | | | | |
| MOVSW | MOVSW | | | | | | | | | | |
| | | ─── COMPARE STRINGS ─── | | | | | | | | | |
| CMPS | CMPS | dest_string,source_string | * | | | | * | * | * | * | * |
| CMPSB | CMPSB | | * | | | | * | * | * | * | * |
| CMPSW | CMPSW | | * | | | | * | * | * | * | * |
| | | ─── SCAN STRING ─── | | | | | | | | | |
| SCAS | SCAS | dest_string | * | | | | * | * | * | * | * |
| SCASB | SCASB | | * | | | | * | * | * | * | * |
| SCASW | SCASW | | * | | | | * | * | * | * | * |
| | | ─── REPEAT PREFIXES ─── | | | | | | | | | |
| REP | REP | string_opcode | | | | | | | | | |
| REPE/ REPZ | REPE | string_opcode | | | | | | | | | |
| REPNE/ REPNZ | REPNE | string_opcode | | | | | | | | | |

Note: * means that the flag is altered by the operation.

## Two Sizes, Two Directions

There are a couple of options that are available with each of these commands. The direction of the pointer adjustment may be either up (toward higher addresses) or down (toward lower addresses), and the adjustment step may be bytes (step by 1) or words (step by 2). The size of the operand is determined either by specifying (optional) labels in the operand field or by appending a "B" (byte) or a "W" (word) to the string primitive mnemonic.

The setting of DF, the CPU direction flag, determines whether the string operation bumps the pointers up or down. Use CLD (CLear Direction) to make sure that the pointers are incremented. STD (SeT Direction) tells the 8088 to decrement the pointers after each operation. In most cases, you will want to start the action at the start of a string (a low address). The exception occurs when you are copying a block of memory into a destination area that overlaps the source area. The following diagram illustrates a case in which you would need to use the STD opcode to work from the end of a string to the start.

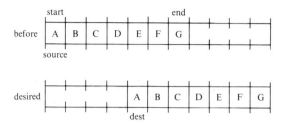

If you started at the low address and moved the bytes successively from the source position to the *dest* position, the very first move would overlay the *E*, the next one would overlay the *F*, and so on. The result would look like this:

Since *ABC* was copied over *EFG*, the last part of the string is invalid.

The secret of this type of overlapping transfer is to start at the *end* of the string and work your way backward toward the address of the *start*. That way, the first move places the *G* into an empty slot, the next move places the *F* into an empty slot, and so on. The only characters that are overlaid are those that have already been transferred.

Although the direction flag is normally in a cleared (UP) state, your program should not make that assumption. However, that doesn't necessarily mean that you must perform a CLD before every string primitive. Once you have specifically forced DF to UP, it will remain the same unless you change it. If you must set DF to DN for an overlapping transfer, it's a good idea to reset it back to UP as soon as possible, thereby assuring that the rest of your code can assume that it is in the default state.

## Repeated String Operations

Individually, the string primitives work on only one byte or word of data at a time. The key to the power of the 8088's string operations is the REP (REPeat) prefix. This handy device tells the CPU, "Check if CX is zero. If not, perform the string primitive (adjusting the pointer registers as needed), decrement CX, and start again." Notice that CX is checked *before* the string primitive is executed, then decremented *afterward*. Therefore, if CX starts at 0, the string operation will not be repeated even once. Also note that as with the LOOP command, the decrementing of CX does not affect the CPU flags in any way.

```
MOV       CX,STRING_LEN   ;initialize the counter
REP MOVSB                 ;repeatedly perform the string
                          ;primitive
```

The REP opcode (when present) must be placed directly before the string primitive on the same line of the source text. In the preceding example, I have offset the REP by one space in the mnemonic field so that it doesn't look like a label, but it clearly isn't a complete opcode. Also, because the action of the REP prefix is directly dependent upon the value of CX, it makes sense to initialize CX in the line right before the repeated string primitive.

In some operations, you will want the repeated action to stop *before* CX is decremented to 0. As with the LOOPZ and LOOPNZ, there are two variations of the REP prefix that can be used to terminate the action before CX becomes 0.

The REPNE (REPeat while Not Equal) continues iterating until either CX decays to 0 *or* ZF is set to ZR. The REPE (REPeat while Equal) prefix is identical to REP. It terminates the repeated action when CX becomes 0 *or* ZF has been reset to NZ. REPNE and REPE are meaningful only when used with CMPS and SCAS because these are the only string primitives that affect any of the flags. Examples of these options are examined in the sections "CMPS: Comparing Strings" and "SCAS: Scanning a String."

## MOVS: Copying a String

The MOVS primitive transfers the memory operand addressed by DS:[SI] into the address pointed to by ES:[DI]. This is a memory-to-memory transfer; the memory operand does not need to be funneled through one of the CPU registers. MOVS is a very fast and convenient operation. In using it, remember that the destination address is an offset in the segment pointed to by the ES register.

A couple of options are available when you specify this command in your source code. You will normally use one of the short forms:

```
MOVSB   ;transfer the byte (MOV byte ptr ES:[DI], DS:[SI])

MOVSW   ;transfer the word (MOV word ptr ES:[DI], DS:[SI])
```

You can also specify the labels of the source and destination strings in the operand field:

```
MOVS   DEST_STRING,SOURCE_STRING
```

It is important to realize that the latter form *does not initialize the pointer registers.* The MOVS opcode by itself is ambiguous because it doesn't say whether the operation is on bytes or words. When you specify source and destination labels as operands, the assembler simply looks through its symbol table to determine the operand's types. If both DEST_STRING and SOURCE_STRING are labels of byte operands, then MOVSB is generated. The assembler generates MOVSW when both labels are of word operands.

This format also has one other function. It can be used to force the assembler to create a segment override for the source operand. For instance,

```
MOVS   CS:DATA_BYTE,BUFFER
```

will generate the proper segment override prefix. It is not legal (or possible) to generate an override for the destination operand. Also, there is a grave danger when a segment override is used with the REP prefix. If a background task interrupts the CPU in the middle of the string move, the segment override will be forgotten and the source segment will revert to its default of DS. When that happens, the data that end up in the destination will be invalid.

With either format of this string transfer instruction, it is the responsibility of your program to set up the SI and DI registers. Usually you will do this in the lines directly before the MOVS instruction. The following example will copy a string of characters that is 80 bytes long from IN_BUF to TEXT_AREA.

```
MOV     SI,OFFSET IN_BUF        ;point to the source address
MOV     DI,OFFSET TEXT_AREA     ;point to the destination address
MOV     CX,80                   ;length of string
CLD                             ;make sure the direction is UP
REP MOVSB                       ;transfer all of the bytes
```

This example initializes the pointer registers by giving them the addresses of their operands via the assembler's OFFSET operator. You might find it more convenient to use the LEA instruction like this:

```
LEA     SI,IN_BUF
LEA     DI,TEXT_AREA
```

LEA generates one extra byte of machine code, but it may help you to visualize what is happening. Try saying aloud, "Load the effective address of IN_BUF into the SI register." This way, there can be no doubt that a register has been loaded with an address value.

## CMPS: Comparing Strings

The CMPSB and CMPSW opcodes are used to compare two memory operands and set the CPU flags in order to make decisions in a program. The byte or word at ES:[DI] is compared to the byte or word at DS:[SI]. When used as a repeated operation, it can be used to compare two strings of characters or elements of two tables. The general form is:

```
CMPS     DEST_STRING,SOURCE_STRING
```

As with MOVS, the assembler just uses the DEST_STRING and SOURCE_STRING references to determine whether the operation is on bytes or words. It can also be used to specify an override segment for the source operand.

The shorthand format is one of these:

```
CMPSB   ;byte operation (CMP byte ptr ES:[DI], DS:[SI])
CMPSW   ;word operation (CMP word ptr ES:[DI], DS:[SI])
```

The REP prefix has a special meaning with this string primitive. When used with CMPSB or CMPSW, the operation is not necessarily repeated for the entire count in CX. The repeated action will be aborted according to the result of the comparison, as well as when CX becomes zero.

REPNE (also called REPNZ) will continue the comparisons as long as the characters of both strings are *not* equal. This option has little value when used with CMPSB. It could, however, be used to find the first place in two strings that have a matching character. Used within a program loop, it could be part of a function that located the first occurrence of a given string within a larger block of data.

REP (or REPE or REPZ) will continue comparing only as long as the result of each comparison is equal. This is exactly what you want when you are comparing two strings. As long as both *characters* are the same, both *strings* are the same, but as soon as two characters are different, you know that the strings are different and you don't need to continue comparing the characters.

The REP CMPSB combination is ideal for finding out if two strings of characters are exactly the same, but that is only part of its potential. When the operation is finished, you also know whether the source string is above or below the destination string in the ASCII collating sequence. The conditional jumps can be used to make a decision based upon the relationships of the strings. The following example is part of a string-sorting routine. Two strings of 12 characters are compared. If the first (destination) string is greater than the second (source) string, the two strings must be swapped.

```
        MOV      DI,OFFSET STRING_TABLE            ;point to
                                                   ;string (n)

        MOV      SI,OFFSET STRING_TABLE + 12      ;point to
                                                   ; string (n+1)


        MOV      CX,12        ;set up the length
        REP CMPSB             ;is string(n+1) => string (n)?
        JAE      NO_SWAP      ; yes, strings are in order, so
                              ; don't swap
          .                   ; no, make the change
          .
          .    (code to swap the strings)
          .

  NO_SWAP:
```

Note: The REPE (or REPZ) prefix could be used in place of the REP. They perform exactly the same function.

As with the other string operations, the direction flag determines whether the pointer adjustments are to be *up* or *down*. You would use STD only if you wanted the comparison to start at their final characters and work toward their starting characters, or if you were searching backward through a table for a matching set of elements.

Also, remember that the destination string must reside in the memory segment pointed to by the ES register. If both operand strings are in the same segment, you will want to make sure that DS and ES have the same value.

### SCAS: Scanning a String

The 8088 has the powerful capability to check through a string or table to look for a match-up with a specific character or word. SCASB and SCASW compare the AL or AX register with the byte or word at ES:[DI]. When used with the REPNE prefix, they will continue comparing successive memory operands until the CX register is decremented to 0 or the value in the accumulator is found to be an exact match.

The general format is one as follows:

```
SCASB                 ;byte operation (CMP ES:[DI],AL)

SCASW                 ;word operation (CMP ES:[DI],AX)

SCAS    DEST_STRING   ;byte or word, depending on DEST_STRING
```

The REPNE SCASB sequence is most often used to check through a series of characters in order to find a match with a specific character. For example, many PC-DOS commands include provisions for "switches" or special parameters that may be entered in the command line. The switch is often specified in the format /x where x is a single character. The SCASB instruction simplifies the search through the command line for any occurrence of the slash (/) character.

```
FIND_SLASH:
        MOV      AL,'/'            ;specify the character
                                   ;to search for
        MOV      DI,OFFSET CMD_LINE ;point to the string
                                   ;to search
        MOV      CX,CMD_LINE_LEN   ;set a maximum search
                                   ;length
        REPNE SCASB                ;try to locate a slash
        JCXZ     NO_SLASH          ;if end-of-string,
                                   ;then '/' wasn't found
                                   ; else, slash was found
        MOV      AL,ES:[DI]        ; get the switch
```

```
                                              ;character into AL
            .
          . (process the specified switch)
            .
   NO_SLASH:                                 ;label taken when slash
                                             ;is not found
```

There are two important techniques illustrated in the preceding example. First, the JCXZ conditional jump is used here in the application for which it was designed. It determines whether the string search was aborted because a matching character was found, or whether it was ended because the end of the string was reached. A JNE conditional jump could also be used to make the same decision because ZF will be set to the value of the most recent comparison. The other notable point is this: After the REPNE SCASB is terminated, ES:[DI] holds the character that directly *follows* the character that matched AL.

REP SCAS (or REPZ SCASB) can be used to search through a string until a character is located that *doesn't* match a specified character. This capability could be used, for example, in a program that compresses the spaces in a text file before writing it to disk.

## STOS: **Initializing a Block of Memory**

The STOSB and STOSW instructions are used to store the value in an accumulator in a memory address. The value in AL or AX is copied into the address pointed to by ES:[DI], and DI is adjusted to point to the next memory address. As a repeated operation, this capability can be used to initialize a series of memory addresses with the same value.

This operation is useful in graphics programs when the entire screen must be blanked out. In fact, a REP STOSW sequence is the fastest possible way to clear the graphics screen.

```
   CLEAR_GRAPHICS PROC NEAR
            MOV      AX,VIDEO_SEG   ;VIDEO_SEG is at 0B800H
            MOV      ES,AX          ;STOS destination is in ES
                                    ;segment
            MOV      DI,0           ;starting at the upper left
                                    ;corner
            MOV      AX,0           ;16 bits of 0 to be stored
            MOV      CX,2000H       ;count of words in all of
```

```
                                  ;screen memory
          REP STOSW               ;fill'em up!
          RET
     CLEAR_GRAPHICS ENDP
```

## LODS: Fetching One Element of a String

The LODS instruction is used primarily to process individual characters of a string or individual elements of a table. It copies the byte or word in the memory location pointed to by DS:[SI] into the accumulator register AL or AX. The REP prefix can be used with LODSB and LODSW, but there is little reason to do so because the accumulator would be overwritten with each iteration.

LODSB is often used as part of a loop to process characters of a string. For instance, to move a string from one place to another, forcing every character into uppercase as you go, you might use a sequence of LODSB and STOSB as follows:

```
          MOV   SI,OFFSET IN_BUF    ;point to string to upshift
          MOV   DI,OFFSET OUT_BUF   ; and area to place it
                                    ; afterward
          MOV   CX,STRING_LEN       ;set up counter for LOOP
     NEXT_CHAR:
          LODSB                     ;get the source character
          CMP   AL,'a'              ;
          JB    SAVE_IT             ;if not in range 'a' to 'z'
          CMP   AL,'z'              ; then don't change it
          JA    SAVE_IT
          AND   AL,11011111         ; reset bit 5 to force it UPPERCASE
     SAVE_IT:
          STOSB                     ;place character at destination
          LOOP  NEXT_CHAR
```

## 3.2.6 CPU Control Instructions

CPU control instructions are a potpourri of opcodes that have special effects on the 8088 microprocessor. Some of these opcodes are commands to alter directly certain CPU flags. Others are used only when there is more than one microprocessor in the system. One opcode does nothing at all. Table 3.6 lists these instructions.

**Table 3.6**
**CPU Control Instructions**

| Mnemonic | Format | | O | D | I | T | S | Z | A | P | C |
|----------|--------|---|---|---|---|---|---|---|---|---|---|
| | | | | | | CPU flags affected | | | | | |

```
                                                    CPU flags affected
Mnemonic            Format                   | O | D | I | T | S | Z | A | P | C |

                    ——— NO OPERATION ———

NOP        NOP

          ——— EXTERNAL CONTROL AND SYNCHRONIZATION ———

ESC        ESC    external_opcode,source

WAIT/      WAIT
  FWAIT

HLT        HLT

LOCK       LOCK

               ——— FLAG CONTROL ———

STC        STC                                                              1
CLC        CLC                                                              0
CMC        CMC                                                              *
STD        STD                    1
CLD        CLD                    0
STI        STI                        1
CLI        CLI                        0
```

Note: * or 1 or 0 means that the flag is altered by the operation.

## No Operation

NOP (No OPeration) forces the CPU to do nothing for three clock cycles. It is a 1-byte instruction (90H) that secretly performs an XCHG AX,AX. NOP can be used in a program to hold open a code area so that you can make changes or patches with DEBUG. It is handy for overwriting opcode bytes while debugging so that the effect of an operation can be nullified. You might also want to use NOPs to fine-tune a timing delay.

## Flag Manipulation

There are several opcodes that directly influence the CPU flags. As discussed in the section "String Manipulation Instructions," DF (direction flag) controls the direction of the automatic adjustments to DI and SI that occur when the string primitives are executed. STD (SeT Direction flag) sets the direction to DN so that the adjustments go backward from higher to lower addresses. CLD (CLear Direction flag) resets DF to its normal state of UP.

STI (SeT Interrupt flag) tells the CPU to accept and process hardware interrupts. It enables normal interrupt processing. CLI (CLear Interrupt flag) resets IF so that hardware interrupts will be ignored until the subsequent execution of STI. CLI disables normal interrupt processing. You would use this command in processing high-priority tasks that are timing-sensitive. INT 2, the *nonmaskable interrupt* is always enabled, regardless of the state of IF. Also, the state of the interrupt flag has no bearing on software interrupts.

CF (the carry flag) is used in so many arithmetic and logic operations that the designers of the 8088 chose to include special instructions to alter the state of this flag.

STC (SeT Carry) sets CF to 1 and CLC (CLear Carry) clears (or resets) CF to 0. These opcodes are often used to force CF to a known state before executing bit rotation commands RCR and RCL. CMC (CoMplement Carry) flip-flops the state of CF. If it is a 1, then it is reset to a 0, and vice versa.

## Coprocessor Control

The ESC and WAIT opcodes are used in interfacing the 8088 with separate coprocessors (namely, the 8087 number cruncher or the 8089 input/output processor).

ESC (ESCape) is used to instruct a coprocessor to start doing some work. It can optionally force the BIU part of the 8088 to fetch a memory operand for the coprocessor to work with. The format for ESC is unusual because there are actually eight different ESC opcodes, ESC0 through ESC7 (although the assembler doesn't accept these mnemonics), and the addressing mode byte that follows it is not interpreted in the normal way. The assembler expects to see this format:

```
ESC     external_opcode,source
```

EXTERNAL_OPCODE is a 6-bit number (0-3FH) that names both the external processor and the operation that must be performed. This 6-bit value is actually broken into two 3-bit fields that are spliced into the opcode itself and into the REG field of the addressing mode byte.

The SOURCE operand is any memory reference or register name. It defines the MOD and R/M fields of the addressing mode byte, indicating just where to find the data that will be passed to the coprocessor. The SOURCE operand may in fact end up being used as a destination for output from the coprocessor. As far as the 8088 is concerned, it is just an address expression that must be placed on the bus and then ignored.

The following statement is a command to the 8087 NDP to read two bytes from memory into its internal stack:

```
ESC     38H,[DI]      ;generate 8087 FILD opcode
```

The EXTERNAL_OPCODE is 38H and the SOURCE operand is [DI]. The assembler will generate the 2-byte opcode DF 05 as follows:

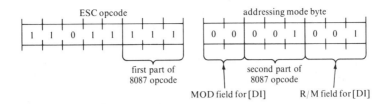

The SOURCE operand may indicate a more complex addressing mode that includes a direct memory offset such as MY_TABLE[BX+DI+3]. In that case, the offset byte (or bytes) will follow the ESC opcodes, just as with any such memory reference. The memory operand may also be specified with a segment override.

When the 8088 executes ESC, it actuall performs no calculation and takes no action, except to fetch the memory operand (actually, the first word or doubleword) so that the coprocessor can read the value of the operand.

## Coprocessor Synchronization

The ESC opcode tells the coprocessor to begin executing its instruction immediately. At the same time, the 8088 continues executing the next opcodes in its stream of instructions. That is, unless you tell the 8088 otherwise, you will have two processors working at the same time. This is very desirable when the result of a coprocessor operation is not immediately needed. For example, some versions of the FORTH language make extensive use of the 8087's very fast stack operations, even when the 8087's number-crunching ability is not needed.

Because the two processors are working simultaneously and at varying rates of speed, the 8088 needs a way to find out when the coprocessor is finished with its task. Otherwise, your 8088 program might try to instruct the coprocessor to do something when it's already busy with another task. You might also make the mistake of trying to fetch a result before the coprocessor is finished calculating that result.

WAIT tells the 8088 to put itself in an idle state until the coprocessor finishes its current operation. It is usually placed on the source text line before the ESC command to ensure that ESC's external opcode is "seen" by the coprocessor. It may also be used at some point *after* the ESC opcode to make sure that the coprocessor has finished its assigned task so that the 8088 can continue to process the result.

WAIT requires no operands. It actually tests the state of the 8088's TEST pin, which the coprocessor will enable whenever it is ready for a new instruction. WAIT will continue checking the TEST line at 5-clock intervals until it becomes active (goes high).

## Sharing Resources

The designers of the 8088 made a special provision so that it can be used in conjunction with one or more other microprocessors. When two 8088's share the same database in RAM, there is some danger that one will step on the toes of the other.

Consider what would happen if both processors wanted to alter a certain byte in memory. If both processors fetched the byte and changed it at the same time, one of them would be working with invalid data.

The LOCK opcode is a prefix byte that can be placed before any operation. It locks the system bus so that for the duration of that opcode, no other processor can access memory. This procedure makes it possible to set up a "semaphore" (a busy/not-busy flag) protocol so that two or more processors can be sure that they are working with valid data. LOCK would be used before an instruction to read the semaphore. If the semaphore indicated that the shared resource was currently being updated, the processor should wait until that update is finished. Whenever a processor finds that the resource is not being used, it must set the semaphore before, and reset it after, altering the data.

This setting and resetting of the semaphore would need to be accomplished using an XCHG instruction such as this:

```
            MOV        AL,1             ;1 means database is busy

TEST_READY:

            LOCK XCHG AL,BUSY_FLAG     ;fetch current value and set
                                        ;to busy

            CMP        AL,1             ;was it already busy?
            JE         TEST_READY       ; yes, wait until not busy
            .                           ; no, okay to update now
            .(process database update)

            .

            MOV        BUSY_FLAG,0      ;let other processors update
                                        ;the database
```

LOCK locks the system bus only for the duration of one opcode. Thus, the XCHG opcode is ideal because it can be used both to fetch the value of the semaphore and to set it to a busy state. Consider the consequences of the alternate sequence:

```
TEST_READY:

            LOCK CMP   BUSY_FLAG,0
            JNE        TEST_READY
            LOCK MOV   BUSY_FLAG,1
```

This won't work because the state of BUSY_FLAG might change between the CMP and the MOV instructions, defeating the purpose of the semaphore.

**THINGS TO DO**

1.  Write a sequence that copies the block of memory starting at DS:AX and ending at DS:DX to addresses starting at DS:DI. Be sure to handle the possibility that the blocks might overlap.

2.  Write a sequence that forces all lowercase characters in a string into uppercase. Assume that the string starts at DS:SI and the length of the string is in CX.

3.  Extend the sequence so that it may be called as a subroutine.

4.  Have the subroutine test the string and pass a parameter back to the caller in the carry flag. If the string contains any characters that are below an ASCII space (20H), CF should be set; otherwise, it should be cleared.

# Chapter 4

# Using the Assembler and Linker

## 4.1 THE TOOLS OF THE TRADE

The IBM-PC's MACRO Assembler translates program lines into machine language opcodes. It reads a *source* text file and outputs an *object code* file. The object code must be processed by the linker (the PC-DOS LINK utility) before it becomes an *executable code* file.

Let's assume, for the moment, that you have worked out the logic of an assembly language program and drawn up a suitably detailed flowchart. Let's also assume that you have recorded the program on paper and are ready to see if it will do what you expect it to do (never a certainty until it is actually tested!). The next step is to create a text file that contains your source code.

### The Editor

You can use the EDLIN program to enter lines if this is your only editor. However, it's a much better idea to buy and become familiar with one of the many fine screen-oriented editors that are available for the IBM PC. The limitations of EDLIN make assembly language programming even more complex than necessary. Most word processing programs will work fine. In fact, most text entry programs for the IBM PC create standard PC-DOS files. The assembler expects files to be broken into lines of fewer than 132 ACSII characters, each ending with a carriage return and linefeed (0DH followed by 0AH). This format is typical of all text files on the IBM PC—BASIC programs saved in ASCII (with the ,A option), Pascal source files, batch files, and so on.

You will normally name the source file with an ASM extension, the default file extension ASseMbly language source files. Let's say that you have created a file called MYPROG.ASM.

### The Assembler

Once you have a file containing the source line, you are ready to assemble it. The assembler is invoked with the ASM or MASM command line described in the *MACRO Assembler Manual*. This book assumes that you will always be using MASM, but if you have only 64K bytes of memory, you will need to use the small assembler, ASM. In either case, the assembler does not turn out a finished product. The result of the assembly, the OBJ (object code) file, must be processed by the linker.

There are many different ways to invoke the assembler, but the most common command is

        A>MASM MYPROG;

This instructs PC-DOS to load and execute the MASM.EXE program, and instructs MASM to assemble a file called MYPROG.ASM and to output an object file named MYPROG.OBJ.

If you have a two-drive system, you will find it convenient to keep the editor, assembler, and LINK on drive A and to keep all program files on drive B. In that case, you should set drive B as the default drive (use the B: command) and then invoke the assembler with

        B>A:MASM MYPROG;

The file B:MYPROG.ASM will be assembled with an output file of B:MYPROG.OBJ. This is a good setup because the output files of each step of the assembly will always go to drive B:, your data diskette.

Sometimes you will want to see a listing of the output file. This gives you a chance to see the hexadecimal representation of the bytes of the output file. A printed listing also provides you with a hardcopy record of the assembly that you can use in debugging your code. If you want to watch the listing file scroll down the screen as it is assembled, you may invoke the assembler via

        B>A:MASM MYPROG,,CON:;

You can temporarily suspend the scrolling by pressing Ctrl-NumLock or Ctrl-S, and then press any key to continue the listing. Pressing Ctrl-Break or Ctrl-C will abort the job immediately. You can send all or part of the listing to your printer by pressing Ctrl-PrtSc. This action will cause PC-DOS to echo the listing to the printer as well as the screen. Another option is to send the listing file directly to the printer:

        B>A:MASM MYPROG,,LPT1:;

Finally, you may invoke the assembler without specifying any parameters. In that case, the assembler will prompt you for (1) an input filename, (2) an object filename, (3) a listing filename (or device), and (4) a cross reference filename; the cross reference file is needed only in huge assemblies, so we can ignore it for now. Once you have become familiar with the assembler command line, you will probably avoid this 4-input option because it is faster and easier to specify all of the selected options from the DOS command line.

As the assembly progresses, the listing device will display all errors that the assembler encounters. If you are forced to use the small assembler, you will be given only an error number. The MACRO Assembler displays a line of text describing the error. Some of these error messages are cryptic, and you may want to look them up in Appendix A of the assembler manual.

At the end of the assembly listing, you will see a symbol table summary that names all of the labels and symbols that you used in the source file. The last thing the assembler prints is the error summary. It gives a count of warning errors and severe errors. Warning errors are rare; for example, you will get one if your editor places a nonprintable character into the text file. You will get used to seeing one or more severe errors on your initial assembly. These errors are caused by typographic errors in your source text, as well as incorrect usage of opcodes and assembler directives. Whenever the error summary indicates any errors of either kind, you will need to go back to your editor, correct the mistakes, and then reassemble.

## The Linker

After you have obtained an error-free assembly, you are ready to convert the object file into an executable program file. The object code produced by the assembler is not yet ready to execute because it is in its "relocatable" format. Think of your object file as a pile of loose pages. Before they are ready to be read, they should be organized into the proper sequence, have holes punched in the edges, and be placed in a three-ring binder. That's what the linker does.

To carry the analogy a little further, imagine that you must insert a new chapter into the middle of the book. The linker handles the job of inserting the new pages and rewriting the table of contents, as well as renumbering the pages and the chapters that were moved forward in the book. What's more, it adjusts every page and chapter number reference in the text that was changed by the insertion.

The assembler has the job of "printing" the pages, but the linker must always be used before the book is "published." Thus, every program must first be assembled, and then must be linked before it may be executed—even if it doesn't need to be linked to anything.

As with the assembler, you can invoke LINK without any parameters and just answer each of the prompts. For now, there is no reason to do this. Assuming that drive B is the current default drive containing your ASM and OBJ files, and you are keeping your utility program on drive A, you will normally invoke the linker via

```
B>A:LINK MYPROG;
```

This command automatically creates a file named MYPROG.EXE, which is ready to execute. For short, simple programs, the entire linking step may seem excessive. However, the linker provides a number of important options that make sophisticated programming tasks easier to handle. For one thing, it allows us to write programs that are composed of short modules that can be individually assembled and tested. The linker also provides a means for adding assembler code to compiled BASIC and Pascal programs. We will discuss these options in depth when we need to use them.

### A Convenient Batch File

Because creating an assembly language program is a multiple-step task, you will find it convenient to use a batch file to take care of the intermediate steps. You can create a simple batch file in 30 seconds, and the lost time is compensated for the first time you use it. You can write a batch file with your editor, or you can use the method described in the DOS manual of copying from the keyboard to a batch file:

```
A>COPY CON: ALD.BAT

A:MASM %1;

pause—press Ctrl-Break if there are errors ---

A:LINK %1;

A:DEBUG %1.EXE

[F6] ENTER      (or CTRL-Z ENTER)
```

This ALD (Assemble, Link, and Debug) batch file should be invoked with one parameter, the filename of the MASM source text. For example:

```
B>ALD MYPROG
```

Every occurrence of %1 in the batch file is replaced with the characters MYPROG. So the batch file automatically assembles the MYPROG.ASM file, creating MYPROG.OBJ, and links the MYPROG.OBJ file, creating MYPROG.EXE. It then loads DEBUG, which loads that executable code in preparation to test it. You can halt the process by pressing Ctrl-Break when prompted.

### DEBUG

DEBUG is an essential utility for assembly language programmers; it is just as important as the assembler and the linker. Rarely do programs run perfectly after the first assembly, and the 8088 forgives very little. The slightest error can send your computer into the never-never land of infinite loops, disabled interrupts, and the Big Red Switch.

DEBUG allows you to examine your program's data in hex and ASCII so that you can see where your messages and variables are stored. It allows you to disassemble your program's code (display the opcode bytes as 8088 mnemonics), so that you can see what part is about to be executed and make sure that it matches the code you wrote with the assembler. It shows you the current value of each register, as well as the setting of the CPU flags.

The most important DEBUG features are its ability to (1) set breakpoints and halt a program's execution and (2) single-step trace through a program one opcode at a time. These tools provide a means of tracking down program logic errors.

DEBUG 2.00, the version that comes with PC-DOS 2.0 and 2.1, provides an excellent means of experimenting with the 8088. The A (Assemble) command allows you to enter short sequences of instructions to see just how the 8088 operates.

DEBUG goes to the heart of assembly language, placing opcode bytes directly into memory and executing them on command. Before we dive into the complexities of the assembler, let's try one short experiment with the DEBUG assembler to give you a taste of assembly language programming. The following discussion assumes that you are using DEBUG version 2.00 under DOS 2.0 or 2.1. If you are still working with an older version of DOS, you won't be able to do everything, but read along anyway.

First, execute DEBUG by entering its name at the DOS prompt:

```
A>DEBUG

-_
```

The minus sign (-) and the blinking cursor are DEBUG's way of saying that it's ready. Let's begin by entering some lines of assembly language. In the following lines, the things that are underlined are to be typed in at the keyboard. Everything else is displayed by DEBUG.

One thing should be noted carefully: DEBUG displays everything in hexadecimal, and it expects all user inputs to be in hex—but it won't accept the *H* at the end of the number. So when we enter a value such as 20, we really mean 20H. The MACRO Assembler, on the other hand, *must have that H,* so don't fall into the bad habit of omitting it.

```
-A 100

0939:0100 MOV AH,2

0939:0102 MOV DL,21

0939:0104 INT 21

0939:0106 INT 20

0939:0108 ENTER
```

This is about the shortest program you can write that does anything visible. It uses a PC-DOS *service call* to display an exclamation point (!) on the screen. The INT 21 is the command that does the work. When INT 21H is executed with AH = 2, the character in the DL register (21H here) is displayed at the current cursor location. The INT 20 is the PC-DOS service that is used to terminate a program. If you forget to enter that line, the 8088 will blindly continue executing whatever random bytes were in memory before we started DEBUG.

The A command takes our input text—assembly language mnemonics—and generates 8088 opcode bytes. Before executing this code, let's use the U command (almost like the BASIC LIST command) to see that everything we entered has been assembled into memory.

```
-U 100 106
0939:0100 B402          MOV     AH,02
0939:0102 B221          MOV     DL,21
0939:0104 CD21          INT     21
0939:0106 CD20          INT     20
```

This command displays, in opcodes and mnemonics, the area of memory that we altered with the A command. The leftmost column shows the address of each opcode. On your machine, the first four digits (i.e., the code segment address) may be different. The next column shows the hex values of the opcode bytes. The rest of the line is DEBUG's disassembly of those bytes. Before we start, let's examine the register display with the R command.

```
-R

AX=0000 BX=0000 CX=00000 DX=0000 SP=FFEE BP=0000 SI=0000 DI=0000
DS=0939 ES=0939 SS=0939 CS=0939 IP=0100   NV UP DI PL NZ NA PO NC
0939:0100 B402          MOV     AH,02
```

This display shows the initial value of each of the registers and flags. Notice that all of the general registers have been set to 0 by DEBUG. All the segment registers have the same value, so that the code segment overlaps the data segment as well as the stack segment. Note that the SP (stack pointer) has been set to a high value, so the program's stack has almost 64K bytes available (remember that the stack grows *downward* in memory). The current execution address is displayed as the values of the CS and IP registers, and the opcode at that address is displayed in the one-line disassembly beneath the registers.

As we do these experiments, you should enter the R command frequently. It always shows the current status of the 8088 and, most importantly, it shows which opcode is to be executed next. In this case, the next opcode is the first one we entered with the A command. We can execute that opcode with the T command.

```
-T

AX=0200 BX=0000 CX=0000 DX=0000 SP=FFEE BP=0000 SI=0000 DI=0000
DS=0939 ES=0939 SS=0939 CS=0939 IP=0102   NV UP DI PL NZ NA PO NC
0939:0102 B221          MOV     DL,21
```

The MOV AH,2 opcode was executed, and DEBUG again displays the registers. Compare this new register display with the previous one. There are two differences. First, the AX register has been altered in accordance with the MOV instruction (AH is the first two digits of the AX register). Also, note that IP (instruction pointer) has been updated to point to the next opcode. Let's try T one more time.

```
-T

AX=0200 BX=0000 CX=0000 DX=0021 SP=FFEE BP=0000 SI=0000 DI=0000
DS=0939 ES=0939 SS=0939 CS=0939 IP=0104   NV UP DI PL NZ NA PO NC
0939:0104 CD21            INT      21
```

Again, note that the opcode altered the DL register, setting it to 21H (the ASCII value of an exclamation point). Tracing the next opcode would invoke an INT 21H, so we won't use the T command. If we did, we would have to step through the reams of code written by the programmers at Microsoft and IBM. So we'll just use the G command to tell the 8088 to "GO!"

```
-G

!

Program terminated normally
```

The exclamation point is printed, and then DEBUG displays a reassuring message to let us know that all went well. When you see this message, you will know that your program executed the INT 20H. This PC-DOS service normally transfers control back to the PC-DOS prompt, but since DEBUG is resident, it grabs control first.

You have already executed your first assembly language program, and you could quit and call it a day. But for the strong-hearted, let's try one more experiment. We're going to modify the program so that it performs a loop, printing out a series of characters.

```
-A 106

0939:0106 INC DL

0939:0108 CMP DL,5F

0939:010B JNE 104

0939:010D INT 20

0939:010F ENTER

-U 100 10D

0939:0100 B402          MOV     AH,02

0939:0102 B221          MOV     DL,21

0939:0104 CD21          INT     21

0939:0106 FEC2          INC     DL

0939:0108 80FA5F        CMP     DL,5F
```

```
0939:010B 75F7          JNZ     0104

0939:010D CD20          INT     20
```

Look this program over carefully and apply what you learned in Chapter 3. The first part is the same as before; it prints the character named in the DL register. But now, the program doesn't immediately end. Instead, it adds 1 to DL, does a comparison to see if DL has reached a terminating value, and branches according to that comparison. If DL has not reached 5FH, the process is repeated; otherwise, execution falls through to the INT 20 instruction, terminating the program.

The loop counter is DL, and the character to be printed by the PC-DOS service is supposed to be in DL. Thus, because the loop counter is incremented with each pass through the loop, the program will print an ascending series of characters, starting with an ASCII 21H and ending with an ASCII 5FH. This program is analogous to the BASIC lines:

```
10 DL=&H21

20 PRINT CHR$(DL)

30 DL=DL+1

40 IF DL<>&H5F THEN GOTO 20

50 END
```

To execute the program, we'll use the special form of the G command to make sure that it starts at the top.

```
-G=100

!"#$%&'()*+,-./0123456789:;<=>?@ ABCDEFGHIJKLMNOPQRSTUVWXYZ[\]

Program terminated normally
```

As you can see, the loop performed as expected, and control returned to DEBUG. Thus, after working with DEBUG for only a few minutes, you have written not one but two programs. You can save the program by issuing the following sequence:

```
-N MYPROG.COM

-R CX

CX 0000

:0010

-R BX

BX 0000
```

```
:0

-W

Writing 0010 bytes

-Q

A>
```

The first command sets up a name for the file, and the second sequence defines the length (the number of the file to be written with the W command is specified by the setting of BX and CX). The W command writes the file onto the disk. Finally, the Q command exits DEBUG, returning control to PC-DOS. The program can be executed by entering MYPROG at the PC-DOS prompt:

```
A>MYPROG

 !"#$%&'()*+,-./0123456789:;<=>?@ ABCDEFGHIJKLMNOPQRSTUVWXYZ[\]
```

This discussion gave us a taste of assembly language, but we have sidestepped many of the most important issues. When we use the MACRO Assembler, we work in a rigidly defined environment; there are many "overhead" details that cannot be overlooked. For instance, we've avoided segments and procedures, and we let DEBUG handle the details of defining and setting up the stack. So remember that the preceding experiments were just experiments. Real assembly language starts with the MACRO Assembler.

**THINGS TO DO**

1.  Change the experiment program so that it prints all of the ASCII characters 20 through FEH.

2.  Write and execute a sequence of code that prints a series of characters in a *descending* sequence.

3.  Use the G *address* command to set a breakpoint in the code. Using the example program, try this sequence to watch the steps of the loop:

```
G=100 106   (Go, starting at 100H, with a breakpoint at 106H)

T           (single-step, note that DL is incremented)

T           (single-step, note how CMP affects the flags)

T      (single-step, note that control is transferred to 104H)

G 106   (Go, stopping at 106H; avoid single-stepping INT 21H)

I           (. . . etc.)
```

4.  (*) Rewrite the program so that it uses a *nested* loop. Have it print letters A to Z ten times.

## 4.2 A PROGRAMMING GESTALT

So far, we have looked at bits and pieces of coding examples and talked in a general way about the 8088's capabilities. Alas, assembler programs are more than a series of opcode mnemonics. There are many types of assembly language programs and many ways to accomplish any assembly language task.

Perhaps the best way to start learning about the multitude of available options is to look at a short but complete assembly language program. Listing 4.1 is just such a program. This program clears the screen and displays a message.

**Listing 4.1**
**MESSAGE.EXE**

```
; ---------------------------------------------------------------------
; Listing 4.1  MESSAGE.EXE
; This program clears the screen, displays a short message,
;  And exits to DOS.

;--- equate section defines some literals for the assembler ----------------

vid_mem          equ  0b800H  ;use 0b000H for monochrome adapter
normal_attribute equ  7       ;symbol for screen attribute
screen_words     equ  80*25   ;  number of memory words on one text screen
eom              equ  0       ;  end-of-message character


;=== set up a segment block for the stack ====================== ================
stack_seg segment para stack                                              ;==
          db  256 dup(0)        ;set aside 256 bytes for the stack        ;==
stack_seg ends                                                            ;==
;==========================================================================


;=== set up a segment block for message data ===============================
data_seg segment para public                                              ;==
message db 'This is the message'   ;the message to print                  ;==
        db eom                     ; end-of-message delimiter             ;==
data_seg ends                                                             ;==
;==========================================================================


;=== set up a segment block for program code ===============================
code_seg segment para public                                              ;==
         assume cs:code_seg, ds:data_seg        ;indicate segment usage   ;==
                                                                          ;==
;------ this procedure sets up return to DOS and calls the other procs -------
main     proc    far          ;start of main procedure block
         push    ds           ;establish "pseudo return address" of the
         mov     ax,0         ; first byte in the PSP
         push    ax           ; ...a method to exit back to PC-DOS.

         mov     ax,data_seg  ;set the DS register to point to data segment
         mov     ds,ax        ; so that program can fetch the message
```

**Listing 4.1
(continued)**

```
        mov     ax,vid_mem    ;use the ES register to point to
        mov     es,ax         ; video memory (destination of output)

        call    cls           ;subtask 1: clear the screen
        call    print_msg     ;subtask 2: print the message
        ret                   ;"return" to address pushed at start (back to DOS)
main    endp                  ;end the main procedure block
;--------------------------------------------------------------------------

;-------------------- this procedure clears the screen --------------------
cls     proc    near          ;first subtask procedure
        mov     di,Ø          ;destination reg points to start of video
        mov     al,' '        ;character is ASCII space
        mov     ah,normal_attribute ;attribute is white on black
        mov     cx,screen_words ;counter is total words of screen memory
        cld                   ;direction is forward (UP)
        rep stosw             ;fill screen memory.  Pronto!
        ret                   ;back to caller
cls     ENDP
;--------------------------------------------------------------------------

;------------------ this procedure displays the message -------------------
print_msg PROC  NEAR          ;second subtask procedure
        mov     si,offset message ;Source Index points to start of message
        mov     di,line_bytes*2 ;destination is third line (first is Ø)
msg_loop:
        cmp     byte ptr [si],eom ;is this the end of the message?
        je      pm_exit       ; yes, skip to exit
        movsb                 ; no, move it to the screen, update SI
                              ;     and DI for next character,
        inc     di            ;     point beyond the attribute byte,
        jmp     msg_loop      ;     then repeat for next character
pm_exit:
        ret                   ;back to caller
print_msg endp
;--------------------------------------------------------------------------
                                                                        ;==
code_seg ends                 ;end the segment block                   ;==
        end                   ;end the assembly                        ;==
;==========================================================================
```

To see this program in action takes three steps:

1. Use an editor to enter the lines of Listing 4.1 into a text file. Name the file MESSAGE.ASM.

2. Assemble the file using the DOS command:      MASM message;

3. Link the file using the DOS command:           LINK message;

4. Run the program using the newly created DOS command: MESSAGE

Now, let's take a look at the program. The following discussion is a gestalt experience: We are examining the *whole* program before taking a detailed look at the individual parts.* Look at the fundamental parts of Listing 4.1. There is a comment header, an equate area, and three segment definitions. The final segment definition defines the executable code, and it is made up of three separate procedures. At the start and end of each segment and procedure block there are lines containing some unfamiliar words. These words are assembler directives or *pseudo-ops,* and they are discussed in Sections 4.4 and 4.5. You will recognize the other lines that contain opcode mnemonics and comments.

Now take a closer look at each of the segment definitions. They all begin with a segment name and the SEGMENT pseudo-op. At the end of each segment block is the ENDS pseudo-op. Farther down in the listing, you will see the three procedures. They begin with a procedure name and the PROC pseudo-op, and they each end with the ENDP pseudo-op. This pattern of grouping related items into blocks is repeated over and over. Any programming instrument that simplifies the complexities of assembly language is treasured. Dividing and subdividing a program into separate units of data and code is just such a tool. Only the most trivial programming exercises can be written in a single procedure in a single segment.

The first lines are a "header" of comments. These comments have no effect on the assembler, but they can hardly be considered optional. Every program you write should start with a similar block of comments to identify the program's function.

The next section defines several *equates.* This program could have been written about these equates, but by assigning certain literal values as assembler symbols, you can make your programs more readable and easier to change. For instance, this program is written for the color/graphics adapter, but if the value of the VID_MEM equate is changed, it will work with the monochrome adapter.

Next, the program sets up its three segment blocks. Each segment delineates an area of memory that is used for a specific type of storage. The STACK_SEG segment is the special area that is set aside for the 8088's stack. This area will be affected every time the program uses a PUSH, POP, CALL, or RET. If you look through the program, you will see that it never uses more than three words of stack space at one time. Nevertheless, 256 bytes have been set aside for stack operations. This is to provide stack space for *background* processes, which will share the program's stack while it is executing.

This program uses the DATA_SEG memory block to hold the characters of the message that it will print. The segment definition describes DATA_SEG as being PARA and PUBLIC. In this case, both of these descriptions are superfluous. PARA is the default type for a segment label. It tells the linker to be sure to start the segment at a 16-byte boundary (notice the implication that there must be segments that *don't* start on a 16-byte paragraph). PUBLIC is meaningful only when you have several program modules. If several modules are linked together and each contains a definition of DATA_SEG, the data of each will be grouped together as a single segment.

Within the DATA_SEG segment block, there are two lines that create storage for a message. The DB pseudo-op is used here to break a string of characters into ASCII

---

* In this book, the opcodes, registers, and labels are shown in lowercase in the listings, but uppercase is used for the program examples in the text. The assembler does not differentiate between lowercase and uppercase for these items. Your own programs can be written completely in uppercase, completely in lowercase, or in a mixture of uppercase and lowercase.

values. These bytes are stored in the object file and will eventually occupy memory addresses in the executable program file. The MESSAGE label will allow us to fetch the characters of the message. The second DB allocates a single byte, the EOM (End of Message) value. This special character is included so that when we process the string, we will be able to determine when the last character is reached. This is only one of many different ways to work with string data.

Finally, we come to the CODE_SEG segment. Notice that this segment, too, is defined as being PARA and PUBLIC. In many ways, it is identical to DATA_SEG. The only difference is that instead of generating bytes of data and messages with DB pseudo-ops, we will use mnemonics to generate machine language opcodes. The rest of the program is included within the CODE_SEG segment block.

The first line of code in the code segment is not code at all. The ASSUME pseudo-op is a sort of error-checking and correcting feature of the MACRO Assembler. It tells the assembler to assume that you will use the DS segment register when you access the bytes in the DATA_SEG segment block. The opcodes in CODE_SEG will be at addresses offset from the CS register.

We are more than 20 lines into the assembly, and we haven't yet written a single opcode mnemonic! Even so, there is still more overhead that must be attended to before we can get to the actual code of the program. The program is made of three procedures: initialization, clearing the screen, and printing the message.

The MAIN procedure handles the initialization code and invokes the procedures for clearing the screen and printing the message. This procedure is defined as being FAR, causing the assembler to generate an intersegment return. The intersegment return is used to pass control back to DOS after the program is finished executing (DOS resides in its own segment). The other procedures are NEAR because they are in the same segment as the CALL instruction that invokes them.

Now let's take a look at the code itself. The very first lines in the MAIN procedure push some data onto the stack. This action sets up the path back to the operating system. We won't go into the details here, but for now, just accept the idea that the best way for a program to exit to DOS is to push DS and 0 onto the stack at the start of the program, and then issue a FAR return at the end of the program.

```
PUSH      DS

MOV       AX, 0

PUSH      AX

     .

     .

     .

RET          ;FAR return to DOS
```

We didn't need to go through this procedure in our DEBUG experiments because DS, CS, ES, and SS all started and ended with the same value. We created a COM format program. But now that we are working with the assembler, we are creating an EXE format program, and the segment registers will be set to different values. The only path back to DOS is through a program segment prefix (PSP), which DOS builds before passing control to your program. The two values pushed onto the stack ensure that we can find the address of the PSP when we need it.

With that complication behind us, let's look at the rest of the program. The next step is to initialize the segment registers. Notice that the program does not try to move values directly into the DS and ES registers. Instead, a value is always moved into a general register (AX, here), and then that value is copied into the segment register. This is just a limitation of segment registers that you'll need to get accustomed to.

## Performing Procedures

Once the segment registers are pointing to their respective memory blocks, the program performs each of the procedures and then exits to the operating system with the FAR return described earlier. We know that this is a FAR return because it resides within a FAR procedure.

The two remaining procedures are short and simple. The CLS procedure uses a repeated string store command to fill video memory with blanks. In the IBM PC, characters can be displayed by placing ASCII codes into memory at the correct addresses. Along with each character location is an attribute byte that defines the color, blink, and other special effects.

In the CLS procedure, we place ASCII spaces (20H) into every character position on the screen, with the normal attribute (white character on a black background) next to it. (Note: Screen characters and attributes are discussed in Chapter 8.) The use of the NORMAL_ATTRIBUTE symbol helps to clarify what is happening in this procedure.

The second procedure, PRINT_MSG, displays the message on the screen. It uses the string move command to copy the characters of the message defined in DATA_SEG into the video memory addresses pointed to by ES:[DI]. In most cases, we will use the PC-DOS and ROM-BIOS services to print characters on the screen. But this procedure illustrates how to bypass these services for very fast screen access.

The final lines of the program tie up the loose ends. ENDP closes the PRINT_MSG procedure; ENDS closes the CODE_SEG segment; and END tells the assembler that there is no more code to be processed.

Look over this program closely. Although it doesn't do much, it contains all the elements needed in virtually every program you will write. It uses equates to create assembler symbols that make the program easier to understand. And there are plenty of comments that document the purpose of the program and the function of each line. It contains data in the data segment and procedures in the code segment. It defines memory segments and initializes segment registers. It has a main procedure that sets up a standard return to DOS, invokes subprocedures, and exits when the task is finished.

## THINGS TO DO

1. When you assemble Listing 1, specify LPT1: as the listing file to obtain a hard copy printout. Then use DEBUG to load the MESSAGE program and the U command to examine the opcodes. Compare the listing to mnemonics and opcode bytes displayed by DEBUG.

2.  Try single-stepping through parts of the code. Use the G *address* command to set a breakpoint after the first CALL (this is the call to the CLS procedure), and execute all of the code up to that point.

3.  Try changing the NORMAL_ATTRIBUTE equate and reassembling the code. An attribute of 87H makes every character blink. An attribute of 70H causes every character to be displayed in reverse video.

## 4.3 ASSEMBLER EXPRESSIONS

The assembler is a very powerful and flexible tool. Two of its most convenient features are its ability to evaluate complex arithmetic expressions and to perform conversions from one numbering system to another. We can use these abilities to save a great deal of time and effort.

In the MESSAGE program, we saw a typical expression evaluation when the PRINT_MSG procedure initialized the DI register. For the message to be printed on the third screen line, the DI register needed to start by printing to byte 320 (160 * 2) in video memory (the first screen line is really line 0). You could have done the calculation manually, but by leaving the math to the assembler, you avoid errors and the formula tends to document the action.

In the CLS procedure, the AL register had to be loaded with the ASCII value of a space. Instead of getting out an ASCII-to-decimal conversion chart and coding the number manually, just enclose the character in quotation marks and let the assembler do the conversion.

### Program Constants

The assembler can convert a variety of numbering systems into the binary values expected by the 8088. Thus, you can write program constants in many different ways:

Decimal (base 10): the digits 0 through 9, with or without a trailing letter *D* (or *d*); optionally preceded by a minus sign (-) for negative values; for example,

        123; -123; 123D

Hexadecimal (base 16): the digits 0 through 9 and the letters *A* through *F* (and *a* through *f*), with a trailing letter *H* (or *h*); positive or negative. The first digit must be a number (0-9), so values that begin with a letter must be preceded by a 0; for example,

        1FH; -23H; 0b800H; 0DH

Binary (base 2): the digits 0 and 1, with a trailing letter *B* (or *b*); positive or negative; for example,

        11010000B; 101b; -101B

Octal (base 8): includes the digits 0 through 7, with a trailing letter *Q* (or *q*) or *O* (or *o*); positive or negative; for example,

```
123Q; -1777Q; 20q; 123o
```

Character: a string of one or more ASCII characters enclosed in single or double quotation marks. Numeric conversions can only be of strings that are one or two characters long. The DB pseudo-op will break multiple-character strings into a series of bytes; for example,

```
'a'; "A"; "it's a string!"; 'He said, "Hi there!"'
```

Decimal scientific notation: floating point decimal numbers (MASM only). The storage format is not compatible with 8087 data types; for example,

```
1E3; 20.327E1; -123.456
```

Hexadecimal real: digits 0 through 9 and letters *A* through *F* (or *a* through *f*), with a trailing *R* (or *r*). There must be 8, 16, or 20 such digits unless the first digit is a 0, in which case there may be 9, 17, or 21 digits in the number (MASM only). This system is used mainly in defining numbers that will be processed by the 8087 NDP coprocessor; for example,

```
12345678R; 0FFFFFFFFFFFFFFFFR; -12345678r
```

When a number contains invalid digits, the assembler will indicate a syntax error. If you forget to place a leading 0 on hexadecimal numbers that begin with the letters *A* through *F*, the assembler will think you are referring to a symbol and will indicate an undefined symbol error.

## .RADIX

Base 10 is the default numbering system for constant evaluation, so numbers such as 123 are correctly evaluated without needing to append a *D* at the end. However, at any time you may set a new default base for constant evaluation. This procedure allows you to specify a number without appending the specific base ID letter. For example, the following sequence loads the AX register with 255 in each case:

```
MOV      AX,255         ;default is decimal

MOV      AX,0ffH        ;append H for hex

MOV      AX,11111111B   ;append B for binary

.RADIX 16               ;switch to hexadecimal default

MOV      AX,0FF          ;look mom, no H

.RADIX 2                ;switch to binary default

MOV      AX,11111111    ;the B is not needed at the end

MOV      AX,255D        ;D must be used for decimal values
                        ;now
```

After using the .RADIX pseudo-op, remember that all subsequent numeric values will be evaluated in the new base. You may switch back to a decimal default with the .RADIX 10 command. Note: After issuing a .RADIX 16 pseudo-op, you will need to watch out for hexadecimal numbers that end with $D$ (0D generates 0 rather than 0DH). The assembler will treat these numbers as decimal numbers. A number such as 01AD generates a syntax error because $A$ is not a valid decimal digit.

The .RADIX pseudo-op has more than casual value when you are working with graphics. By specifying base 4 as the default, you can provide an easy way to define bytes to be displayed on the medium-resolution graphics screen. For example, the sequence

```
.RADIX 4

MOV     SCREEN[DI]              ,3333

MOV     SCREEN[DI+2000H]        ,3003

MOV     SCREEN[DI+80D]          ,3003

MOV     SCREEN[DI+2000H+80D],3333
```

will display a small white (or yellow) box that is four lines high, starting at the byte pointed to by DI.

## 4.4 ASSEMBLER OPERATORS

The assembler supports a wide selection of arithmetic, logical, and relational operators. These operators allow you to specify operands as complex expressions as well as simple program constants. They simplify your work by allowing you to skip the process of manually calculating constant values. Table 4.1 lists the operators that the assembler supports in its expression evaluation.

It is important for assembly language novices to realize that these operators are different from the 8088's arithmetic opcodes. A line such as

```
AX    EQU    AX+BX
```

will give the assembler fits. Just remember that these operators are used to evaluate expressions *during the assembly*—not when the program is being executed.

Perhaps the most valuable aspect of using arithmetic operators is that they can be used in conjunction with assembler symbols to define values that would otherwise need to be coded as constants. In Listing 4.1, changing the LINE_SIZE symbol from 160 to 80 would make the program compatible with 40-character screens.

The assembler automatically does some arithmetic when you specify indexed addresses in some of the more exotic formats. For instance, in the address expression

```
MOV    AX,MY_TABLE[BX+SI][3]
```

the address of MY_TABLE is added to 3 to create the true offset that is saved in the object code file. When the opcode is executed, that offset value will be added to the current value of SI and the sum added to the value of BX, forming the effective address

**Table 4.1**
**Assembler Operators**

| Operator | Format/Function |
|---|---|

### Arithmetic

**+**
    *operand1* + *operand2*
      Returns sum of *operand1* plus *operand2*

**-**
    *operand1* - *operand2*
      Returns difference of *operand1* minus *operand2*

**\***
    *operand1* \* *operand2*
      Returns product of *operand1* multiplied by *operand2*

**/**
    *operand1* / *operand2*
      Returns integer quotient of *operand1* divided by *operand2*

**MOD**
    *operand1* MOD *operand2*
      Returns remainder of integer division of *operand1* by *operand2*

**SHL**
    *operand1* SHL *operand2*
      Returns value of *operand1* shifted left by *operand2* bit positions

**SHR**
    *operand1* SHR *operand2*
      Returns value of *operand1* shifted right by *operand2* bit positions

### Logical

**AND**
    *operand1* AND *operand2*
      Returns binary logical product of *operand1* and *operand2*

**OR**
    *operand1* OR *operand2*
      Returns binary logical sum of *operand1* and *operand2*

**XOR**
    *operand1* XOR *operand2*
      Returns binary logical difference of *operand1* and *operand2*

**NOT**
    NOT *operand*
      Returns one's complement of *operand* (toggles all bits of *operand*)

### Relational

**EQ**
    *operand1* EQ *operand2*
      Returns TRUE if *operand1* = *operand2*, else returns FALSE

**NE**
    *operand1* NE *operand2*
      Returns TRUE if *operand1* <> *operand2*, else returns FALSE

**LT**
    *operand1* LT *operand2*
      Returns TRUE if *operand1* < *operand2*, else returns FALSE

**GT**
    *operand1* GT *operand2*
      Returns TRUE if *operand1* > *operand2*, else returns FALSE

**LE**
    *operand1* LE *operand2*
      Returns TRUE if *operand1* <= *operand2*, else returns FALSE

**GE**
    *operand1* GE *operand2*
      Returns TRUE if *operand1* >= *operand2*, else returns FALSE

Notes:  TRUE = ØFFFFH and FALSE = Ø
        All relational operators work with 16-bit *unsigned values*.
        For example: (-2 GT Ø) is TRUE because -2 is unsigned ØFFFEH.

**Table 4.1
(continued)**

| Operator | Format/Function |
|---|---|

### Attribute Override

**PTR**
*type* PTR *expression*
Overrides the *type* (BYTE, WORD, DWORD, FAR, NEAR etc.) of a label or address *expression*.

**CS:**      CS:*addr_expression*
**DS:**      DS:*addr_expression*
**ES:**      ES:*addr_expression*
**SS:**      SS:*addr_expression*
*seg_name:*    *seg_name:addr_expression*
*group_name:* *group_name:addr_expression*
Overrides the segment attribute of the *addr_expression*. This normally results in the generation of a SEG prefix opcode.

**SHORT**
JMP SHORT *address_label*
Overrides the NEAR attribute of the target *address_label*. Used to force the assembler to generate the 2-byte form of the JMP opcode.

**THIS**
THIS *attribute*
Overrides the normal *attribute* (BYTE, WORD, DWORD, FAR, NEAR etc.) of a label to generate a symbol with the specified attibute at the current location (segment and offset) in the assembly.

**HIGH**
HIGH *variable*
Isolates the high-order byte of a 16-bit memory variable.

**LOW**
LOW *variable*
Isolates the low-order byte of a 16-bit memory variable.

**DUP**
*expression* DUP(*value*)
Used with a DB, DW, DQ, or DT pseudo-op to allocate repeated occurences of a storage value. The *value* is duplicated *expression* times.

### Attribute Value

**OFFSET**
OFFSET *variable* or OFFSET *label*
Returns the segment offset address of a variable or a label.

**SEG**
SEG *variable* or SEG *label*
Returns the segment address of a variable or a label.

**TYPE**
TYPE *variable* or TYPE *label*
Returns the numeric code of the type attribute of a variable or a label.

**LENGTH**
LENGTH *variable* or LENGTH *structure_name*
Returns the number of units allocated to a variable (e.i., the DUP count (if any, or 1 if none) of a DB or DW data declaration).

**SIZE**
SIZE *variable*
Returns the number of bytes allocated to a variable; i.e., the product of LENGTH*TYPE.

**$**
$ (no operands)
Returns the offset of the assembler's location counter within the segment currently being processed.

**Table 4.1
(continued)**

| Operator | Format/Function |
|---|---|
| | **Record Specific** |
| MASK | MASK *rec_field*<br>Returns a binary mask value that has 1s in each of the positions of a bit record that are defined for *rec_field* in a RECORD pseudo-op. |
| WIDTH | WIDTH *rec_field* or WIDTH *rec_name*<br>Returns the number of bits that have been allocated to a bit field or a bit record as defined with the RECORD pseudo-op. |
| SHIFT<br>COUNT | *rec_field* (no operands)<br>Returns the number of right shifts that will place the relevant bits of *rec_field* into the least significant bits of an operand. |

of the memory operand that is loaded into AX. This procedure may appear somewhat clearer if you specify the address in a different but equally valid format:

```
MOV     AX,[BX+SI+MY_TABLE+3]
```

## 4.4.1 Arithmetic and Logical Operators

Addition, subtraction, multiplication, and division are self-explanatory. The only thing you need to watch for is arithmetic overflow that the assembler does not flag as an error. The assembler does all of its internal calculations with signed values ranging from -FFFFH to FFFFH. Therefore, the expression in

```
MOV     AX,(0FFFFH*10)/10
```

will be incorrectly evaluated. In this case, AX will end up with a value of 1998H because 0FFFFH*10 creates an overflow, losing significant digits. You will rarely calculate such constants, but be aware that the assembler will drop significant digits if you do.

The MOD operator divides a value, and then discards the quotient and returns the remainder. For instance, 5 MOD 2 equals 1.

The SHL and SHR operators shift the bit pattern of an operand by a specified number of bit positions. Like the 8088 operations with the same names, these assembler operators are used to move a set of bits into a desired position.

The AND, OR, XOR, and NOT operators are also used to manipulate bit patterns in an expression. AND is used in masking off unwanted bits; OR is used to turn on certain bits; XOR toggles a group of bits, and NOT toggles each of the bits in its single operand. AND, OR, and NOT can be used in evaluating the relational expressions described in the following section.

## 4.4.2 Relational Operators

The EQ, NE, LT, GT, LE, and GE operators compare their two operands and return either a true (FFFFH) or a false (0) value. There is little reason for an operation such as

```
MOV     CX,VERSION_NUM LT 3
```

which will generate one of

```
MOV     CX,0FFFFH      ;when VERSION_NUM is 0, 1, or 2
MOV     CX,0           ;when VERSION_NUM is 3 or more
```

However, when used in conjunction with the conditional pseudo-ops, they add a lot of flexibility to the range of questions that the assembler can answer about program symbols. If you want to generate a different message to be displayed in only certain versions of a program, you could use the relational operators in an expression such as this:

```
IF ((VERSION EQ1) AND NOT DEBUGGING) OR (VERSION GT 3)
  DB 'Super Ultra Program for the IBM-XT'
ELSE
  DB 'IBM-PC Version'
ENDIF
```

Note: The IF, ELSE, and ENDIF pseudo-ops are discussed in Chapter 6.

In MACRO Assembler version 1.0, the relational operators incorrectly evaluate some expressions. They ignore the sign of their operands, working entirely with absolute values. This means, for example, that an expression such as

```
MOV     AX,-1 LT 0 ;erroneously evaluated expression
```

is evaluated as false even though -1 is obviously less than 0. Keep this problem in mind when you try to evaluate expressions that contain negative constants or symbols.

## 4.4.3 Attribute Operators

Attribute operators allow you to extract information from and specify certain things about assembler symbols. A little background information is in order: Every symbol or label defined in a program is placed in the assembler's symbol table. Each entry contains more than a name and a numeric value. For every symbol, there is an associated *segment, offset,* and *type* attribute. The attribute operators provide a means of retrieving the attributes of a symbol or overriding the attributes of a symbol.

### PTR: Overriding a Symbol's Type

PTR (PoinTeR) is one of the most often used operators. It is used to override the type (BYTE, WORD, etc.) or distance (NEAR, FAR) of variables and labels. The general format is:

```
type PTR expression
```

The *type* field is one of BYTE, WORD, DWORD, QWORD, TBYTE, NEAR, FAR, or an expression that extracts the *type* attribute of a previously declared symbol. The *expression* is an address identifier.

PTR is misnamed; it isn't necessarily used in conjunction with a pointer or index register, although it is most often seen in that context. Perhaps OVRIDE or ATTRIB would have been a better name.

PTR is most often used to clarify ambiguities that arise in referencing memory operands. For instance,

```
INC        [SI]
```

could mean increment the byte pointed to by SI or increment the word pointed to by SI. The only way to resolve this ambiguity is to use one of the following:

```
INC     BYTE PTR [SI]

INC     WORD PTR [SI]
```

Similar ambiguities can arise in data transfers, additions, and subtractions when the destination operand is a base-relative or indexed memory reference and the source is an immediate operand. The PTR operator must also be used to clarify multiplications and divisions that use a base relative or indexed memory operand as a multiplier or divisor.

```
LDS     SI,DWORD PTR [BX] ;get SI=[BX], DS=[BX+2]

FBLD    TBYTE PTR [SI]     ;8087 opcode: use with 8087

                           ;macros only

CMP     WORD PTR [SI],30   ;30 could be BYTE or WORD

MUL     BYTE PTR [DI]      ;multiplier is BYTE

DIV     WORD PTR [DI]      ;divisor is WORD
```

Note that these ambiguities occur only when the assembler is unable to identify an operand's type from the instruction. The line

```
ADD     AL,[SI]            ;no override needed
```

clearly specifies addition of an 8-bit memory operand because the destination is an 8-bit register. Also, if the memory address is specified as an offset within a table, then the *type* attribute is taken from the type of table that is being accessed:

```
BYTE_TABLE DB   100H DUP(0)     ;DB indicates bytes

            .

            .

            .

    INC     BYTE_TABLE [SI] ;type is taken to be BYTE
```

PTR is also used when you want to reference a symbol by other than its original definition. For instance, the command

```
WORD_VAR DW       1234H
```

allocates 16 bits of memory to a variable that has a type attribute of WORD. If you need to increment only the first eight bits (the low byte), you can use

```
    INC     BYTE PTR WORD_VAR
```

You use the FAR and NEAR types when using memory operands for jumps and calls:

```
JMP         NEAR PTR [BX]       ;[BX] is used as a 2-byte,

                                ;NEAR vector

CALL        FAR PTR [DI]        ;[DI] is used as a 4-byte,

                                ;FAR vector
```

Occasionally, you may not be sure of what type of override is needed, but you know that it is the same type as another label. You can use the TYPE operator to determine the distance of the known label as follows:

```
JMP         (TYPE MY_PROC) PTR [DI]
```

## Segment Override

The 8088 supports an opcode that was not mentioned in Chapter 3 and is not supported by the MACRO Assembler. The SEG opcode is actually one of four different opcode bytes that tell the CPU, "If the next instruction accesses memory, don't calculate the effective address using the default segment register. Instead, use this other segment register."

The MACRO Assembler implements this opcode by allowing the inclusion of a segment override for any memory operand expression. The assembler accepts any of these formats:

```
seg_reg:addr_expr

seg_name:addr_expr

group_name:addr_expr
```

*Addr_expr* is an address expression in any one of the familiar addressing mode formats.

*Seg_reg* is one of CS, DS, ES, or SS.

*Seg_name* is a name that has been specified with a SEGMENT pseudo-op.

*Group_name* is a name that has been specified with a GROUP pseudo-op.

The most common usage is with a segment register directly:

```
MOV     AX,ES:[BX+DI]

MOV     BYTE PTR CS:[DI],0
```

You can also use the name of a segment or a group of segments for the override, as long as the ASSUME pseudo-op has been used to tell the assembler which segment is associated with *seg_name* or *group_name*. (The ASSUME pseudo-op is discussed in Section 4.4.5.)

```
ASSUME    CS:CODE_SEG, ES:COM_GROUP

  .

  .

  .

MOV     AX,CODE_SEG:[BX]

INC     BYTE PTR COM_GROUP:[BX]
```

If the assembler believes that no segment override is needed, it will not generate the special prefix byte. For instance, if DATA_TABLE has been defined in the DATA_SEG and an ASSUME pseudo-op has indicated that DS is pointing to that memory segment, neither of the following will generate a SEG prefix for its opcode:

```
MOV     AX,DATA_SEG:DATA_TABLE[BX+20]

MOV     DS:DATA_TABLE[5],AX
```

Sometimes you want to address a memory variable that has not been defined in your program. The ROM-BIOS data area is full of useful variables that contain such information as the keyboard shift status and the type of display monitor that is currently active (color graphics or monochrome). You know from reading the technical reference manual that the BIOS keeps the keyboard shift status at 0040:0017. It may seem like you should be able to set DS to 40H and access the byte at offset 17H, but the assembler will generate an error message if you try to access that byte directly. This happens because the assembler does not have a type or segment attribute for the variable. So instead of

```
MOV     AX,40H

MOV     DS,AX        ;ROM-BIOS data area

MOV     AL,[17H]     ;--- generates an error ---
```

change the MOV instruction to

```
MOV     AL,BYTE PTR DS:[17H];--- generates correct code --
```

At some point, you will wish that you could override the segment registers that the 8088 uses in its string operations. This operation is possible, but only in a limited sense. You may specify a segment override for the source string (i.e., override the normally used DS register), but you cannot override the segment of the destination string. In other words, STOS and SCAS cannot be overriden at all; they always work with the memory addressed by ES:[DI]. The other operations, MOVS, CMPS, and LODS, can have a segment override prefixed to their source memory operands.

The problem is that if these string primitives are used in a repeated string operation, the segment override will be forgotten in the event of a hardware-generated interrupt. After an interrupt, the CPU remembers only the single prefix directly before the string primitive operation. So if the code is arranged as

```
MOV  CX,1000

REP

SEG  CS:

MOVSB
```

and a background task interrupts after, say, 500 iterations of the MOVSB opcode, then after returning from the interrupt, the CPU will have forgotten the REP prefix, and control will fall through without completing the string operation. If the prefixes are rearranged as

```
MOV  CX,1000

SEG  CS:

REP

MOVSB
```

and the CPU is interrupted after the 500th iteration, the first 500 bytes will come from the CS segment and the final 500 bytes will be moved from the DS segment. The CS: segment override will be forgotten, and the REP MOVSB will revert to using the default source segment register.

As long as you know that this problem may arise, you can take steps to prevent it. If you halt the background interrupts before starting the repeated action and then restart them afterward, you can be relatively certain of achieving the desired result:

```
CLI

REP MOVS CS:source,ES:destination

STI
```

### Short Jumps

The SHORT operator is used to tighten up code. Two different JMP instructions will perform identically in many cases. The 3-byte JMP opcode can force execution to any place within the current code segment. A 2-byte JMP opcode can be used to transfer control to within +127 to -128 bytes of the jump instruction.

The assembler will use the shorter form whenever it knows that the short jump is valid, that is, when the jump is backward to a label it has already processed. But the assembler has no way of knowing if a forward jump can use the 2-byte opcode. The purpose of the SHORT operator is to tell the assembler that the short form of the JMP opcode is possible.

```
JMP      SHORT TAG ;force assembler to generate
                   ;the 2-byte opcode
(less than 128 bytes)

         .

TAG:

         .

(less than 128 bytes)

         .

JMP      TAG    ;automatically a short, 2-byte
                ;opcode
```

### THIS and $: Where Am I?

The THIS operator creates a symbol of any type (BYTE, WORD, DWORD, QWORD, or TBYTE) or distance (NEAR or FAR) at the location of the assembler's internal location counter. The symbol is given a segment attribute of the enclosing segment block.

THIS is useful for creating a symbol with a special type, often to avoid using the PTR operator in address expressions. For instance, the following sequence will define a memory variable as both a byte and a word.

```
BYTE_VAR  EQU  THIS BYTE
WORD_VAR  DW   0
```

It can also be used to define a FAR label in a NEAR procedure, and vice versa:

```
FAR_TAG   EQU  THIS FAR
MY_PROC   PROC NEAR
```

The use of the dollar sign ($) is another way to retrieve the value of the assembler's location counter. It comes in handy in many situations in which you would like to have the assembler count addresses. For instance:

```
MSG1        DB  'THIS IS A STRING OF ASCII BYTES'

MSG1_LEN  EQU $ - MSG1

             .

             .

             .

            MOV         CX,MSG1_LEN       ;get the length for a

                                          ;string transfer

        REP MOVSB
```

This sequence will let you determine the length of a string without having to count its characters manually. If you change the string and make it longer or shorter, the value of MSG1_LEN will remain valid in the next assembly.

The $ may also be used in address expressions. For example,

```
    JE          $+5
```

will perform the same as a jump to a label that is exactly five bytes from the current location counter. The $ equates to the address of the location counter *just before the line is assembled.* In the preceding example, the expression $+5 points to the opcode that is exactly three bytes from the end of the jump instruction because the jump instruction itself is two bytes long.

## HIGH and LOW

The HIGH and LOW operators are used to isolate a single byte from a 2-byte word variable. The LOW operator specifies the LSB (low order) and the HIGH operator specifies the MSB (high order). Both of these bytes can be simulated with the BYTE PTR operator:

```
MOV     AL,LOW WORD_VAR          ;is the same as . . .

MOV     AL,BYTE PTR WORD_VAR

MOV     AH,HIGH WORD_VAR         ;is the same as . . .

MOV     AH,BYTE PTR WORD_VAR+1
```

## OFFSET

The OFFSET operator returns the offset attribute of a variable or label within the segment in which it is defined. It provides a means of finding out where a variable is stored rather than what value is stored at that address. When you want to use a register as an index into a memory table, you may need to point that register to the start of the table.

```
MOV      BX,OFFSET MY_TABLE   ;point to the base of the
                              ;table
MOV      SI,CUR_ELEMENT       ;point to the desired table
                              ;element
MOV      AX,[BX+SI]           ;fetch the element value
```

You will often use OFFSET to initialize the SI and DI registers for addressing strings:

```
MOV      SI,OFFSET INPUT_BUFFER    ;point to source
MOV      DI,OFFSET STORAGE_AREA    ;point to destination
MOV      CX,STRING_LENGTH          ;fetch the length
REP MOVSB                          ;transfer the string
```

Note: The LEA command may also be used to initialize base and index registers for processing strings or tables. The resulting object code is one byte longer than the corresponding immediate move, but you may find it conceptually easier to deal with. The following two examples both point SI to the start of the INPUT_BUFFER:

```
MOV      SI,OFFSET INPUT_BUFFER    ;functionally the same
                                   ;as . . .
LEA      SI,INPUT_BUFFER
```

OFFSET is automatically implied when a variable name or label is used in DW or DD pseudo-op commands. For instance, this sequence will create a table of jump vectors:

```
JMP_TABLE DW     EDIT_PROC    ;same as OFFSET EDIT_PROC
                              ;(a 2-byte NEAR address)
          DW     PRINT_PROC   ;same as OFFSET PRINT_PROC
          DW     READ_PROC    ;same as OFFSET READ_PROC
```

Version 1.0 of the MACRO Assembler has a slight but nasty bug associated with the OFFSET operator. As we will see when we discuss the SEGMENT and GROUP pseudo-ops, the offset of a variable may be changed drastically by the linker. Therefore, any reference to a variable or its offset must be relocatable to be dynamically adjusted at link time. Usually when the OFFSET operator is used to form an address expression, the assembler will correctly record a relocatable reference in the object file. However, in some cases, the assembler will simply create a "hard-coded" value that the linker can't relocate. This problem occurs only when an OFFSET is used to form an address expression that is stored as an immediate operand for arithmetic and logical opcodes:

```
ADD       BX,OFFSET MY_TABLE      ;erroneously assembled
```

If you use this kind of expression and then combine the segment that contains MY_TABLE with an external segment of the same name, or with other segments via the GROUP pseudo-op discussed in Section 4.5.4, the value that is added (or subtracted or ANDed or ORed) will be incorrect. You overcome this bug to make certain that the correct, relocatable offset is generated by using a group or segment name override:

```
ADD       BX,OFFSET COM_GRP:MY_TABLE     ;correctly
                                         ;assembled

ADD       BX,OFFSET DATA_SEG:MY_TABLE    ;correctly
                                         ;assembled
```

### Offsets with Group or Segment Register Overrides

When you are using the GROUP pseudo-op to instruct the linker to combine several logical segments into a single physical segment, you will need to use a group name as a segment override to the label or variable. For instance:

```
COM_GRP GROUP     CODE_SEG,DATA_SEG

CODE_SEG SEGMENT

          ASSUME  CS:COM_GRP, DS:COM_GRP, ES:COM_GRP
          MOV     SI,OFFSET COM_GRP:INPUT_BUFFER
                            ;override with group name

          LEA     SI,INPUT_BUFFER
                            ;LEA works without override

          .
          .

CODE_SEG ENDS

DATA_SEG SEGMENT

INPUT_BUFFER    DB 80 DUP(' ')

          .
          .

DATA_SEG ENDS
```

### SEG: Fetching the Value of a Variable's Segment

The SEG operator can be used to isolate and fetch the segment attribute of a variable or label. It is one quick way to avoid searching through a source file to locate the segment in which a variable is enclosed:

```
MOV     AX,SEG STORAGE_AREA    ;find the correct segment
                               ;for source
MOV     ES,AX                  ;initialize ES
LEA     DI,STORAGE_AREA        ; and DI for MOVSB
```

Its most powerful use is to fetch a segment address that is not in the source file. This operation is performed when you are linking external code and data to a module. In the following example, an external module contains a look-up table. The SEG operator is used to set up the segment register to access those data:

```
EXTRN     DATA_TABLE:WORD
ASSUME    DS:SEG DATA_TABLE
MOV       AX,SEG DATA_TABLE
MOV       DS,AX
MOV       SI,OFFSET DATA_TABLE
MOV       AX,[SI]
```

The ASSUME and EXTRN pseudo-ops are discussed in Section 4.6.

### TYPE: Fetching a Symbol's Type Attribute

The TYPE operator returns a value indicating the type attribute of a variable or label. For variables, that value is the size in bytes of the variable:

```
type        bytes
BYTE        1
WORD        2
DWORD       4
QWORD       8
TBYTE       10

structure   number of bytes declared in STRUC block
```

For procedure and other address labels, TYPE returns either NEAR or FAR:

```
NEAR      -1   (FFFFH)
FAR       -2   (FFFEH)
```

The TYPE operator comes in handy while processing tables of data. Regardless of the size of each element, you can move an index register pointer from element to element by adding or subtracting the table's TYPE value from the pointer:

```
LEA     SI,MY_TABLE+(TYPE MY_TABLE * 4)  ;point to
                                         ;fifth element
ADD     SI,TYPE MY_TABLE                 ;point to
                                         ;next element
```

TYPE is especially useful in programs that employ structures (see the STRUC pseudo-op in Section 4.5.3).

## LENGTH and SIZE

The LENGTH operator fetches any DUP count value that is associated with a variable. The SIZE operator is simply the product of LENGTH times TYPE. Experienced programmers will use these operators to give a program flexibility in order to allow for future changes. For instance, a program that has a disk input buffer might contain statements such as these:

```
INPUT_BUFFER  DB 128 DUP(0)   ;allocate space for the
                              ;buffer

        .

        .

        .

MOV     CX,SIZE INPUT_BUFFER

REP MOVSB
```

At some future point, the size of the input buffer may need to be changed. If references to the size of that buffer are hard-coded (as in MOV CX, 128), updating would require a careful search through a program (or group of program modules) to locate and change every such reference. If the references are tempered by using the SIZE operator, a single change in the definition of the input buffer (i.e., an alteration of the DUP count) will change every reference in the program.

These operators reference only the DUP count. There is no single operator for retrieving the size or length of a literal message or string of characters. In the following example, the variable MESSAGE will have a TYPE of 1, a SIZE of 1, and a LENGTH of 1; in other words, these operators have no meaning for character string data definitions.

```
MESSAGE DB  'THIS IS A MESSAGE',0DH,0AH
```

## Record Operators

There are several special operators that are used to extract information about RECORD bit fields. A record field name is used as an operator that retrieves a SHIFT

COUNT that can be used to move bit positions of a record into a certain position within a byte or word. The MASK operator returns a bit mask that has 1s in all bit positions that are significant to a particular bit field and 0s in the other bit positions. The WIDTH operator returns the number of bit positions that are allocated to an individual field of a record.

These operators are illustrated in Section 4.5.3, along with the discussion on the RECORD pseudo-op.

## 4.5 PSEUDO OPERATIONS

Assembler directives, usually called *pseudo-ops*, are used like opcode mnemonics. They are placed in the opcode field of a line of source text, may be labeled with a name, most often have one or more operands, and may be followed by a comment. The major difference is that pseudo-ops instruct the assembler; they do not generate code that is executed by the CPU.

The MACRO Assembler has a large selection of pseudo-ops that handle a variety of functions, including defining data, grouping code into segments and procedures, assigning values to assembler symbols, building macro instructions, and formatting the listing of an assembly. Table 4.2 gives a brief summary of each function. This section discusses the fundamental pseudo-ops and those that are particularly important or difficult to understand. It also describes in detail the more complex RECORD and STRUC pseudo-ops. Macros, repeating, and conditional pseudo-ops are examined in Chapter 6.

**Table 4.2**
**General Pseudo-Ops**

```
Pseudo-op                               Format/Function

                      Data Definition

  DB          DB expression [,...] or DB 'text'  (Define Bytes)
  DW          DW expression [,...]               (Define Words)
  DD          DD expression [,...]               (Define Doublewords)
  DQ          DQ expression [,...]               (Define Quadwords)
  DT          DT expression [,...]          (define 10-byte packed BCD values)
              Allocates and optionally initializes storage for data.
              Expression may contain a DUP clause: count DUP expression

  RECORD      rec_name RECORD field_name:width[=expression][,...]
              Defines a bit-field to format bytes and words for bit-packing.
              Rec-name may later be used to allocate and initialize data.

  STRUCT      structure_name STRUC
              Begins the definition of a data structure; ended by ENDS.
              STRUC block contains DB,DW,DD,DQ,and/or DT data pseudo-ops.
              Structure-name may later be used to allocate and initialize data.

                      Symbol Definition

  EQU         name EQU expression
              Assigns the value of expression the the symbol name.
              Name cannot be redefined with a different value.
```

**Table 4.2
(continued)**

| Pseudo-op | Format/Function |
|---|---|

=           *name = expression*
                Like EQU except the value of *name* can be redefined.

LABEL       *name* LABEL *type*
                Creates a symbol with attributes of *type* at the current offset
                in the current segment.

PUBLIC      PUBLIC *symbol* [,...]
                Declares *symbol* to be publicly available to external modules.

EXTRN       EXTRN *name:type* [,...]
                Describes symbols used in this module whose attributes are defined
                in a different module.

### Segment and Procedure Definition

SEGMENT    *seg_name* SEGMENT [*align_type*][ *combine-type*][ '*class*']
                Declares the start of a segment block and its attributes.
                *Align_type* is one of: PARA, BTYE, WORD, PAGE
                *Combine_type* is one of: PUBLIC, COMMON, STACK, MEMORY, AT *exp*
                '*class*' is text enclosed in single quotes.
                Default arguments are: paragraph, private, and '' (no *class*)

ENDS        *name* ENDS
                Indicates the end of a SEGMENT or STRUC block.

ASSUME     ASSUME *seg_reg:seg_id*
                Specifies which segment register is associated with a particular
                logical segment or group of segments.

GROUP       *name* GROUP *seg_name* [,...]
                Used to collect logical segments into a single physical segment.

PROC        *proc_name* PROC [NEAR] or *proc_name* PROC FAR
                Begins the definition of a block of procedure code.

ENDP        *proc_name* ENDP
                Indicates the end of the *proc_name* procedure block.

### Miscellaneous

COMMENT    COMMENT *delimiter text delimiter*
                *Delimiter* is any non-blank character (same in both places).
                Provides a way to write multi-line comments.

INCLUDE    INCLUDE *filespec*
                Reads source statements from a disk file.

EVEN        EVEN (no arguments)
                Adjusts the assembler's location counter to an even boundary.

END         END [*start_label*]
                Forces assembler to halt assembly and optionally sets up the
                address for the program to begin executing. (Default = offset 0)

NAME        NAME *module_name*
                Gives a name to a module so that it may be accessed by an object
                module librarian utility.

ORG         ORG *expression*
                Alters the assembler's internal location counter.

.RADIX      .RADIX *expression*
                Sets the default radix (normally decimal) to a value from 2 to 16.

## 4.5.1 Symbol Definition Pseudo-Ops

One of the most powerful features of the assembler is its flexible options for creating symbols. The most common type of symbol is the one that gives a name to a program address. Just think up a good symbol, affix a colon to the end, and place it on a source line. The symbol can be used as a target label for any intrasegment jump or call.

But experienced programmers use symbols for much more than address labels. A symbol can be used in place of a complex addressing expression in order to simplify your coding. Symbolic names tend to document code much better than literal values. And the first law of assembly language is, "Thou shalt document thy code."

### EQU and =: Creating Symbolic Names

The symbol definition pseudo-ops EQU and = assign an expression to a symbolic name. The general format is:

```
name    EQU expression

name    =    expression
```

The *name* is any valid assembler symbol. The *expression* may be an address reference (using any addressing mode expression), a numeric constant, or any combination of symbols and operations that can be evaluated as a numeric value.

The primary use for EQU (equate) is to define program constants to make program listings more self-documenting and easier to change:

```
LINE_SIZE      EQU  80

SCREEN_SIZE    EQU  LINE_SIZE * 25

LF             EQU  0AH

CR             EQU  0DH
```

You can make complex address expressions easier to use by creating a symbolic name which encompasses the entire expression:

```
ADDR_PTR    EQU  [BP+6]

CUR_CHAR    EQU  BYTE PTR DATA_GROUP:[SI]

    .

    .

    .

    MOV    SI,ADDR_PTR    ;point to the string

    CMP    CUR_CHAR,CR    ;is current character a
                          ;carriage return?
```

EQU is useful when you need to access a variable as if it had a different type attribute. By using the PTR operator, you may assign a new name to a previously declared variable or address label, giving it new attributes:

```
LOW_BYTE     EQU BYTE PTR WORD_VAR      ;create two 1-byte
                                        ;variables from a
                                        ;word
HIGH_BYTE    EQU BYTE PTR WORD_VAR+1
FAR_TAG      EQU FAR PTR MY_NEAR_TAG    ;make a FAR name for
                                        ;a NEAR procedure
FAR_PROC     EQU THIS FAR               ;use the THIS
                                        ;operator to create a
                                        ;tag
```

The expression associated with a name created with EQU cannot be changed. That is, once you have defined a symbol as being one value, it must remain the same value throughout the program.

The = (equal sign) pseudo-op functions the same as EQU, except that the value of the symbol can be redefined. This distinction is made because the assembler has more work to do when it needs to treat a symbol as a variable rather than as a constant. For example:

```
RADIUS = RADIUS+1
CIRCUM = PI*(RADIUS*RADIUS)
```

This assembler directive is handy in iterative assembler operations (as within a REPT block) and in macros. See Chapter 6 for examples of its use.

## LABEL: Naming an Address

The LABEL pseudo-op is a convenient tool for assigning multiple names to a variable or address label. It may be used to place a tag at any point in a program or data area. The format is:

```
name    LABEL    type
```

The *name* is any valid assembler symbol. It will be used as a reference to the offset of the label within the enclosing segment. The *type* is either an address type of FAR or NEAR or a data type of BYTE, WORD, DWORD, QWORD, TBYTE, a *structure name*, or a *record name*. The latter two options refer to the special user-defined data types created with the RECORD and STRUC pseudo-ops.

The following example shows a way to give names to all four bytes as well as both words of a 32-bit doubleword variable.

```
DWORD_VAR   LABEL DWORD      ;could be used in
                             ;LES  DI,DWORD_VAR

LOW_WORD    LABEL WORD       ;could be used in
                             ;MOV  AX,LOW_WORD

BYTE_1      DB    0          ;could be used in
                             ;MOV  AL,BYTE_1

BYTE_2      DB    0

HIGH_WORD   LABEL WORD

BYTE_3    ' DB    0

BYTE_4      DB    0
```

## 4.5.2 Storage Allocation Pseudo-Ops

The assembler provides a variety of formats for defining program variables and allocating memory for variable storage. The DB, DW, DD, DQ, and DT directives are used to reserve memory for program variables and, optionally, to assign them initial values. The format is:

```
[name] DB expression      ;allocates single bytes of data

[name] DW expression      ;allocates 2-byte words

[name] DD expression      ;allocates 4-byte doublewords

[name] DQ expression      ;allocates 8-byte quadwords

[name] DT expression      ;allocates 10 bytes of packed
                          ;decimal data
```

The *name* entry is optional. If used, it is the name by which a program will thereafter refer to the variable. The *expression* can be one of:

* A question mark (?)

* A single constant expression

* A series of constant expressions separated by commas

* A duplication expression

The question mark indicates that you don't care about the initial values stored in the object code file and loaded with the executable file.

```
WORK_VAR    DW     ?        ;this 16-bit word variable must be
                            ; initialized by the program
```

A constant expression is used to specify an initial value for the storage area. The evaluated expression will be stored in the load module along with the opcodes of the program.

```
CONST_80    DB      80              ;constant used in
                                    ;multiplication
TEXT_PTR    DW      STORAGE_AREA ;initially the address of
                                    ;STORAGE_AREA
```

The constant expression in a DB pseudo-op may also be a string of characters enclosed in single or double quotation marks. The assembler will break the string into its component ASCII values and allocate storage for each of them. In this case, any name specified to label the string will refer to the address of the first byte of the string.

```
ERR_MSG_1 DB    '?NEXT without FOR'

ERR_MSG_2 DB    '?Syntax error'
```

If a string expression must contain the single quotation mark (an apostrophe), you can surround the string with double quotation marks:

```
ERR_MSG_3 DB    "Can't Continue"
```

A series of constants separated by commas can be used to set up an initialized table. This format can be used to create a table of values that will be used in a look-up table in your program, as well as add special characters to a string expression:

```
SQUARE_TBL DW 0, 1*1, 2*2 ,3*3, 4*4, 5*5, 6*6
           DW 7*7, 8*8, 9*9

HELLO_MSG  DB 'Hello there!',0DH,0AH,'$'
```

A duplicated expression (or duplicate clause) is used to allocate a series of identical expressions. The syntax is

```
repeat_count DUP (expression[, . . .])
```

*Repeat_count* is a constant or an expression containing symbols and arithmetic operations. The *expression* of a DUP clause is the same as the expressions described above, including multiple-argument and string expressions.

```
TEXT_AREA    DB  1000 DUP(0)          ;1000 bytes,
                                      ;initially all 0
TEXT_AREA    DB  1000 DUP(?)          ;1000 bytes,
                                      ;not initialized
EMPTY_SPACE DB  10   DUP('EMPTY   ') ;highly visible
                                      ;with DEBUG
PHONE_TABLE DB  100  DUP(20 DUP(' '), '(000)000-0000')
```

The last example shows how to nest DUP clauses. In this case, a table is created to hold 100 entries, each with room for a 20-character name followed by the ASCII digits of a phone number.

### DD: Defining Doubleword Storage

While DB and DW are the most common variable allocation pseudo-ops, there are some very important uses for the DD, DQ, and DT directives. DD allocates and optionally initializes a 32-bit doubleword. These doublewords can be used to set up storage for multiple-precision arithmetic results. DD creates the type of variable that the assembler needs in order to perform indirect FAR jumps and FAR calls. The variables referenced by the LDS and LES opcodes must also be defined as doublewords.

```
SAVE_VECT    DD    ?             ;storage to save a 32-bit
                                 ;interrupt vector

TEXT_PTR     DD    TEXT_AREA     ;stores both the segment and
                                 ;offset values

PROC_TABLE   DD    CMD_MODE, BREAKPOINT, FILL
             DD    ENTER_BYTES, DSPLY_REGS
```

The pointer set up in the latter example can be used in indirect intersegment jumps and calls:

```
MOV     DI,CMD_NUM        ;number of user-selected command
SHL     DI,1
SHL     DI,1              ;times 4 to point to table element
CALL    PROC_TABLE[DI]    ; call DIth FAR procedure in
                          ; PROC_TABLE
```

### DQ and DT: Data-Types for the 8087

DQ (Define Quadword) allocates storage for and optionally initializes 64 bits (8 bytes or 4 words) of memory. DT (Define Tenbytes) defines storage for 10 bytes of packed Binary Coded Decimal (BCD) (i.e., 20 digits). These storage options correspond to two of the data formats that are used by the 8087 coprocessor.

The DQ pseudo-op can be used to reserve storage for an 8087 *long real* floating point value (an 80-bit number in a special binary format). Alas, the assembler has its own internal floating point format that doesn't jibe with that of the 8087, and it places these bytes into the source code. Therefore, you can't expect floating point values initialized with DQ to be meaningful to the 8087. You can, however, use DQ to initialize storage for very large integers up to 1E20.

The DT pseudo-op can be used both to allocate and to initialize storage for the 8087's 18-digit packed BCD format. The initial value (if specified) will be held in 10 bytes of memory composed of one byte for the sign and nine bytes of packed BCD digits (two BCD digits per byte). That format gives business applications a precise representation of dollar values as high as $9,999,999,999,999,999.99 (one cent less than 10 thousand trillion dollars).

```
INCOME   DT        1000                 ;the decimal point
                                        ;position
OUTGO    DT        999999999999999999   ; must be handled
                                        ; by software
```

### 4.5.3 Advanced Data Definitions

Two of the data-defining pseudo-ops allow the creation of complex data types. The RECORD and STRUC pseudo-ops are systems that allow you to create your own data-defining pseudo-ops. These pseudo-ops are not supported by the small version of the MACRO Assembler (ASM).

If you are new to assembly language, feel free to skip over the following discussion of the RECORD and STRUC pseudo-ops. You can become a perfectly efficient assembly language programmer without knowing how to use MACRO Assembler records and structures. But as you begin to write more sophisticated applications, you will eventually work with bit fields and data structures. You can set up complex data types through a combination of pseudo-ops and program logic, or you may choose to wield the powerful tools that the assembler provides.

#### RECORD: Defining Packed Bit Fields

The RECORD pseudo-op creates a *template* for a user-defined bit pattern. RECORD does not allocate bytes of memory. Rather, it sets up a framework within which odd-sized bit fields may be packed. Once defined, the record name becomes both a pseudo-op that allocates and initializes memory storage and an operator that can be used for working with bit fields. The RECORD pseudo-op is not supported by the small version of the assembler. The MASM syntax is:

```
record_name RECORD field_name:width[, . . .]
```

or

```
record_name RECORD field_name:width[=expression][, . . .]
```

The *record name* and the *field name* can be any valid assembler symbol name. The colon (:) must be entered between the *field name* and the *width* parameter. The *width* parameter is a number from 1 to 16 that declares the number of bits defined by *field name*. The *=expression* is optional. When used, it sets up a default value for the field.

Let's begin with a typical example. Every file that PC-DOS stores on a diskette is given a date stamp in the diskette directory. The entire date is stored as a series of three bit fields held in a 16-bit word. The format of the date stamp is:

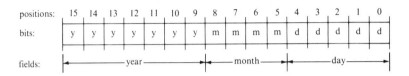

The day is a number from 1 to 32, the month is 1 to 12, and the year is 0 to 119 (added to 1980 to achieve a range of 1980 to 2099).

To set up a template of this date stamp, we'll define a record with YEAR, MONTH, and DAY fields, in that order—with the most significant bits first.

```
DATE_REC RECORD year:7, month:4, day:5   ;define bit
                                         ;fields
```

Once the record is defined, we can create a program variable by using a *record_name* of DATE_REC as if it were a DW pseudo-op, except that we can easily specify initial values for each of the bit fields. The syntax for this type of data allocation is:

```
[name] record_name <[expression][, . . .]>
```

The *name* is an optional label that can be used as a reference to the data. The *record name* is the symbol created via the RECORD pseudo-op. The angle brackets are required. A list of expressions, separated by commas, will be used to fill in the bit fields. One or more fields may be left blank, in which case the default value (if any) is applied to the field. If there is no default value for a field and its corresponding expression is blank, then the initial value of the allocated memory will be indeterminate.

```
FILE_DATE DATE_REC <10,2,17>  ;year 10 (from 1980),
                              ;month 2, day 17
```

This program line creates a 16-bit variable named FILE_DATE that has an initial value of February 17, 1990. The alternative method of using DW to allocate and initialize the variable would require a complex arithmetic expression.

Perhaps the greatest advantage of using a record is that the assembler supplies three operators that simplify the process of storing a value in and extracting data from a byte or word defined as a record.

The WIDTH operator returns the size, in bits, of an individual record field. The value returned is the same value that was used as a field's width parameter in a RECORD definition.

The MASK operator returns a binary value with 1s in only those positions that define a certain field. The value returned by MASK provides an effective screen to mask off all other bit fields in the record. For instance,

```
AND      FILE_DATE,MASK MONTH
```

will clear out all of the bits of the variable FILE_DATE except those that define the month. In our example, the value in FILE_DATE is 1250H (Feb. 17, 1990) and the MASK value of MONTH is 01D0H, making the AND operation work like this:

```
    FILE_DATE  = 1250H = 0001 0010 0101 0000 = 0001001 0010 10000
AND   MASK MONTH = 01D0H = 0000 0001 1110 0000 = 0000000 1111 00000
---------------  -----------------------------------------------
         RESULT = 0040H = 0000 0000 0100 0000 = 0000000 0010 00000
```

Thus, the AND opcode has isolated the bits of the MONTH field. The next step is to bring those bits to the far right side of the operand. We want to end up with a number from 1 to 12 that can be used as a reference to a month.

The *field name* of any field of a record is also a value-returning operator that may be used as a SHIFT COUNT. It describes the number of shifts that will be required to move the relevant bits to the right side of an operand. In our example, the MONTH *field name* returns a value of 5. In order to derive a useful number from the value 0040H (the result of the masking operation), that value must be shifted to the right by five places. The usual practice is to place the shift count value into CL and perform a repeating shift opcode:

```
MOV      CL,MONTH      ;get the SHIFT COUNT of the MONTH

                       ;record field

SHR      FILE_DATE,CL  ;move the relevant bits into position
```

The value held in the variable FILE_NAME will now be a number from 1 to 12; in this case, it is exactly 2—representing the month of February.

Now let's put the parts together and write a sequence that will break down a PC-DOS date stamp into a year, month, and day. The following procedure illustrates how to break down our example record into its components and store each in a separate word variable. It assumes that the date stamp of a file has been stored in a 16-bit variable FILE_DATE. The procedure isolates the individual fields and stores the correct values in the variables SAVE_DAY, SAVE_MONTH, and SAVE_YEAR.

```
;  IN THE DATA SEGMENT

DATE_REC RECORD   YEAR:7, MONTH:4, DAY:5   ;define the

                                           ;fields of

                                           ;the record

SAVE_DAY   DB    ?                         ;define storage

                                           ;for results
```

```
SAVE_MONTH DB      ?

SAVE_YEAR  DW      ?

; IN THE CODE SEGMENT

UNPACK_DATE PROC NEAR
        MOV     AX,FILE_DATE      ;get the 16-bit date stamp
        AND     AX,MASK DAY       ;isolate the day field
        MOV     SAVE_DAY,AX       ;save the day (1-31)

        MOV     AX,FILE_DATE      ;fetch the date stamp again
        AND     AX,MASK MONTH     ;shave off all but month
                                  ;bits
        MOV     CL,MONTH          ;use the shift count
        SHR     AX,CL             ; and move the bits into
                                  ; position
        MOV     SAVE_MONTH,AX     ;store the month (1-12)

        MOV     AX,FILE_DATE
        AND     AX,MASK YEAR      ;isolate year bits
        MOV     CL,YEAR
        SHR     AX,CL             ;move the bits into
                                  ;position
        ADD     AX,1980           ;make it a complete year
                                  ;reference
        MOV     SAVE_YEAR,AX      ;store the year
                                  ;(1980-2099)
        RET                       ;back to caller
UNPACK_DATE ENDP
```

There are a few more facts about using records that need to be discussed. First, when you define a record in which all of the field width parameters add up to less than eight (or 16), the fields will be right-justified in the byte (or word). Therefore, you may need to supply a dummy value if you want the record to define only the leftmost bits.

For instance, the ROM-BIOS keeps track of a keyboard status flag that is a group of bit fields describing the current state of the various shift keys. When bit 7 is set, the

Ins key is being pressed, bit 6 echoes the state of the CapsLock key, and so on. The lowest three bits of this flag have no meaning. Any record that defined the relevant bit fields would need to have a dummy field to hold the defined bits to the left side:

```
KB_FLAG1_REC RECORD INS:1, CAPS:1, NUM:1, SCROLL:1,
    HOLD:1, DUMMY:3
```

With a record such as this, you could, for example, find out if the NumLock key is being pressed with this test:

```
TEST      KB_FLAG1 MASK NUM

JZ        NOT_PRESSED          ;skip if not being pressed

                               ; else, process for

                               ; NumLock key
```

Records can be used to good advantage in graphics-intensive programs. Colorful graphics shapes are difficult to work with because each byte needs to be broken into its 2-bit pixels and then reassembled into bytes for storage. You can save time and effort by defining a record that does the work:

```
COLOR_REC RECORD c7:2=0,c6:2=0,c5:2=0,c4:2=0,c3:2=0,
                 c2:2=0,c1:2=0,c0:2=0

BL      EQU     1    ;blue

RD      EQU     2    ;red

WH      EQU     3    ;white

                          ;Blanks default to the background color

TORPEDO COLOR_REC <BL,  ,  ,RD,RD,  ,  , >

        COLOR_REC <BL,BL,  ,  ,RD,RD,  , >

        COLOR_REC <  ,WH,WH,WH,WH,RD,RD, >

        COLOR_REC <  ,  ,WH,WH,WH,WH,RD,RD>

        COLOR_REC <  ,WH,WH,WH,WH,RD,RD, >

        COLOR_REC <BL,BL,  ,  ,RD,RD,  , >

        COLOR_REC <BL,  ,  ,RD,RD,  ,  , >
```

## STRUC: Defining Data Structures

The STRUC pseudo-op provides a means of creating complex, user-defined data structures. Once a structure is defined, the structure name becomes a pseudo-op used to define and allocate storage. STRUC is a block command; that is, it begins a series of lines that define a structure. The ENDS pseudo-op closes or ends the block. The general syntax is:

```
structure_name STRUC

[field_name]   DB | DD | DQ | DT  expression

                .

                .

                .

structure_name ENDS
```

The body of the STRUC block is composed of one or more of the data definition pseudo-ops (DB, DW, DQ, and DT). Each such pseudo-op may be preceded by a field name. The field names allow you to access the various parts of a structure. Here's a simple example:

```
PHONE_STRUC     STRUC

PH_INDEX        DW ?            ;16 bits for a unique index #
                                ;of this person

PH_NAME         DB 30 DUP (?)   ;30 bytes for a person's name

PH_NICKNAME     DB '          ';10 bytes for a nickname or
                                ;personal code

PH_NUM          DB 10 DUP (?)   ;10 bytes for an ASCII number
                                ;(000)000-0000

PHONE_STRUC     ENDS
```

As with the RECORD pseudo-op, a sequence such as this does not allocate any storage. Rather, it sets up a template that you may use to "overlay" bytes in memory in order to give them meaning and make them easy to access. Here's the special format used to address memory as elements of a structure:

```
address_exp.field_name
```

The *address_exp* refers to any program variable name or any of the assembler's addressing mode notations. The period (.) is required.

Pretend for the moment that you have just read a disk file that has 50 phonebook entries. The file was loaded at an address labeled PHONEBOOK. Assuming that you have defined the PHONE_STRUC previously described, you could access the data with any of the following commands:

```
MOV    AL,PHONEBOOK.PH_NUM        ;first digit of first
                                  ;phone number

MOV    AL,PHONEBOOK[SI].PH_NAME ;get the address via an
                                  ;index register
```

```
MOV     AL,PHONEBOOK.PH_NAME[SI]  ; and in another format
MOV     BX,OFFSET PHONEBOOK       ;set up a base register
MOV     AL,[BX][SI].PH_NAME       ;go through both a base
                                  ;and an index
MOV     AL,[BX+SI].PH_NAME        ; another notation
```

Perhaps the most important use of structures is to access subroutine parameters that have been placed on the stack prior to the call to the subroutine. Data structures are ideal for this application because the actual address of any parameter is never known by the caller; only a stack-relative address is known. By setting up a structure that is a template for the parameters, you make them easy to access. For instance, if a Pascal program passes four 16-bit arguments and one 8-bit argument to your assembly language line-drawing procedure, you could access them with:

```
LINE_PARMS STRUC

X_START     DW   ?

Y_START     DW   ?

X_STOP      DW   ?

Y_STOP      DW   ?

COLOR       DB   ?

LINE_PARMS ENDS

            PUSH   BP              ;6 extra bytes now on the
                                   ;stack

            MOV    BP,SP
            ADD    BP,6            ;SS:[BP] addresses first
                                   ;parameter

            MOV    CX,[BP].X_START
            MOV    DX,[BP].Y_START
            MOV    AL,[BP].COLOR
            CALL   PLOTDOT
```

See Chapter 7 for a full description of the standard parameter-passing convention used when interfacing with high-level languages.

Now let's look at the situation from the other direction. In addition to using the PHONE_STRUC as a template for accessing data, you may use it as a fill-in-the-blanks form to allocate and initialize data. The procedure is similar to that used with the fields defined with the RECORD pseudo-op:

```
[name] structure_name <[expression][, . . .]>
```

The *name* is an optional label you may use to identify the address of a particular structure allocation. The *structure_name* is used like a pseudo-op that allocates all of the bytes defined in a structure definition. A series of *expressions*, surrounded by angle brackets, are optionally used to initialize the storage area.

You may allocate an empty block of bytes for a single PHONEBOOK entry by simply omitting the *expression* parameters:

```
ONE_PHONE PHONE_STRUC <>            ;1 entry, no data
                                    ;initialized

PHONEBOOK PHONE_STRUC 500 DUP[<>]   ;500 entries, no data
                                    ;initialized
```

A major difference between the way RECORDs and STRUCs are allocated is that there are certain limitations on the fields that may be overridden when a structure is allocated. That is, the default values in a structure (the values that have been coded in the DEFINE pseudo-ops within the STRUC declaration) may or may not be overridden when the *structure_name* is used to allocate data for a structure. The rule is: Fields that contain a duplication clause or have multiple entries may not be given new values when allocated. Fields with single-expression entries, including string expressions, may be overridden.

```
PH_INDEX        DW 0            ;may be overridden with a
                                ;numeric expression

PH_NICKNAME     DB '       '    ;may be assigned a
                                ;different string

PH_NAME         DB 30 DUP(?)    ;may not be overridden
```

In order to make PHONE_STRUC useful for setting up a series of initialized PHONEBOOK entries, it will need to be redefined:

```
PHONE_STRUC     STRUC       ;using strings that may be
                                overridden

PH_INDEX        DW ?                            ;index

PH_NAME         DB '         '                  ;name

PH_NICKNAME     DB '         '                  ;nickname
                                                ;or code

PH_NUM          DB '0000000000'                 ;phone
                                                ;number

PHONE_STRUC     ENDS
```

Now the assembler will allocate storage for PHONEBOOK entries with:

```
PHONEBOOK  PHONE_STRUC  <1,'Baggins,Bilbo','hobbit',
   '8001234567'>

            PHONE_STRUC  <2,'Mouse,Michael',,'7149994565'>
                                       ;no nickname

      PHONE_STRUC <3,,,>              ;index number only

      PHONE_STRUC <>                 ;empty entry
```

A string expression used to override a string field may be longer or shorter than the size of the string defined in the STRUC. If it is shorter, the assembler will pad the right side of the field with ASCII 20H blanks. If it is longer, the string will be truncated to the defined number of characters.

## Complex Nested Structures

In essence, structures and records subdivide chunks of memory into predefined groups of bytes and bits. No huge intuitive leap is needed to realize that you can use lower-level structure and record templates to break up higher-level structure fields. This "nesting" of structures is not physical; one STRUC block can't contain another STRUC block. However, any structure that defines subfields within fields of another structure is conceptually a nested data construct. We can't use a secondary structure to initialize data for a primary structure, but when we access the data, this nested structure concept will make those data easier to visualize.

In our PHONE_STRUC example, we may find it convenient to be able to access separate parts of the PH_NUM field. This ability would allow us to determine the three parts of a phone number. The following example defines a PHONE_NUM substructure and uses its fields to access the individual fields within a PHONE_STRUC structure:

```
PHONE_NUM       STRUC
                ;used as template over PH_NUM data of PHONE_STRUC

PH_NUM_AREA    DB 3 DUP (?) ;3-digit area code

PH_NUM_EXCH    DB 3 DUP (?) ;3-digit exchange

PH_NUM_CODE    DB 4 DUP (?) ;4-digit phone code

PHONE_NUM       ENDS

        MOV     DI,OFFSET PHONEBOOK.PH_NUM
                        ;these both point to

        MOV     DI,OFFSET PHONEBOOK.PH_NUM.PH_NUM_AREA
                        ;  the first element

        MOV     BX,OFFSET PHONEBOOK
                        ;set up a base pointer
```

```
MOV      SI,0                    ;point to first entry
CMP      [BX+SI].PHONE_NUM.PH_NUM_AREA,'8'
                                 ;access the area code

LEA      DI,[SI+TYPE PHONE_STRUC]
                                 ;point to next element
MOV      CX,LENGTH PH_NUM_EXCH + LENGTH
         PH_NUM_CODE   ;set up a counter

  REP CMPSB                      ;compare the 7-digit parts
```

This example also illustrates how to use the TYPE and LENGTH operators with structures and substructures. As you know, the SIZE operator returns a variable's DUP count times the unit size of the duplicated expression. It is used in the example to calculate the combined size of the PH_NUM_EXCH and PH_NUM_CODE subfields.

The TYPE operator returns a count of the number of bytes allocated to a variable. For structures, it returns the number of bytes allocated to all of the fields of the structure. Adding the value of a structure's TYPE to an index register is a good way of bumping that register to point to the next element of an array of structures.

## 4.5.4 Code Block Pseudo-Ops

The CPU does things in very tiny steps, but programmers need to think about a project in larger steps—as a series of tasks and subtasks. The assembler provides powerful tools to help you divide your program into manageable modules. It also provides the tools needed to work with the segmented structure of the 8088's memory.

### Procedures

Procedures are the building blocks of assembly language programs. They perform discrete units of work that, when combined with other procedures, accomplish a programming task. Only the most trivial programming tasks can be written without being broken into procedures—program modules. In assembly language, modular programming is more than an abstract concept to be argued among academicians; it's a way of life.

The PROC pseudo-op is a tool that helps you to write programs modularly. You use it to declare a block of code to be a procedure. This tool also provides the mechanism needed to code the different types of subroutines (i.e., intrasegment and intersegment). The code for each procedure in a program must reside within a block that is declared as follows:

```
procedure_name PROC [NEAR]

  or

procedure_name PROC FAR
```

```
         .

(opcode mnemonics and pseudo-op directives)

         .

[RET]

         .

procedure_name ENDP
```

The *procedure_name* can be any valid assembler symbol. If there is no distance attribute (FAR or NEAR) in the PROC declaration, the procedure will be treated as a NEAR procedure.

The code in a procedure does not necessarily need to refer to a called subroutine. It may be jumped to or simply executed in-line. In fact, it makes sense to create a procedure block for *any group of opcodes that performs a distinct function*, whether that task is to be invoked via the CALL opcode or not.

If a procedure is a subroutine, all RET opcodes that lie within the procedure block will be affected by the procedure declaration. A RET within a NEAR procedure will be a NEAR return (i.e., only the instruction pointer will be POPped off the stack). If the procedure is FAR, RET opcodes will be assembled as FAR returns (i.e., both CS and IP will be POPped off the stack). Likewise, all calls to procedures declared NEAR will be intrasegment calls, and all calls to FAR procedures will be assembled as intersegment calls. For example,

```
FAR_SBRTN    PROC      FAR

             CALL      NEAR_RTN     ;NEAR, intrasegment linkage

             .

             .

             RET                    ;a FAR, intersegment return
FAR_SBRTN    ENDP

NEAR_SBRTN PROC      NEAR

             .

             .

             RET                    ;a NEAR, intrasegment return
NEAR_SBRTN ENDP
```

As we saw in Listing 4.1, the MAIN procedure (the procedure that takes control as soon as a program is loaded) must be declared FAR. Normally, this master routine will invoke NEAR procedures—subroutines that reside in the same code segment. It is perfectly possible (and often desirable) to write programs that use more than one code segment. Any procedures called or jumped to from a different segment, and any routines invoked via a software interrupt, must be declared FAR.

Procedures may be assembled and stored on a disk and then linked with other procedures to form a complete program. Such library procedures must be named in a PUBLIC declaration. The assembler must encounter an EXTRN pseudo-op in order to process calls to external procedures or access data defined in an external module. See Section 4.6 for details on the PUBLIC and EXTRN pseudo-ops.

## Segment Pseudo-Ops

The SEGMENT, ENDS, ASSUME, and GROUP pseudo-ops are the tools provided to implement and take advantage of the 8088's segmented memory scheme. These commands offer a regular smorgasbord of options—some of them tasty and delightful, others that may lie heavy in your stomach. Until you become familiar with the techniques of using memory segments to simplify a programming task, these options might seem confusing and frustrating.

Let's start with a few basic premises:

* In one sense, a segment is a physical block of memory that begins on a 16-byte paragraph of memory and has a length of 64K bytes. This definition is the familiar one associated with segment registers. We will refer to this 64K block of memory as a *physical segment.*

* In another sense, a segment is a logical grouping of code or data in your program. These segment blocks may start anywhere in memory, and may be any size up to 64K in length. They are called *logical segments.* Logical segments are composed of procedures and opcodes (a code segment) or data defined by the DB, DW, and other pseudo-ops (a data segment).

* Logical segments are constructed and named by your program. Physical segments are constructed by the linker according to the way you define the logical segments in a program.

* Your program may contain one or more *partial* logical segments that will be combined by the linker into physical memory segments, or it may consist of one or more *complete* logical segments that may be treated as if they were physical segments.

* Every bit of data or code that is defined by your program must reside within a segment block.

The general format for defining a logical segment is as follows:

```
segment_name SEGMENT [align_type]        ;optional

                     [combine_type]      ;parameters

                     ['class_name']
```

```
segment_name ENDS
```

The *segment_name* is any valid assembler symbol. It is a good practice to use a *segment_name* that includes the letters 'seg.' CODE_SEG, DATA_SEG, PROGRAM_ VARIABLES_SEG, VIDMEM_SEG, and LIBRARY _SEG are good examples.

Everything that lies between the SEGMENT and ENDS pseudo-ops will be tagged in the OBJ file as being part of a segment. Every symbol (procedure name, jump label, or variable name) that lies within the segment block is listed in the assembler's internal symbol table as having a segment attribute of the enclosing segment.

The optional parameters are passed to the linker to give it instructions on how to load and relocate a segment block. For instance, you may say "combine this logical segment with other similar segments," "this logical segment will overlap another segment," "this segment is the physical segment to be used by the stack," or "start this segment at a certain address in memory."

Let's take a look at each of the optional segment-defining parameters:

### Segment *Align_type*

The *align_type* parameter describes the physical memory boundary that the linker should start loading a segment block. It may be one of:

PARA (or blank): The segment will be loaded beginning at an address that is evenly divisible by 16. This is the *align_type* default. Any segment that will be directly addressed by a segment register should be given this attribute. When this segment is loaded into memory, the linker will precede its code (or data) by up to 15 bytes of filler to be sure that it begins on a paragraph boundary.

BYTE: The segment may begin anyplace in memory. This *align_type* is used solely in the definition of a logical segment that will be combined with other segments, one of which must be aligned on a paragraph boundary. The linker will not insert any filler bytes before this block of code.

WORD: The segment must begin at an address that is evenly divisible by 2. As with BYTE alignment, this type must be used with logical segments that will be combined with a segment with PARA alignment. This option will be used mainly in programs that are specifically written for the 8086 (the 8086 will fetch 16-bit data much faster if it begins on an even boundary). The linker will insert up to one filler byte before this segment block.

PAGE: The segment will be loaded on a page boundary (i.e., an address evenly divisible by 256). The linker will insert up to 255 filler bytes before it loads a segment with the PAGE *align_type*.

As we saw in Listing 4.1, the *align_type* of simple segments will always be PARA. BYTE alignment is the only other significant *align_type* for 8088 programming. It is needed when you use external library procedures or when you employ the GROUP pseudo-op to combine logical segments.

## Segment *Combine_type*

The *combine_type* parameter of the SEGMENT pseudo-op indicates the manner in which a logical segment should be combined with other segments in the run file. Simple programs may omit this parameter entirely. The *combine_type* options include:

(blank): The segment is private; it may not be combined with any other segments. This is the option to select unless you expect to group segments or link external segments to the program.

PUBLIC: The segment will be concatenated to any other segments that have the same name. This is the *combine_type* used when you are linking external logical segments so that they will be treated as a single physical segment. Specifically, when you write a library procedure, you may want all other library procedures to reside in the same physical segment. In that case, you should enclose each procedure with the same *segment_name* and a *combine_type* of PUBLIC, and then use the linker to link them together.

You will also want to use an *align_type* of BYTE so that the assembler doesn't insert a bunch of unusable bytes between the combined procedures. See Appendix C for examples of the various ways to create and use library procedures.

COMMON: All segments declared COMMON will begin at the same physical memory address. A COMMON segment overlays other segments of the same name. This *combine_type* is used to redefine variables and data in another program module in order to give a program a means of accessing those data in more than one way. Chapter 7 demonstrates how to use a COMMON segment in an assembler module to access variables declared COMMON in a compiled BASIC program.

AT *expression*: This parameter allows you to create symbolic references to specific areas in memory. The *expression* is evaluated as a segment address (i.e., a paragraph number). Data and procedures defined within a segment declared this way *will not be loaded into memory*. However, labels and variable names that are declared within such a segment block will have the desired attributes and addresses.

The AT *combine_type* is most often used to set up symbolic references to ROM addresses and data that are known to be found at a certain address in memory (the interrupt vector table and the ROM-BIOS data areas, for example). It does not specify a particular address at which code should be loaded.

STACK: A segment declared with this attribute will define the memory area that will be used by the 8088's stack while the program is being executed. When an EXE program is loaded by the DOS loader, the stack segment (SS) register will automatically be set to point to this value, and the stack pointer (SP) register will be set to point to the last byte defined in the segment. All data pushed onto the stack (via PUSH, PUSHF, INT, and CALL opcodes) will be stored in this segment.

The linker expects every program to contain a STACK segment and will issue an error if one is not found in the linked object file(s). However, there need be no STACK segment if (1) your program sets up its own stack segment or (2) the program is converted into a COM format file by the EXE2BIN utility.

If several object modules that each contain a STACK segment are linked, the size of the stack segment will equal the combined sizes of all of those segments. In other words, all segments with the STACK *combine_type* will be treated as if they each had the same *segment_name* and were declared PUBLIC.

MEMORY: This *combine_type* is supposed to force a segment to be loaded at higher addresses than all segments with other combine types. However, the linker does not support this definition. The linker treats MEMORY segments as if they were PUBLIC segments.

### Segment *Class_name*

The *class_name*, if included, must be enclosed in single quotation marks. This parameter is passed to the linker, which uses it to group segment blocks physically in memory. As with the other SEGMENT parameters, only complex programs (i.e., programs with external segments brought in at link time) need to include this declaration. The linker will place all segments with identical *class_names* together. That is, they will still be separate segments residing in their own physical segment and addressed using different values for the segment registers, but they will be loaded as a group. This option allows a multiple-module program to keep its data, code, and stack segments in separate areas of memory. Most such complex programs will define 'data' and 'code' classed segments. A 'stack' class segment is superfluous because STACK segments are automatically grouped.

Here are some example SEGMENT declarations:

```
MYCODE_SEG  SEGMENT
            ;default to PARA alignment; noncombinable

MYCODE_SEG  SEGMENT PARA PUBLIC
            ;may be combined with other MYCODE_SEG segments

MYCODE_SEG  SEGMENT BYTE PUBLIC
            ;contains near PROCs combined into above segment

CODE_SEG    SEGMENT PUBLIC 'CODE'
            ;these two are separately addressed
```

```
LIB_SEG    SEGMENT PUBLIC 'CODE'
               ;   but will reside next to each other

STACK_SEG SEGMENT STACK
               ;combined with all other STACK segments

COMMON  SEGMENT COMMON 'BLANK'
               ;this segment overlays BASCOM's COMMON area

BIOS_DATA_SEG SEGMENT AT 40H
               ;defines BIOS_DATA_SEG for the assembler
KBD_FLAG1 DB       0
               ;the 0 is NOT loaded into memory at run time

BASIC_ROM_SEG    SEGMENT AT 0F600H
               ;segment to define labels in ROM

           ORG     3

FLT2BIN    PROC    FAR
               ;now okay to call FLT2BIN (invoke a ROM procedure)

FLT2BIN    ENDP
```

## Nesting Segments

Code and data blocks created with the SEGMENT pseudo-op are never physically nested; however, a segment block may be defined within an enclosing segment. When the assembler encounters the start of an inner segment as it processes an outer segment, it puts aside the outer block, assembles the inner block, and then takes up where it left off in the outer segment. Thus, the enclosed segment is complete unto itself, having no relationship to the enclosing segment.

This situation is quite handy in certain cases. Consider this scenario: As you write a procedure (in a code segment), you realize that it must print a message. That process could entail going back to the data segment and inserting the DB to define the message and a label to use as a reference to it. That's not so hard when you are writing a simple program that defines all of the data and code in a single assembler source file. But when the data segment is defined in an external module, the task becomes more difficult, giving many opportunities for making errors.

The alternative is quite simple: Without closing the current code segment, begin and end a data segment that contains just the one-line definition of the message to print. *Voila!* As long as the data segment has the same name as the main data segment (possibly in an external module), and both have a *combine_type* of PUBLIC, the linker will automatically concatenate the second segment to the main segment. This feature is quite convenient for developing high-level macro commands such as

```
PRINT 'this text'
```

## The GROUP Pseudo-op

The difference between a logical segment and a physical segment is most clearly explained in terms of the GROUP pseudo-op. This directive tells the linker to combine segments of different names as if they were PUBLIC segments with the same name. That is, GROUP collects two or more segments into a single 64K physical segment. The syntax is:

```
group_name GROUP segment_name [, . . . ]
```

or

```
group_name GROUP SEG name [, . . . ]
```

The *group_name* is a unique identifier that allows you to control all the segments named in the GROUP command. The *segment_name* entries can be a *segment_name* declared in a SEGMENT pseudo-op or an expression that extracts the SEG attribute of any variable or label.

GROUP provides the very desirable ability to combine data with code without depriving a programmer of the convenience of segments. Specifically, the GROUP pseudo-op is the primary instrument with which COM programs and installable device drivers are written. Both of these types of programs must go to the linker with a single physical segment.

One option for creating a 1-segment program is to enclose the entire assembly in a single code segment. The disadvantage of this technique is that data and code become inseparably merged; you lose all the advantages of segments. Furthermore, all memory references will need to be modified with segment overrides.

The other technique for writing COM format and device driver programs is to code in the normal manner, using as many different logical segments as you please, and then combine them using GROUP. The following example contains three logical segments that are concatenated via the GROUP pseudo-op. As shown, this is a valid COM format file (although useful only for illustration purposes). It just needs to be assembled, linked, and processed by the EXE2BIN utility.

```
COM_GROUP GROUP ZETA_SEG, CODE_SEG, MSG_SEG
                        ;order here does not mean anything

ZETA_SEG SEGMENT BYTE MEMORY 'DATA'
                        ;this segment will be highest in memory

LINE_NUM DW   0

TEXT_BUF LABEL BYTE    ;this label names the highest address
                        ;in the program

ZETA_SEG ENDS

MSG_SEG   SEGMENT PARA 'DATA'
                        ;this will be next to (below) ZETA_SEG
```

```
MSG_1     DB    'Ultra-Super-Incredulo Program.'
          DB    'Patent Pending.',0
MSG_2     DB    'Sorry, internal error. Hit the
          DB    Big Red Switch',0
MSG_SEG ENDS

CODE_SEG SEGMENT PARA PUBLIC 'CODE'
                          ;this segment will be first

          ASSUME CS:COM_GROUP, DS:COM_GROUP, ES:COM_GROUP

          ORG   100H       ;ORG 100H is required for COM programs
MAIN      PROC  FAR
          MOV   AX,LINE_NUM                  ;fetch the variable
          MOV   AX,COM_GROUP:LINE_NUM          ; same thing
          LEA   SI,MSG_1            ;get offset of MSG_1 into SI
          MOV   SI,OFFSET COM_GROUP:MSG_1       ; same thing
          MOV   SI,OFFSET MSG_1  ; this notation doesn't work
          MOV   SI,OFFSET CS:MSG_1            ; nor does this
          INT   20H                   ;immediate exit back to DOS
MAIN      ENDP
CODE_SEG ENDS
          END   MAIN              ;starting point label needed
                                  ;for COM files
```

Important note: The segment ZETA_SEG will be loaded at the highest address in memory, making it ideal for buffering disk files of unknown size. ZETA_SEG is positioned highest because the *class_name* of 'DATA' and the *segment_name* of ZETA_SEG are both higher in the alphabet than all others in the module. The MEMORY attribute is meaningless; its only purpose is to help document the segment's usage.

## The ASSUME Pseudo-op

The ASSUME pseudo-op is another feature of the MACRO Assembler that is unfamiliar to even experienced microprocessor programmers. Recall from Chapter 1 that each physical memory segment can be accessed only through a segment register.

The ASSUME pseudo-op lets the assembler know which segment register is associated with which memory segment. ASSUME is an error-detecting device masquerading as a housekeeping chore. If the assembler sees that you are using an addressing mode that can't possibly access the data you want, it will issue an error notice. In some cases, it will correct your code so that it contains the necessary segment override. The assembler syntax is one of:

```
ASSUME seg_reg:segment_name [, . . . ]

ASSUME seg_reg:SEG name [, . . . ]

ASSUME seg_reg:NOTHING [, . . . ]
```

or

```
ASSUME NOTHING
```

The *seg_reg* is either CS, DS, ES, or SS, and the colon(:) is required. The *segment_name* is either a label defined via the SEGMENT pseudo-op, a *group_name* declared via the GROUP pseudo-op, an expression that uses the SEG operator, or the keyword NOTHING.

The minimum requirement for all programs is a declaration that the CS register points to the segment that contains the procedures and opcodes that are being assembled:

```
ASSUME CS:CODE_SEG      ;minimum required for all programs
```

Without this declaration, the assembler will spew out error notices every time it encounters a procedure name or a label for a jump. That occurs because it won't be able to decide whether a jump or call to that address is to be intersegment or intrasegment. The same is true for any accesses to memory variables that, for lack of an ASSUME declaration, apparently reside in no segment.

By placing an ASSUME at the start of your code, the assembler can automatically generate a segment override when you attempt to access an address that cannot be reached with the CPU's default segment register. For example, recall from the discussion of addressing modes in Chapter 2 that any access to MY_TABLE[DI] will automatically use the DS register as the segment (direct indexed addressing). But if MY_TABLE[DI] is defined within the code segment and DS is pointing elsewhere, a CS: segment override is needed in order to access that address. Knowing this, the assembler will automatically generate the proper segment override opcode for you. Let's look at a couple examples:

```
VIDMEM_SEG   SEGMENT AT 0b800H
                          ;the color/graphics memory segment
SCREEN       DB    80*25 DUP (?,?)
                          ;set up a SCREEN array symbolic name

VIDMEM_SEG   ENDS

DATA_SEG     SEGMENT PARA PUBLIC 'DATA'
```

```
        PRIME_TABLE DW   1,2,3,5,7,11,13,17,23,31
                                 ;a look-up table

        MSG_1       DB 'THIS IS A MESSAGE',0Dh,0AH
                                 ;and an ASCII string

        DATA_SEG    ENDS

        CODE_SEG    SEGMENT 'CODE'
                    ASSUME  CS:CODE_SEG, DS:DATA_SEG, ES:VIDMEM_SEG
                    JMP     START
                                 ;START is seen to be in this segment

        VECTOR_TBL  DW      SBRTN1,SBRTN2,SBRTN3,SBRTN4
                                 ;table in code segment

        START:      MOV     AX,PRIME_TABLE[5]
                                 ;direct address in
                                  DATA_SEG (no override)

                    MOV     SCREEN[DI],0FFH
                                 ;will generate SEG ES override

                    CALL    VECTOR_TBL[SI]
                                 ;will generate SEG CS override

                    MOVS    SCREEN,MSG_1
                                 ;assembler verifies that
                                  DS and ES are ok

                    STOS    MSG_1
                                 ;ERROR! MSG_1 is in ES, STOS uses ES

                        .

                        .

                        .
```

Notice how friendly the assembler is. It verifies that the CPU will access the desired address, and it even corrects you when you make an error. If it is unable to correct you (as in the STOS example), it calls the error to your attention.

In the preceding example, no assumption is indicated for the SS register. This is because the program makes no direct reference to data in the stack segment. Unless your program is likely to be doing unusual things with the stack (beyond PUSH, POP, and fetching and storing data via the BP register), you will usually be able to omit an ASSUME SS:STACK_SEG.

If you use the NOTHING keyword in lieu of a *segment_name*, you defeat the entire purpose of the ASSUME pseudo-op. In that case, you would need to prefix manually every reference to memory with a segment register or segment name override.

Finally, there are two important topics that should be mentioned in regard to the ASSUME pseudo-op. This pseudo-op *does not initialize the segment registers.* You must write code that does the initialization of the DS and ES registers. (The SS and CS registers are always initialized by the DOS program loader.)

This second point may save you some precious debugging time: Placing the declaration of a data segment at the end of an assembly causes several problems. First, the assembler will not know the sizes and types of the variables in that segment until after it attempts to process the code segment. In the previous example, the SCREEN[DI] reference would need to be prefixed with a BYTE PTR operator because the reference is ambiguous—at least until the SCREEN array is seen to be of type BYTE. Second, the assembler is likely to come up with a mysterious "Phase Error" during the assembly. On the first pass, it will process all memory references as if they needed no segment override. On the second pass, it may discover that a memory reference does need the 1-byte segment override. Inserting the opcode that makes that adjustment will cause all of the subsequent offsets in the assembler's symbol table to be misaligned.

## Where Segments Are Loaded

The assembler and linker provide no mechanism for specifying an absolute address for a program to be loaded. This is not a major drawback because 8088 programs are relocatable to any segment boundary. When a program is loaded, only the references to segment addresses need to be adjusted, a function neatly handled by the PC-DOS program loader. However, knowing that segments are mobile is sometimes not enough. It may be essential to know the order in which logical segments will be concatenated and the order in which physical segments are to be loaded into memory.

This need is most critical when you have to define a buffer for varying amounts of data. The segment that defines the start of that buffer should be at the highest addresses—above the code and stack segments. Unfortunately, the MEMORY *combine_type* doesn't work. The sole documented way to specify a relative position for a segment is to create a series of assembled object modules and then specify the module names to the linker in the desired order:

```
A>LINK

Object Module(s) [.OBJ]: code1+ code2+ stack+ data

Run File [CODE1.EXE]: myprog;
```

If each of those modules defines exactly one segment, the segments will be ordered in memory as input to the linker. In this case, the segment defined in CODE1.OBJ will be located lowest in memory and the segment defined in DATA.OBJ will be located highest in memory.

If you need to specify the order in which the modules are loaded, you can use a roundabout way to obtain the desired sequence. Let's say that you have a program, MYPROG, that defines three segments—CODE_SEG, DATA_SEG, and STACK_SEG—and you want CODE_SEG to be lowest in memory and DATA_SEG to be highest. First, you must write three short programs that do nothing but define three empty segments:

```
;PROGRAM 1: CODE.ASM

CODE_SEG SEGMENT PUBLIC 'CODE'          ;same name and class as in
                                        ;  MYPROG

CODE_SEG ENDS
        END
--------------------------------
;PROGRAM 2: DATA.ASM

DATA_SEG SEGMENT PUBLIC 'DATA'          ;same name and class as in
                                        ;  MYPROG

DATA_SEG ENDS
        END
--------------------------------
;PROGRAM 3: STACK.ASM

STACK_SEG SEGMENT STACK                 ;same name and class as in
                                        ;  MYPROG

STACK_SEG ENDS
        END
```

Next, assemble all three programs and MYPROG into their OBJ versions. Finally, invoke the linker with:

```
A>LINK  CODE+ STACK+ DATA+ MYPROG,MYPROG,CON;
```

The linker will display the start and stop addresses of each segment, showing that they are indeed ordered in the desired sequence. You may want to hide the details of this procedure by placing them into a batch file:

```
REM LO.BAT BATCH FILE LINKS %1.EXE IN THE DESIRED ORDER

LINK CODE+ STACK+ DATA+ %1, %1, CON;
```

You could also create a linker response file that contains the names of the dummy files, separated by plus marks (+), in the desired order. Then use

```
@filename.ext
```

as the first response to the linker "Object Module(s)" prompt.

Here are the criteria by which the linker orders segments. The first two are documented; the rest were discovered by trial and error:

* Segments defined in the first modules input to the linker are lowest in memory.

* Segments with matching *class_names* are loaded next to one another.

* Segments in the same group are placed next to each other unless there is a *class_name* conflict.

\* Where two or more modules meet one of the preceding criteria, they are ordered alphabetically, first by the segment name and then by the class name.

The alphabetic ordering is the one that is most likely to affect your program. For instance, ZZZZ_SEG will always be loaded at the highest address of all the segments in an individual module (unless you have also defined ZZZZZZ_SEG!).

## THINGS TO DO

1. Write a short program that defines a variety of segment types. Assemble it. Then link the program, specifying CON as the list file. Examine the link map, paying special attention to the order in which the segments are placed.

2. Change the preceding program so that it uses the GROUP pseudo-op to collect certain segments. Try varying the segment attribute parameters. Change the names of the segments. Notice the changes in the link map after each experiment.

3. (\*) Use DEBUG (or any file examination tool) to look at OBJ files that are created by the assembler. You'll recognize quite a bit of the information including segment, group, and class names.

## 4.6 EXTERNAL PROCEDURES AND DATA

The assembler and linker provide a simple yet powerful mechanism for combining a series of program modules into an executable file. The complex nature of assembly language virtually forces a programmer to think in terms of tasks and subtasks. You can save an enormous amount of program development time by isolating common subtasks and creating a library of procedures. The assembler has three pseudo-ops that make this possible: INCLUDE, PUBLIC, and EXTRN.

## INCLUDE

INCLUDE is the simplest of the external module development tools. It simply specifies the filename of an assembly language text file that the assembler reads and inserts into a program. The format is

```
INCLUDE filespec
```

The *filespec* is any complete filename, including a drive specifier. If no drive is specified, the default drive is searched. MACRO Assembler version 1.0 does not allow DOS 2.0 pathnames. If the file is not found, an error message is displayed. If the file is found, the source statements are assembled into the program as if they were part of the source text. When the assembler reaches the end of the included file, it continues the assembly where it left off in the original file. The listing of the included file will have a *C* preceding each statement.

This feature is most often used to read a series of macros into an assembly that uses them. However, it is perfectly possible to create an "include library" of STRUC and RECORD definitions, data allocations, or EQU symbol assignments.

You may even keep source files of commonly called procedures and INCLUDE them in the assemblies that call them. This method is slower and clumsier than the PUBLIC/EXTRN method described in the following section. The two-pass assembler will need to open and close each included file twice, considerably slowing the assembly.

## PUBLIC and EXTRN

PUBLIC and EXTRN are pseudo-ops that work together to allow you to pass information from module to module via the linker. Information about variables and procedures declared PUBLIC will be included in the OBJ file. When the linker processes several OBJ modules, it will look through its list of PUBLIC symbols in order to satisfy any EXTRN symbol references.

In other words, a program module may call external procedures (i.e., procedures that have already been assembled and tested). You can create a *library* of procedures. After a procedure (or module) has been assembled and tested, it need never be assembled again. Therefore, you can write program source files that contain only *the code that is unique to that program*. The result is shorter listings, faster assemblies, and fewer errors. Simply stated, the PUBLIC and EXTRN pseudo-ops are two of the most important tools in your toolbox.

We'll discuss these two pseudo-ops together because you'll never use one without the other. The syntax for the PUBLIC pseudo-op is

```
PUBLIC symbol [, . . . ]
```

where *symbol* is any symbol defined in a program, including procedure names and other labels, variable names, and symbols created with the EQU and = pseudo-ops, but excluding segment, macro, structure, and record names.

The syntax for EXTRN is

```
EXTRN symbol:type [, . . . ]
```

The *symbol* is usually the name of a procedure, but it may be any valid assembler symbol. The *type* is either BYTE, WORD, DWORD, NEAR, FAR, or ABS. NEAR and FAR are used with procedure names.

ABS is a special operand used to define 16-bit integer constants. An external declaration such as EXTRN X:ABS is the same as the X EQU *expression*, except that the expression is filled in by the linker from a PUBLIC value in an external module.

The PUBLIC declaration may appear anywhere in the source file of the library module that defines the symbol. But it's a good practice to place all of your PUBLIC declarations at the top of your listing so that you can find them at a glance. There should be only one PUBLIC declaration for any symbol.

Each symbol in an EXTRN declaration must match a symbol listed in a PUBLIC declaration in one of the linked modules; otherwise, the linker will display an "Unresolved External Reference" error and create an invalid EXE file.

Important: Each EXTRN declaration must appear inside the segment to which it belongs. For example, if an external module contains a PUBLIC NEAR procedure, the EXTRN declaration should be in the same segment as the call opcode. If the external procedure is in a different segment (as with FAR library procedures), the external declaration must be enclosed by a PUBLIC segment with the same name as that of the library procedure.

If you place an EXTRN data declaration outside of all segment blocks, you will need to override each access of those data with a segment override or use

```
ASSUME DS:SEG variable_name
```

Listing 4.2 demonstrates techniques for passing external data, procedure, and constant references between modules. Appendix C has several "program templates" that illustrate public and external declarations for many of the most common types of complex programs.

## Library Modules

Your first library modules will be very low-level procedures that you will need to use in many programs. For instance, any program that displays data on the screen will need to set the cursor position. The ROM-BIOS has a function that sets the cursor to the coordinates defined by the DH and DL registers, so why write a module that performs the same function?

The answer is *transparency*. Your own cursor-positioning routine can be written so that you never again need to "see" the details of how the cursor is positioned. You "look through" these details to see the underlying function. The BIOS SET_CUR_POS function requires that a video page number be placed in BH, that AH be loaded with 2, and that an INT 10H be invoked. That's three different parameters that need to be set and three different ways to make an error. Furthermore, every time you invoke that service, you will lose the values of AL and BH unless you explicitly PUSH them before the INT and POP them afterward. Here's what the ROM-BIOS service call looks like:

```
MOV    DH,ROW
MOV    DL,CLM    ;or use constant values
PUSH   AX        ;save the registers
PUSH   BX
MOV    BH,0      ;specify video page number (don't forget)
MOV    AH,2      ;or is that 3? Let me get out the Tech Ref manual...
INT    10H       ;or is that 10 decimal?   "    "   "    "    "    "
POP    BX
POP    AX        ;restore the registers (in the right order!)
```

## Listing 4.2
## Using PUBLIC and EXTRN

```
;----------------------------------------------------------------------------
; SLAVE MODULE: Examples of PUBLIC declarations.
;               Public values will resolve external references in the
;               MASTER module and segments will be combined by the linker.

public far_proc, near_proc, msg, msg_len  ;these are passed to the linker

;============================================================================
data_seg segment byte public   ;no gap between this and DATA_SEG in master
msg      db 'this is a message' ;the address of a string
msg_len  equ $-msg              ;a constant expression
data_seg ends

;============================================================================
code_seg segment byte public   ;concatenated with CODE_SEG in master module
near_proc proc near            ;the address of a NEAR procedure
         ret                   ; (within CODE_SEG)
near_proc endp
code_seg ends

;============================================================================
lib_seg segment public         ;the address of a FAR procedure
far_proc proc far              ; (within LIB_SEG)
         ret
far_proc endp
lib_seg ends
         end

;----------------------------------------------------------------------------
; MASTER MODULE: Examples of using EXTRN
;                The external references in this module are resolved by the
;                linker from the public declarations in the SLAVE module.

;============================================================================
data_seg segment para public
         extrn msg:byte, msg_len:abs   ;BYTE for address, ABS for a constant
data_seg ends

;============================================================================
lib_seg  segment para public         ;Surround FAR procedure with "empty" segment
         extrn far_proc:far          ; to give assembler a segment attribute.
lib_seg  ends                        ;LIB_SEG is defined before CODE_SEG to
                                     ; avoid "forward reference" error.
;============================================================================
code_seg segment para public
         extrn near_proc:near        ;define NEAR procedure inside master segment
my_proc  proc far
         mov   cx,msg_len            ;refer to the external constant
         mov   si,offset msg         ;refer to address of external data
         call  far_proc              ;call a FAR procedure (in LIB_SEG)
         call  near_proc             ;call a NEAR procedure (in this segment)
my_proc  endp
code_seg ends
         end
```

Now compare an alternative method. In the following example, the details that surround the ROM-BIOS service call have been neatly packaged into a single external routine that has been declared PUBLIC.

```
MOV    DH,ROW

MOV    DL,CLM

CALL   SET_CURSOR_POS      ;Presto!
```

The difference goes way beyond the 10 bytes of code that your program saves each time it calls the SET_CURSOR_POS procedure. By eliminating all of the "main line" overhead and placing it in a fully debugged procedure, you have eliminated many potential sources of error, shortened the listing, and sped up the assembly. You can safely call the procedure without worrying about saving or restoring any registers; nothing is changed by the call. What's more, a call to SET_CURSOR_POS is self-documenting. It does exactly as its name indicates; the statement doesn't even need a comment.

The SET_CURSOR_POS module is a typical procedure found in a personal library of object files. A library module may contain a complete subprogram. For instance, you could write a separate module for each command of a word processing program. This technique would allow you to make minor changes to, say, the move block function without reassembling the entire program.

More often, a library will consist of a series of general-purpose routines that might be called from any program. Given a set of low-level modules such as one to set the cursor position and one to write a character at the current cursor position, you can begin to write more complex modules such as one to print an entire string, updating the cursor as each character is printed.

Some overhead is required to make a library system work. The name of the library module must be declared external with the EXTRN command. That entails knowing whether the procedure is FAR or NEAR and placing the EXTRN declaration in the proper segment. My policy is to create a LIB_SEG in all of my programs and place all library external declarations in it. The procedures are all NEAR, so I use the GROUP pseudo-op to tack the LIB_SEG onto the code segment that makes the call.

## Linking Modules

Every call to an external library module must be resolved at link time. That is, if your programs calls CLS, SET_CURSOR_POS, and PRINT_MESSAGE, each of these separate object modules must be fed into the linker. Normally, you will have a main module that calls the library modules. Let's say that this program has been assembled into an object file called MYPROG.OBJ and that the three library procedures are in the three files $CLS.OBJ, $LOCATE.OBJ, and $PRT_MSG.OBJ (the $ makes the filenames stand out in the directory). You link them all together into a program called MYPROG.EXE with this simple command:

```
LINK MYPROG+ $CLS+ $LOCATE+ $PRT_MSG;
```

That's all; it's almost as if the folks at Microsoft created the linker for just this purpose (ahem). You may also simply enter the LINK command and then answer each of the prompts. Just enter each of the module filenames separated by plus signs (+) or spaces when the linker prompts for object modules. Note that the linker prompt for libraries should be ignored. At the time of this writing, IBM has not released a library management tool for the IBM PC. So we will have to use a separate file for each library module.

Here are a few notes for advanced use of library modules. When a program calls so many external procedures that their filenames won't all fit on a single 80-character line, you have a few options. First, you may enter some of the filenames at the object modules prompt and end the line with a plus sign (+). The linker will come right back with another object modules prompt. Another (and very convenient) method is to create a linker response file, which is a text file containing responses to any or all of the linker prompts, including the object module filenames. Just instruct the linker to read the response file instead of the keyboard. At any of the linker prompts, type the "at" sign (@) followed by the name of the linker response file. For example,

```
A>LINK @MYPROG.LNK    <invoke linker response file A:MYPROG.LNK

        MYPROG+ MOD1+ MOD2+ MOD3+
        MOD4+ MOD5                        <name the modules

        MYPROG:                           <name the output file
-------------------------------------
A>LINK B:MYPROG+@C:MYLIB:LNK              <invoke response file

        C:MOD1+ C:MOD2+ C:MOD3+               <name the library
        C:MOD4+ C:MOD5+ C:MOD6               <modules

        B:                                 <send MYPROG.EXE to drive

        CON:;                              <send link map to screen
```

The latter example is especially helpful when drive C is a RAM drive. You can automate the process even more by writing a simple batch file that substitutes a filename parameter for the name of the main module in the LINK command line. This procedure allows flexibility in naming different versions of the program.

Another hint: Instead of placing each procedure in a different file, you can place interrelated procedures into a single object file. For instance, a $CLS module is likely to call a $LOCATE module to set the cursor to the top left corner of the screen after clearing it. You may simply choose to assemble both procedures, along with other screen-related code, into a single object module and call it $DSP_LIB. That operation would allow you to bring the whole set of procedures into a program as a single module. The disadvantage is that the resulting program would contain the code for all of your screen-related functions, even if you only wanted one or two of them.

**THINGS TO DO**

1. Rewrite Listing 4.1 so that it is composed of three separate modules. Have the main module include the stack and data segments as well as the MAIN procedure of the code segment. Make two separate modules for the CLS and PRINT_MSG procedures. Use the templates in Appendix C as a guide. Be sure to declare PUBLICs and EXTRNs for all data addresses and equates as well as procedure names. Hint: The values of EOM and MESSAGE will need to be passed to the PRINT_SEG module with an ABS declaration. Assemble, link, and execute the combined program.

2. Once you have completed task 1, link the modules again, specifying a different order for the two "satellite" modules. Respond to the list file prompt with CON:/MAP to get a detailed listing of all PUBLIC values passed between modules.

3. Begin writing your own procedure library. Start with common, low-level functions and use them as the building blocks in more powerful functions. Keep a 3-ring binder with a listing of each module so that you can quickly reference the comments that describe each procedure.

# Chapter 5

# Interfacing with BIOS and PC-DOS

## 5.1 A PROGRAMMER'S TOOLBOX

As you have seen in the previous chapters, assembly language programming is not a task for the fainthearted. Assembler programs are lengthy and complex. Someday Intel will make a chip—the 80003208, perhaps—that will directly execute high-level language statements. Until then, individual assembly language commands will always perform very small units of work. Therefore, in order to accomplish any worthwhile goal, larger and more complex tools must be written; the smaller, general-purpose tools must be used to write larger, more specific tools. Chapter 4 introduced a way to create your own library of tools. In this chapter, we will look at the extensive toolboxes that are provided with the IBM PC, namely, the ROM-BIOS and PC-DOS service routines.

The ROM-BIOS (Read Only Memory-Basic Input and Output System) is a set of tools that provide an interface between the software and the hardware that make up the IBM-PC system. This toolbox includes services that range from reading diskette sectors to writing individual pixels on a graphics display. The routines themselves are stored in ROM locations starting at F000:E000, but that fact is irrelevant. Unlike your own library routines, these supervisor calls are invoked with software interrupts. The interrupt vector table is automatically set up with pointers into each separate routine. You may generally ignore the location of a BIOS or PC-BIOS routine; you need only know the number (or type) of the interrupt and what service it provides.

The PC-DOS (generally synonymous with MS-DOS) services are a more powerful set of tools that build in the fundamental services provided by the ROM-BIOS. Sometimes referred to as *supervisor calls* or *function calls*, these services include such powerful tools as opening and closing files, reading entire strings of keyboard input, and determining the current time and date. The PC-DOS routines reside in low memory, at addresses that are determined at power-up. This operating system code is stored in the "invisible" files IBMBIO.COM and IBMDOS.COM and is automatically loaded into memory when the system boots up. As with the ROM-BIOS routines, it is never necessary to know exactly what addresses are occupied by these routines because their services are obtained via software interrupts.

It is as important to know the ROM-BIOS and PC-DOS service protocols as it is to know the 8088's opcode mnemonics. These tools do so much with so little program overhead that without them, even the simplest programs would be monstrous tasks. The alternative is to write an entire library that duplicates the functions. And while there is good reason to bypass certain BIOS and DOS functions in favor of your own more efficient code, you would need to be a lunatic to tackle something like file I/O when tens of thousands of programmer-hours have already been spent so that you can avoid this task.

This chapter introduces the general procedures for invoking BIOS and DOS services, gives some background, discusses selected services, details how to use DOS file I/O, and explains the DOS 2.0 installable device driver protocol. Appendix B lists the BIOS and DOS services, giving short descriptions of each service and the input parameters and output actions of each. That appendix should be used as a quick reference supplement to your DOS and technical reference manuals.

## 5.2 HOW TO USE BIOS AND DOS SERVICES

Many of the services provided by the PC-DOS overlap those provided by the ROM-BIOS. When a particular service is duplicated by both, it is always wiser to select the DOS version. The idea is to try to make your code as portable as possible. If you use a lot of ROM-BIOS service calls, when you decide to transport your program to a different machine (even an IBM-PC look-alike), you may need to make massive changes in your code. By sticking to the DOS functions, you can guarantee that your program will run directly on any machine that uses MS-DOS. Of course, many programs *must* be written specifically for one machine. For instance, arcade-style programs must use every trick to make graphics routines as fast and efficient and possible. Text editing programs will also probably need to go beyond the simple (and slow) DOS and BIOS routines that display characters on the screen. However, it is advisable to keep such machine-specific activities isolated to a certain easily modified section of a program.

The general procedure for invoking any service routine involves issuing a software interrupt. Most functions have many different options, or subfunctions. One rare exception is the BIOS memory size determination service. This service is used to find out how much total memory has been installed in the system that is running your program. Appendix B lists this service as interrupt 12H. It also shows that the memory size is returned in AX as a number of 1K blocks. Here's one way to find out if the system contains 128K or more:

```
INT     12H

CMP     AX,128          ;is there 128K or more?
```

```
JB        ERROR_ABORT        ; no, write message that program

                             ; won't run

.                            ; yes, continue

.

.
```

Notice how much easier it is to use this interrupt than it would be to go through all of memory looking for an address that won't accept a value (i.e., an address that contained no RAM). Even when you know that the memory size value is stored in the word at 0040:0013, it is easier to invoke the interrupt than it would be to read that value directly from memory.

The MEMORY_SIZE service is one of the few that provide only a single function. When an interrupt provides two or more functions, the calling program must indicate which subfunction is desired. The standard protocol for multifunction services is to use the AH register to select the desired function. That is, the value of AH is used as an input parameter for the service. Thus, for the great majority of services, your program must first set the AH register to a subfunction number before invoking the interrupt. For example, subfunction 0FH of the VIDEO_IO interrupt (ROM-BIOS service 10H) specifies a request for information about the current state of the screen. This service returns a video mode code in AL, the screen width in AH, and a video page number in BH. Here's a sequence that will find out if the screen is currently in 40- or 80-character mode:

```
MOV       AH,0FH        ;select CURRENT_STATE subfunction

INT       10H           ;invoke VIDEO_IO service

CMP       AH,40         ;is the screen in 40-character mode?

JNE       CHAR_80       ; no, skip to 80-character screen
                        ;width code

.                       ; yes, process code for 40-character
                        ;screen

.

.
```

The two previous examples were chosen for their relative simplicity. Most BIOS and DOS services require more than a single parameter. Most often, there is a sophisticated protocol that involves setting a series of registers to desired values before invoking the interrupt. Because each service is different, there is no rule of thumb as to which register will be used in which capacity. You can be sure that AH is used to select a subfunction, but the only way to know exactly which of the other registers have meaning in the context of a particular service call is to read the specifications for that service.

Here's a more complex call to the BIOS VIDEO_IO interrupt. The WRITE_DOT subfunction of this service will set a single graphics pixel to a desired color. This service expects three parameters in addition to the subfunction code in AH. The DX register is a row (or line) value of 0 to 199; the CX register is a column number ranging from 0 to 319 (or 0 to 639 for high-resolution mode); the AL register is expected to hold a color value of 0 to 3 (or 0 to 1 in high-resolution mode). In addition to providing these register parameters, this service will take special action according to a bit flag that may be set in the AL register. When bit 7 of AL is a 1, the pixel will be XORred with the pixel that is currently on the screen. The following example sets a single dot dead center in the mid-resolution screen:

```
MOV     DX,100     ;select the middle line

MOV     CX,160     ;select the center column

MOV     AL,2       ;select color RED (omit XOR flag)

MOV     AH,0CH     ;select WRITE_DOT subfunction

INT     10H        ;invoke the VIDEO_IO service
```

Remember that if any one of these parameters is omitted, the program will malfunction (unless, by a miracle, a register contained a valid value). In particular, the value in AH is easy to misplace. For instance, if you are using a loop to draw a series of dots, you must be sure to reinitialize the AH register before every call to WRITE_DOT because the routine may destroy its value. Also, the WRITE_DOT routine is meaningful only when the video display is in graphics mode. Thus, there is at least one precondition that must be satisfied before the service is invoked.

Some of the PC-DOS services are equally complex, requiring as many as four registers to specify all of the parameters. And often there are a number of preconditions for any call. For instance, you can't open a PC-DOS 1.10 file unless there is a specially formatted filename within an unopened file control block (FCB). What's more, many of the DOS functions return information that cannot be held in registers. For instance, as you read a sequential file, the system brings whole blocks of data into memory. It updates a record counter in memory, and it returns a code in the AL register indicating whether the end of the file was reached. DOS 2.0 adds a new level of complexity by introducing such esoteric objects as ASCIIZ strings, standard I/O devices, and a DOS "environment."

On the other hand, many of the DOS functions are straightforward and easy to use. For one thing, you needn't worry about the interrupt number; all but four of the 78 DOS 2.0 services are vectored through INT 21H. Also, some of the services perform a very limited task such as sending a character to the printer. Unlike the BIOS equivalent, the DOS printer service does not read a printer number parameter; it selects the printer that has been previously declared the "standard printer device" (or LPT1: for DOS 1.10). That makes sending data to the printer conceptually easier; you simply place the character in the DL register and invoke the function:

```
MOV     DL,TEXT_BUFFER[SI]      ;fetch a character to print
MOV     AH,5                    ;select PRINTER_OUTPUT
                                ;subfunction
INT     21H                     ;invoke the PC-DOS service
```

## 5.3 WORKING WITH PC-DOS FILES

Perhaps the most important services that PC-DOS provides are those that read and write files. It is no coincidence the DOS stands for Disk Operating System. The services are powerful and flexible, providing a wide range of options. You may access a file sequentially, byte by byte (or block by block), beginning at the start of the file and stopping at the end. Or you may reach out to any part of a file and read or write any size block of data. You may specify exactly how large a block to read and exactly where in memory you want its data placed when it is read in. You may determine the size of an existing file and the date and time that the file was last modified.

DOS provides services for determining if a file already exists (or how many files match a "wild card" filename), renaming a file, creating new files, and erasing old ones. This avalanche of file control options may seem a bit overwhelming at first. The trick is to absorb some background information and apply it to a simple procedure. Then as you get a feel for how the system operates, advance to the more complex tasks. We will begin by discussing the fundamentals of file I/O as used in DOS 1.10. We'll look at the individual steps of opening, reading, writing, and closing a sequential file. Then we'll put all of the functions together into a simple program. Afterward, we'll look at random access files and the specialized calls that are available with DOS 2.0.

### The File Control Block

Everything you need to know (or want to specify) about a PC-DOS file has been collected into a single block of information. Referred to as a *file control block (FCB)*, this 32-byte collection of data may reside anywhere your program places it. An FCB begins as an "unopened FCB." All it contains is a drive number, a filename, and a filename extension. After you invoke an OPEN_FILE or CREATE_FILE function, the FCB is filled in by DOS with various kinds of information pertaining to the file. Such an "opened FCB" contains the number of bytes that the file contains, the date that the file was created (or most recently updated), two pointers that keep track of what part of the file was last read (or written), and a *record size* that determines how much of the file should be read (or written) at a time.

Figure 5.1 illustrates the internal structure of an FCB. Before it is opened, only the first three fields are present: the drive number, the filename, and the filename extension. The filename is one to eight characters long. If it is less than eight characters, the rightmost bytes will be blanks (20H). Likewise, the three characters in the extension field are left-justified and padded with blanks. The extension field may be composed of all blanks, and the filename may include blanks between the other characters. Notice that in the FCB, there is no period between the filename and the extension.

**Figure 5.1**
**PC-DOS File Control Block (FCB) Format**

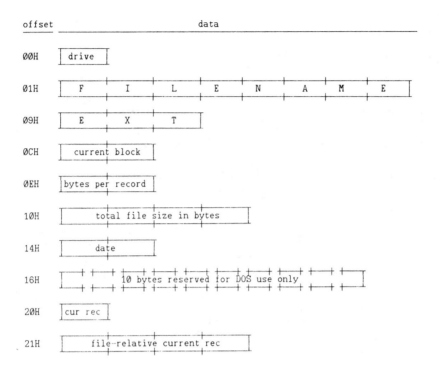

Before the file is opened, the drive number may be either 0, 1, 2, 3, or 4. When the drive number is 0, DOS assumes that the default drive is requested. After the file is opened, DOS will replace the 0 with the correct drive number (A = 1, B = 2, etc.).

When you open a file, DOS fills in several of the other fields. The file size field is obvious. It contains an exact count of the number of bytes in the entire file. As might be expected, this doubleword value is stored with the least significant byte followed by the next significant byte, and so on.

The 2-byte value that indicates the date a file was created or most recently updated is actually a set of three bit fields. You will recall the format of these bytes from our discussion of the RECORD pseudo-op in Chapter 4. In brief, the two bytes contain a 7-bit year field, a 4-bit month field, and a 5-bit day field.

In order to discuss the file pointers and record size, we need some background on how DOS perceives a file. A file is a collection of *blocks*, each containing exactly 128 *records*. Each record in a file contains the same number of bytes—from 1 to 32,767, depending upon the application. Thus, files are made of blocks, which are made of records, which are made of bytes. Figure 5.2 illustrates this scheme.

**Figure 5.2**
**Blocks, Records, and Bytes**

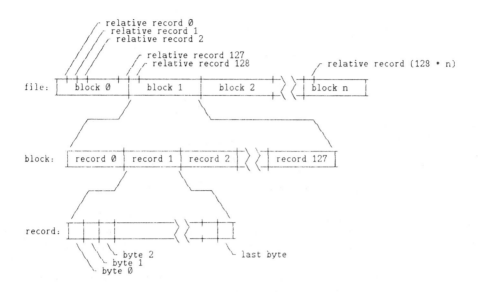

The bytes-per-record field must be initialized by your program unless you want to use the system default of 128 (80H). For sequential files, it makes sense to set this field to a value of 1. Then every time you invoke the READ_SEQ service, DOS will return a single byte from the file. That way, you simplify the task of keeping track of your current position in the file; the number of records read corresponds exactly to the number of bytes read. The $n$th record is also the $n$th byte. When you have read the last record, you have read the last byte.

The other critical FCB fields for sequential file access are the current block and current record (cur rec) fields. By manipulating these two values, you may specify any part of a file. The record that is accessed is found by multiplying the current block by 128 and then adding the value of the current record field. In practice, sequential access techniques never need the exact location in the file—only whether the current record (i.e., byte) is at the end of the file. Before you begin to read a sequential file, both of these fields must be set to 0 so that they point to the first byte. DOS automatically sets the current block field to 0, so your program need only initialize the current record field to 0. After each call to the READ_SEQ service, these fields are automatically updated to point to the next record.

A question still remains: Where does DOS place each record as it is read from the disk? In other words, after the READ_SEQ call, where can I find the byte that was just read? The answer requires the introduction of another acronym: The record is read into the disk transfer area (DTA). It is the responsibility of your program to tell DOS (via the SET_DTA service) exactly where you want the DTA buffer to be placed.

Each call to READ_SEQ brings a single record into the buffer, starting at the DTA. That is, each record is overlaid at the same address. Your program can process each record as it is read in or bring an entire file into memory at once by changing the DTA after each read. In the upcoming example, we will use the former method because we need to work with only one character at a time. However, many programs will work more efficiently when an entire file is read into memory at once.

The steps for reading a sequential text file, one byte at a time, are:

1. Format an unopened FCB that contains the desired drive number, filename, and extension.

2. Invoke the OPEN_FILE service.

3. Set the (now opened) FCB current record field to 0.

4. Set the FCB bytes-per-record field to 1 (to process single characters).

5. Invoke the SET_DTA service to point to a 1-byte buffer.

6. Repeatedly invoke the SEQUENTIAL_READ_SEQ service until an ASCII 1AH is read or DOS returns an end-of-file code.

Writing a sequential text file is almost identical, except that the WRITE_SEQ service is used to send each byte to the disk and the CLOSE_FILE service must be called after writing the last byte.

Fortunately for assembly language programmers, PC-DOS does some preliminary steps that take much of the work out of file manipulation. Before we begin coding a program that uses the DOS file services, let's look at the environment in which a program exists when it first takes control.

## The Program Segment Prefix

Before COMMAND.COM passes control to a program, it first sets up a 256-byte block of code and data at the lowest available memory address. This area is called the *program segment prefix (PSP)*. It contains such important items as a way to get back to DOS when the program terminates, the addresses of the code that will take control when Ctrl-Break is pressed or a critical error occurs while the program is executing, the amount of memory that is available for the program to use, and all of the characters that were entered after the name of the program in the DOS command line. Additionally, COMMAND.COM has gone to the trouble of creating unopened FCBs for the first two filenames that were entered as program parameters.

When a program takes control, the DS and ES registers will both point to the PSP; they are set up to process any parameters and FCBs in the PSP. The AX register will contain codes indicating the validity of the drive specifiers in the FCBs (AL is for the first filename, and AH is for the second: FFH means that the drive number is invalid, and 0 means that the drive exists). The DTA has been set to point to PSP offset 80H (the DOS default DTA).

In COM format programs, all segment registers point to the segment of the PSP, and the IP register is initially set to 100H (i.e., the first byte following the PSP). The SP register (the top of the stack) is set to the highest available byte in the segment of the PSP. (See Appendix C for examples of how to create COM format programs.)

In EXE programs, the CS and IP registers will be initialized to the values specified by the linker (i.e., the values specified via the assembler's END pseudo-op or 0 if no value is set). The SS register will initially point to your STACK segment, and SP will point to the highest byte you defined in that segment. Remember that DOS leaves DS and ES pointing to the PSP. If your program contains a separate data segment, you must initialize the values of DS and ES.

Figure 5.3 diagrams the various fields of the PSP. The first two bytes in the PSP are an INT 20H opcode. This opcode is part of the DOS's cryptic system of passing control between programs. In previous example programs, we have seen the mysterious sequence

```
PUSH      DS
MOV       AX,0
PUSH      AX
          .
          .
          .
```

in the first few lines of code. These lines are done in preparation for the eventual program exit.

The only way to terminate an EXE program is to execute an INT 20H with CS pointing to the segment of the PSP. In COM format programs, CS *starts* by pointing to the PSP, so an INT 20H can be used at any time. But in EXE programs, CS points to a different segment altogether and must somehow be set to the right value.

Now consider how difficult it is for us to get any value into CS. There is no MOV CS, operand, nor is POP CS a valid opcode. Using it would be like mailing a package to the right street in the wrong city! Instead, the program prepares the stack for an intersegment return to the first address in the PSP—which contains the 2-byte opcode INT 20H. Thus set up, a RET from a FAR procedure will terminate the program. However, this method has the drawback that there must be no extraneous data on the stack when the FAR return is taken. For instance, you can't easily terminate a program while it is executing a called subroutine.

Note: Programs written to run under DOS 2.00 may use the new EXIT service (function 4CH of INT 21H). This service correctly terminates the program regardless of the value of CS.

The next most important piece of information (as far as an application programmer is concerned) is held in the bytes starting at offsets 5CH, 6CH, and 80H. The field starting at 80H is the *unformatted parameter area (UPA)*. It identifies, for the inspection of your program, all of the characters that a user has entered as parameters to your program. The byte at 80H is the number of characters in this string (less the carriage return at the end), and the bytes beginning at offset 81H are the characters themselves. By examining these characters, a program can find out such things as whether the user entered a filename after the command, or whether an optional parameter was specified.

**Figure 5.3**
**Program Segment Prefix (PSP)**

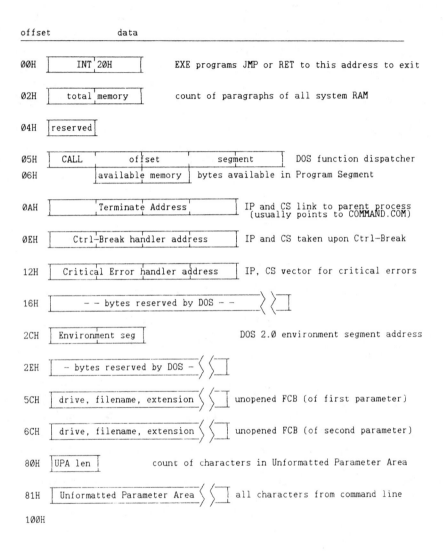

**Command Line Parameters**

The great majority of external DOS commands (EDLIN, DEBUG, etc.) manipulate one or more files. The standard procedure is to enter the command, the name of an input file, a space (or comma), the name of the output file, and then any specially formatted parameters. Because this practice is so common, the DOS command processor always attempts to format two unopened FCBs from the first two command line parameters. This is very considerate of DOS because it saves us a lot of work. When we type a command line such as

```
A>MYPROG infile.txt,b:outfile.txt /m:5000 /p
```

the bytes starting at offset 5CH will contain an unopened FCB for INFILE.TXT on the default drive (A, in this case), and offset 6CH will have a properly formatted FCB for OUTFILE.TXT on drive B. The byte at 80H will contain 36 (the number of characters following the MYPROG command), and the bytes starting at 81H will contain

```
(space)infile.txt,b:outfile.txt /m:5000 /p(carriage return)
```

A command line such as

```
A>MYPROG A:*.BAS /W
```

will result in an unopened FCB at offset 5CH that contains a 1 in the drive number field, question marks (wild card characters) in all eight positions of the filename field, and the characters "BAS" in the extension field. The /w parameter can be found by looking through the string that starts at offset 81H.

The PSP also includes a count of the number of bytes available in the program segment (found at PSP offset 6). If your machine has only 64K of memory, this field reflects the amount of memory you have as a work area. Another field (found at PSP offset 2) indicates the total amount of memory available for your program (inside and outside of the program segment). It is expressed as a count of memory paragraphs; the true byte count may be obtained by multiplying this value by 16.

## 5.3.1 Sequential Text Files

A majority of sequential files are text files made entirely of ASCII characters. PC-DOS uses four special characters inside of a text file. The end of each line is specified by the two bytes CR (0DH), followed directly by LF (0AH). The last character in the file is always a byte of Ctrl-Z (1AH). Thus, when a program reads a byte of 0AH, the end of a line has been reached; a 1AH byte indicates that the end of the file was reached.

The fourth special character that we may encounter in a PC-DOS text file is the TAB (09H) character. This byte stands for a series of spaces. It is used by many programs (including EDLIN and MASM) to conserve bytes in a file. In order to display a TAB character properly, you need to replace it with the number of spaces that will bring the printing device to the next position that is a multiple of eight. That is, if you have printed four characters on a line and then you encounter a tab, you must print four spaces instead of the tab. Likewise, if you have printed 17 characters before encountering a tab, you must print seven spaces to "expand" the line to the 24th position (the next multiple of eight). The DOS TYPE command automatically expands the tabs, but a command such as

```
COPY FILENAME.TXT LPT1
```

will simply send the unexpanded tabs to your printer. Thus, columns won't line up on the printout. Aside from occasionally needing to print files with expanded tabs, it may be necessary to expand the tabs in a file so that a text processing program will not be bothered by them. The example program for this section reads an input file, expands the tabs, and writes a second file containing the expanded text.

Listing 5.1 is the pseudo-code I used to outline the steps needed to accomplish this task. There is no particular "language" for pseudo-code; it is just a way to block out the major steps of a program in order to make it easier to visualize the sequence. You may use any combination of Pascal, BASIC, C, assembly language, and your own made-up statements. Pseudo-coding is an important part of writing assembly language. Some programmers prefer to start with a block flowchart to get an even more general visual picture of the flow of a program (see Figure 5.4 for an example), but in any case, the pseudo-code is an essential step.

**Listing 5.1**
**Pseudo-Code of UNTAB Program**

```
Set up the FCBs for the input and the output files.
Open both files
Set the FCB bytes_per_record field to 1
Set the DTA to point to CUR_CHAR
Intitialize program variables
   NEW_LINE = true
   CHAR_CNT = 0
   END_OF_FILE = false

Repeat until END_OF_FILE = true
   Read byte from input into CUR_CHAR
   Case CUR_CHAR of
     1AH:  end_of_file reached
              (Set END_OF_FILE = true
               Write byte)

      0AH:  end_of_line reached
              (Write byte
               Set NEW_LINE = true
               Set CHAR_CNT = 0)

      09H:  expand tabs
              (Repeat until (CHAR_CNT mod 8) = 0
                 Write 1 space
                 CHAR_CNT = CHAR_CNT + 1
               Endo)

      Else: normal character
              (write_byte)
   Endcase
Enddo
Close output file
Exit to DOS
```

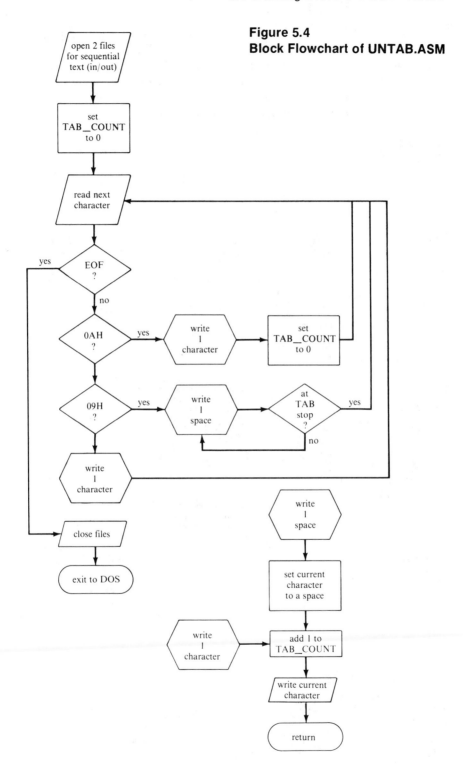

**Figure 5.4
Block Flowchart of UNTAB.ASM**

Listing 5.2, UNTAB.ASM, in effect copies one file to another, expanding tabs as it goes. Notice, that the program moves the unopened FCBs from the PSP into its own work area. Most applications using only one file will be able to leave the FCB right there in the PSP and even use the default DTA. But UNTAB (and any program that opens two files simultaneously) must put the second FCB elsewhere in memory, because when DOS opens the first FCB, it overwrites part of the second one.

**Listing 5.2**
**UNTAB.ASM**

```
;-----------------------------------------------------------------------
; Listing 5.2    UNTAB.ASM
;
; This program expands all of the tab characters in an input file, sending the
; resulting text to an output file (or device).  From DOS use:
;
;          UNTAB source,destination
;
; Expects a standard PC-DOS text file as the source file.
; If destination is omitted, default is CON: (output to screen).
;
;----- equates and structures -----

lf              equ     0AH
cr              equ     0DH             ;simplify making messages

eof             equ     1AH             ;ASCII Ctrl-Z (end-of-file marker)
eol             equ     0AH             ;ASCII linefeed (end-of-line marker)
tab             equ     09H             ;ASCII TAB character
fn_open_file    equ     0FH             ;simplify calling DOS services
fn_create_file  equ     16H
fn_close_file   equ     10H
fn_read_seq     equ     14H
fn_write_seq    equ     15H
fn_set_dta      equ     1AH
fn_print_str    equ     09H

fcb_struc struc
  drive_num  db    ?                    ;0 = default drive, 1 = A, 2 = B, etc.
  filename   db    '        '           ;8 spaces for filename
  extension  db    '   '                ;3 spaces for extension
  cur_block  dw    ?                    ;current 128-record block
  rec_size   dw    ?                    ;bytes per record
  file_size  dd    ?                    ;doubleword count of bytes in file
  file_date  dw    ?                    ;date file was created/updated
  dos_res    db    10 dup(?)            ;DOS reserved area
  cur_rec    db    ?                    ;0-127 current record in current block
  rel_rec    dd    ?                    ;relative record from start of file
fcb_struc ends

stack_seg segment para stack
        db  100H dup(?)          ;recommended stack size
stack_seg ends

data_seg segment para public

back_to_dos label dword         ;vector of indirect jump to DOS
save_offset dw   0              ;stores the offset (PSP:0 is INT 20H)
save_psp    dw   ?              ;stores the PSP address

input_pos   db   128            ;set counter to "prime for first read"
output_pos  db   0              ;count of bytes written in current line
```

**Listing 5.2
(continued)**

```
infile_fcb   fcb_struc <>           ;allocate storage for first FCB
outfile_fcb  fcb_struc <0,'CON'>    ;and second FCB (with default)
in_buf       db    80H dup(?)       ;input file uses 128-byte record buffer
cur_char     db    ?                ;all bytes are funneled through this address

;---- messages -------

bad_infile_msg db "Can't find input file",        cr,lf,'$'
bad_name_msg   db 'Missing or invalid filename',  cr,lf,'$'
bad_drive_msg  db 'Unknown drive error',          cr,lf,'$'
same_file_msg  db "Can't UNTAB to same file",     cr,lf,'$'
disk_full_msg  db 'Disk Full! Operation aborted', cr,lf,'$'
read_err_msg   db 'Diskette read error',          cr,lf,'$'
success_msg    db 'File activity successful',      cr,lf,'$'

data_seg ends

code_seg segment para public
        assume cs:code_seg, ds:nothing, es:data_seg  ;(DS points to PSP)

main    proc    far
        mov     bx,data_seg
        mov     es,bx              ;ES points to DATA_SEG

;--- copy the formatted parameter areas to the data segment ---
        mov     si,5CH                  ;point to formatted parameter area 1
        mov     di,offset es:infile_fcb
        mov     cx,type fcb_struc       ;get the size of the structure
        rep movsb                       ;copy the first unopened FCB
        mov     si,6cH
        cmp     byte ptr ds:[si+1],' '  ;second parameter entered?
        je      parms_done              ; no, use the default (CON:)
        mov     di,offset es:outfile_fcb ; yes, copy the filename
        mov     cx,type fcb_struc
        rep movsb                       ;copy the second unopened FCB
parms_done:

;--- establish normal DATA_SEG addressing ---
        mov     es:save_psp,ds    ;save segment of PSP (for exit to DOS)
        mov     es:save_offset,0  ;and make sure indrect JMP offset is 0
        mov     ds,bx             ;DS points to DATA_SEG
        assume  ds:data_seg       ; let MASM know it

;--- test for bad drive in either filename parameter ----
        or      al,ah                   ;are both 0? (0 = drive# is okay)
        jz      drive_ok                ; yes, go
        mov     dx,offset bad_drive_msg ; no, point to message
        jmp     msg_exit                ;print message and exit to DOS
drive_ok:

;--- see if both filenames are the same -----
        mov     si,offset infile_fcb    ;both DS and ES point to DATA_SEG
        mov     di,offset outfile_fcb   ; for this comparison
        mov     cx,12                   ;count = chars in drive + name + extension
        rep cmpsb                       ;compare strings... same?
        jne     not_same                ; no, continue
        mov     dx,offset same_file_msg ; yes, abort with a message
        jmp     msg_exit
```

**Listing 5.2
(continued)**

```
not_same:
        call    open_2_files    ;open INFILE and OUTFILE (record length = 1)
        mov     output_pos,0    ;initialize character counter to first column

;---- copy the file, expanding the tabs -------
        call    process_files                   ;input, process, and output

;---- close the output file and exit to DOS ----

        mov     dx,offset outfile_fcb
        mov     ah,fn_close_file
        int     21H
        mov     dx,offset success_msg           ;announce successful operation

;-------------------------------------------
; MSG_EXIT
; Jump here from any part of the program to exit to DOS.
; Must set DX to offset of a message (terminated with '$')
;
msg_exit:
        mov     ah,fn_print_str
        int     21H                     ;print the message
        jmp     back_to_dos             ;take FAR jump to PSP:0 (go to DOS)
main    endp

;-------------------------------------------
; OPEN_2_FILES near procedure
; Opens the files that have unopened FCBs at INFILE_FCB and OUTFILE_FCB.
; Aborts with an error message if something goes wrong.
; Input file uses 128-byte records.  Output file uses 1-byte records.

open_2_files proc near
        mov     dx,offset infile_fcb    ;open the input file
        mov     ah,fn_open_file
        int     21H
        cmp     al,0                    ;was the input file found?
        jz      file1_ok                ; yes, continue
        mov     dx,offset bad_infile_msg ; no, take error exit
        jmp     msg_exit
file1_ok:
        mov     dx,offset outfile_fcb   ;open (create) the output file
        mov     ah,fn_create_file
        int     21H
        cmp     al,0                    ;was the file created ok?
        jz      file2_ok                ; yes, continue
        mov     dx,offset bad_name_msg  ; no, take error exit
        jmp     msg_exit
file2_ok:
        mov     infile_fcb.rec_size,80H ;set up for 128-byte input records
        mov     infile_fcb.cur_rec,0    ;and current record = beginning

        mov     outfile_fcb.rec_size,1  ;use 1-byte output records
        mov     outfile_fcb.cur_rec,0

        ret                             ;back to MAIN procedure
open_2_files endp

;-------------------------------------------
; PROCESS_FILES near procedure
; Reads each byte in the input file and copies it to the output file.
; If a TAB character (09H) is found in the input file, then spaces are output
;  until a tab-stop is reached (device position becomes a multiple of 8).
; Returns after writing the last byte of the output file.
;
process_files proc near
```

**Listing 5.2
(continued)**

```
next_char:
        call    read_char               ;get input character into CUR_CHAR

        cmp     cur_char,eof            ;is it a Ctrl-Z (end-of-file)?
        jnz     not_eof                 ; no, continue
        call    write_char              ; yes, write it and exit
        ret                             ; back to MAIN
not_eof:
        cmp     cur_char,eol            ;is it a ØAH (end-of-line)?
        jnz     not_eol                 ; no, continue
        call    write_char              ; yes, write the byte
        mov     output_pos,Ø            ; character counter to first column
        jmp     next_char               ; loop back for next character
not_eol:
        cmp     cur_char,tab            ;is it a Ø9H (TAB character)?
        jnz     not_tab                 ; no, continue
        call    expand_tab              ; yes, expand the tab
        jmp     next_char               ; loop back for next input
not_tab:
        call    write_char              ;not EOF, EOL, or TAB, so just write it
        jmp     next_char               ;and loop back for next character
process_files endp

;-------------------------------------
; EXPAND_TAB near procedure
; Writes spaces to the output file until the device position becomes
; a multiple of 8.
; Uses the OUTPUT_POS variable.
;
expand_tab  proc near
        mov     cur_char,' '            ;set up to write spaces
        call    write_char              ;always output at least 1 space
next_space:
        test    output_pos,7            ;at tab-stop (low bits all = Ø)?
        jz      done_tabbing            ; yes, exit loop
        call    write_char              ; no, output another space
        jmp     next_space              ;     and loop back
done_tabbing:
        ret                             ;back to caller
expand_tab endp

;-------------------------------------
; READ_CHAR near procedure
; Fetches a character from the input record and places it in CUR_CHAR.
; When the end of the input record is reached, reads a new 128-byte record.
;
read_char  proc near
        mov     bh,Ø
        mov     bl,input_pos            ;set up pointer in record buffer
        cmp     bx,127                  ;already used last character in buffer?
        jbe     read_ok                 ; no, just send it out

        mov     dx,offset in_buf ; yes, must read a new record
        mov     ah,fn_set_dta
        int     21H                     ;set DTA to input buffer
        mov     input_pos,Ø             ;set pointer to first byte in record
        mov     bx,Ø
```

**Listing 5.2
(continued)**

```
                mov     dx,offset infile_fcb   ;name the file to read
                mov     ah,fn_read_seq
                int     21H                    ;read a 128-byte record
                cmp     al,1                   ;data found in record?
                jne     read_ok                ; yes, continue
                mov     dx,offset read_err_msg ; no, write message and exit
                jmp     msg_exit
read_ok:
                mov     al,in_buf[bx]          ;transfer current character
                mov     cur_char,al            ; into global variable
                inc     input_pos              ;point to next address in IN_BUF
                ret
read_char endp
;----------------------------------------
; WRITE_CHAR near procedure
; Writes the character in CUR_CHAR to the output file.
; Updates the OUTPUT_POS variable.
;
write_char  proc near
                mov     dx,offset cur_char     ;point to DTA for output
                mov     ah,fn_set_dta
                int     21H                    ;set up to write

                mov     dx,offset outfile_fcb  ;use FCB for output file
                mov     ah,fn_write_seq
                int     21H                    ;write the byte

                cmp     al,0                   ;any problem with write?
                je      write_ok               ; no, continue
                mov     dx,offset disk_full_msg ; yes, exit with message
                jmp     msg_exit
write_ok:
                inc     output_pos             ;update device position
                ret
write_char endp

code_seg ends
                end     main                   ;specify starting address
```

Notice also that the STRUC pseudo-op is used to simplify access to these FCBs. Either of the following statements could be used to initialize the bytes-per-record field of an FCB:

```
MOV     WORD PTR INPUT_FCB + 0EH,1

MOV     INFILE_FCB.REC_SIZE,1
```

The second one is self-documenting, and the size of the field doesn't need to be explicitly named; it is defined in the structure. The structure definition also makes it easier to initialize storage for both FCBs and to copy the unopened FCBs from the PSP to the program's work area. Examine the program's data segment to see an example of using a string to override a field in a structure. The "empty" filename field of the FCB_STRUC is overridden with CON (console device). This practice makes it easier for the program to give the user a default output file.

The file manipulation is the most important thing to watch for in this program. UNTAB.ASM is a complete framework for any program that reads and/or writes sequential files. It demonstrates single-byte as well as multibyte records. The input file is read in groups of 128 bytes, and the output file is written one byte at a time. Examine the READ_BYTE and WRITE_BYTE procedures. WRITE_BYTE actually invokes the DOS WRITE_SEQ service as each byte is processed. The READ_BYTE procedure goes out to the disk only every 128th time the procedure is called.

Listing 5.2 also contains the error-handling code needed in any program that processes one or more filename parameters. It issues error messages when the input file is not found or an invalid drive number or filename is specified. It also checks for and informs the user of errors such as those that might be encountered during disk-reading operations—such as disk-full errors and trying to process a file that doesn't end in a Ctrl-Z. Other errors, such as trying to write to a write-protected disk, are handled by the critical error handler in DOS (i.e., you see the normal "Write protect error: Abort, Retry, Ignore" prompt).

A final note on UNTAB: This program needs to exit back to DOS when it encounters an error. That error may not be noticed until the program is three levels deep in calls to subroutines. Therefore, the usual method of exiting back to DOS won't always work (a far RET works only when you know that the top two words on the stack will be a 0 followed by the segment of the PSP). UNTAB simply stores the PSP segment in a data variable named BACK_TO_DOS. Then, regardless of the state of the stack, the program can always bail out with

```
JMP     BACK_TO_DOS     ;take indirect FAR jump to exit to DOS
```

In order for this operation to work, BACK_TO_DOS must be defined as a label for a DWORD variable. When the JMP is taken, the DS register must point to the segment in which the variable is stored—DATA_SEG, in this example.

## THINGS TO DO

1. Try some experiments with DEBUG to see how DOS formats the PSP and passes input parameters to an application. Using any existing text or code file as MY_PROG, try entering these sequences at the DOS prompt:

```
DEBUG MY_PROG *.*

DEBUG MY_PROG *.TXT

DEBUG MY_PROG TEMPFILE.TXT

DEBUG MY_PROG A:INFILE.TXT,B:OUTFILE:TXT /QQQ
```

Then use the DEBUG D command to examine the bytes starting at 5CH, 6CH, and 80H.

2. Look through Listing 5.2 (UNTAB) and examine the technique used for displaying error messages. Try writing a simpler version of UNTAB that displays the single message "File Error" if any file error is encountered.

3. Add code to the UNTAB program to read and write to the same file (make a temporary .BAK file and rename it).

4. Read the UNTAB command line to check for and process special options:

   a. To write a margin of space on the left side of each line.
   b. To break lines longer than 80 characters into two or more lines.
   c. To write a line number to the left of each line.

5. Read the entire input file into memory before processing the output file.

### 5.3.2 Random Access Files

In the preceding example of sequential access, the program reads and writes every byte via the READ_SEQ service. We know that every time that service is invoked, DOS will read the next byte (or multibyte record) from the disk and place it into the DTA. But what if we need to access records 1, 17, 23, and 3—in that order? The READ_RANDOM and WRITE_RANDOM services allow a program to specify exactly which record should be read or written.

Like the sequential access commands, these commands demand the precondition that a file has been opened and that the bytes-per-record field of the FCB has been set to the size of the record. The two differences between random access and sequential access are as follows:

1. The random access DOS services demand that the file-relative current record field of the FCB be initialized before the call.

2. Neither the relative record, current record, nor current block fields are updated after the access.

The BLOCK_READ and BLOCK_WRITE services make it easy to read and write large groups of bytes with one call to DOS. These calls are just like the READ_RANDOM and WRITE_RANDOM services in that the file-relative current record field of the FCB must be initialized before invoking the service. The difference is that another parameter, held in the CX register, determines how many records to read or write. Thus, if you want to write 32,178 bytes from memory to disk, you would set the bytes-per-record field to 1, set the file-relative current record field to 0, and set CX to 32,178 before invoking the service. The entire 32,178 bytes that begin at the memory address specified as the DTA will be recorded on the disk.

### 5.3.3 PC-DOS 2.0 Filing System Enhancements

Of the many features that make DOS 2.0 easier to work with than DOS 1.1, the concept of *standard input* and *standard output* devices and (redirection thereof) are perhaps the most significant. In effect, this concept allows the user to open and close any files that the program employs. That's right—no FCBs, no setting of the bytes-per-record or current record fields, no error handling for bad filenames, no OPEN_FILE, CLOSE_FILE, READ_SEQ, WRITE_SEQ calls—the most complicated parts are eliminated.

By letting the user decide upon the input and output devices, the scope of many programs can be narrowed to doing only file processing. For instance, the UNTAB program is shortened by half when you allow the program to omit handling all of the details about FCBs. In particular, the sequential file output can be handled via the same call that prints characters on the screen. The input file will need to be opened, but as shown in Listing 5.3 (UNTAB2.ASM), this is just a matter of duplicating the "handle" of the standard input device and then reading characters from that device until DOS indicates that the end of the file is reached (DOS 2.0 files don't necessarily end with a Ctrl-Z; otherwise, we could use DOS service 2 for input). Compare Listings 5.2 and 5.3, and see how easy the redirected I/O makes the processing of sequential files.

## Listing 5.3
## UNTAB2.ASM

```
;-------------------------------------------------------------------------------
; Listing 5.3    UNTAB2.ASM
;
; This version of UNTAB is written to work with DOS 2.0.  It expands the
; TAB characters that are read in from the standard input device and
; writes the resulting characters to the standard output device:
;
;          UNTAB [[ <source] >destination]
;
; It may also be used as a DOS 2.0 filter:
;
;          DIR | UNTAB | SORT > sorted.txt
;
; Note: This is a COM format file: ignore "no STACK segment" warning of linker.
;       The file requires processing by EXE2BIN after linking.

lf              equ       0AH
cr              equ       0DH          ;simplify making messages

eof             equ       1AH          ;ASCII Ctrl-Z (end-of-file marker)
eol             equ       0AH          ;ASCII linefeed (end-of-line marker)
tab             equ       09H          ;ASCII TAB character
fn_preview      equ       0BH          ;give names to the DOS services
fn_input        equ       07H
fn_output       equ       02H

code_seg segment para public
        assume cs:code_seg, ds:code_seg, es:nothing

        org       100H                 ;required for COM format programs
main    proc      far

        mov       di,0                 ;DI counts characters processed in current line
        call      process_files        ;do all of the work
        int       20H                  ;exit back to DOS
main    endp
```

**Listing 5.3
(continued)**

```
;-------------------------------------------
; PROCESS_FILES    NEAR procedure
; Reads each byte in the input file and copies it to the output file.
; If TAB character found (09H) in input file, then spaces are written
;  until tab-stop is reached (device position becomes a multiple of 8).
; Returns after writing the last byte of the output file (Ctrl-Z).
;
process_files proc near

next_char:
        call    read_char
        cmp     al,eof          ;is it a Ctrl-Z (end-of-file)?
        jnz     not_eof         ; no, continue
        call    write_char      ; yes, write it and exit
        ret                     ;<<----- procedure exit ----------
not_eof:
        cmp     al,eol          ;is it a 0AH (end-of-line)?
        jnz     not_eol         ;  no, continue

        call    write_char      ;  yes, write the byte
        mov     di,0            ; character counter to first column
        jmp     next_char       ; loop back for next character
not_eol:
        cmp     al,tab          ;is it a 09H (TAB character)?
        jnz     not_tab         ; no, continue
        call    expand_tab      ; yes, expand the tab
        jmp     next_char       ; loop back for next input
not_tab:
        call    write_char      ;not EOF, EOL, or TAB, so just write it
        jmp     next_char       ;and loop back for next character
process_files endp

;-------------------------------------------
; EXPAND_TAB    NEAR procedure
; Writes spaces to the output file until the device position becomes
;  a multiple of 8.
; Expects DI to be a pointer to the current position in the output line.
;
expand_tab  proc near
        mov     al,' '          ;set up to write spaces
        call    write_char      ;always output at least 1 space
next_space:
        test    di,7            ;at a tab-stop (low bits all = 0)?
        jz      done_tabbing    ; yes, exit loop
        call    write_char      ; no, output another space
        jmp     next_space      ;      and loop back
done_tabbing:
        ret                     ;back to caller
expand_tab endp

;-------------------------------------------
; READ_CHAR near procedure
; Fetches a character from the standard input device.
; returns: AL = character or AL = 1AH (if end-of-file).
;
read_char  proc near
        mov     ah,fn_preview
        int     21H
        cmp     al,0ffH         ;any characters waiting?
        je      char_ready      ; yes, read one
        mov     al,eof          ; no, indicate end of file
        ret
```

**Listing 5.3
(continued)**

```
char_ready:
        mov     ah,fn_input     ;DOS service returns a character
        int     21H             ; in AL
        ret                     ;return it to the caller.
read_char endp

;-------------------------------------------
; WRITE_CHAR   NEAR procedure
; Writes the character in AL to the standard output device.
; Updates DI (output position pointer)
;
write_char  proc near
        mov     ah,fn_output
        mov     dl,al
        int     21H                     ;set up for write
        inc     di                      ;update device position
        ret
write_char endp

code_seg ends
        end     main                    ;specify starting address
```

DOS 2.0 also simplifies the open and close operations for files that must be accessed randomly or when the standard I/O can't be redirected. You can open, read, write, and close any file (or device) without ever having heard of an FCB. The trick is to set up an ASCII string of a filespec (including a pathname if necessary) and terminate the string with a byte of 00H. Such a 0-terminated string is usually referred to as an ASCIIZ string; DOS 2.00 uses them in many operations.

Once the ASCIIZ string is set up, use DOS service 3DH to open the file according to the access code specified in the AL register (1 = read, 2 = write, 3 = read and write). That service returns a 16-bit *handle* with which you thereafter refer to the file:

```
FILESPEC DB     'c:wordproc/book/chap5/list5-3.asm',0

HANDLE   DW     ?        ;storage for DOS file handle

BUFFER   DB     80 DUP(?)

            .

            .

            .

         MOV    DX,OFFSET FILESPEC
                    ;(assuming DS is set to data segment)

         MOV    AL,0    ;open for reading

         MOV    AH,3DH   ;OPEN_HANDLE service
```

```
INT     21H

MOV     HANDLE,AX
                ;save HANDLE for use with READ or WRITE

        .

        .
```

DOS service 42H replaces the manual setting of FCB fields by introducing the concept of a *read/write pointer*. You invoke the service with register parameters that indicate what part of the file you will next be reading from or writing to. Reading and writing are simplified because the DTA and the byte count are specified with each invocation of the read or write services (3FH and 40H) rather than as a separate preliminary step:

```
MOV     BX,HANDLE            ;fetch the HANDLE

MOV     DX,OFFSET BUFFER     ;point to place to read data

MOV     CX,80               ;number of bytes to read

MOV     AH,3FH              ;specify READ service

INT     21H                 ;80 bytes are read into BUFFER
```

See Appendix B for a quick reference on all PC-DOS and ROM-BIOS services. Study the DOS manual for further details on handles, pathnames, and so on.

## 5.4 INSTALLING AN INTERRUPT SERVICE ROUTINE

You already know that the 8088 can be interrupted to process tasks specified by the system hardware. The keyboard interrupts the CPU to process any keyboard activity; the real-time clock stops everything 18.2 times per second to run a little program that keeps track of the system time and date; tasks such as printer spoolers run in the "background" during the time that other programs spend waiting around for a user to enter characters. How do all these operations take place? The secret is in the architecture of the 8088 and the 8259 interrupt controller chip.

All hardware interrupts are vectored through the 8259 before the CPU ever gets wind of them. This controller *prioritizes* interrupts in order as they come in. It makes sure that the most important interrupt is executed first, and that any interrupts that occur simultaneously are queued so that all of them will eventually be handled by the CPU. The 8259 also decides the type or number of the interrupt that is to take place. Just as when you place an INT 10H in your code to specify the VIDEO_IO BIOS service, the 8259 specifies a number from 8 to 0FH that tells the CPU which interrupt handler to execute.

The standard IBM PC uses only three of these available hardware interrupts. The diskette interrupt (INT 0EH) is vectored to a tiny ROM routine that sets a flag at 40:003E that other programs (specifically, the INT 13H DISKETTE_IO service) may examine to find out the status of various operations of the disk controller.

The keyboard interrupt (INT 9) is forced whenever the 8259 senses some activity from the IBM PC's keyboard. This sophisticated routine decodes the *scan codes* that the keyboard returns and places ASCII characters into a circular queue where other programs may examine and use them. This is a critical operation; it provides us with a 15-character type-ahead buffer so that regardless of how busy the CPU may be, it always finds the time to process a pressed (or released) key.

The timer interrupt (INT 8) takes place every 55 milliseconds (about 18.2 times per second). The routine that processes this interrupt keeps track of the number of interrupt "ticks" that have occurred since the computer was turned on. The timer interrupt handler performs two other important functions. It turns off the motors of the floppy disk drives if they have been inactive for two seconds. It also provides a "hook" by which any properly written interrupt service routine may perform a background task at every timer interrupt.

This hook is built into ROM-BIOS (it is sanctioned by IBM), so we may feel free to use it as we see fit. Just after the TIMER_INT has completed its primary duties (updated the clock and turned off the disk drive motors), it invoked INT 1CH. Normally, this software interrupt consists entirely of a single IRET instruction; that is, the INT 1CH usually does nothing. Putting this interrupt to work is a simple 2-step procedure. First, you write an interrupt procedure and load it someplace where no other program will touch it. Then you alter the entry in the interrupt vector table to point to your routine. The program you install will run at the same time as BASIC, DOS, or any other program.

Finding a place to put an interrupt handler is easier than you might think. The only problem that an interrupt service routine faces is that DOS might load a program into a program's data area or (horror of horrors) right over the interrupt handling code. The folks who wrote PC-DOS provided a mechanism that ensures that a program can be placed in memory without fear of being overwritten with subsequent programs. The trick is to exit the program by a means other than the normal INT 20H. The FIX_IN_MEMORY service, INT 27H, does just that. In effect, it makes your program and its data a permanent part of DOS.

Altering the current interrupt vector to patch your program into the real-time clock interrupt is only as hard as changing two words of memory. First, set a segment register to point to the bottom of the 8088's memory; then place a segment and offset value into the vector table element that you wish to change. However, there are two complications. Because we are changing the vector of a routine that is invoked in the background, we must make sure that the vector is not taken before we have changed both the segment and the offset. (Imagine the disaster if an INT forced execution to a new segment but to the old offset!) By disabling interrupts (with CLI) just before making the change, and then enabling them (with STI) afterward, we can be sure that this error will never occur.

Another thing to keep in mind when you alter the timer interrupt vector is that you might not be the only one who wants to capture the interrupt. Print spoolers or other background tasks may also be installed and expect to be called every 18.2 seconds. If you install your own routine without keeping these other processes in mind, you may end up with devices or systems that no longer function. The trick is to save the value of the original vector before changing it, and then exit from the interrupt service routine by jumping to that original vector. This way, you insert your routine into a chain of processes rather than completely ignoring someone else's code. It's the standard practice, and it's the nice thing to do.

### Creating a Background Task

Listing 5.4, LOCKKEYS.COM, uses the previously discussed techniques to install a background task on the IBM PC. It sets up an interrupt service routine that constantly displays the status of the keyboard's NumLock, Ins, and CapsLock toggle states. This procedure lets you know, for example, whether pressing the keys of the numeric keypad will result in a cursor movement or a digit. And the function is present whether you are running an editor, a BASIC program, VisiCalc, or anything else.

### Listing 5.4
### LOCKKEYS.COM

```
;---------------------------------------------------------------------
; Listing 5.4    LOCKKEYS.COM
;
; This program installs an interrupt service routine that "captures" INT 1CH
; to perform the background task.  It displays the status of several keyboard
; "mode" keys.  The program displays NUM, CAPS, and/or INS depending on the
; status of the NumLock, CapsLock, and Ins keys.
;
; Press Ctrl and Alt (together) to toggle the display off or back on.
;
; This is a COM format file, so it must be processed by EXE2BIN after
; being assembled and linked.
;

;---- equates-----
vid_mem    equ     0b800H  ;use 0b000H for monochrome display adapter
disp_addr  equ     132     ;use 0 for upper left corner

abs_seg    segment at 0
           org     1CH * 4
old_vect           dd      ?       ;label for the INT 1CH vector
           org     417H
kbd_flag           db      ?       ;label for the shift key states
ins_state  equ     80H     ;equates for the relevant bits
caps_state equ     40H
num_state  equ     20H
state_keys equ     num_state or caps_state or ins_state ;all of the above
ctrl_alt   equ     8 or 4    ;press Ctrl and Alt together to stop display
abs_seg    ends

code_seg segment para public

;set up some labels in the PSP to be used as data for this program
           org     80H
exit_int   label   dword   ;used to save exit address to return from interrupt
save_offset label  word    ; get a handle on the low-order word
           org     82H
save_seg   label   word    ; and the high-order word
           org     84H
old_state  label   byte    ;variable checked to find if any state has toggled
           org     85H
on_off_flag label  byte    ;checked to see if display should be updated
on         equ     0FFH    ;(altered by pressing Ctrl-Alt)
off        equ     0
```

**Listing 5.4
(continued)**

```
;-----------------------------------------------------------------------
; INSTALL_PROC
; This procedure is executed only once -- when first invoked from DOS.
; It installs the INTERRUPT_PROC and leaves it resident.  The only
; way to eliminate the installed routine is to reboot DOS.

        org     100H                ;COM programs must start at 100H
        assume cs:code_seg,ds:abs_seg
install_proc proc   far
        mov     ax,abs_seg          ;establish vector-table addressing
        mov     ds,ax
        les     ax,old_vect         ;get doubleword vector into ES:AX
        mov     save_offset,ax      ;store the offset
        mov     save_seg,es         ;store the segment address

        mov     on_off_flag,on      ;initiate display mode
        mov     old_state,0         ;and start assuming all states off

;--- point the interrupt vector to INTERRUPT_PROC in this segment ---
        cli                         ;interrupts off
        mov     old_vect,offset interrupt_proc ;store the new offset
        mov     old_vect+2,cs       ;store the new segment
        sti                         ;interrupts back on

;--- exit to DOS with FIX_IN_MEMORY service ---
        mov     dx,offset last_addr+1  ;get address of last byte in program
        int     27H                 ;FIX_IN_MEMORY and exit to DOS
install_proc endp

;--- message data used to display states of keys
rev       equ   70H
blanks    db    '|',rev,' ',rev,' ',rev,' ',rev,'|',rev
num_str   db    '|',rev,'N',rev,'u',rev,'m',rev
caps_str  db    '|',rev,'C',rev,'p',rev,'s',rev
ins_str   db    '|',rev,'I',rev,'n',rev,'s',rev,'|',rev

;-----------------------------------------------------------------------
; INTERRUPT_PROC
; Once installed, this program is executed at every tick of the
; real-time clock (18.2 times per second).
; It displays the keys only when one is changed, or when the LOCKKEY
; display has scrolled off the screen.
; Checks for Ctrl and Alt keys for toggling LOCKKEY display off and on.

interrupt_proc proc far
        assume  ds:code_seg, es:nothing

        push    es
        push    ds
        push    ax
        push    cx
        push    si
        push    di

        push    cs
        pop     ds                  ;address the string data

        mov     si,abs_seg          ;address the keyboard flag area
        mov     es,si
        mov     al,es:kbd_flag      ;fetch the flags
        mov     ah,al               ;copy of flags in AH for next step
```

**Listing 5.4
(continued)**

```
;--- see if user wants to toggle LOCKKEY display on or off

            and     ah,ctrl_alt         ;mask unwanted bits
            cmp     ah,ctrl_alt         ;are both Ctrl and Alt pressed?
            jne     no_toggle           ; no, continue
            not     on_off_flag         ; yes, toggle the flag (Ø -> FF; FF -> Ø)
            mov     cx,Ø
delay:      loop    delay               ; and "debounce" to avoid switching twice
no_toggle:
            cmp     on_off_flag,on      ;should key states be displayed?
            jne     all_done            ; no, exit
                                        ; yes, process the display
            and     al,state_keys       ; mask off all but relevant key bits

            mov     si,vid_mem          ;establish screen memory addressing
            mov     es,si               ;ES for destination of MOVS commands
            mov     di,disp_addr        ;and address to write first character

            cmp     byte ptr es:[di],'|' ;has screen scrolled?
            jne     display_all         ;  yes, display all keys
            cmp     al,cs:old_state     ;  no, has any state changed?
            je      all_done            ;     no, exit interrupt handler
display_all:                            ;     yes, process all keys
            mov     si,offset blanks    ;assume lock state not true
            test    al,num_state        ;state true?
            jz      disp_num            ; no, use blanks
            mov     si,offset num_str   ; yes, use characters
disp_num:
            mov     cx,4
            rep movsw                   ;copy '|Num' or '|   ' to screen
            mov     si,offset blanks
            test    al,caps_state
            jz      disp_caps
            mov     si,offset caps_str
disp_caps:
            mov     cx,4
            rep movsw                   ;copy '|Cps' or '|   ' to screen

            mov     si,offset blanks
            test    al,ins_state
            jz      disp_ins
            mov     si,offset ins_str
disp_ins:
            mov     cx,5
            rep movsw                   ;copy '|Ins|' or '|   |' to screen

all_done:
            mov     cs:old_state,al     ;save the flags for next pass
            pop     di
            pop     si
            pop     cx
            pop     ax
            pop     ds
            pop     es
            jmp     cs:exit_int   ;take indirect FAR jump to exit <--- exit ---
interrupt_proc endp
last_addr equ   $               ;end of program -- for FIX_IN_MEMORY service

code_seg ends
            end     install_proc  ;must have END address in COM format programs
```

The first part of the program is called the *installation* of the interrupt. It includes the code that saves the original vector and changes it to point to the new procedure. It uses the FIX_IN_MEMORY service to make sure that the code remains resident after it returns to DOS.

The rest of the program is the interrupt portion. This part is executed every 55 milliseconds or as often as the BIOS TIMER_INT procedure calls it (the 8259 may queue several requests and then invoke them faster than that until they are all satisfied). The procedure reads the low-memory addresses where the BIOS (i.e., the KB_INT routine) stores the bit patterns of the keyboard shift states.

LOCKKEYS could simply test the keyboard bits and display a corresponding string at every 55-ms juncture (i.e., 18.2 times per second), but that would place a lot of overhead strain on the system. Instead, the program lies dormant until one of two things happens: Either the status of a key changes, or the top line is scrolled off the screen. When either of these events occur, the program reads and interprets the keyboard flags and then displays the status of all three keys. The strings: Num, Cps, and Ins are displayed in reverse video on the top right-hand corner of the screen. The program assumes that the color/graphics card is installed and active and that it is functioning in text mode. (See the program comments on how to change the program for the monochrome adapter and how to reposition the key display.)

LOCKKEYS also contains logic to turn itself off and on. It looks for the Ctrl and Alt keys being pressed at the same time. When this occurs, it toggles from on to off or vice versa. Whenever you are using a program that needs the upper right-hand corner of the screen, or you find that you need to switch to graphics mode, this feature lets you temporarily stop the key display. You may also want to turn it off while performing any operation that you want to execute very quickly (background tasks steal time from foreground tasks).

Notice that in the INSTALL_PROC the registers are not saved, but the INTERRUPT_PROC is very careful to preserve the environment. There's no telling how much damage you can do if your interrupt handler neglects to save and restore every register it uses.

Pay special attention to how the program accesses its data. Several variables are declared within the PSP. That entire 256 bytes is waiting to be used; it becomes resident just like the program's opcodes. The other data, the strings that are displayed, are allocated within the code segment at addresses that will never be executed. Examine how the segment registers are "floated" from memory area to memory area. Always keep a close eye on those gadgets!

LOCKKEYS is written as a COM program to simplify the use of the FIX_IN_MEMORY service. Thus, after the program is assembled and linked, it must be processed by the EXE2BIN utility and given a .COM extension. After creating the file LOCKKEYS.ASM with your editor, use the following commands:

```
MASM LOCKKEYS;   (until there are no errors listed)

LINK LOCKKEYS;   (ignore the "no STACK" error)

EXE2BIN LOCKKEYS LOCKKEYS:COM      (convert to COM format)

ERASE LOCKKEYS.EXE
                 (get rid of the useless EXE format file)
```

```
        LOCKKEYS              (install the interrupt handler)

                              (display should show the key states)
   < NUMLOCK >                (display should show 'Num' in reverse video)
   < CTRL-ALT >               (toggle display off; no change till scroll)
   < CTRL-ALT >               (toggle display back on)
```

Several special commands are used to make a COM format program. There is no STACK segment because COM programs must be written as a single physical segment. The ORG pseudo-op is used to create labels for variables in several different areas. In COM programs, ORG must be used to set the assembler's program counter to 100H at the beginning of the executable code. That procedure ensures that all addresses mentioned in the program will be at the offsets in effect when the program is loaded; it will be loaded directly after the 256-byte PSP. The END pseudo-op is used to specify the starting address as being the first statement in the code section (a requirement of the EXE2BIN utility).

Because the program will be installed with the FIX_IN_MEMORY service, it sets up a label, LAST_ADDR, at the end of the code. This value is passed back to DOS in the DX register to indicate the address where subsequent programs may safely be loaded. Be aware that if you repeatedly invoke the LOCKKEYS program, it will use up about 500 bytes of memory each time and insert itself into the chain of actions that take place at each timer interrupt. Eventually, you will either run out of memory or your computer will be overloaded with interrupt processes and slow down to a crawl.

The background process created in Listing 5.4 intercepts the USER_TIMER_INT, but it illustrates the techniques used to intercept any BIOS interrupt. For instance, if your printer doesn't have exactly the same character set as that of the IBM printer, it's not difficult to write a short program that intercepts the BIOS PRINTER_IO interrupt. You could write the routine so that it filters out the offending characters, or you could substitute a certain character (or group of characters) for any character that is routed through that BIOS printer service interrupt.

A program that performs such a filtering action will have a section just like the INSTALL_PROC in Listing 5.4 to set the filter in place. The interrupt handling procedure will also have two things in common with that listing; it will preserve all registers that it uses, and it will pass control to the normal interrupt handler via an indirect FAR jump. The actions that are taken can range from ignoring a service request to executing a lengthy series of commands, including multiple calls to the original interrupt routine.

For example, a print spooler program will likely intercept both the PRINTER_IO and KB_INT routines. As characters come into PRINTER_IO, they are routed into a buffer area. Then, when the spooler senses that a program is waiting for a keyboard input, it slips a character from the buffer out to the printer. (Since most programs spend a majority of their lives waiting for sluggish humans, it's sensible to get some real work done between keystrokes.)

All of this intercepting and capturing of interrupts can lead to a spaghetti-like tangle of interlocking procedures. When you need to modify the way that the BIOS perceives a device, DOS 1.10 requires that you take control of that BIOS interrupt—and heaven help those programs that expect the interrupt to be handled normally. Fortunately for assembly language programmers, DOS 2.0 has a powerful alternative to this underhanded device-napping: a bona fide, fully sanctioned mechanism for installing device drivers.

**THINGS TO DO**

1.  Modify LOCKKEYS so that before the code is fixed in memory, the program checks to see if it has already been installed.

2.  If LOCKKEYS has already been installed, have it check the DOS command line (starting at PSP:0081) for the keywords ON or OFF. If either or both are found, have it modify the ON_OFF_FLAG variable accordingly and take a normal exit to DOS.

3.  (*) Write a timer interrupt procedure that displays a message and sounds the bell at a time set by the user. This "alarm clock" would be helpful for absentminded assembly language programmers who forget important appointments (Who, me?).

4.  (**) Write a timer interrupt that flashes a subliminal message on the screen every five minutes or so. The message should remain on the screen for about 1/30th of a second—just long enough for the mind to perceive it without the eyes seeing it.

## 5.5  PC-DOS 2.0 INSTALLABLE DEVICE DRIVERS

DOS 2.0 provides a means for creating specialized device handlers that are fully integrated into the PC-DOS system. These installable device drivers are programs, written in a special format, that are read in when DOS boots up. They become a resident part of DOS, just like the internal device handlers for CON, LPTn, and disk drives. You may write device drivers that replace the normal DOS devices, and you may add new devices to the system.

Considering the differences between, say, a disk drive and a line printer, you have to give credit to the folks at Microsoft. Standardizing every conceivable action that a device might be requested to do is something less than a monumental breakthrough (although UNIX has done this for years). But the format for device drivers may seem very confusing precisely because of this flexibility.

The first step toward understanding this type of program is realizing that there are two very different types of devices: block data and single-character devices. Block devices are complex, and character devices are simple.

The DOS 2.0 manual gives an example of a silicon floppy driver that adds a RAM drive to the system. Like all disk drive device handlers, it works with blocks of data, specifically disk sectors. Writing this type of driver involves setting up a BIOS parameter block (BPB) within the program data area. A BPB must contain such trivia as information on file allocation tables, directory sectors, a bytes-per-sector count, and so on. A block device handler must also contain the code to answer queries such as: "has the user removed the diskette that was in the drive earlier?" and "how many directories are on this diskette?" The listing in the DOS manual is a good example of what is involved in writing a block device driver. In this section, we will discuss a much simpler device driver, one that handles individual characters.

Character devices are considerably simpler because they send and receive only one character at a time. You may make them as sophisticated as you like. The ANSI.SYS file on the DOS 2.0 diskette is a character device driver for the keyboard that is able to redefine a single keystroke so that it becomes an entire string of characters.

The following tutorial will illustrate a bare-bones device so that you may use it as a framework upon which to build your own more complex code. Before we get into the specifics of character devices, let's take a look at device handlers.

### The Theory of Device Drivers

When DOS wants to fetch a character from a device (be it the keyboard, the serial port, or an electronic thermometer), it needs to have:

* A way to request the character.

* A mechanism to carry the character back to DOS.

* A way to know whether or not the character was transferred correctly.

It must also be able to check for errors by the user. For instance, if the user tries to copy the LPT1 device to the CON device, DOS must be able to recognize that error and write an error message. In other words, DOS must be able to *identify* the device, *make requests* of it, *retrieve* data from it, and *retrieve its status*. The mechanism for handling all of these actions turns on two types of data structure: the *device header* and the *request structure*.

The device header is a block of data that identifies the device. It declares the name and type of the device and contains pointers to the addresses of the code that processes requests. Figure 5.5 shows the format of this header. Notice that a device header contains a pointer to the next device in the system. When you ask DOS to

```
COPY CON: LPT1:
```

it looks through all of its device headers until it finds a device with "CON" in the name field. That is, it checks to see if the first device is named CON; if not, it uses the next-device-pointer field of the first device header to find the segment and offset of the next device. It then checks the bytes starting at offset 8 from that address. If they don't match CON, the next-device-pointer field of that device is used to access the next device header—and so forth. When DOS encounters a device header that has a next-device-pointer that contains a -1 (FFFF:FFFF), it knows there is no device by that name.

Similarly, as DOS *installs* drivers, it alters the next-device-pointer field of each existing driver so that it points forward along the chain (see Figure 5.6). When there are two or more devices with the same name, only the first one will be used. DOS installs its default devices last, so that user-installed devices take precedence.

**Figure 5.5**
**Device Header Fields**

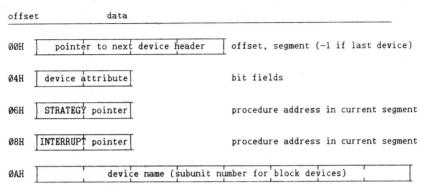

**Figure 5.6**
**The PC-DOS 2.0 Device Header Chain**

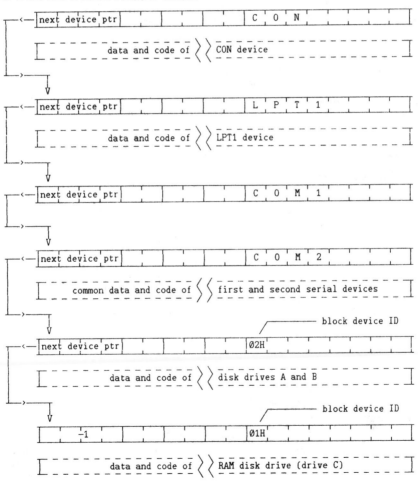

Once the CON device is located, DOS will start back at the beginning of the device header chain and try to locate a device named LPT1. The copy operation will consist of repeated requests to input characters from CON and repeated requests to output each character to the LPT1 device.

The request structure is a chunk of information (sometimes called a *data packet*) that is shuttled back and forth through the system. Every transaction between CON and LPT1 (in the preceding example) passes this request structure first to the source device and then to the destination device. DOS, sitting in the middle, moderates these transactions. It tells the source device that it wants a character, and it tells the destination device to accept a character. It also looks for error codes that either device may indicate in the transaction, and it checks for the end-of-file condition that terminates the sequence of transactions.

When I said that the data packet is shuttled around the system, I was simplifying to make the concept clearer. Actually, DOS only passes a pointer to the structure from device to device. But conceptually, a device driver owns the data while it is processing a request. Now let's take a look at the data held in a request structure.

Examine Figure 5.7. The first part of the structure is referred to in all of the DOS literature as the *request header*. It contains the basic ingredients needed by every device for every type of transaction. The two most important fields in the request header are the *command code* and the *status word*. The command code tells the device which type of action it should take (remember, this system must be flexible enough to handle many types of commands, even if a particular device can process only one or two different commands). The status word is a bit field that is passed back to DOS after the device takes the action specified in the command code.

**Figure 5.7**
**Request Structure Fields**

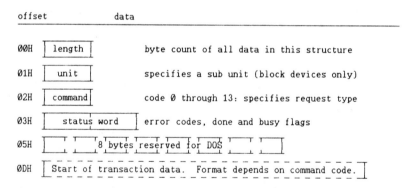

Following the request header is an area whose meaning depends upon the context set by the command code. It may contain several words and doublewords of data, a single byte, or nothing at all. Thus, the request header is always the same, but the structure of the data packet varies according to the command. For instance, if the command code indicates that the device should return a block of information, the variable data area will contain (among other things) a doubleword field that points to the address where the data should be placed. If the device is asked to declare whether the user has changed a diskette in a drive, the request structure provides a place to put a 1-byte yes/no/don't know flag.

The formats of the various structures are detailed in the DOS manual, so we won't go into them here. Besides, most of them don't apply to a simple character device driver. Getting back to the bare-bones definition of a device, let's look at the minimum amount of code and data that is required for a character device driver.

## The Components of a Device Driver

All drivers begin with a data area. It includes the mandatory *device header*, any messages it will display, and a list of pointers to the addresses of the various functions it may be asked to perform. If it is a block device, it must also contain a 13-byte BPB (we can ignore this area when writing character device drivers). At the very minimum, the device driver data area will contain a 13-byte request header and a doubleword storage area to enqueue requests.

DOS makes requests in a 2-step process. Harking back to Figure 5.5, you will see two fields in the device header that are pointers to two different procedures. DOS uses these pointers to invoke two separate procedures in a device driver. It first invokes a strategy procedure and then an interrupt procedure. The strategy procedure is very simple. All it needs to do is save a pointer to the request structure so that the interrupt procedure can process the request.

Currently, the strategy of any device is simply to save ES:BX in a doubleword at an address where the interrupt procedure can find it. It is called the *strategy* because the routine could be given the "intelligence" to buffer or queue a series of requests and then pass a strategically organized list to the interrupt handler. This list could be used in a disk device driver to optimize disk accesses, minimizing the amount of head travel. Also, in a multitasking environment, the strategy routine might be called twice before the interrupt routine is called. It would therefore need to save a first-in-first-out queue, and the interrupt routine would need to be able to read requests from that queue.

After invoking the strategy procedure, DOS immediately invokes the interrupt procedure to handle the request. The interrupt procedure first retrieves the doubleword that has been stored by the strategy procedure. Then it looks to the indicated request structure to determine exactly what DOS wants. Depending on that request, it then routes control to the procedure that can perform the indicated function. These procedures satisfy the request by moving data into and out of buffers and passing a status word back to DOS.

Thus, a device driver program will contain three parts: the data area, the strategy procedure, and the interrupt procedure. The interrupt procedure does all of the work. It saves all registers, interprets the command code, invokes the indicated subfunction, restores the registers, and then returns to DOS. Figure 5.8 illustrates how these components fit together to make a complete device driver.

**Figure 5.8**
**The Components of a Device Driver**

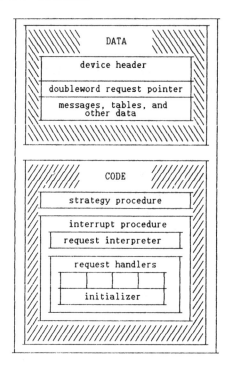

## CHARDEV: A Sample Device Driver

Listing 5.5 is an example of a simple character device driver. It performs no particularly useful function, except to illustrate the basic concepts of DOS 2.0 installable device drivers. The "device" that is created by this procedure is not a piece of hardware at all. It just calls the already existing PC-DOS and ROM-BIOS services for the keyboard and the display. It is both an input and an output device. When requested for an input, the CHARDEV device turns around and invokes the ROM-BIOS interrupt 16H to wait for a key, and then displays the ASCII value of the key pressed. Output requests are handled by displaying a character via PC-DOS service 2. CHARDEV also displays a message that indicates what type of request is being made.

Looking at the listing, you will see several structures and bit records defined. They make it easy to access the various fields of the request structures, and the code is self-documenting. The first part of the program allocates and defines the bytes and words of the device header. Notice that the entire program is written to reside in a single physical segment, just like a COM program. Unlike a COM format file, a device driver must not contain the normal ORG 100H statement (device drivers are not preceded by a PSP, as are all normal PC-DOS programs).

Following the device header data is the allocation of the doubleword that is used as the 1-element queue that saves the pointer to the request structure. This section is followed by the messages that are printed by the various request handlers as they are

## Listing 5.5
## MYDRIVER.ASM (creates CHARDEV.SYS)

```
;-------------------------------------------------------------------
; Listing 5.5  MYDRIVER.ASM (creates CHARDEV.SYS)
;
; Simple device driver illustrates the fundamental structures and
; actions of a DOS 2.0 installable device driver.
; CHARDEV is both an input and and output character device.

;=====================================================================
;---- structures, records, and equates for character device drivers ----
;=====================================================================
request_hdr_struc struc        ;"template" for the data passed by DOS (at ES:BX)
rh_len            db  ?
rh_unit_code      db  ?
rh_cmd_code       db  ?
rh_status         dw  ?
rh_reserved       db  8 dup(?)
request_hdr_struc ends

init_block_struc  struc         ;data structure used by function 0 (INIT_FN)
ib_req_hdr        db  13 dup(?)
ib_unit_count     db  ?
ib_end_addr       dd  ?
ib_bpb_ptr        dd  ?
init_block_struc  ends

io_struc          struc         ;used by functions 3, 4, 8, 9, and 12
io_req_hdr        db  13 dup(?)
io_media_desc     db  ?
io_transfer_addr  dd  ?
io_data_count     dw  ?   ;bytes or sectors
io_start_sector   dw  ?   ;used only with block devices
io_struc          ends

attr_rec  record  dev_type:1, ioctl:1, format:1, dummy:10, nul:1, sto:1, sti:1

                  ;DEV TYPE = 1 for character device, 0 = block device
                  ;IOCTL    = 1 if IOCTL system calls are supported
                  ;FORMAT   = 1 if block device is non-IBM format
                  ;DUMMY      is unused bits in record
                  ;NUL      = 1 if this is the NUL device
                  ;STO      = 1 if this is the Standard Output device
                  ;STI      = 1 if this is the Standard Input device

status_rec record err_flag:1, res:5, busy:1, done:1, err_code:8

                  ;ERR_FLAG = 1 if error occured (ERR_CODE defines error)
                  ;RES      = unused bits in record
                  ;BUSY     = 1 if device is busy
                  ;DONE     = 1 when operation is complete (always 1 on exit)
                  ;ERR CODE = the type of error that occurred (see below)

write_protect      equ  0    ;DOS prints a message when error code is returned
unknown_unit       equ  1
device_not_ready   equ  2
unknown_cmd        equ  3    ;<-- only error used by this device ---
crc_error          equ  4
bad_drive_req_len  equ  5
seek_error         equ  6
unknown_media      equ  7
sector_not_found   equ  8
out_of_paper       equ  9
write_fault        equ  0AH
read_fault         equ  0BH
general_failure    equ  0CH
```

**Listing 5.5
(continued)**

```
;================================================================
;------------ data and code of the file begins here -------------
;================================================================

dev_seg segment
char_device   proc   far     ;following data must be contained in a procedure
                             ;so that the END pseudo-op will accept the label
         assume cs:dev_seg, ds:dev_seg, es:dev_seg

;------------------------------
; The following lines are the device header that must exist for
;  every device.  This file has only one device, and it works with
;  character I/O.

chardev_header:        ;label for the start of the device driver

next_dev_ptr          dd   -1    ;only 1 device is defined in this file
dev_attribute         attr_rec <1,0,0,0,0,0,0>  ;see ATTR_REC record definition
strategy_ptr          dw   strategy  ;the installation procedure
interrupt_ptr         dw   interrupt ;the procedure that handles function calls
device_name           db   'CHARDEV ' ;8-byte string of device name

request_ptr      DD   ?    ;STRATEGY stores ES:BX request header pointer here
                          ;INTERRUPT retrieves it

; this table is used to jump to the procedure that is indicated
; by DOS in the command code (third byte of the request header)

fn_table dw   init_fn           ;  0: initialization procedure
         dw   media_check_fn     ;  1: media check procedure
         dw   build_bpb_fn       ;  2: build Bios Parameter Block
         dw   ioctl_in_fn        ;  3: IOCTL Input
         dw   input_fn           ;  4: read from device
         dw   nd_input_fn        ;  5: Non-Destructive, no-wait read
         dw   input_status_fn    ;  6: return status of input device
         dw   input_flush_fn     ;  7: flush (clear) the input buffer
         dw   output_fn          ;  8: write to device
         dw   output_verify_fn   ;  9: write and verify
         dw   output_status_fn   ; 10: return status of output device
         dw   output_flush_fn    ; 11: flush (clear) the output buffer
         dw   ioctl_out_fn       ; 12: IOCTL Output

;The following messages are displayed by CHARDEV when DOS
;makes a request.

cr       equ     0DH
lf       equ     0AH

fn0_msg  db 'Initializing CHARDEV Driver ',cr,lf,'$'
fn4_msg  db 'Input request : $'
fn8_msg  db 'Output request : $'
crlf     db cr,lf,'$'

;================================================================
; STRATEGY procedure
; Just saves the request header pointer for the INTERRUPT procedure

strategy proc far
         assume cs:dev_seg
         mov     cs:request_ptr,bx
         mov     cs:request_ptr+2,es
         ret                        ;FAR return to DOS
strategy endp
```

## Listing 5.5
## (continued)

```
;================================================================
; INTERRUPT procedure
; Processes the command indicated in the request header.

interrupt proc far
        assume  cs:dev_seg, ds:nothing, es:nothing
        push    ds                      ;preserve all registers
        push    es
        push    ax
        push    bx
        push    cx
        push    dx
        push    di
        push    si
        mov     di,cs
        mov     ds,di                   ;address the program data area

        les     bx,request_ptr          ;get the pointer saved by STRATEGY
        mov     ah,0
        mov     al,es:[bx].rh_cmd_code   ;fetch the command
        shl     ax,1                    ; * 2 to point to jump vector
        mov     di,ax
        jmp     fn_table[di]            ;invoke that function procedure

nd_input_fn:                    ;requests for any of these services
media_check_fn:                 ; will result in DOS issuing an error message
build_bpb_fn:
ioctl_in_fn:
input_status_fn:
input_flush_fn:
output_verify_fn:
output_status_fn:
output_flush_fn:
ioctl_out_fn:
error_exit:
        or      es:[bx].rh_status,mask err_flag  ;set the ERROR_FLAG bit
        or      es:[bx].rh_status,unknown_cmd    ;name the error

;--- interrupt service request has been handled.
;--- Set the "done flag" and return to DOS.

common_exit:
        or      es:[bx].rh_status,mask done    ;indicate completion
        pop     si                             ; by setting DONE bit
        pop     di
        pop     dx
        pop     cx
        pop     bx
        pop     ax
        pop     es
        pop     ds
        ret                             ;FAR return

;-------------------------------------
; INTERRUPT procedure function calls
; Only three types of requests are handled by CHARDEV.  All other
;  requests are routed through the ERROR_EXIT.

;-----------------------------------------------------------------
; INPUT_FN
; Reads (waits for) 1 character from the keyboard, and displays it,
; then returns it (within the I/O structure) to DOS.

input_fn proc near
        mov     dx,offset fn4_msg       ;"Input request: "
        mov     ah,9                    ;DOS print string service
        int     21H

        mov     ah,0            ;indicate BIOS AWAIT_KEY function
        int     16H             ;get AL = ASCII character, AH = scan code

        mov     es:[bx].io_data_count,1       ;store the character count
        push    ds
        lds     di,es:[bx].io_transfer_addr   ;get offset of destination
        mov     [di],al                       ;point to destination segment
        pop     ds

        mov     dl,al
        mov     ah,2                    ;display the character
        int     21H

        mov     dx,offset crlf   ;start a new line
        mov     ah,9             ;invoke DOS print string service
        int     21H
        jmp     common_exit
input_fn endp
```

**Listing 5.5
(continued)**

```
;-----------------------------------------------------------------
; OUTPUT_FN  sends the character passed to it from DOS out to the
; standard output device.
output_fn proc near
          mov      dx,offset fn8_msg     ;"Output request :"
          mov      ah,9                  ;DOS print string service
          int      21H

          push     ds
          lds      si,es:[bx].io_transfer_addr
          mov      dl,[si]      ;retrieve the character
          pop      ds           ;leave something on the stack and you die

          mov      ah,2         ;display the character
          int      21H

          mov      dx,offset crlf   ;print new line characters
          mov      ah,9             ;DOS print string service
          int      21H
          jmp      common_exit
output_fn endp
;-----------------------------
; INIT_FN procedure
; Passes the end-of-driver address back to DOS.  Other block-related
;   fields aren't required by character devices such as this one.
; Note that the address of this procedure is passed back to DOS as the
;   address of the end of the driver.  After one invocation, INIT_FN
;   is never called again; thus, it doesn't need to be saved with the
;   rest of the function procedures.

init_fn  proc  near
          mov      dx,offset fn0_msg     ;"Initializing CHARDEV"
          mov      ah,9                  ;DOS print string service
          int      21H

;-- specify the end of this driver -------
          mov      es:[bx].ib_end_addr,offset init_fn ;offset is this procedure
          mov      es:[bx].ib_end_addr+2,cs           ;segment is current CS
          jmp      common_exit
init_fn  endp

interrupt endp
char_device endp
dev_seg ends
          end      chardev_header    ;must specify end for EXE2BIN
```

invoked. The final data are a look-up table that defines the addresses of each of the device request handlers. Most of them are NOP procedures; they are vectored to ERROR_EXIT because CHARDEV ignores the block-related functions and contains only the minimum amount of code.

The rest of the listing defines the code that is executed when DOS makes requests of CHARDEV. The STRATEGY procedure performs its single task of saving the ES and BX registers (passed by DOS) that point to the request structure. Then it returns (always by a FAR return) to DOS.

The INTERRUPT procedure is considerably more complex. It saves all of the registers, and then sets up the DS register so that it can access the request structure pointer that was saved by the STRATEGY procedure. It retrieves that value with a 32-bit load of ES and BX via the LES opcode. Next, the INTERRUPT procedure finds out which type of request is being made, and then executes an indirect jump to the procedure that is indicated in the table. CHARDEV handles only three of the 13 possible requests, so it *could* route execution via a compare-and-jump chain. However, this "computed *goto*" system demonstrates how more sophisticated drivers should operate.

The only three requests that CHARDEV handles are INPUT, OUTPUT, and INIT. Let's look at the INIT procedure first. DOS requests a driver to initialize itself as soon as it is loaded into memory (i.e., when DOS reads the filename from the CONFIG.SYS file as it boots up). There is no hardware to initialize in this case, so the INIT_FN procedure is relatively simple. It displays the message that lets you know it is being invoked, and then it changes a single field, the END_ADDR doubleword, in the request structure before it skips back to the common exit to return to DOS.

DOS expects to receive an ending address at which it may begin loading other device drivers and programs. You will recognize this function as being similar to what happens when we use the INT 27H FIX_IN_MEMORY service. That service expects the ending address to be in CS:DX, but the DOS device driver processor expects to find a segment and an offset value in bytes 15 to 19 of the request structure. The INIT_FN procedure simply places the value of the CS register into the segment field and places the offset of the start of INIT_FN into the offset field. This action tells DOS that all addresses beyond that segment and offset are available for new operations. Note that the INIT_FN procedure itself will be overwritten by the next file that DOS loads. The manual promises (cross its heart!) never again to invoke the INIT_FN procedure, so it's OK to free this memory.

The other two request handlers are INPUT_FN and OUTPUT_FN. These routines both display a message on the screen via the PC-DOS service 9. Then they each process the request by fetching or storing a single character in the buffer named in the request structure. Notice that special care is taken to make sure that the segment registers are always pointing at the right segments.

All three request handlers return (via a NEAR jump) to a common exit where the DONE bit is set in the request header status word, the registers are popped to restore the CPU to its prerequest state, and execution is passed back to DOS via a FAR return.

The other 10 commands are processed by setting an error flag and naming the "Unknown command" error in the request header status word. DOS commands such as COPY will never invoke any of these NOP request handlers, but it is possible that some program may ask for an output-with-verify or request a preview of an input character via the nondestructive input service. In any case, all of the requests that are not handled by CHARDEV return an error code to DOS to let it figure out what to do.

Installing CHARDEV as a new device on your system is a 5-step process:

```
MASM MYDRIVER;           (assemble the file)

LINK MYDRIVER;           (link it. Ignore the No STACK error)

EXE2BIN MYDRIVER MYDRIVER.SYS
                         (convert it to a device file)
```

Note: You don't want to name the ASM file (or any file) CHARDEV because after the driver is installed, there will be no way to specify that filename; the device by that name will always take precedence.

Next, place the command

```
DEVICE=MYDRIVER.SYS
```

into the CONFIG.SYS file. If you don't already have such a file, create one that has only that line. Finally, you must reboot the system to force DOS to install the driver. The first thing you will see is

```
Initializing CHARDEV driver
```

Now try some experiments with the new device. In the following example sessions, the words enclosed in square brackets are displayed by CHARDEV; the underlined characters are entered at the keyboard. This example uses CHARDEV as an output device:

```
COPY CON: CHARDEV:ENTER

ABC 123ENTER                    this text is entered at the
                                keyboard

^ZENTER

[Output request: a]            these lines are immediately
                                displayed

[Output request: b]

[Output request: c]

[Output request:  ]

[Output request: 1]

[Output request: 2]

[Output request: 3]

[Output request:  ]

[Output request:  ]

        1 file(s) copied
```

In this example, CHARDEV answered nine output requests by sending nine characters to the screen. A command such as copy MYFILE.TXT CHARDEV: might take hours as each character in the file MYFILE.TXT is painfully scrolled down the screen. In the following example, CHARDEV is used as an input device:

```
COPY CHARDEV: CON: ENTER

[Input request: ] t          these characters were entered
                             one at a time

[Input request: ] e

[Input request: ] x

[Input request: ] t

[Input request: ] ENTER

[Input request: ] ^Z

[Input request: ] ENTER

text                         these characters are immediately
                             displayed

        1 file(s) copied
```

You may try using CHARDEV as a file to be edited or try copying it to a file, or even opening and reading from it or writing to it from BASIC. You will soon tire of these antics and remove CHARDEV from your configuration file. But do comb through Listing 5.5 and compare it to the RAM drive listing in the DOS 2.0 manual. Use it to understand the device driver documentation in that manual. This will give you some real insight into how PC-DOS perceives devices and will give you a head start when you need to write your own keyboard, disk, or printer device driver.

**THINGS TO DO**

1. Use DEBUG to disassemble the ANSI.SYS keyboard driver. Use the D command to examine bytes 106H and 108H in order to find the addresses of the strategy and interrupt procedures. Remember that DEBUG will create a PSP, which DOS won't do when it installs the driver. Thus, every address in the program will differ by 100H from what it would be if it had been loaded as a device driver.

2. Write a more sophisticated CHARDEV that will handle an input request by reading (buffering) an entire line of text via PC-DOS service 0AH. Then have it transfer one character from that buffer back to DOS for every output request.

3. Change the STRATEGY procedure so that it truly enqueues requests into a circular buffer. Write the corresponding code for the INTERRUPT procedure so that it will dequeue the oldest request.

4.   Use DEBUG to search through low memory until you locate the device headers for CON, LPT1, and the block device drivers for the disk drives. (Hint: The first driver starts somewhere above 500:0000. Use DEBUG's S command to search for a recognized device name. Once you've found the first driver, use the next-device-pointer to work your way through the chain of device headers.) Use your knowledge of device drivers to figure out how they operate.

5.   (*) Write your own standard input device driver that won't allow anyone into your system until a password has been entered.

6.   (**) Write a printer driver that contains page-formatting functions. Have it check for lines that begin with a recognizable sequence and format the pages accordingly. Have it check for and handle the following commands:

```
.S:n            to set line spacing to n blank lines
                between lines

.N:nnn          to set the current page number

.H:text[###]    to create a header on each page (### =
                include current page)
```

You can make this device as sophisticated as you'd like, including having it scan through each line for special sequences such as "Ital" for setting your printer into the Italics mode. It can map the embedded commands to a set of strings for various printers on your system.

# Chapter 6

# Macros and
# Super Macros

## 6.1 INTRODUCTION TO MACROS

One of the most powerful features of the IBM-PC MACRO Assembler is its advanced macro capability. Macros are used like opcode mnemonics; the difference is that these are opcodes that *you* define. Simply stated, a *macro* is a predefined set of assembler instructions that can be used in different parts of a program with some optional modifications each time it is used.

Macros can be used as simple shorthand for often used sequences of commands, but that is only the tip of the iceberg. Macro programming can be as complex and fascinating as any programming language. In fact, the IBM-PC MACRO Assembler offers so much flexibility in its macro capability that a program that uses macros extensively may strongly resemble a high-level language.

It should be noted that many programmers prefer to avoid using macros. For one thing, 64K IBM PCs host only the small assembler (ASM), which doesn't support macros. Also, programs that employ macros tend to take longer to assemble because the assembler has more work to do. Finally, programming with macros can be tricky; a macro can hide a program error and make debugging more difficult.

On the other hand, proper care in defining and testing a macro can eliminate the most common types of errors: mistyped and duplicated label names, loop control errors, and incorrect operating system calls. A library of macros may be kept in a separate file (brought in with the INCLUDE pseudo-op) to shorten the length of a listing. The IF1/ENDIF conditional pseudo-ops can surround the macro definition to speed up assembly.

First, we'll examine the components of a macro and look at some simple shorthand macros. Then we'll move into the abstract realm of complex macro programming.

### Components of a Macro

There are four parts to a macro definition. All macros have a *name*, a *beginning*, a *body*, and an *end*. They can, and most often do, specify a list of one or more *dummy names*. Here is an outline of the basic macro:

```
name MACRO [[dummy][,dummy]...]        ;the beginning

    .

    .                                  ;the body

    .

    ENDM                               ;the end
```

The *name* is a standard assembler symbol (1 to 31 alphanumeric characters, including the special characters: ? @ _ $). It is used to invoke the macro, just as an opcode mnemonic is used to invoke a CPU function. In fact, the *name* can be the same as some assembler reserved words (such as an opcode mnemonic) in order to redefine what that word does.

The *dummy* names are a list of values, separated by commas, that will be used within the macro. They are the names of temporary variables whose values may be changed with each new macro invocation. When you invoke the macro, you specify parameters that correspond to each of the dummy names. These parameters can be numeric or text, including register names, opcode mnemonics, other macro names, and program labels. Normally, you separate the parameters with commas, but the assembler also recognizes spaces and tabs as valid delimiters.

The body of the macro consists of labels, opcodes, pseudo-ops, and comments—in other words, lines of assembler source code. When the macro is invoked, it is expanded so that dummy names referenced in the body are replaced with the characters entered as macro parameters. Let's look at a specific example. The following macro uses a BIOS interrupt to set the cursor position.

```
LOCATE MACRO    LINE,COLUMN
       MOV      BH,0        ;select video page 0
       MOV      DH,LINE     ;select desired screen line
       MOV      DL,COLUMN   ;  and column
       MOV      AH,2        ;BIOS SET_CUR_POS function
       INT      10H         ;invoke the service
       ENDM
```

For example, if you invoke this macro like this:

```
       LOCATE   0,25
```

then *line* will be replaced by the single character '0' and *column* will be replaced by the character '25'. The code that is generated will look like this:

```
MOV      BH,0

MOV      DH,0

MOV      DL,25

MOV      AH,2

INT      10H
```

Whenever your program must change the position of the cursor, you can use LOCATE as if it were an opcode. If you expect to do a lot of cursor manipulation, this macro will come in quite handy. Here are some examples:

```
LOCATE   10,0         ;set cursor to line 10,
                      ;leftmost column

LOCATE   10,AL        ;line 10, column specified
                      ;by AL register

LOCATE   CUR_LINE,0   ;use a memory variable

LOCATE   0,CENTER     ; or an equate established
                      ; earlier
```

### Pros and Cons of Using Macros

There are several advantages to using this macro instead of entering the individual opcodes. You will avoid some typing; you won't need to look up the interrupt number or service code; and you won't make errors such as forgetting to specify the video page number. What could be safer?

The LOCATE macro is a "little black box" that handles the details of positioning the cursor. Although that is its strength, it is also its weakness. The macro is opaque; you can use it without seeing what it does. Consider the problem that could occur if you used the following loop to print lines of characters on the screen.

```
        MOV      BH,0

AGAIN:  LOCATE   BH,0          ;invoke LOCATE macro,

                               ;specifying line BH

        CALL     PRINT_LINE ;print next line of text

        INC      BH

        CMP      BH,24         ;done with screen?

        JBE      AGAIN         ; no, loop back
```

The BH register is used here to indicate the screen line; it is also used as the loop counter. Everything looks fine until the macro is expanded, and you can see that BH is altered on every pass through the loop. In this example, the consequences would be disastrous: The program would enter an endless loop (oops, reach for the Big Red Switch).

This problem can be compounded by using the .SALL (Suppress ALL macro expansion listings) pseudo-op. You could use it to shorten lengthy listings that contain many macro expansions. If you do, you'll have a hard time tracking down the bug. One way to avoid these invisible errors is to be sure that a macro saves and restores (PUSHes and POPs) any registers that it alters. Another possibility is to place a comment line within the macro body indicating that registers have been altered:

```
.LALL   ;***** NOTICE! AH and BH have been changed! *****
.SALL
```

So, knowing the possible hazards of macro programming, we forge on.

### THINGS TO DO

1. Identify two errors in this macro. One is a macro syntax error, and the other is a typical programming oversight.

   ```
   DOS_INT   MACRO   SERVICE_ID
             MOV     AH,SERVICE_ID
             INT     21
             END
   ```

2. After correcting the macro, determine why it would be unwise to make it totally transparent by saving and restoring AX.

3. Write a series of macros that handle the most often used DOS and BIOS service calls.

### Synthetic Opcodes

The name of the macro can be the same as an opcode mnemonic. Therefore, you can redefine what any opcode does. Additionally, macros can be used to synthesize new opcodes and extend the 8088 instruction set. The 8088 instruction set does not include any conditional CALL or RET opcodes (i.e., CALL Z,MY_SBRTN). If you want to call a routine only when a condition is met, you must test for the reverse condition and use a conditional jump to branch around the call instruction. In other words, when you want to call a subroutine only after a comparison comes out equal, you would need to code this sequence:

```
        CMP     AX,BX       ;are they equal?

        JNE     SKIP        ; reverse the Equal criteria

                            ; and go if not

        CALL    MY_SBRTN    ; else, it's your nickel
SKIP:

        ;program continues
```

It is surprising to see such a fundamental omission from the otherwise rich 8088 instruction set. One immediate drawback is that we programmers are required to make up ever more meaningless label names to avoid a code 4 "Redefinition of Symbol" error. However, it is easy to create a macro that performs the correct sequence.

### The LOCAL and Ampersand (&) Macro Operators

There are two important macro programming tricks needed to write a conditional call macro. One is to use a LOCAL label as the landing pad of the jump. LOCAL labels are generated by the assembler and are unique to an individual invocation of a macro. The LOCAL declaration must be the first command following the head of the macro. Specifically, you must avoid placing comment lines between the MACRO line and the LOCAL line.

The other trick is to use the ampersand (&) special macro operator to "build" the correct conditional jump. The ampersand is used to concatenate pieces of text in a macro. By using it, you can put part of an opcode or label in the body of a macro and specify the rest of it as a parameter. The following macro definition adds conditional calls to the 8088 instruction set.

```
CALL_IF MACRO   COND,SBRTN

        LOCAL   SKIP

        JN&COND SKIP

        CALL    SBRTN
SKIP:

        ENDM
```

The COND parameter must be one of A, AE, B, BE, G, GE, L, LE, E, C, O, S, Z, or P, that is, any set of characters that, when preceded by a JN, will constitute a valid conditional jump mnemonic. The SBRTN is the name of a procedure defined elsewhere in the program. Here's how to use CALL_IF in a program:

```
        CMP     CUR_LINE,24

        CALL_IF AE,SCROLL_SCREEN     ;call only if it's

                                     ;Above or Equal to 24
```

When the macro is expanded, it generates this code:

```
    JNAE      ??0000
    CALL      SCROLL_SCREEN
??0000:
```

Note: The ??0000 symbol is the assembler's way of creating a unique temporary label or variable name. Subsequent uses of the CALL_IF macro would create label names such as ??0001, ??0002, and so on. These labels are listed in the symbol table summary at the end of the source code, just as if you had created them yourself.

If you have ever wondered why the assembler allows so much latitude in specifying conditional jumps, this example may make it clear. The flag test of every jump mnemonic can be reversed just by inserting an *n* before the character of the condition. The people who wrote MACRO Assembler were aware of the shortcomings of the 8088 vis-à-vis conditional jumps (e.g., the 127-byte reach of a conditional branch and the lack of conditional CALL and RET opcodes). This flexibility in specifying the condition takes the pressure off of the people at Intel.

## Conditional DO Macro

Some ancient 4-bit microprocessors included a condition prefix opcode. In effect, this opcode says, "if this condition is met, do the following opcode; otherwise, skip it." We can synthesize this prefix by defining a DO_IF macro:

```
DO_IF    MACRO     COND,TEXT
         LOCAL     SKIP
         JN&COND   SKIP
         TEXT
SKIP:
         ENDM
```

Note: If TEXT is more than one word, it must be surrounded by angle brackets to keep it as a single parameter: <MOV AX, BYTE PTR [DI]>.

The DO_IF "synthetic" opcode can become one of the most often used devices in your toolbox. The test-and-skip sequence is integral to assembly language programming, and quite often branches skip a single opcode. The DO_IF macro introduces the concepts of conditional data transfers and conditional arithmetic. A typical example will illustrate the point. This code is part of a binary to hexadecimal-ASCII conversion routine. It converts the 4-bit binary value in the AL register into a one of the hex digits 0-9 and A-F.

```
CMP       AL,9                              ;will it convert to
                                            ;ASCII correctly?
DO_IF     A,<ADD    AL,7>                   ; if not, adjust
                                            ; for conversion
OR        AL,30H                            ;AL becomes '0'-'9'
                                            ;or 'A'-'F'
```

## Macros and the 8087 Coprocessor

Synthetic opcodes are often seen in programs that instruct the 8087 number cruncher or the 8089 input/output processor chips. These coprocessors work in tandem with the 8088 (or 8086) microprocessor and take their instructions directly from the stream of opcodes that normally affect only the 8088 CPU. For example, to instruct the 8087 to perform an 80-bit floating point division, a program will contain a series of bytes beginning with the WAIT and ESC opcodes and ending with numeric values specifying the action for the 8087 to take and the registers (or memory operands) to use. We might specify a floating point divide with:

```
WAIT
ESC       6,0F1H
```

As you can see, this instruction is far from meaningful. It doesn't look much like a division instruction. The beads of an abacus could tell you more! We can make programming of the 8087 much easier by preparing a set of macros that define each of its instructions.

```
FDIV   MACRO
       DB   9bH,0deH,0f1H
       ENDM
```

Here's another example that uses an addressing mode argument as part of the macro. The FBLD opcode loads a 10-byte packed BCD value into the 8087's internal stack for further manipulation. The following macro generates instructions to do so and specifies the address of the 10-byte argument:

```
FBLD   MACRO  ADDR
       WAIT
       ESC    3CH,TBYTE PTR ADDR
       ENDM
```

This instruction will generate the correct opcodes to FBLD data addressed with any valid addressing mode:

```
FBLD    PACKED_DATA

FBLD    PACKED_ARRAY[SI]

FBLD    CS:PACKED_DATA

FBLD    ES:[DI+BX].FLOAT_ACCUMULATOR
```

Knowing that you can define mnemonics for coprocessors, you can see that it is possible to define the instruction set for any microprocessor. It would take some effort, but you could define the entire Z-80 instruction set as macros, and then use the MACRO Assembler to assemble Z-80 mnemonics into Z-80 machine language. With even more work, you could define macros that would assemble Z-80 mnemonics into 8088 opcodes. This cross-assembly capability is often used in hardware development laboratories for writing code for new processors. It is likely that the first 8088/8086 programs were written using the macro capabilities of an 8080 or Z-80 assembler.

### Enhanced Assembler Mnemonics

Finally, macros can be used to mask the differences between two slightly different assemblers. Some assemblers, including the tiny assembler that is used in the A command of DEBUG 2.0, do not keep track of procedure blocks. In order to code a FAR return from a subroutine, you must use the RETF opcode. You can create your own RETF opcode for use with the MACRO Assembler with a simple macro:

```
RETF    MACRO

        DB          0CBH

        ENDM
```

The conditional pseudo-ops discussed later in this chapter provide the means to generate a RETF with the optional stack displacement (an intersegment return that discards parameters that have been PUSHed onto the stack).

The MACRO Assembler provides no way to make a direct FAR call to an absolute address. That is, you can never say:

```
CALL    0F600:0003   ;not allowed
```

A direct call such as this requires the definition of a dummy segment and a label within that segment. Then you can make a call to that label. The following CALLF macro will overcome this inconvenience.

```
CALLF   MACRO    SEG_ADDR,OFFSET_ADDR

        DB       9AH     ;generate the intersegment FAR call

        DW       OFFSET_ADDR

        DW       SEG_ADDR

        ENDM
```

This instruction will not allow you to specify a segment and offset in the normal manner (i.e., separated by a colon). Like all macros, this one expects the two values to be separated by either a comma or a space:

```
CALL     0F600H  0003H
```

## THINGS TO DO

1.  Write a RET_IF macro (a counterpart to the CALL_IF macro) that will force a return from a subroutine depending on a given condition.

2.  Extend the DO_IF macro so that it will execute up to five opcodes when a condition is met. (Hint: When the macro is expanded, all dummy names that correspond to blank parameters will be ignored.)

3.  Try experimenting with nested macros. That is, within the body of one macro, invoke a second macro. Try passing parameters from the outermost to the innermost macro.

## 6.2 SELF-MODIFYING MACROS

Macros can contain any number of program lines using any of the opcodes, pseudo-ops, labels, or macros that the assembler knows. Thus, you can define macros that include segment, procedure, and data definitions. You can even write a macro that defines a new macro or redefines itself.

A macro that redefines itself can be used to place the source code of a subroutine into a program. One argument against writing a lengthy macro is that every time it is invoked, the entire piece of code is assembled into the program. This operation is faster than calling a subroutine; but it can be less than efficient when program size is significant. This problem can be circumvented by using a macro that generates a subroutine the first time it is invoked, and then redefines itself so that thereafter it generates a call to that subroutine. Listing 6.1, the CLS macro, does just that.

The CLS function is a good example because it defines a procedure that requires no parameters. Once it is in place, it need only be called to perform its task. The first time the CLS macro is invoked, it generates the CLS_SUB procedure and then creates a new CLS macro that calls that procedure. The first code generated by the macro is a branch around the CLS_SUB code. It ensures that the procedure will never be executed except when it is called. It is interesting to note that once the macro has been redefined, it invokes itself. You're looking at a self-modifying and self-invoking macro.

Note: A self-invoking macro has the potential of putting the assembler in an infinite loop. Be sure that if a macro invokes itself, either it is redefined (so that the modified version does not invoke itself) or a mechanism is provided to exit from the loop. (See the discussion of the IFDEF pseudo-op in Section 6.3.)

## Listing 6.1
## CLS Macro

```
;-----------------------------------------------------------
; Listing 6.1  CLS macro
;
; Example of a self-modifying macro.
; Clears the page 0 video screen, leaving each position
;  with a normal attribute (white character/black background),
;  and places the cursor in the top left-hand corner of the screen.
;
; Preserves all registers
;
; The first time this is invoked, a NEAR procedure is created,
;  starting at the point of the invocation, and the procedure is
;  executed.  Thereafter, a CLS directive is just a call to that
;  procedure.
;
; Note: Can't be defined between IF1 and ENDIF.

cls       MACRO
          LOCAL   skip
          jmp     short   skip
cls_sub proc      near
          push    ax
          push    bx
          push    cx
          push    dx

          mov     cx,0        ;top left-hand corner of "window"
          mov     dh,24
          mov     dl,79       ;bottom right-hand corner
          mov     bh,7        ;attribute for the screen
          mov     al,0        ;special parameter:  blank entire window
          mov     ah,6
          int     10H

          mov     dx,0        ;cursor to top left-hand corner
          mov     ah,2
          int     10H

          pop     dx
          pop     cx
          pop     bx
          pop     ax
          ret
cls_sub endp

  cls       MACRO             ;second definition of the macro
            call    cls_sub
            ENDM

skip:   cls                   ;invoke the newly defined macro
        ENDM
```

The value of this self-modifying technique is dubious for two reasons. First, it needlessly introduces some confusion into the program (a CALL CLS command is just as clear as a CLS macro invocation). Second, a self-modifying macro must be available on both passes of the assembler, so the IF1 pseudo-op can't be used to speed up the assembly and shorten the listing. The upcoming discussion of the IF1 pseudo-op will clarify the reasons for this limitation.

## 6.3 CONDITIONAL PSEUDO-OPS

Although conditional pseudo-ops are not exclusively associated with macros, only the simplest uses of this assembler feature have any meaning outside of the context of macro programming. Conditional assembly is an advanced feature of the MACRO Assembler and, like macro definition, it is most useful to experienced programmers with special needs. Table 6.1 lists the conditional pseudo-ops with a brief description of each.

**Table 6.1**
**Conditional Pseudo-Ops**

```
IF expression
    The following source code is assembled only when expression is
    evaluated as being not 0.

IFE expression
    The following source code is assembled only when expression is
    evaluated as being 0.

IF1
    The following source code is assembled only during the first pass
    of the assembler.  IF1 has no argument.

IF2
    The following source code is assembled only during the second pass
    of the assembler.  IF2 has no argument.

IFDEF symbol
    When symbol has been defined or declared external, the following
    lines are assembled.  MASM only.

IFNDEF symbol
    When symbol has not been defined or declared external, the following
    lines are assembled.  MASM only.

IFB <argument>
    If argument is blank, then the following lines are assembled.
    Used mainly to determine if an argument has been passed to
    a macro.  The angle brackets are required.  MASM only.

IFNB <argument>
    If argument is not blank, then the following lines are assembled.
    Used mainly to determine if an argument has been passed to a macro.
    The angle brackets are required.  MASM only.

IFIDN <argument_1>,<argument_2>
    If all characters of argument_1 are identical to those of
    argument_2, the following lines are assembled.  The angle brackets
    are required.  MASM only.

IFDIF <argument_1>,<argument_2>
    If the characters of argument_1 are not identical to those of
    argument_2, the following lines are assembled.  The angle brackets
    are required.  MASM only.

ELSE (no paramters)
    Begins a block of code that will be assembled only if a preceding
    conditional pseudo-op was evaluated as being false.  Usage is optional.

ENDIF (no parameters)
    Ends a block started by a Conditional pseudo-op.
```

The IF and IFE conditionals can open up whole new realms of possibilities to macro programming. When used in conjunction with the assembler's internal variables, it is possible to write sophisticated macros—macros that test values established in other macros, macros that ascertain whether input parameters are in range, even macros that can modify code that has been assembled earlier. Because macros can assign and test variables as well as use iteration structures, macro programming is a language unto itself. Before moving on to these more advanced concepts, we'll establish a foundation by discussing the basics of conditional pseudo-ops.

Each of the IF constructs must be ended with an ENDIF. An ELSE can be placed between the IF and the ENDIF to handle instances of the opposite condition. Use of ELSE is optional, and only one ELSE is allowed per IF.

It's easy to get tangled up in a maze of nested IFs. It is helpful to visualize the consequences of an IF/ELSE/ENDIF construct by indenting the code as you write it. The best way to do that is to enter the IF line and immediately drop down to the next line and enter the corresponding ENDIF. Then *insert* lines between the two, indenting them all to the same depth. When you nest another IF, repeat the action, indenting the inserted lines more deeply. This action ensures that every IF will have an ENDIF and that all steps that take place will stand out for easy recognition.

```
IF CONDITION1
    IF CONDITION2   ;condition1 must be true
       (COMMAND)    ;condition2 is also true
       (COMMAND)
    ELSE
       (COMMAND)    ;condition1 is true,
                    ;but condition2 is false
    ENDIF           ;end of inner nest level
ELSE
    (COMMAND)       ;condition1 is false
    (COMMAND)
ENDIF               ;end of outer nest level
(COMMANDS)          ;always assembled
```

## Misuse of Conditional Pseudo-Ops

It must be clearly understood that conditional pseudo-ops of themselves do not generate machine language instructions. I have seen a novice programmer puzzle over this piece of code, wondering why it wouldn't assemble:

```
      IF        CX = 0
         JMP       DONE
      ENDIF
```

Just remember that conditional pseudo-ops make decisions *about* your program. They do not generate code that makes decisions *in* your program.

I have also seen that error in reverse. A novice programmer was attempting to use a conditional jump mnemonic to control the action of a macro expansion. The following example was supposed to generate one of two different messages in the data segment, depending on a macro parameter:

```
DEF_MSG MACRO    MSG_NUM
            CMP      MSG_NUM,1
            JNE      MSG_2
            DB       'THIS IS MESSAGE NUMBER 1'
            JMP      EXIT
    MSG_2:  DB       'THIS IS MESSAGE NUMBER 2'
    EXIT:
            ENDM
```

The programmer thought that JNE would redirect the flow of assembly of the macro. Conditional jump mnemonics do not control the actions of the assembler as it processes your source text.


## IF1: Macros and the 2-Pass Assembler

We have already seen the only real use of the IF1 condition: It allows the assembler to skip through macro definitions on the second pass through the source code. Once the assembler has coded a macro internally, it doesn't need to do so again. The one exception occurs when a macro redefines itself. To understand why the CLS macro (Listing 6.1) must be assembled on both passes, we must have some understanding of what the assembler does on each pass.

Pass 1 does not generate any machine language opcodes. Its purpose is to build a symbol table containing a name, segment, type, and offset reference for each label in the source code. Pass 2 looks to that symbol table whenever it encounters a reference to a label. For example, in order to generate the object code for CALL MY_PROC, the assembler must know where MY_PROC is relative to the calling instruction.

In pass 1, the CLS macro generates 36 opcode bytes the first time it is invoked, and only three bytes thereafter. But in pass 2, it generates exactly three bytes *every time it is invoked.* Therefore, the symbol table created on pass 1 will contain offsets that differ from the offsets encountered on pass 2. The assembler recognizes this condition and calls it a "phase error."

The point is that when you use the IF1 conditional, you run the risk of creating a phase error. Therefore, you should "play assembler" to see if any address labels will be altered between passes.

### Different Versions of One Program

IF and IFE are most often used when writing programs that come in more than one version. There are many IBM-PC "work-alike" computers on the market and even more 8088-based computers. It is likely that a program written for the IBM PC will need only slight modifications to make it work on one of these other machines. A simplified example illustrates how these pseudo-ops are usually used:

```
VERSION EQU        0         ;change to 1 for XT version

        .

        .

DATA_SEG SEGMENT PARA PUBLIC 'DATA'
IFE VERSION
 TITLE_MSG     DB    'Ultra Program for the IBM PC'
ENDIF
IF VERSION EQ 1
 TITLE_MSG     DB    'Extra Ultra Deluxe Program for the IBM XT'
ENDIF

        .

        .

DATA_SEG ENDS
```

In the first conditional, the expression that is evaluated is the single operand VERSION. When it is 0, the following code is generated. The second conditional shows a more complex expression, and this is where BASIC programmers may run into some problems.

In BASIC, the equals sign (=) has the dual purpose of assignment and relational testing. The MACRO Assembler uses EQU and = only for assigning values to internal variables. When you write an expression to be evaluated by the conditional pseudo-ops, you must use the relational operators EQ, NE, LT, LE, GT, and GE (see Chapter 3).

In this example, when the value of VERSION is 1, the expression is evaluated as being true, so the following code is assembled. (Note: MACRO Assembler release 1.00 incorrectly evaluates some expressions containing relational operators. These operators work only with unsigned numbers, so the assembler does not recognize that -1 is LT 0. See Listing 6.11 at the end of this chapter for an example of how to overcome the problem.)

As you begin to write more complex programs, you will often place debugging code into your source file. For example, you may insert instructions to print the values of certain variables or indicate that a certain procedure was executed. By surrounding these debugging aids with IF DEBUGGING and ENDIF, and setting up an equate (DEBUGGING EQU 1), you won't need to keep two copies of the source code. To switch from debugging copy to production copy, you only need to change the equate to read DEBUGGING EQU 0.

Another example of the IF pseudo-op is demonstrated in Chapter 7. It is used there to mask the differences between interpreted and compiled BASIC. This procedure makes it possible to write only one version of a routine that can be interfaced with either form of BASIC.

### IFDEF and IFNDEF: Checking for External Symbols

IFDEF (IF DEFined) and IFNDEF (IF Not DEFined) are most often used in conjunction with calls to external subroutines. Assume you have a text file that contains a procedure that is usually brought into a program via the INCLUDE command. Normally, you have complete control of this action:

```
CALL    MY_PROC
.
.
INCLUDE MY_PROC.ASM
```

But a call to MY_PROC might be "hidden" in a macro (for example, a CLS macro might finish up by calling a LOCATE procedure to position the cursor in the top left-hand corner of the screen). It makes sense to code the macro to contain the INCLUDE command that will bring the file into the program. However, we don't want the LOCATE code to be included every time we invoke the CLS macro. The IFNDEF pseudo-op can be used to include the LOCATE procedure only the first time CLS is invoked.

```
CLS     MACRO
        LOCAL TAG

        .

        . (CODE TO CLEAR THE SCREEN)

        .

        MOV     DX,0
        CALL    LOCATE
        IFNDEF  LOCATE
        JMP     SHORT TAG
```

```
            INCLUDE  B:LOCATE.ASM   ;all the lines of LOCATE
                                    ;are included here
      ENDIF
TAG:
      ENDM
```

## IFIDN and IFDIF: Testing Macro String Parameters

The IF pseudo-op must always evaluate numerical arguments. When you want the condition to depend on the comparison of two strings, use the IFIDN (If IDeNtical) and the IFDIF (IF DIFferent) conditional pseudo-ops. They are most useful for testing string parameters that have been inputted to a macro. The following example generates a special message when certain persons' names are used as input parameters.

```
SAY_HI_TO MACRO PERSON
      IFIDN <PERSON>,<FRED>
        DB   'Hiya Fred! How's Wilma and Pebbles?'
      ELSE
        IFIDN <PERSON> <YOGI>
          DB   'Hello, Yogi. Hungry for a pik-a-nik'
          DB   'basket?'
        ELSE
          DB   'Good afternoon, whoever you are!'
        ENDIF
      ENDIF
```

Usage examples:

```
      SAY_HI_TO  FRED     ;generates special greeting
      SAY_HI_TO  MATILDA  ;generates general greeting
```

You should recognize a very powerful potential here. The IFIDN conditional pseudo-op checks for a match with any character or string of characters. You can use it to write macros that interpret keywords to generate code like a high-level language compiler. For example, you could write a SCREEN macro that looks for the keywords *text* or *graphics* and then invokes the ROM-BIOS service to set the correct screen mode. The keywords could include special symbols such as the plus (+) or division (/) signs. Remembering that macro parameters can be separated by spaces, envision a macro that parses and generates code for a line such as MY_VARIABLE = AX + CX.

## IFB and IFNB: Checking for Optional Parameters

The IFB (IF Blank) and IFNB (IF Not Blank) conditional pseudo-ops are very useful in defining flexible macros. These conditionals can be used to determine if all of the parameters were specified when the macro was invoked. Depending on that determination, the macro can assume that certain defaults were requested, take (or omit) special actions, or simply flag the code as an error.

BASIC programmers are accustomed to using commands that have a series of optional parameters. For example, the graphic LINE command will draw a line in the default color unless a different color is specified. If the command ends in 'B', a box is drawn. If it ends in 'BF', a box is drawn and filled with the specified color. The result is that a single command does a lot of things. Microsoft could have included a BOX command, but most of the code would be a duplicate of the line command.

The LOCATE command is another case in point. BASIC programmers most often use it to set the cursor position, but if some additional parameters are tacked onto the command, it will also change the shape of the cursor. Listing 6.2 is a macro that simulates the BASIC command by combining both of these cursor-related functions into a single extended command that allows optional parameters.

The SET_CURSOR macro uses IFNB several times in order to determine what it needs to do. Let's walk through the steps of this macro "program." First, the macro generates code to save the values of the registers that will be altered. Then it takes care of the cursor-type arguments. You'll notice from the comments that if the cursor size is to be changed or the cursor is explicitly made visible, both of the cursor size parameters must be specified. The FLAG variable is used here because the assembler won't allow a question such as "IF CURSOR EQ 0" when CURSOR is a dummy name that hasn't been given a value.

When CURSOR has been given a value of 0, the ROM-BIOS SET_CUR_TYPE call is made, indicating a START value of 16. This procedure makes the cursor invisible. Alas, there is no way to keep the cursor from blinking except through software-controlled cursor management (i.e., displaying a character at the cursor position and updating its position with each keystroke). If you go through this procedure, the first step is to make the blinking "hardware" cursor invisible.

The next thing SET_CURSOR does is to generate the code to set the cursor location. That is somewhat complicated. I wanted this macro to have all of the flexibility of the LOCATE command in BASIC. If the command line specifies one but not both of the screen coordinates, code must be generated to fetch the value of the other ordinate. That is, if LINE but not CLM *or* CLM but not LINE, the macro must invoke the ROM-BIOS INT 10H, service 1. An *either/or* question is harder to code than a simple *and* condition. I chose to use a truth flag that indicates which possibilities are true. The FLAG variable is set to 0, 1, or 2 to show whethere neither, only one, or both parameters were entered.

Once the value of FLAG has been determined, the macro fetches the current line and column by calling the ROM-BIOS service (if needed). It then sets up the registers to prepare to call another ROM-BIOS service to set the cursor position (if needed). Finally, all the registers that were used during the process are restored to their original values, and the macro expansion is finished. Notice that SET_CURSOR is flexible enough to interpret correctly up to 15 different combinations of blank and nonblank parameters.

## Listing 6.2
## SET_CURSOR Macro

```
;--------------------------------------------------
; Listing 6.2  (SET_CURSOR macro)
;
; SET_CURSOR [line] [,[clm] [,[cursor] [,start,stop]]]
;
; Calls the ROM-BIOS service to position the cursor and
; (optionally) change the size of the cursor or turn it off.  The
;   cursor> default is 1 (visible).  If it is 0, then the cursor is
;   invisible.
; The start,stop option indicates the size of the cursor.
; Examples:
;    SET_CURSOR 20,10        ;line 20, clm 10
;    SET_CURSOR 20           ;line 20, current clm
;    SET_CURSOR ,10          ;current line, clm 10
;    SET_CURSOR ,,0,7        ;size of cursor is 8 scan lines
;    SET_CURSOR ,,0          ;cursor is invisible
;    SET_CURSOR ,,1,6,7      ;cursor is visible, lowest 2 scan lines
;
; Either or both of line or clm may be blank.
; Both start and stop must be specified if either is, or
;   if cursor is specified and is not 0.

SET_CURSOR  macro   line, clm, cursor, start, stop

        push    ax
        push    bx
        push    cx
        push    dx

        flag = 1
        ifnb <cursor>
          flag = cursor
        endif
        ife flag       ;if cursor is 0 then . . .
         mov    ch,16
         mov    cl,0
         mov    ah,1
         int    10H     ;make cursor invisible
        endif

        ifnb <start>
         ifnb <stop>    ;if both these parameters are present
          mov   ch,start
          mov   cl,stop
          mov   ah,1
          int   10H     ; . . . then set cursor type
         endif
        endif

        flag = 0
        ifnb <line>
          flag = 1
        endif
        ifnb <clm>
          flag = flag + 1
        endif
```

**Listing 6.2
(continued)**

```
      if flag EQ 1    ;if one, but not the other
        mov     bh,0
        mov     ah,3
        int     10H   ;get position into DH,DL
      endif           ;skip point if both line and clm specified

      if flag GT 0        ;skip if both are blank or both are specified
        ifnb <line>
          mov     dh,line ;alter line position
        endif
        ifnb <clm>
          mov     dl,clm  ;alter clm position
        endif

        if flag NE 1    ;BH is already set from above
          mov       bh,0
        endif
        mov       ah,2    ;call to set cursor position
        int       10H
      endif

      pop     dx
      pop     cx
      pop     bx
      pop     ax
    endm
```

**THINGS TO DO**

1. Improve the SAY_HI_TO macro so that it generates "Hello *name*" even if the person's name is not recognized.

2. Write a macro that sets the screen mode and clears the screen, and optionally sets each display attribute to a specified color (defaulting to white on black), and optionally sets the screen border color. Use Appendix B-1 to find the BIOS services that need to be invoked.

3. (*) Write a MATH macro that will generate the correct code for adding, subtracting, multiplying, or dividing two operands (memory or register) and storing the result in an indicated operand. The macro should generate the correct code for

```
MATH   WORD_VAR1 = WORD_VAR1 + WORD_VAR2

MATH   <WORD PTR [DI]> = WORD_ARRAY[SI+5] - 5F0H

MATH   CX = BL * BYTE_VAR
```

Try to preserve the values of all registers (except the destination, if it is a register). If you must alter any registers, be sure to display a message that will stand out in the listing.

4. (*) A challenge to idle programmers: Write a *recursive* macro that calculates factorial numbers. The macro should repeatedly invoke itself until all of the components of the number have been multiplied together, and then store the result as a 2-byte variable. For example,

```
FACTORIAL 5
```

should generate

```
DW      0078H
```

which is the product of 5 * 4 * 3 * 2 * 1.

## 6.4 REPEATING PSEUDO-OPS

The MACRO Assembler has a set of exotic tools that even the most experienced programmers may never use. The repeating pseudo-ops are used to replicate a series of source lines, with some optional modifications on each repetition. Although these pseudo-ops can be used just to save the typing of repetitious sequences and need not necessarily reside within a macro, they are most often used to give the macro programmer a form of loop control within the body of a macro.

The REPT (REPeaT), IRP (Iteration RePeat), and IRPC (Iteration RePeat by Character) pseudo-ops delineate the start of a block of code that is ended by an ENDM pseudo-op.

### REPT: Macro Iteration Control

The REPT pseudo-op is the simplest form of repetition. Its syntax is:

```
REPT      expression
```

It forces the assembler to process the block of source lines repeatedly. The number of passes is specified by the value of the *expression*. This procedure gives you a form of iteration control over the way the assembler processes your source text.

For instance, one feature the 68000 microprocessor has that the 8088 lacks is multiple incrementing and decrementing of register and memory operands. We could implement multiple incrementing on the 8088 with a macro as follows:

```
MINC    MACRO     OPERAND,COUNT
        IFB  <COUNT>
          INC   OPERAND
        ELSE
          REPT COUNT
            INC   OPERAND
```

```
        ENDM

    ENDIF

    ENDM
```

Perhaps the best use for REPT is in building look-up tables to speed program execution. For example, screen graphics programs often need to convert an X,Y coordinate pair into a video memory address. Part of this conversion involves multiplying a row (or line) value by 80 and then adding a constant of 2000H to odd-numbered lines (Chapter 8 gives the details). You can use MUL for the multiplication, but that is one of the most time-consuming opcodes.

You can shave precious milliseconds off the conversion routine by defining a look-up table that holds the starting addresses of each graphic line. Then, instead of calculating the address of the bits to be altered, you need only read a value from the table. The REPT pseudo-op can take the drudgery out of defining that table.

```
    .SALL               ;save some paper by suppressing the listing
ROW_TBL LABEL WORD
        LINE_NUM = 0
        REPT 100    ;define 2 line addresses per iteration
          DW    LINE NUM * 80           ;even lines
          DW    2000H + LINE_NUM * 80   ;odd lines
          LINE_NUM = LINE_NUM + 1
        ENDM
```

A program using this method can calculate the start of a graphics line with the following statement:

```
    MOV     SI,ROW_NO               ;get the Y ordinate
    SHL     SI,1                ;times 2 for word entries
    MOV     DI,ROW_TBL[SI]          ;fetch relevant line
                                    ;address into DI
```

This procedure takes exactly 24 clock cycles and can be shortened to 20 cycles if the table begins at the start of the data segment. Contrast that to the 130 cycles (143, worst case) that are needed when MUL is used. By letting the assembler do the calculations, we can save the program millions of cycles over the course of a game. Similar savings can be obtained in other graphics operations as well. Of course, the table requires 400 bytes of storage, but silicon is cheap. And the time savings can mean the difference between a game that sells and one that can't make the grade.

### IRP: Interpreting Multiple Macro Parameters

The IRP pseudo-op has great potential for use in sophisticated macros. It will read a sequence of parameters so that a macro can interpret each in turn. The syntax is

```
IRP     dummy,<argument[,argument . . .]>
```

The number of times the assembler will reassemble the block is determined by the number of arguments between the (required) angle brackets. For each repetition, the characters of the corresponding *argument* are used to define the value of the *dummy* in the body of the macro.

You can use IRP to aid in writing commands that have the flavor of a high-level language. You can even write macros that interpret a special "language" such as that of the DRAW and PLAY commands in BASIC. Imagine a macro that could read a command line and draw the shape represented by the arguments. For example, suppose that the letters U D L R mean to move Up, Down, Left, and Right and that C means to change the current default color. Further assume that you have a routine that will plot a dot at the screen coordinates specified by DX and CX in the color specified in AL (these are the parameters of the BIOS WRITE_DOT service of INT 10H).

Listing 6.3, the DRAW macro, will interpret a series of commands by generating a sequence of calls to a PLOT_DOT routine, altering the line and column pointers with each call. This is the most sophisticated macro we've examined, but its action is quite straightforward. It actually reads the parameters two at a time in two separate passes. When the CMD_PASS flag is false (0), the dummy argument CUR_ARG is interpreted as a number and saved for the next pass.

On alternate passes through the macro repeat loop, when the CMD_PASS flag is true (1), the CUR_ARG is interpreted as a motion or color command. For example, if it is U, the line ordinate (DX) is decremented (moved closer to the top of the screen) and the PLOT_DOT subroutine is called to light the pixel pointed to by DX and CX. This action of adjusting the pointer and plotting the dot is repeated the number of times specified by the previous numeric argument. For example, the command line

```
DRAW <1,C,  2,U,  1,L,  2,D>
```

generates this code:

```
MOV     AL,1         ; the 1,C

DEC     DX           ; the 2,U
CALL    PLOT_DOT     ;
DEC     DX           ;
CALL    PLOT_DOT     ;

DEC     CX           ; the 1,L
CALL    PLOT_DOT     ;

INC     DX           ; the 2,D
```

**Listing 6.3**
**DRAW Macro**

```
;------------------------------------------------------
; Listing 6.3  DRAW macro
;
; Uses IRP and REPT to interpret a "Shape Language" in the format:
;
;     num,command[,num,command...]
;
; where command is either a direction (U, D, L, R) or C (to change color)
; and num is either the number of pixels to draw in the direction, or the
; color selected for the C command.
; Works in conjunction with a PLOT_DOT subroutine that writes the color
; specified in AL to the screen coordinates in DX and CX (row,column).
; Example:
;         mov   cx,screen_clm
;         mov   dx,screen_row
;         DRAW <3,C, 4,U, 4,R, 4,D, 4,L> ;will draw a box in color 3 (white)
;
; Calls: PLOT_DOT
; Alters: AL, CX, DX

draw    MACRO cmd_text
        cmd_pass = 0        ;first parameter must be a number
        num = 0
        IRP cur_arg,<cmd_text>
          ife cmd_pass
            num = cur_arg     ;when not a command, save as num count

            cmd_pass = 1      ;set a flag so the next pass is command
          else
            cmd_pass = 0

            ifidn <cur_arg>,<C>
              mov   al,num        ;put the color into AL
            endif

            ifidn <cur_arg>,<U>  ;if Up
              REPT  num
                dec  dx
                call plot_dot
              ENDM
            endif

            ifidn <cur_arg>,<D>  ;if Down
              REPT  num
                inc  dx
                call plot_dot
              ENDM
            endif

            ifidn <cur_arg>,<R>  ;if Right
              REPT  num
                inc  cx
                call plot_dot
              ENDM
            endif

            ifidn <cur_arg>,<L>  ;if Left
              REPT  num
                dec  cx
                call plot_dot
              ENDM
            endif

          endif          ;end of the test for command pass
        ENDM             ;end the IRP
        ENDM             ;end of the DRAW macro
```

```
        CALL      PLOT_DOT  ;

        INC       DX        ;

        CALL      PLOT_DOT  ;
```

This macro does not generate concise code; a routine that sets up a software loop rather than in-line code would require less space. However, the DRAW macro generates the very fast code that would be needed for drawing small shapes in arcade-type games.

### IRPC: Manipulating a String Parameter

The IRPC pseudo-op can be used in applications similar to those of the DRAW macro. The assembler syntax is:

```
        IRPC dummy,string
```

The number of times the assembler will reassemble the block is determined by the number of characters in the *string* argument. For each repetition, all occurrences of *dummy* within the block will be replaced by the next character of the string.

I have seen this capability used to program a 4-bit microcomputer that controlled a hand-held data terminal. Predefined messages had to be broken down into a series of nibbles before being stored into the 4-bit PROM. The IRPC pseudo-op helped automate the process by breaking down that message into bytes so that each character could be further broken down into nibbles.

But the value of IRPC is not limited to special applications. Consider the labor that goes into defining the colorful shapes that are displayed in arcade-type games. The previous DRAW macro worked with individual pixels, but most shapes must be defined as groups of bytes in a shape table (again, refer to Chapter 8 for the particulars on IBM-PC graphics).

Each midresolution pixel on the IBM-PC graphics screen is defined by two bits. Manually breaking down a shape into its component bits and reassembling them into bytes can become a lengthy and cumbersome task. Macro Listing 6.4, COLORS, interprets a string of input characters as colors. It builds a table of bytes for a shape-drawing subroutine to move directly into video memory.

### Listing 6.4
### COLORS Macro

```
;----------------------------------------------------
; Listing 6.4 COLORS macro
;
; Uses the IRPC repeating pseudo-op to define bytes of a shape table.
; Interprets a string as mid resolution pixel colors:
;
; (space) = color 0
;    +        = color 1
;    #        = color 2
;    *        = color 3
;
; Example:
;          COLORS <****  #+>
;
; This invocation generates two DBs, the first is four pixels of
; color 3 (DB FFH) and the second will be four pixels of
; colors 0, 0, 2, 1 (DB 09H).
```

**Listing 6.4
(continued)**

```
colors  MACRO    color_text
        cur_byte = 0
        pel_count = 0

        IRPC  pel,<color_text>
          cur_byte = cur_byte * 4    ;shift it left by 2 bits

          ifidn  <pel>,<+>           ;+ is color 1
            cur_byte = cur_byte or 1
          endif

          ifidn  <pel>,<#>           ;# is color 2
            cur_byte = cur_byte or 2
          endif

          ifidn  <pel>,<*>           ;* is color 3
            cur_byte = cur_byte or 3
          endif

          pel_count = pel_count +1

          if pel_count EQ 4          ;when 4 pels are in place . . .
            db   cur_byte            ; store the accumulated value
            cur_byte = 0             ; and reinitialize counters
            pel_count = 0
          endif

        ENDM                    ;end the IRPC (loop back for next pel)
        if pel_count NE 0
        .lall ;*** error in COLOR macro: not defined in multiples of 4 ***
        .sall
        endif
        ENDM                        ;end the COLORS macro
```

The COLORS macro makes defining a complex shape as easy as this:

```
        .SALL     ;save paper on the listing

FACE    COLORS <   ************    > ;start of face shape

        COLORS <  **+++++++++++++**  >

        COLORS < *+++##+++++++##+++*  >

        COLORS <*+++#   #+++++#   #+++*>

        COLORS <*+++++##+++++++##+++++*>

        COLORS <*+++++++++*++++++++++*>

        COLORS <*++++++++++*++++++++++*>

        COLORS <*++   +++******+++   ++*>

        COLORS < *++    ++++++    ++* >

        COLORS <  **++           ++**  >

        COLORS <    ************    >
```

**THINGS TO DO**

1.  Write a REPT block that allocates and initializes storage for a table of square numbers (i.e., 1, 4, 9, 16, and so on).

2.  Write a subroutine that looks through that table and determines the square root of the value specified in AX.

## 6.5 DEBUGGING MACROS

Complex macros can be a time-saving and error-eliminating tool, a dream come true for the assembly language programmer. They can also turn into a nightmare. When you begin writing your own high-level function macros, be prepared for a major programming task. It is of paramount importance that the macro be fully tested and debugged so that when your program has a bug, you can be sure that it is not hidden in the macro expansion.

To test a macro, you must try it with a variety of parameters and carefully examine the code that is generated to be sure that it is performing as expected. When you find unexpected code in the expansion, or the assembler begins spewing error messages all over the listing, there are several tools at your disposal to track down the error.

While debugging a macro, use the .LALL (List ALL macro expansions) pseudo-op. Then trace through the expansion step by step. At this stage, it helps to have plenty of comments in the body of the macro. Later, you will want to use the .SALL (Suppress ALL macro expansions) pseudo-op so that your listings aren't cluttered with ENDIFs, DBs, and so on. You can also speed up the assembler by removing comments and spaces and abbreviating dummy names. But do that only after you are sure that the macro is flawless.

If the listing shows a phase error between passes, you can use the /D input parameter when you start the MACRO Assembler to create a listing for both passes. Try to find where the label offsets begin to vary. Finally, you can use the .LFCOND (List False CONDitional text) pseudo-op to see exactly which branch is being taken during each expansion of a macro.

Many macro errors can be traced to improper use of the IF and IFE pseudo-ops. Be sure to remember that the relational operators work only on unsigned (absolute) values.

## 6.6 MACROS FOR STRUCTURED PROGRAMMING

This section presents and discusses a group of related macros that may revolutionize the way you program. We have already discussed the merits of modular programming and seen that writing programs in discrete modules will increase your productivity by making them easier to read and debug. The techniques of *structured programming* go hand-in-hand with those of modular programming.

Most high-level languages encourage (even enforce) GOTO-less programming. They contain commands that make control of the flow of execution much less painful than it is in assembly language. Typical examples are WHILE/WEND, FOR/NEXT, and IF/ELSE/ENDIF structures. Programmers who write in both Pascal and assembly language are forced to change hats and write in two very different styles. Pascal programs have a clear structure; everything is done in blocks of code, so that the programmer is able to think in terms of program modules. Assembly language programs must explicitly specify every detail of the flow of execution; the simplest looping construct can be a spaghetti-like maze to trace and debug.

Program control structures are such handy gadgets that it makes sense to try to implement them in assembly language with macros. Let's take a look at what is required to set up a WHILE/WEND structure in assembly language. The following example will perform a series of steps until the DL register becomes 80.

```
TOP:
                CMP       DL,80    ;is terminating condition true?
                JNE       BODY     ; no, skip to the code to execute
                JMP       EXIT     ; yes, skip past the end of the loop
BODY:

                .
                . (the body: code to execute while DL  <> 80)
                .

                JMP       TOP      ;loop back for next pass
EXIT:
                (code to execute after DL becomes 80)
```

So, the elements of a flexible WHILE/WEND construct are:

* A label for the top of the structure                         (TOP)

* A label for the executable code                              (BODY)

* A label for the exit from the loop                           (EXIT)

* An opcode to compare two operands                      (CMP DL,80)

* A condition to be met                                       (Not Equal)

* A jump to execute the body when the condition is true   (JNE BODY)

* A jump to skip the code when the condition is false     (JMP EXIT)

* Code to execute while the condition is true             (the body)

* A jump code to get back to the top of the loop
  after each iteration                                       (JMP TOP)

It isn't possible to write a single macro to handle all of these requirements, mainly because a macro is unable to generate the jump needed to exit from the loop; it can't know the size of the body of the loop. The trick is to get two macros to work together, one to generate the condition-testing code and another to close the loop and provide an exit from it.

The macros used to implement full-featured WHILE/WEND structures are quite complex, so we will discuss them in three steps. The first step introduces the fundamental mechanisms. The second step shows how to make the macros reusable by assigning label addresses to internal assembler variables. Finally, we'll discuss (and solve) the problems of nesting in structured macros. By the end of the chapter, we'll have developed an entire system of interlocking macros that implement a spectrum of structured programming constructs, including WHILE/WEND, IF/ELSE/ENDIF, and FOR/NEXT loops.

## Step 1: Simple WHILE/WEND Structure

Let's begin by examining the mechanisms used to generate a single WHILE/WEND structure. The first macro, called WHILE, must be invoked with three parameters—two operands and a condition. It must generate the code that will compare the two operands. Then it must create a conditional jump to the body of the loop to be used when that comparison is true. When the condition is false, execution must fall through to an unconditional jump to exit the loop. However, when the WHILE macro is invoked, there is no way to know how far that jump will be. Therefore, this macro simply generates three NOPs to reserve an area for the correct jump opcode to be generated when it is known.

The WEND macro is the counterpart of the WHILE macro. It must first generate a backward jump that closes the loop. Then it starts the job of tying up the loose ends left by the WHILE macro, placing a loop-exit jump in the area reserved for that purpose. First it creates an exit label at the end of the code body. Then it instructs the assembler to go back, via the ORG pseudo-op, to the area reserved by the WHILE macro. There it generates a jump to the exit label. Finally, it instructs the assembler to resume assembling at the address it left off.

This is a complex procedure, so you should trace through the code very carefully and understand each of the steps involved. Listing 6.5 shows a preliminary version of the WHILE and WEND macros. These macros refer to address labels that are hard-coded into the program, so that nesting or even reuse in the same program is not allowed. Peruse this listing to get a feel for the fundamentals of the mechanism by which one macro alters the code created by another.

Listing 6.6, ASC2BIN, is an example of a procedure that uses a WHILE/WEND construct. It converts a string of ASCII digits into a binary number. The WHILE and WEND macros keep the program looping until the end of the string is reached (indicated by a 0DH carriage return).

Examine the parameters that are specified for the WHILE macro. In plain English, they say "while the byte pointed to by SI is Not Equal to a carriage return . . ." Notice that the body of the structure has been indented. This indentation makes it easier to see

**Listing 6.5**
**Simplest (Preliminary) Version of WHILE and WEND Macros**

```
;------------------------------------------------------------
; Listing 6.5   Simplest (preliminary) version of WHILE and WEND macros
;
; expects: two operands (either, but not both is a memory operand)
;        : a condition of A, AE, B, BE, G, GE, L, LE, or E (and all Nxx)
;
; example: while dl NE 80
;
; warning: This demonstration version can be invoked only once.

while   MACRO     op1,cond,op2
loop_top:                       ;label jumped to after each iteration
        cmp       op1,op2       ;generate comparison opcode
        J&cond    body          ;generate conditional jump to the body of code
back_up:                        ;label of area reserved for exit jump
        nop
        nop                     ;reserve space for JMP  EXIT opcode
        nop
body:                           ;the body begins here
        ENDM
;----------------------------------
; simple version of WEND
; expects no parameters

wend    MACRO
        jmp       loop_top      ;close the loop
exit:                           ;label the end of loop exit
        org       back_up       ;go back to the NOPs above
        jmp       exit          ;replace them with JMP opcode

        org       exit          ;restart assembler back down here
        ENDM
```

just what is done on each iteration. The WEND macro stands alone to indicate the end of the loop. Finally, notice that the entire routine contains no explicit branches, and the only visible label is the name of the procedure.

Here's the code of Listing 6.6 after it has been processed by the WHILE and WEND macros:

```
LOOP_TOP:

        CMP     BYTE PTR [SI],0dH

        JNE     BODY

        JMP     SHORT EXIT

        NOP

BODY:

        MOV     DX,10

        MUL     DX

        MOV     DL,[SI]
```

## Listing 6.6
## ASC2BIN Procedure

```
;-----------------------------------------------------------
; Listing 6.6  ASC2BIN procedure
;
; Demonstration of WHILE/WEND macros
; Converts a string of ASCII digits (terminated by 0DH)
; into a 16-bit binary number
;
; expects: SI points to start of string if digits ending with 0DH
; returns: AX is binary value (mod 65536) of ASCII string
; calls  : none (uses WHILE/WEND macros)
;
; alters only AX register

asc2bin proc near
        push    dx
        push    si
        mov     ax,0            ;zero accumulator

        while   <byte ptr [si]>,NE,0dH
        mov     dx,10
        mul     dx              ;AX = AX * 10
        mov     dl,[si]         ;get the next ASCII digit
        and     dx,0fh          ;make it binary in DX
        add     ax,dx           ;add into accumulator
        inc     si              ;point to next character
        wend

        pop     si
        pop     dx
        ret
asc2bin endp
```

```
        AND     DX,0fH

        ADD     AX,DX

        INC     SI

        JMP     SHORT LOOP_TOP

EXIT:
```

If you are wondering about the NOP that comes right before the body of the loop, it is the last of the three NOPs that were generated by the WHILE macro. The first two NOPs have been replaced with the JMP EXIT code generated by the WEND macro. In this case, EXIT was only a few bytes from the jump opcode, so the assembler generated a 2-byte short jump. If the body of the loop had been more than 127 bytes long, the assembler would have generated a 3-byte jump. Since WHILE can't tell in advance just how far the jump will be, it plays it safe by reserving three bytes for this purpose.

**THINGS TO DO**

1. Determine what ASC2BIN would do if the first character in the buffer pointed to by SI was a carriage return. What value is returned in AX if the buffer holds the characters '65536' plus a carriage return?

2. Write a version of WHILE that will be used only for loops that are less than 128 bytes in length. (Hint: Both jumps can be combined into a single conditional jump.)

3. (*) Rewrite the ASC2BIN procedure so that it will return a 32-bit value in the DX:AX register pair. Have it skip over leading spaces and return an error code if a nondigit character is found in the input string. (**) Have it correctly evaluate a string containing a leading plus (+) or minus (-) sign.

**Step 2: Reusable WHILE/WEND Macros**

The previous WHILE/WEND structure is limited by the fact that it can be used only once in a program. If it is invoked more than once, the assembler will indicate a code 3, "Redefinition of symbol" error because each invocation generates the labels LOOP_TOP, BACK_UP, BODY, and EXIT. These labels are essential to the communication that takes place between the macros, so they can't be declared LOCAL to either macro. A method must be developed to get around this problem.

The assembler has two features that make it possible to use WHILE/WEND more than once. The first is the equal sign (=) assignment of symbol values. Symbol values assigned this way may be changed later in the program. The other essential feature is the ability to find the value of the assembler's internal location counter. This value can be determined by using the THIS operator or the dollar sign ($) in an address expression.

```
BACK_UP = THIS NEAR
```

This instruction says, "Store the offset of the location counter in the internal variable BACK_UP and give it the same attributes that are associated with a NEAR label." The dollar sign can also be used to refer to the assembler's location counter. For example:

```
JMP        $+10
```

is interpreted by the assembler as meaning "Jump to the address that is 10 bytes beyond the current location." Listing 6.7 shows the WHILE and WEND macros after they have been recoded using this technique.

The major difference between Listings 6.5 and 6.7 is that each occurrence of

```
label:
```

has been replaced with

```
label = this near
```

Also note that the BODY label is missing in the second listing. It is not needed because the conditional jump has been recoded so that it doesn't need a label. It simply

## Listing 6.7
## Modified Version of the WHILE and WEND Macros

```
; ------------------------------------------------------------------------
; Listing 6.7
;
; Modified version of the WHILE and WEND macros
; Expects: two operands (either, but not both is a memory operand)
;        : a condition of A, AE, B, BE, G, GE, L, LE, or E (and all Nxx)
;
; example: while ax NE 0
;
; warning: This demonstration version does not support nesting.

while   MACRO   op1,cond,op2

loop_top =      this near   ;save offset for jump after each iteration
        cmp     op1,op2     ;generate comparison opcode
        J&cond  $ + 5       ;generate conditional jump to the body of code
back_up =       this near   ;label of area reserved for exit jump
        nop
        nop                 ;reserve space for JMP  EXIT opcode
        nop
                            ;the body begins here
        ENDM
; ----------------------------------------
; modified version of WEND
; does not support nesting
; expects no parameters

wend    MACRO
        jmp     loop_top    ;close the loop
exit    =       this near   ;label the end of loop exit
        org     back_up     ;go back to the NOPs above
        jmp     exit        ;replace them with JMP opcode

        org     exit        ;restart assembler for next instructions
        ENDM
```

sends execution to just beyond the three NOPs. This works out to be exactly five bytes from the location counter: three NOPs plus the two object code bytes of the conditional jump.

By keeping all of the jump references variable, we can invoke the macros with wild abandon—as long as every WHILE is followed by a WEND, and there is no other WHILE/WEND interposed between them. Imagine what would happen if we try to nest a second WHILE/WEND within another. Answer: The second WHILE would destroy the values of LOOP_TOP and BACK_UP that had been defined by the first. Therefore, the outer WEND macro would generate a jump back to the wrong position when it was invoked to close the outer loop.

### Step 3: Nested WHILE/WEND Macros

What we need is a mechanism to save the values of LOOP_TOP and BACK_UP for each invocation of the WHILE macro. We also need a corresponding mechanism so that the WEND macro can retrieve the most recently saved address. The solution involves implementing an assembler *symbol stack* and a set of macros to manipulate that stack. That is, we need to have a macro that will save the current location counter and one that will retrieve the most recently saved location counter value.

Listing 6.8 is a collection of macros that initialize and manipulate a stack of internal assembler symbols. These macros are complex, but they are very easy to work with. When you want to save the current location, you invoke the SAVE_THIS_ADDR macro. When you want to retrieve the last address that was saved, simply invoke the GET_LAST_ADDR macro and that address will be placed in the LAST_ADDR variable. Keep in mind that neither the CPU stack nor the program variables are changed by these macros. Only the assembler's internal symbol table is manipulated.

## Listing 6.8
## Structure Macro Support Macros

```
;-----------------------------------------------------------------
; Listing 6.8  Structure macro support macros
;
; These macros are used to allow nesting of structure macros:
;
; SAVE_THIS_ADDR, PUSH_ADDR
; GET_LAST_ADDR, POP_ADDR
; DISPLAY_MACRO_ERR
;

addr_num = 0  ;used as a symbol stack pointer

addr_1 = 0    ;These define the symbol stack used to pass data
addr_2 = 0    ; between macros.  Maximum nesting level is
addr_3 = 0    ; determined by the number of variables here.
addr_4 = 0    ; Each nesting of FOR/NEXT and WHILE/WEND requires
addr_5 = 0    ; two variables.  $IF/$ELSE/$ENDIF structures require
addr_6 = 0    ; only one variable per nest level.  Thus, these 10
addr_7 = 0    ; variables will support four levels of FOR/NEXT plus
addr_8 = 0    ; two levels of $IF/$ELSE/$ENDIF, and so on.
addr_9 = 0
addr_10= 0

;--------------------------------
; SAVE_THIS_ADDR   (no parameters)
; PUSH_ADDR %addr_num
;
; "Primitive" macros invoked by FOR, WHILE, $IF, and $ELSE.
; to store address values temporarily on a symbol stack.

SAVE_THIS_ADDR macro
  addr_num = addr_num +1
  PUSH_ADDR %addr_num
endm

PUSH_ADDR macro num
  ifndef addr_&num
    .lall ;**** structure macro ERROR: nesting too deep ****
    .sall
    %out    **** structure macro ERROR: nesting too deep ****
  endif
  addr_&num = this near
endm
```

**Listing 6.8**
**(continued)**

```
;--------------------------------
; GET_LAST_ADDR   (no parameters)
; POP_ADDR %addr_num
; "Primitive" macros retrieve addresses stored by SAVE_THIS_ADDR.

GET_LAST_ADDR  macro
  POP_ADDR  %addr_num
  addr_num = addr_num -1
endm

POP_ADDR macro num
  ifndef addr_&num
    .lall ;**** structure macro ERROR: too many NEXT,WEND,$ENDIF ****
    .sall
    %out   **** structure macro ERROR: too many NEXT,WEND,$ENDIF ****
  endif
  last_addr = addr_&num
endm

;--------------------------------
; DISPLAY_MACRO_ERR %addr_num
; Invoke at end of assembly to display if all nested
; structures were properly closed.
;
display_macro_err macro num
  %out macro nesting errors: num
endm
```

The first lines of Listing 6.8 define the size of the symbol stack. Each of the ADDR_n variables must be made part of the assembler's symbol table. This step is accomplished by assigning each variable a value of 0. If you find yourself nesting deeper than five levels, you can increase the size of the stack by adding ADDR_11, ADDR_12, and so on.

The SAVE_THIS_ADDR macro adjusts the *stack pointer* to point to the next higher number. It then passes that number, by value, to the PUSH_ADDR macro. Remember that when a macro is expanded, each of the dummy names is replaced by the characters of each parameter. Then the assembler evaluates the resulting lines of code. In this case, we want to pass a number between 1 and 10 to the PUSH_ADDR macro, a number that can be appended to the characters "addr_" to distinguish it from other variables of similar format. The percent (%) special macro operator allows us to perform this operation. The digit of the value of ADDR_NUM is passed to the PUSH_ADDR macro, where it is used to replace all occurrences of NUM in the body of the macro. The ampersand (&) operator is used to append the identifying digit to the name of the variable.

For example, the first invocation of SAVE_THIS_ADDR will change ADDR_NUM from 0 to 1 and will assign ADDR_1 with the offset of the current location counter. The second time the macro is invoked, ADDR_2 receives the value of the location counter, and so on.

The mechanism used by the GET_LAST_ADDR is similar. The same sequence of operations is used to identify the requested variable. Once it has been identified, its value is passed to the global variable LAST_ADDR. Then the symbol stack pointer is adjusted back to where it pointed before the most recent invocation of SAVE_THIS_ADDR. An error message is displayed if GET_LAST_ADDR is invoked without having previously invoked the SAVE_THIS_ADDR macro.

The DISPLAY_MACRO_ERR macro can be used at the end of an assembly to determine if all structures were properly closed. It simply displays the value of ADDR_NUM, which should be 0 at the end of an assembly.

Try mentally tracing the actions that take place when these macros are invoked. The mechanism is complex (the macros are nested three deep), but we now have all the tools necessary to implement structure macros that can be nested to a satisfactory depth. Listing 6.9 is the final version of WHILE/WEND.

### Listing 6.9
### WHILE/WEND (Final Version: Can Be Reused and Nested)

```
;-----------------------------------------------------------------
; Listing 6.9  WHILE/WEND (final version: can be re-used and nested)
;
; WHILE op1, condition, op2
;
; With WEND, sets up a loop that repeats as long as the
;  comparison of op1 and op2 meets the condition.
;
; condition is: E, NE, L, LE, B, BE, G, GE, A, AE (and all Nxx)
; op1 is       : memory variable, register
; op2 is       : register, immediate (,memory if op1 is register)
;
; Must resolve ambiguous memory references.  Example:
;     WHILE <byte ptr [SI]>, L, 'Z'
; ( <> used here to keep op1 as a single parameter)
;
; Uses SAVE_THIS_ADDR, GET_LAST_ADDR macros

WHILE   macro   op1,cond,op2

        SAVE_THIS_ADDR       ;save LOOP_TOP
        cmp     op1,op2
        J&cond  $ + 5        ;if condition true, execute body of loop
        SAVE_THIS_ADDR       ;save BACK_UP address
        nop
        nop
        nop
        endm

;--------------------------------------
; WEND (no parameters)
; The continuation point after exit from a FOR or WHILE loop.
; Same action is taken for WEND and NEXT (invoked either way)
; Preserves all registers.

WEND    macro

        GET_LAST_ADDR        ;retrieve BACK_UP
back_up =       last_addr    ;save it for now
        GET_LAST_ADDR        ;retrieve LOOP_TOP
        jmp     last_addr    ;code jump to top of loop
exit    =       this near    ;here's the end of the loop
        org     back_up      ;alter NOPs into a
        jmp     exit         ; a jump to the exit

        org     exit         ;get assembler back on track
        endm
```

Listing 6.10 is an example of nested WHILE/WEND loops. This subroutine will repeatedly print an error message and wait for the Esc key to be pressed. If any other key is pressed, the process is repeated. The outer loop checks for the Esc key. If it hasn't been pressed, the inner loop prints each character of a message.

### Listing 6.10
### Use of Nested WHILE/WEND

```
;-----------------------------------------------------------
; Listing 6.10    Use of nested WHILE/WEND
; ERR_TRAP
; Call this subroutine whenever the user makes an input error.
; It displays the error message and beeps.  It waits for a key
;  and won't return to the caller until [Esc] is pressed.
; Set up as an EXTERNAL library routine.  Use a near call.

        public  err_trap

data_seg segment byte public 'data'     ;to be added to main program's DATA_SEG

msg     db 'ERROR! press [Esc] to return to menu',0AH,0DH,07,00  ;07 is BEL

data_seg ends

lib_seg  segment byte public 'code'
err_trap proc near
        mov     cx,1
        mov     al,0
        while   al NE 27     ;repeat until ESC pressed
          mov     si,offset msg
          lodsb
          while   al NE 0    ;repeat till end of message
            mov     bl,7
            mov     bh,0
            mov     ah,14    ;parameters for WRITE_TTY BIOS service
            int     10H      ;write the character in AL
            lodsb
          wend
          mov     ah,0
          int     16H        ;read (wait for) one key
        wend
        ret
err_trap endp
lib_seg  ends
```

Although you could write more efficient code by hand, the most you could save would be about 15 clock cycles per loop iteration. This is negligible compared to the amount of overhead involved when using ROM-BIOS input/output services. The important thing is that the source code clearly describes a pair of nested loops based on conditions that can be easily read in the source code. The disassembly (Figure 6.1) is a tangle of compares and jumps.

**Figure 6.1**
**Disassembly of ERR_TRAP (Listing 6.10)**

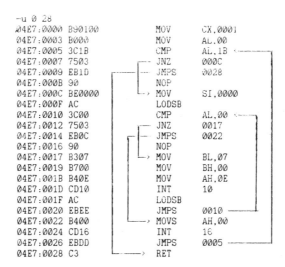

```
-u 0 28
04E7:0000 B90100          MOV     CX,0001
04E7:0003 B000            MOV     AL,00
04E7:0005 3C1B            CMP     AL,1B
04E7:0007 7503            JNZ     000C
04E7:0009 EB1D            JMPS    0028
04E7:000B 90              NOP
04E7:000C BE0000          MOV     SI,0000
04E7:000F AC              LODSB
04E7:0010 3C00            CMP     AL,00
04E7:0012 7503            JNZ     0017
04E7:0014 EB0C            JMPS    0022
04E7:0016 90              NOP
04E7:0017 B307            MOV     BL,07
04E7:0019 B700            MOV     BH,00
04E7:001B B40E            MOV     AH,0E
04E7:001D CD10            INT     10
04E7:001F AC              LODSB
04E7:0020 EBEE            JMPS    0010
04E7:0022 B400            MOVS    AH,00
04E7:0024 CD16            INT     16
04E7:0026 EBDD            JMPS    0005
04E7:0028 C3              RET
```

**THINGS TO DO**

1. Generalize the ERR_TRAP routine in Listing 6.10 so that it requires an error code in the AL register that specifies which of several error messages to print.

2. Have the message printed on the bottom of the screen in reverse video and erase the message after Esc is pressed.

**FOR/NEXT Structure Macros**

Listings 6.11 and 6.12 are further examples of structure macros. The FOR/NEXT construct (Listing 6.11) uses all of the techniques seen in WHILE/WEND. In fact, the NEXT macro is identical to the WEND macro. FOR/NEXT also handles the overhead involved in initializing, updating, and testing a loop index. Like BASIC's FOR command, it allows a step size that defaults to +1 when omitted in the command line. The step size can be a positive or a negative integer (not a register or memory label).

All parameters must be of the same type (all 8-bit or 16-bit values) and are treated as *signed* integers. Thus, you must be aware that numbers above 8000H (above 80H for byte operands) will be treated as being less than numbers from 0 to 7FFFH (0 to 7FH for byte operands). The start and finish bounds can be register, memory, or numeric (immediate) operands. The index can be either a memory operand or a register, but if it is a memory operand, both the start and the finish must be either registers or numbers.

FOR/NEXT makes its completion test at the top of the loop, so if the start is greater than the finish and the step is positive, then the loop will not be executed even once.

## Listing 6.11
## FOR/NEXT Macros

```
;-------------------------------------------
; Listing 6.11  FOR/NEXT macros
;
; FOR, with NEXT, sets up a repeating loop with an automatic index.
;
; FOR   index,start,finish [,step]
;
; Repeats code beterrn FOR and NEXT, altering index by step until index
; exceeds finish.  If step < 0, then the loop executes until index
; becomes less than finish.  The step should not be 0 unless another exit
; is provided.
;
; index  is: memory variable, register
; start  is: register, immediate
; finish is: register, immediate signed value (,memory if index is register.
; step   is: positive or negative immediate (if omitted, default is +1)
;
; Examples:
;     FOR my_variable, 1, 20    (FOR my_variable = 1 TO 20 STEP 1)
;     FOR ax, bx, 500, -1       (FOR ax = bx TO 500 STEP -1)
;     FOR byte_var, al, 90, 10  (FOR memory = al TO 50 STEP 10)
;     FOR cx, ax, bx, 30        (FOR cx = ax TO bx STEP 30)
;
; Memory operands must be defined before the macro call, or their
;  size must be known.  Example: FOR <byte ptr [si]>,1,15,2
; All parameters must match in type (all 8-bit or 16-bit operands).
; The test is on signed numbers (i.e., FFFFH is less than 0) and the test
;  occurs before the first pass through the loop.
; It's OK to exit loop at any time with a jump.
; If finish is a register, changing it will alter loop control.
; Requires at least three parameters, alters index, flags register.
;
; uses: SAVE_THIS_ADDR, GET_LAST_ADDR, WEND macros

FOR macro index, start, finish, step
  local  skip

  step_size = 0       ;must initialize
  ifb <step>
    step_size = 1
  else
    step_size = step
  endif

  cmp_step = (step_size+0ffffH)+1  ;fix so relational operators work

  mov    index,start
  jmp    short skip   ;don't change index first time through

  SAVE_THIS_ADDR         ;resume here from NEXT

  if cmp_step LE 7fffH  ;adjust index on each iteration
    if cmp_step EQ 1
      inc  index
    else
      add  index,step_size
    endif
  else
    if cmp_step EQ 0ffffH
      dec  index
    else
      add    index,step_size
    endif
  endif
```

## Listing 6.11
## (continued)

```
  skip:
  cmp   index,finish      ;the test

  if cmp_step LE 7fffH ;when step is positive,
     jle $+5              ; do loop when index <= finish
  else                    ;when step is negative
     jge $+5              ; do loop when index >= finish
  endif

  SAVE_THIS_ADDR
  nop                     ; (NEXT macro modifies these bytes)
  nop
  nop                     ;reserve bytes for JMP to exit loop
endm

;--------------------
; NEXT macro is identical to WEND macro

NEXT macro
     WEND
endm
```

## Listing 6.12
## $IF/$ELSE/$ENDIF Macros

```
;-----------------------------------------------------------
; Listing 6.12  $IF/$ELSE/$ENDIF macros
;
; Sets up a structured IF. . .ELSE. . .ENDIF construct.
;
; $IF op1, condition, op2
;
; condition is: E, NE, L, LE, B, BE, G, GE, A, AE (and all Nxx)
; op1 is     : memory variable, register
; op2 is     : register, immediate (,memory if op1 is register)
;
; When condition is true, the following code is executed up to
;  a matching $ELSE or $ENDIF macro invocation.  For every $IF,
;  there must be a $ENDIF.  The $ELSE is optional, and only one
;  $ELSE is allowed per $IF/$ENDIF pair.
;
; Examples:
;           $IF ax, L, bx   (if ax < bx)
;              ...           (code executed if true)
;           $ELSE           optional
;              ...           (code executed if false)
;           $ENDIF
;              ...           (code executed in either case)
;
; Nesting of $IF/$ENDIFs is allowed, up to the limit of the symbol stack
;
; Uses SAVE_THIS_ADDR, GET_LAST_ADDR macros

$IF macro op1,condition,op2
     cmp op1,op2
     j&condition $+5
     SAVE_THIS_ADDR
     nop
     nop
     nop
endm
```

**Listing 6.12
(continued)**

```
;--------------------------------
; $ELSE (no parameters)
; Indicates the start of code to be executed when an $IF test
;   fails. Use is optional. (Note: Use only one $ELSE per $IF.)
; Alters no registers or flags.
;
$ELSE macro
      local end_else,else_code
      end_else:

      GET_LAST_ADDR
      org   last_addr
      jmp   else_code

      org   end_else
      SAVE_THIS_ADDR
      nop
      nop
      nop
      else_code:
endm

;--------------------------------
; $ENDIF (no parameters)
; Indicates the start of code to be executed when the matching
;   $IF fails or the (optional) $ELSE code is finished.
; There MUST be a $ENDIF for every $IF or $IF/$ELSE combination.
; Alters no registers or flags.
;
$ENDIF macro
      local exit
      exit:
      GET_LAST_ADDR
      org   last_addr
      jmp   exit
      org   exit
endm
```

## IF/ELSE/ENDIF Structure Macros

Listing 6.12 includes three interactive macros that combine to make an IF/ELSE/ENDIF construct. These macros have been named $IF, $ELSE, and $ENDIF to differentiate them from the assembler conditional pseudo-ops. As with assembler pseudo-ops, there must be exactly one $ENDIF to match each $IF. Nesting is allowed up to the limits of the SAVE_THIS_ADDR and GET_LAST_ADDR symbol stack.

The comments in these listings, along with the foregoing explanation of the WHILE/WEND macros, should provide enough information to allow you to study the macros in order to see exactly what they do. But as with high-level language commands, you don't need to know exactly how they operate. Just become familiar with what they do and how to use them.

These macros allow you to write self-documented code with an easily perceived structure. The following example will give you some ideas of the possibilities created by structure macros. It reads each dot on the midresolution graphics screen, starting in the upper left-hand corner and working across the screen to the right and then down to the bottom. If it encounters a yellow dot, it replaces it with a blue one. If the dot is blue, it replaces it with a yellow one. The process is repeated until the space bar is pressed.

```
        CALL    CHECK_KBD       ;fetch AL = pressed key (0 if no key)
                WHILE AL NE 32  ; repeat until space bar is pressed
                    FOR   DX,0,199  ;for each row of screen graphics
                        FOR   CX,0,319               ; for each column
                            CALL    READ_DOT    ; get color of dot (CX,DX)
                            $IF     AL EQ 3           ;if the dot is yellow
                                MOV     AL,2
                                CALL    WRITE_DOT         ; then make it blue
                            $ELSE
                                $IF     AL EQ 2          ;if the dot is blue
                                    MOV     AL,3
                                    CALL    WRITE_DOT   ; then make it yellow
                                $ENDIF
                            $ENDIF
                        NEXT
                    NEXT
                    CALL    CHECK_KBD           ;fetch any key during loop
                WEND
```

This example demonstrates a complex series of nested structures including a WHILE/WEND loop, two FOR/NEXT loops, and two IF/ELSE/ENDIF constructs.

To assemble a program such as this, you should create a macro file that contains Listings 6.8, 6.9, 6.11, and 6.12. Use the INCLUDE pseudo-op to assemble the file into your source text:

```
        IF 1
            INCLUDE STRUCS.MAC
        ENDIF
```

If you take the time to build a library of structure macros and learn to use them regularly, you will be able to write larger, more complex programs in a shorter time. Because you can see the flow of the program at a glance, you can spend more time being creative and less time debugging logic errors.

**THINGS TO DO**

1.  Use DEBUG to disassemble the code generated by the structure macros. See if you can write macros that generate less loop overhead, especially in short loops.

2.  Write an extension to the WHILE macro that could be used to make decisions based on a value returned from a called routine. For example:

```
WHILE CALL_TO INKEY E 0    ; call INKEY, compare result to 0
```

3.  (*) Write a DO macro for loops that do not need to access the loop index. Have it create and test a variable that is stored *within the code segment* (at an address that will never be executed). Although the generated code could never be used in a ROM application, the construct would free a register, and the loop control would be completely invisible:

```
DO    100

   .

   . (code executed 100 times)

   .

NEXT
```

4.  (*) Write macros for a REPEAT/UNTIL construct that performs the condition checking at the end of the loop, thereby ensuring that the loop will be executed at least once.

5.  (**) Write a SWITCH/CASE/ENDCASE/ENDSWITCH system that will work like that of the C programming language. The SWITCH must have a register or memory parameter, and each CASE must specify a value to be compared with the SWITCH parameter. If the case is true, all of the code up to an ENDCASE should be executed. DEFAULT and BREAK are handy options. DEFAULT should capture all cases that weren't specified, and BREAK should force an immediate exit from the SWITCH/ENDSWITCH construct. It should be able to generate the correct code for the following:

```
CALL    INKEY     ;wait for key press

SWITCH AL

   CASE    'Y'

      MOV     AH,-1    ;Y for 'Yes' is true
```

```
        ENDCASE
        CASE      'y'
          MOV     AH,-1     ;y for 'yes' is true
        ENDCASE
        DEFAULT
          MOV     AH,0      ;false
        ENDCASE
ENDSWITCH
```

# Chapter 7

# Interfacing with High-Level Languages

## 7.1 HYBRID PROGRAMMING

It has probably occurred to you that assembly language is too complex for major programming tasks. In fact, the entire computing world is moving toward the exclusive use of higher-level languages, and the reasons are obvious. For instance, obtaining a formatted printout of a list of double precision numbers (decimal point aligned with a floating dollar sign) takes only ten minutes for the experienced BASIC programmer. But even the utterly competent hacker might need weeks to do the same thing in assembly language. On the other hand, a BASIC program that sorts those same numbers will give everyone in the office a good excuse for a coffee break, but its assembly language equivalent will be finished in the blink of an eye.

Fortunately, the choice between high-level and assembly language is not a binary, either/or decision. BASIC, Pascal, C, Forth, and all other high-level languages invariably provide "hooks" into user-provided machine language subroutines. By learning how to graft machine code into a high-level language, you can create "hybrid" programs that provide the best of both worlds. You need not be stifled by BASIC's 64K data area; assembly language has no such limitation. If a high-level language lacks a certain function, you can write your own version and add it to the language's repertory. If a certain subroutine is slowing a program's execution, you may be able to recode it in assembly language and obtain a dramatic increase in speed.

There is plenty to be gained by making the assembly language connection. It can also be a frustrating and time-consuming experience. When you step outside of the domain of a language, you must tread very carefully; it's difficult to know just where the language has laid its land mines, and such traps always exist. Debugging a hybrid program involves knowing the internal workings of the high-level language as well as expertise with the assembler. In particular, you must be very sure that when your assembler routine takes control, it is able to assimilate the information being passed to it. And when it transfers control back to the high-level caller, it must do so gracefully and in the prescribed manner.

## 7.2 PASSING PARAMETERS

Up to now, we have passed parameters by placing them in registers. All of the ROM-BIOS and PC-DOS services require certain registers to be initialized before the interrupt is invoked, and any information that is returned by the call is also via register. But when we write code in BASIC or Pascal, there is no direct way to set up the CPU registers. Besides, routines often require more parameters than can conveniently be held in the registers. The ROM-BIOS listing in the technical reference manual reveals the contortions required to keep track of register parameters. Communication between languages works most smoothly when the data are stored in memory by the calling program and fetched from memory by the subroutine.

There are many ways to pass information from one language to another. BASIC programs can POKE data into a specific memory address for later inspection and modification by the assembly code. BASIC programs may also use the USR command to pass a single 16-bit value to a routine. Compiled BASIC variables may be declared COMMON so that a segment with the COMMON combine type may be used as a template to access those variables from an assembly language module. Pascal variables may be declared PUBLIC to allow an assembler module to access those values by name—just like PUBLIC values in other assembler modules.

All of these methods will work, but there is often an element of risk. For instance, POKEs that work with one version of BASIC may destroy important system code or data in another version. Furthermore, these methods provide no secure way to write reentrant or recursive procedures. When absolute addresses are used to contain parameters, they may be destroyed by subsequent or concurrent calls to the program. By far the safest and most flexible method to pass values from module to module is the one used by all Microsoft and Intel products: placing parameters on the stack.

This method, which has sprung from Intel's handling of PL/M function arguments, involves placing a frame of data into the stack. It is said that one of the design criteria when the 8086/8088 was first on the drawing board was to implement a convenient way to work with the PL/M argument frame. It's not hard to imagine that the specialized BP pointer register and the RET *nnnn* instructions were designed into the 8088 because of this criterion. If that's the case, the 8088 was partially designed around a language, rather than vice versa.

Function parameters are temporary values, just like return addresses. They are needed only during the time a subroutine is being executed. Thus, they qualify as logical items to be placed on the stack. They are PUSHed onto the stack right before the call and then POPped off of the stack by the RET *nnnn* opcode. This system is very flexible, allowing any program to pass information to any other program without worrying about which registers are used. And the exact location of the frame of data is easily found: It will be at addresses in the stack segment, four bytes beneath the address of the

SP register. This convention has worked so successfully for PL/M that all of the Intel and Microsoft languages use it, including interpretive BASIC, BASCOM, Pascal, FORTRAN, and C.

In previous programs, we have had little use for the BP register. It may seem unfortunate that a perfectly good register should be relegated to the back of our assembly language toolbox. Along with the BX register, this one is an integral part of one of the 8088's most powerful features: the base-relative addressing mode. The value of BP can be combined with either DI or SI, plus an offset, in order to generate an effective address of a memory operand.

The reason BP doesn't see much action is that the address to which it points is, by default, in the stack segment. Normal program variables are usually in the memory area pointed to by the DS and/or ES registers, and most programmers prefer to avoid the stack for fear of wiping out return addresses. (There may be an action that is more destructive than returning to an indeterminate address, but it probably involves napalm and grenades.)

But the very fact that BP automatically points to stack data makes it ideal for accessing subroutine parameters. The normal procedure is to copy the value of SP (which always points to the top of the stack) into BP, and then use offsets from that base to fetch the parameters. Listing 7.1 is the outline of two assembly language modules that use this "frame data" method to pass parameters. Figure 7.1 illustrates how the stack looks while the code is being executed.

Pay special attention to the way the BP register is used to access the arguments on the stack and the values of the base-relative offsets that point to that data. Notice that upon entry into PRINT_MSG, the parameters are at offsets 4 and 6 from the top of the stack. But before copying SP into BP, the routine PUSHes BP. That action places the parameters at offsets 6 and 8 from the top of the stack. Likewise, any PUSH that occurs before SP that is copied into BP will change all offsets by two bytes. Once the BP is set up as the frame pointer, the arguments will always be at the same offsets—even if other registers are PUSHed or other routines are called.

Now consider the case of reentrant code: What if the PRINT_MSG routine itself needed to print a message? Or, more likely, what if a background task needed to use the PRINT_MSG procedure? In either case, the same system could be used: The caller simply PUSHes the address and length of the message and then makes a FAR call to PRINT_MSG. Since the frame pointer has been saved at the start of the procedure and restored at the end, PRINT_MSG may be invoked without fear of destroying any partially processed data. Each invocation has its own frame and data set in an area of the stack that will not be disturbed. Thus, in a multiuser environment, several different programs can use the procedure simultaneously.

Even if you never expect your code to be called recursively, it is a good policy to save the BP register before initializing it to the value of the stack pointer. When the BP register has been PUSHed following a FAR call, you may use the following formula to access the arguments in the frame:

```
ARGn offset = 6 + (2 * (total args - ARGn number))
```

**Listing 7.1**
**Partial Program to Illustrate the Intel Standard Method**
**of Passing Parameters Between Program Modules**

```
;--------------------------------------------------------------------------
;Listing 7.1
;Partial program to illustrate the Intel standard method of
; passing parameters between program modules.

data_seg segment
err_msg  db      'ERROR 217: Invalid perbalutational snarficon.'
msg_len  equ     $ - err_msg   ;assembler symbol counts characters of message
data_seg ends

         extrn   print_msg:far  ;in an external segment
code_seg segment
main     proc    far
         mov     ax,offset err_msg
         push    ax             ;place the address of the message on the stack
         mov     ax,msg_len
         push    ax             ; place the length right above it.
         call    print_msg      ;FAR call stacks doubleword return address
         .
         .
         .
main     endp
code_seg ends


;--------------------------------------. .---------------------------------
; Called subroutine expects two 16-bit arguments on the stack
;
         public  print_msg
lib_seg  segment                ;in an externally linked module
print_msg proc   far
         push    bp             ;save the frame pointer
         mov     bp,sp          ;make it the BASE of the parameters
         mov     cx,[bp+6]      ;fetch the length of the message
         mov     si,[bp+8]      ;fetch the address of the message
         .
         .(process the message)
         .
         pop     bp             ;restore the frame pointer
         ret     4              ;back to MAIN, discarding 2 parameters
print_msg endp
lib_seg  ends
```

where *ARGn number* ranges from 1 to *total args*. The first argument placed on the stack is number 1, the second is number 2, and so forth. Thus, if four arguments are passed to a subroutine, the offset from BP that will access the second argument will be:

$$OFFSET = 6+(2*(4-2))$$

$$= 6+(2*2)$$

$$= 6+4$$

$$= 10$$

and the argument itself will be found at [BP + 10]. In other words, the last argument to be PUSHed on the stack will be closest to the frame pointer (have the smallest offset) and the first argument will be at the greatest offset.

**Figure 7.1**
**Diagram Illustrates the Stack During Execution of Listing 7.1**

```
Figure 7.1a  Before MAIN begins
xxxx:010A SP ——>
xxxx:0108                | — free area — |
xxxx:0106                | — free area — |
xxxx:0104                | — free area — |
xxxx:0102                | — free area — |
xxxx:0100                | — free area — |


Figure 7.1b  After first PUSH
xxxx:010A
xxxx:0108 SP ——>         | address of ERR_MSG |
xxxx:0106                | — free area — |
xxxx:0104                | — free area — |
xxxx:0102                | — free area — |
xxxx:0100                | — free area — |


Figure 7.1c  After second PUSH
xxxx:010A
xxxx:0108                | address of ERR_MSG |
xxxx:0106 SP ——>         | length of message |
xxxx:0104                | — free area — |
xxxx:0102                | — free area — |
xxxx:0100                | — free area — |


Figure 7.1d  After FAR call to PRINT_MSG procedure
xxxx:010A
xxxx:0108                | address of ERR_MSG |
xxxx:0106                | length of message |
xxxx:0104                | return address segment |
xxxx:0102 SP ——>         | return address offset |
xxxx:0100                | — free area — |
```

**Figure 7.1
(continued)**

```
Figure 7.1e  After PUSH BP and MOV BP,SP in PRINT_MSG
xxxx:010A
xxxx:0108          | address of ERR_MSG     |   BP + 8
xxxx:0106          | length of message      |   BP + 6
xxxx:0104          | return address segment |   BP + 4
xxxx:0102          | return address offset  |   BP + 2
xxxx:0100 SP ----> | BP (frame pointer)     |   BP + 0
```

```
Figure 7.1f  After POP BP
xxxx:010A
xxxx:0108          | address of ERR_MSG     |
xxxx:0106          | length of message      |
xxxx:0104          | return address segment |
xxxx:0102 SP ----> | return address offset  |
xxxx:0100          | — free area —          |
```

```
Figure 7.1g  After RET 4
xxxx:010A SP ---->
xxxx:0108          | — free area — |
xxxx:0106          | — free area — |
xxxx:0104          | — free area — |
xxxx:0102          | — free area — |
xxxx:0100          | — free area — |
```

Note: It is also possible for a called routine to create *local* stack variables for its own use. For instance, after saving BP and initializing it to the value of SP, a dummy value may be PUSHed onto the stack. It may then be accessed as [BP - 1]. If you use this technique, you must be sure to discard that value before returning to the caller (POP it into an unneeded register or add 2 to the stack pointer).

We'll see these concepts illustrated in several program listings when we discuss the BASIC CALL statement and Pascal EXTERNAL procedures. So, let's put this topic aside for a while and look at the nuts and bolts of interfacing assembler code to BASIC.

## 7.3 INTERFACING TO INTERPRETIVE BASIC

Interpretive BASIC is an alien language. The code you write with the BASIC interpreter is actually just data in a highly specialized format which is processed by the BASIC interpreter. The commands that pass control to assembly language modules are a way of saying, "Okay, Mr. B., If you can't handle this little detail, I'm going to your supervisor." Well, BASIC might get upset and fly off the handle, or maybe it will just be glad to be relieved of the strain. But in any case, it is a touchy situation, one not to be entered lightly. However, with a properly humble attitude, we can step behind BASIC's back and perform magic.

The abracadabras that BASIC provides are the USR*n* and CALL statements. These work in very different ways, and both are useful. The CALL command passes a frame of data, as discussed in the previous section. The USR*n* function does not use the stack to pass values. It passes a single 16-bit argument by placing it in the DX register. Like all arguments passed by BASIC, the value is always a pointer to data, never the data itself.

Both CALL and USR*n* transfer control with the segment registers set up in a standard format: DS, ES, and SS are all the same, and they point to BASIC's work area—the 64K area where the BASIC program and all BASIC variables reside. The CS register will be set to the most recent value specified by the DEF SEG statement. If no DEF SEG has been used, or if the most recent one did not specify a value (DEF SEG by itself), the CS register will have the same value as the other registers.

BASIC invokes the user routine by saving all of the general registers and transferring control with a FAR call. The CALL statement passes control to the address named in the call. That is, CALL MY.PROG transfers control to the offset named by the variable MY.PROG. Setting up for the USR*n* command requires an additional step. You must execute a DEF USR*n* command; DEF USR0 = &HF000 sets up the USR0 function to transfer control to offset F000H in the current DEFault SEGment.

### Finding Where to Put a Routine

The real trick of interfacing assembler code to BASIC is getting the code into memory at a location where you can be sure that it won't disturb BASIC and BASIC won't mess with it. Many tricks have been developed to ensure this compatibility. You can place the code into a BASIC string variable [the transfer address can be found using the VARPTR *(code.strings$)* function and then PEEKing the two bytes above that address]. Unused BASIC file buffers can hold up to 218 bytes of code. Short programs can be read in with the GET command (the address of code read in this way will be 118 bytes beyond the value returned by the VARPTR (#) function). An even more arcane method uses an integer array to hold a machine language program.

All of these techniques are holdovers from earlier versions of Microsoft BASIC and hardly require discussion in this book. The version of interpretive BASIC that comes with the IBM PC includes a command that makes all of these "back door" tricks obsolete. The magic word is CLEAR. One option of the CLEAR command allows you to set aside a portion of BASIC's work area for your own use. For instance, after you issue

```
10 CLEAR ,60000
```

you may use any address above 60000 (EA60H) for any purpose, including insertion of your own code. That figure of 60000 just happens to be a nice round number. You can set aside any amount of memory, just as long as you leave some for the BASIC program.

To determine the high-memory limit needed by your application, read the "Free Bytes" message that comes up when you first enter BASIC. In a 64K machine, this amount will be approximately 32000; a 128K machine displays something like "60865 Bytes Free." Just subtract the length of your assembly language routine from the number of free bytes to determine the maximum value you can use in the CLEAR command. Smaller numbers will just provide more suspenders for those pessimists among you. With an unknown machine, the FRE(0) function can be used by a program to find out how much memory is available.

If your target machine has 128K or more, you may choose to leave all of BASIC's work area intact and place your routine outside of BASIC's segment. You may also choose to use part of BASIC's work area, but view it as being in a different segment. There are certain advantages to placing your code at the start of an unused segment. If your code accesses internal variables or messages, you will be able to determine the addresses of those data more easily. Programs that begin at offset 0 in a segment are fully relocatable (NEAR jumps and calls are always self-relative, but program data are relocatable only in the context of 16-byte memory paragraphs).

The DEF SEG statement sets up an absolute segment address for all POKEs, BLOADs, CALLs, and USR*n* statements, There is some danger in specifying an absolute segment address. For instance, if you expect your program to reside in the upper 4K of an IBM PC with 128K of memory, you can use

```
DEF SEG = &H1B00
```

But if the target IBM PC is equipped with 256K, and part of that area is taken up with a RAM-disk device, BASIC might be loaded at a much higher address. The address 1B00:0000 might be right in the middle of BASIC's work area. You could be courting disaster. What we need is a way to specify an area that is above BASIC— wherever it may be. The following code will set up a segment value that is outside of BASIC's work area, regardless of how much memory a target machine has:

```
10 DEF SEG=0              '** address DOS reserved area
20 BAS.SEG=PEEK(&H510)+PEEK(&H511)*256
                          '** fetch BASIC's segment address
30 MYCODE.SEG=BAS.SEG+&H100
                          '** add 64K in segment notation
40 DEF SEG=MYCODE.SEG '** segment is set up
50 MY.PROG=0              '** offset for POKE, BLOAD, CALL, etc.
```

(Note: Address 0000:0510 is named in the technical reference manual as containing a 16-bit word containing BASIC's segment address.)

This program assumes that the target machine has enough memory to give BASIC a complete 64K work area and have some left over for an external program. The simplest way to make sure that a target machine has enough memory is to see if the segment and offset point to actual RAM (not an empty socket):

```
60 X=PEEK(0) :POKE 0,123
                          '** see if address will accept a value
70 IF PEEK(0)=123 THEN POKE 0,X :GOTO 90
                          '** no problem . . . continue
80 PRINT "ERROR! This program requires 128K of RAM": STOP
90                        '** program continues
```

An alternative to placing your code above BASIC's segment is to place it below BASIC before BASIC starts up. You will recall from Chapter 5 that the PC-DOS FIX_IN_MEMORY service will place program code and data into the lowest available addresses and keep it resident, as if it were a part of DOS. You may use this service to find a secure place for your assembly language subroutines. The trick is to find a way to tell a BASIC program just where the assembler code resides. The only technique that immediately comes to mind is to store the program's address (segment and offset) into memory where it can be PEEKed by the BASIC program. The technical reference manual states that absolute addresses 04F0H through 04FFH may be used as an interapplication communication area. Thus, if the segment and offset of the assembler code are stored in these bytes (and if no other application overwrites them!), a BASIC program could later read that address to determine where the machine code is located. This method is discussed in greater detail in Section 7.4.

### Getting the Code Into Memory

Once you have located an area that you feel is safe from DOS and BASIC, you need to get the opcodes of your program into it. Among the exotic methods that we won't discuss in this section are (1) using GET to read a small program into a BASIC disk input buffer, (2) concatenating a string from the bytes of the opcodes, and (3) reading the bytes of a program into an integer array. All of these methods work, but it is difficult to imagine an application that *must* use these techniques; they all have the very real drawback that BASIC may take some action behind your back. String data are always being shuffled around in memory, and integer arrays are moved every time a new scalar (nonarray) variable is defined.

The only way to be certain that your assembly language routine remains immobile is to place it into addresses that have been reserved with the CLEAR command or addresses that are outside of BASIC's work area. The POKE command may be the easiest to understand: The bytes of your routine are individually POKEd into sequential addresses of the reserved area. Listing 7.2 is a simple example.

## Listing 7.2
## CLREOP

```
1 '** Listing 7.2    CLREOP
2 '**
3 '** Demonstrates how to POKE and CALL a short 8088 subroutine.
4 '** The CALL clears the screen from the current cursor line down.
5 '**
10 CLEAR,60800!                    '** protect memory above 60800
20 CLREOP=60800!                   '** define load and call address
30 ADDR=CLREOP
40 READ BYTE :IF BYTE= -1 THEN 100 '** exit after last byte is read
50 POKE ADDR,BYTE                  '** place opcode into memory
60  ADDR=ADDR+1                    '** point to next address to POKE
70 GOTO 40                         '** loop back to read next byte
100 PRINT "CLREOP program is loaded" :PRINT :PRINT
110 PRINT "To test the program enter:"
120 PRINT "    LOCATE nn :CALL CLREOP"
130 PRINT "This will clear the screen from line NN to the bottom."
140 END
196 '** -------------------------------------------------------------------
197 '** these are the data that make up the CLREOP subroutine
198 '** opcode bytes | opcode mnemonics and comments
199 '** ---------    -------------------------------------------------------
200 DATA &HB7,&H00    :'mov  bh,0  ;specify screen page number
210 DATA &HB4,&H03    :'mov  ah,3  ;specify BIOS sub-function number
220 DATA &HCD,&H10    :'int  10H   ;READ_CURSOR_POS to fetch cursor line into DH
230 DATA &H88,&HF5    :'mov  ch,dh ;setup upper left-hand corner of window
240 DATA &HB1,&H00    :'mov  cl,0
250 DATA &HB6,&H18    :'mov  dh,24 ;setup lower right-hand corner of window
260 DATA &HB2,&H4F    :'mov  dl,79
270 DATA &HB7,&H07    :'mov  bh,7  ;attribute used for blank character
280 DATA &HB0,&H00    :'mov  al,0  ;special function: blank entire window
290 DATA &HB4,&H06    :'mov  ah,6  ;SCROLL_WINDOW service
300 DATA &HCD,&H10    :'int  10H   ;clear the defined window
310 DATA &HCB         :'ret        ;FAR RET to BASIC
320 DATA -1           :'end        ;indicates end of program for line 40 above
```

Listing 7.2, CLREOP, reads and POKEs the bytes of a very short program into the area above address 60000 in BASIC's segment. The program adds a useful command to your BASIC toolbox; it gives you the capability of erasing the screen from the current line to the bottom. It does this by making two ROM-BIOS service calls. The first fetches the current cursor location (INT 10H with AH = 3), and the second uses a special option of the SCROLL_WINDOW service (INT 10H with AH = 6 and AL = 0) to clear the screen from that point down to the bottom.

The advantage of this POKE method is that the bytes of machine code are integrated into your BASIC program; there is no external BLOAD file to fuss with. The disadvantage is that the READ-and-POKE method is slow and cumbersome. And you must be very careful with the bytes of the machine code; you won't be able simply to copy them from the assembler listing file. Some of the bytes seen in the assembler listing are in reverse order, and others are in a relocatable format. One way to overcome this obstacle is to convert the assembled and linked EXE file into a BIN file. Then use DEBUG to print the opcode bytes, and finally include them in DATA lines in the BASIC test driver. It is also possible to write a short BASIC program that reads the BIN file and outputs an ASCII file that may be MERGEd with another BASIC program.

## THINGS TO DO

1. Write and assemble a short subroutine that clears a screen line from the current cursor position to the end (call it CLREOL). Use subfunction 3 (READ_CURSOR_POS) of INT 10H to find the location of the cursor, and use a SCROLL_WINDOW subfunction (06H or 07H) to clear the rest of the line.

2. Link the program and load it with DEBUG. Use the U command to disassemble the code and write down (or print out) the hex values of each opcode byte. Using the technique illustrated in Listing 7.2, POKE the bytes into memory and test the program.

## The BLOAD Connection

By far the easiest and most flexible way to load a subroutine is by using the BLOAD command. If you have read the BASIC manual (Appendix C) on this subject, you may have been turned off by the unnecessary complexity of the method described. The manual suggests using the linker's /D and /H options to create a file that loads into the high end of memory; using DEBUG to load BASIC.COM; writing down the values of the registers; loading the linked EXE file; noting the CS and IP values after the load; restoring the original values of the registers; executing BASIC; and finally, using BSAVE to store the EXE file. This tiresome sequence will slow production to a crawl!

A much easier method is to create a BLOAD file directly from an EXE module. There are several ways to do this, and they all require the single step of placing a "BLOAD header" at the start of the object code. The critical information (not described in the BASIC manual) is that all BLOAD files begin with a 7-byte header; the rest of the file is simply a binary image of the memory that contains the program.

The BLOAD header consists of four items:

1. A BYTE of 0FDH that identifies the file as being in BLOAD format.

2. A WORD that specifies the default *segment* of the load address.

3. A WORD that specifies the default *offset* of the load address.

4. A WORD that indicates the *length* of the file (less the BLOAD header).

Notice that the default segment:offset address is not in the standard doubleword format. This is one of the few instances in which the segment value is specified in the first two bytes of a 4-byte address.

You may examine the format of a BLOAD module by using DEBUG to read a file that was created by the BSAVE command. After loading the file, dump the bytes starting at CS:100 (the address at which DEBUG loads all but EXE files). For instance, the following session BSAVEs all of the bytes in the monochrome adapter's video memory and then uses DEBUG to examine the first part of the file:

```
A>BASICA

The IBM Personal Computer Basic

Version A2.10 Copyright IBM Corp. 1981,1982,1983

60891 Bytes Free


Ok

DEF SEG=&HB000 :BSAVE ''bsave.tst'',0,4000
                              '** save the B/W screen memory

SYSTEM
                              '** exit to DOS


A>DEBUG bsave.tst

-D cs:100

xxxx:0100 FD 00 B0 00 00 A0 0F 54-07 68 07 65 07 20 07 40   }.0.. .T.h.e. .I
xxxx:0110 07 42 07 4D 07 20 07 50-07 65 07 72 07 73 07 6F   .B.M. .P.e.r.s.o
xxxx:0120 07 6E 07 61 07 6C 07 20-07 43 07 6F 07 6D 07 70   .n.a.l. .C.o.m.p
xxxx:0130 07 75 07 74 07 65 07 72-07 20 07 42 07 61 07 73   .u.t.e.r. .B.a.s
xxxx:0140 07 69 07 63 07 FF 07 20-07 20 07 20 07 20 07 20   .i.c... . . . .
xxxx:0150 07 20 07 20 07 20 07 20-07 20 07 20 07 20 07 20   . . . . . . . .
xxxx:0160 07 20 07 20 07 20 07 20-07 20 07 20 07 20 07 20   . . . . . . . .
xxxx:0170 07 20 07 20 07 20 07 20-07 20 07 20 07 20 07 20   . . . . . . . .
```

The first byte is the BLOAD file identification. The next four bytes are the value of the DEFault SEGment and the offset (B000:0000). The following bytes are the hex representation of 4000 (0FA0H). The rest of the file contains the data that are stored in the display memory. In this example, it is the message that appears in the upper left-hand corner of the screen when you start BASIC. (Every second byte is a screen attribute of 07H—the white-on-black video attribute.)

The default load address is used only in one special case. If you BLOAD the file without using the offset parameter of the BLOAD statement, the load address is read from the BLOAD file. For example,

```
10 BLOAD "bsave.tst"
```

will automatically load the file at B000:0000. But if you specify an offset, the file will be loaded at the segment defined by the current DEFault SEGment at the specified offset. A good way to lock up your machine is to enter

```
10 DEF SEG :BLOAD "BSAVE.TST",0
```

This command will load the screen data into offset 0 in BASIC's default segment—right over the top of critical BASIC code and data. Omit the ",0" and it will be loaded from the address from which it was saved. Change the DEF SEG to point to &HB800 and the screen data will be loaded into the color/graphics adapter card memory.

How do we use all of this information to create our own BLOAD file from an assembly language program? First, we must start with a binary image file, such as those created by the EXE2BIN program. This action entails making sure that all of the program's code and data reside in a single logical segment (the simplest way is to place everything in the code segment). Once the file is in the BIN format, several alternatives are available.

**Putting the BLOAD Header in the Source Code**

One method is to use DB and DW pseudo-ops within the assembly language file itself. By inserting the following commands at the top of the code segment, you can specify the required information:

```
HEADER    DB   0FDH        ;the BLOAD identification byte

ADDR_SEG  DW   0B800H      ;the default load address

                          ;segment . . .

ADDR_OFF  DW   0           ;  and offset (this one's in

                          ;video memory)

RTN_LEN   DW   LAST_ADDR   ;BLOAD module size in bytes
```

The symbol LAST_ADDR is a label that is to be placed directly before the ENDS pseudo-op that closes your program's code segment. The ADDR_SEG and ADDR_OFF are set to arbitrary values that will load the program into video memory if you should (heaven forbid!) forget to specify the offset parameter in the BLOAD command. This procedure makes that error highly visible and not fatal.

You must be cautious in using this method, especially when the assembly code contains its own data area (messages, scratch pad variables, etc.). Just remember that the seven bytes of the BLOAD header will bias all address references by seven bytes. Jump and call opcodes are self-relative but references to internal data locations will be invalid (they must be adjusted downward by seven).

### Adding the BLOAD Header with DEBUG

Another way to create a BLOAD file is to load the BIN program with DEBUG; use the M command to move all of the opcodes forward in memory by seven bytes; use Edit or Fill to place the 7-byte header at the top of the file; and finally, use the W command to Write the file back out to disk (be sure to write the entire file by setting CX to seven greater than its initial value). For example:

```
A>DEBUG MYPROG.BIN

-R cx

0040:                   (examine the current length of the file)

47                                (increase the file size by 7)

-M 100 L40 107            (move the bytes upward in memory)

-F 100 L7 fd 00 b8 00 00 20 00   (place the BLOAD header
                                   bytes at the start)

-N myprog.bld             (rename file)

-W                        (save the 47H-byte file)

-Q                        (exit to DOS)
```

This method is almost as complex as the technique described in the BASIC manual, but it does illustrate what needs to be done. The 7-byte header must be inserted at the start of the file, and the file's length must be increased by seven bytes.

### Adding the BLOAD Header by Using COPY

An easier but less flexible method is to create a short, 7-byte file that contains the bytes of the header, and then use the DOS COPY command to add the bytes to the start of the BIN file.

```
A>COPY header.bin/B +myprog.bin myprog.bld
```

The /B option is specified to indicate that this is a binary file as opposed to the ASCII file. The disadvantage of this method is that the HEADER.BIN file must be changed for each program that is converted to the BLOAD format; bytes 6 and 7 must specify the length of the BLOAD module.

### Converting a Binary Image File into BLOAD Format

Finally, Listing 7.3 is a BASIC program that converts a binary-image file to BLOAD format. The program prompts for the filename of the input file (which is assumed to have an extension of .BIN) and automatically creates a file with the same name but a .BLD extension. By using this program, you can create a BLOAD-format file with the following steps:

```
A>MASM MYPROG;

A>LINK MYPROG;

A>EXE2BIN MYPROG

A>BASICA BIN2BLD

Input filename [.BIN]: myprog

Load address segment [B800]: ENTER

Load address offset  [0000]: ENTER

Output file         : myprog.BIN
Default load address: B800:0000
OK
```

Once the file has been converted, you may run your BASIC program that loads and tests the object code. If you selected the default load address, you will need to be sure that the BLOAD command specifies an offset and is preceded by a DEF SEG statement.

For example, to load the BLOAD module into the addresses above EA60H within the BASIC segment, use a sequence such as

```
10 CLEAR ,60000
20 MYPROG=60000
30 BLOAD "myprog.bld",myprog
```

To load the program at the start of a segment that is out of the domain of the BASIC interpreter, use a sequence like this:

```
10 DEF SEG=0 :BAS.SEG=PEEK(&H510)+PEEK(&H511)*256
20 DEF SEG=BAS.SEG+&H100
30 MYPROG=0
40 BLOAD "myprog.bld",MYPROG
```

## Listing 7.3
## BIN2BLD.BAS

```
7 '** Listing 7.3    BIN2BLD.BAS
8 '** program converts a .BIN format file into a BLOAD module
9 '**
10 CLS :INPUT "Input file [.BIN]: ",F$
20    IF F$="" THEN 10
30    T=INSTR(F$,".")
40    IF T=0 THEN IN.FILE$=F$+".BIN" ELSE IN.FILE$=F$
50    IF T=0 THEN OUT.FILE$=F$+".BLD" ELSE OUT.FILE$=LEFT$(F$,T)+".BLD"
60 INPUT "Hex load address Segment [B800]: ",SEGMENT$
64    SEGMENT=VAL("&h"+SEGMENT$) :IF SEGMENT<0 THEN SEGMENT=SEGMENT+65536!
66    SEG.H=INT(SEGMENT/256) :SEG.L=SEGMENT-256*SEG.H        '** break into bytes
70 INPUT "Hex load address Offset  [0000]: ",OFFSET$
74    OFFSET=VAL("&h"+OFFSET$) :IF OFFSET<0 THEN OFFSET=OFFSET+65536!
76    OFF.H=INT(OFFSET/256) :OFF.L=OFFSET-256*OFF.H          '** break into bytes
80 IF (OFF.H+OFF.L+SEG.H+SEG.L)=0 THEN SEG.H=&HB8 :SEGMENT=&HB800 '** default
97 '**
98 '** open the files
99 '**
100 OPEN IN.FILE$ AS #1 LEN=1
110 OPEN OUT.FILE$ AS #2 LEN=1
120 FIELD #1,1 AS IN.B$ :FIELD #2,1 AS OUT.B$
130 COUNT = LOF(1)                                '** size of input file
197 '**
198 '** place the 7-byte header in the output file
199 '**
200 LSET OUT.B$ = CHR$(&HFD)        :PUT #2    '** BLOAD file identfier byte
210 LSET OUT.B$ = CHR$(SEG.L)       :PUT #2    '** default load segment LSB
220 LSET OUT.B$ = CHR$(SEG.H)       :PUT #2    '**                      MSB
230 LSET OUT.B$ = CHR$(OFF.L)       :PUT #2    '** default load offset LSB
240 LSET OUT.B$ = CHR$(OFF.H)       :PUT #2    '**                      MSB
250 LSET OUT.B$ = CHR$(COUNT AND 255) :PUT #2  '** BLOAD file length LSB
260 LSET OUT.B$ = CHR$(COUNT\256)   :PUT #2    '**                   MSB
297 '**
298 '**  copy the rest of the input file to the output file
299 '**
300 FOR J=1 TO COUNT
310    GET #1 :LSET OUT.B$ = IN.B$ :PUT #2
320 NEXT
330 CLOSE
340 PRINT
350 PRINT "Output File          : ";OUT.FILE$
360 PRINT "Default load address: ";
380 PRINT RIGHT$("000"+HEX$(SEGMENT),4);":";RIGHT$("000"+HEX$(OFFSET),4)
390 PRINT
```

## THINGS TO DO

1.  Write a BASIC program that reads a BIN file and outputs DATA lines, in ASCII,
    that define the value of each byte in the file. Use the same type of logic for reading
    the file as that used in Listing 7.3. Each line of output should start with a line
    number (in an ascending sequence), followed by the word "DATA." Write ten
    values to a line, and place a comma between each. Example:

    ```
    1000 DATA 12,78,255,26,224,89,200,111,0,17

    1010 DATA 219,91,200,00,00,71,5,33,71,119
    ```

    .

    .

    .

The resulting file can be inserted into a program with the MERGE command. Given the data lines that define the bytes of a procedure, you need only write the code that READs the data and POKEs each byte into memory.

## USR Programs: Creating a User Service Routine

The general format for the USR function is:

```
variable = USRn(expression)
```

The *n* is one of 0 to 9 user service routines that have previously been defined with a DEF USR*n* = *address* statement.

When BASIC hands control to a USR program, it does not employ the standard parameter-passing convention discussed earlier in this chapter. Instead, it follows this special convention described in the BASIC manual. When a USR program takes control, it finds the following environment:

* The DS, ES, and SS segment registers all point to BASIC's segment.

* The CS and IP registers have the values named by DEF SEG and DEF USR*n*.

* The AL register contains a *variable-type* code.

* Either DX or BX contains a pointer for accessing the parameter.

The variable-type will always be one of four values, and it indicates which register contains the pointer to the data:

* AL = 2 BX points to a 2-byte integer value.

* AL = 4 BX points to a lowest byte of a 4-byte single-precision number.

* AL = 8 BX points to a lowest byte of an 8-byte double-precision number.

* AL = 3 DX points to a 3-byte *string descriptor*.

(See the BASIC manual for details on the exponent and mantissa conventions that BASIC uses for single- and double-precision numbers.)

When the variable type code is 3, you must go through a series of steps to access the characters of the string. The address passed in DX is a pointer to a 3-byte block of data, with the first byte being the length of the string and the last two bytes being a pointer to the actual string data. Figure 7.2 diagrams this structure.

To access the string data, first copy DX into a pointer register (BX is handy). That action makes the BX point to the byte that defines the length of the string (0-255). Copy this byte into the CX register so that it can be used as a counter (i.e., copy the byte into the CL register and clear the CH register to 0). The next two bytes of the string descriptor describe the offset (within BASIC's segment) at which you can find the first character of the string. Copy these two bytes into another pointer register (SI is a good candidate). After these steps have been performed, the SI register points to the first character of the string and the CX register is set up for repeated string operations.

**Figure 7.2**

**Interpretive BASIC USR Function and the String Descriptor Block**

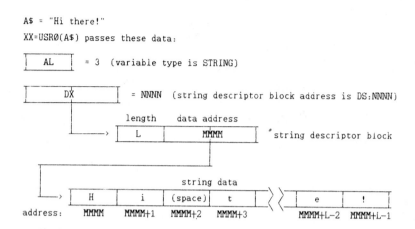

Listing 7.4a, UPSHIFT, gives an example of how to work with this convention. This program goes through an error-checking prologue to make sure that a string variable has been passed to it and that the string is at least one character long. Then the program uses the SI register and the LODSB opcode to access the string data. The processing is very simple. Each byte of the string is tested to see if it is a lowercase alphabetic character. If so, the lowercase bit (bit 5) is masked off the character, forcing it to become uppercase. After all of the characters have been processed, the program exits back to BASIC via a FAR return.

The main advantage of the USR*n* function is the variety of ways that it may be invoked. BASIC treats the USR function just like a SIN(*num_exp*), an ASC(*string_exp*), or any other 1-argument function. It evaluates the expression between the parentheses and then takes the indicated action. USR is different from regular BASIC functions only in that the function is one that you have personally created and interfaced to BASIC.

There is considerable flexibility in terms of how the routine is invoked. Here are some examples of valid ways to invoke the UPSHIFT function:

```
PRINT USR0(A$)              'UPSHIFT before output

LSET B$=USR0(A$)            'UPSHIFT into file buffer

MID$(A$,12,2)=MID$(USR0(A$),12,2)
                              'UPSHIFT a part of the string

A$=USR0(FIRST.NAMES+" "+LAST.NAME$)
                              'UPSHIFT a concatenated string

IF USR0(INPUT$(1))="Y" THEN . . .
                              'UPSHIFT before interrogating
```

## Listing 7.4a
## UPSHIFT User Service Routine

```
;-------------------------------------------------------------------
; Listing 7.4a   UPSHIFT  User Service Routine
;
; This routine changes all lowercase characters in a BASIC string
;  into UPPERCASE characters.
; It is called from BASIC via
;
;         UPCASE$ = USRn(VAR$)
;where:
;         VAR$ is a string variable name or a string expression.
;
; All characters in VAR$ that were between 'a' and 'z' will
;  be converted to the 'A' to 'Z' counterparts.
;
; Note: Assemble and link; then process with EXE2BIN and BIN3BLD.BAS

cseg    segment
        assume  CS:cseg, DS:nothing

upshift proc    far         ;FAR PROC ensures intersegment return
        cmp     al,3        ;must be string argument
        jne     exit        ; exit if not
        mov     bx,dx       ;use base register for memory work
        mov     ch,0        ;preclear upper byte of character counter
        mov     cl,[bx]     ;get the length for string descriptor
        cmp     cl,0        ;is it a null string?
        je      exit        ; yes, exit. Otherwise, get pointer to characters
        mov     si,[bx+1]   ; SI points to first character of string
get_char:
        lodsb               ;fetch a character from the string, increment SI
        cmp     al,'a'      ;below 'a' ?
        jb      save_char   ; yes, leave it alone
        cmp     al,'z'      ;above 'z'?
        ja      save_char   ; yes, leave it
                            ; no, lowercase alphabetic, so upshift it..
        and     al,1011111B ;     by masking the lowercase bit
save_char:
        mov     [si-1],al   ;put the character back where it came from
        loop    get_char    ;decrement CX and loop until done
exit:
        ret                 ;long RET to BASIC
upshift endp
cseg    ends
        end     upshift     ;need start address for .BIN file
```

Listing 7.4b is a BASIC example of how to load and execute the UPSHIFT USR function. The address of the routine is set with the DEF USR0 command in line 30 and the routine itself is invoked in lines 60 and 80. This listing also illustrates an interesting facet of the interpretive BASIC connection. When a machine code subroutine alters a BASIC string, *it may alter program text.* If the string is a literal on a program line, the string descriptor block will point to that program line. The same is true for strings that have been read from DATA lines. If such an alteration occurs and you later save the BASIC program, the changes will become permanent.

The first major drawback of using the USR function to interface code to BASIC is that the compiler's USR function works entirely differently (you lose compatibility when compiling your interpretive program). The other important drawback is that only

## Listing 7.4b
## UPTEST.BAS

```
0 '** Listing 7.4b UPTEST.BAS
1 '** Loads and tests the UPSHIFT USR routine
2 '**
10 CLEAR,60000! :UPSHIFT=60000!
20 BLOAD"upshift.bld",UPSHIFT    '** read file created with BIN2BLD.BAS
30 DEF USR0=UPSHIFT              '** set up the call address
40 CLS
50 INPUT "enter some lowercase characters";A$
60 PRINT USR0(A$)               '** show that the input string is upshifted
70 A$="This program line is lowercase."
80 UU$=USR0(A$)
90 PRINT :LIST                  '** show that line 70 has been altered
```

one value or argument may be passed to your subroutine. In the case of UPSHIFT, this is no problem, but more sophisticated functions will inevitably need more than a single argument. The BASIC CALL statement has no such limitations.

### THINGS TO DO

1.  Write a USR routine that adds 1 to its integer parameter. Make it as fast as possible by using the INC WORD PTR [BX] instruction.

2.  Compare the elapsed time of 10000 executions of each of these statements:

    ```
    X%=X%+1

    X%=USR0(X%)
    ```

3.  (**) Basic program text begins at the offset specified by the word at address 30H in the BASIC segment. That address contains a 2-byte pointer to the start of the next line, followed by a 2-byte value of the line number, followed by one or more bytes of program text. The last line of the program starts with a next-line pointer that points to a word of 0000.

    BASIC's current-line pointer (the period . in LIST .) is stored at offset 349H in the BASIC segment. It names the line number that was last entered or listed or at which an error occurred.

    The challenge: Write a USR routine that accepts a string parameter and looks through the BASIC program (from the current-line to the end) for a match with that string. If it finds a match, it should change the current-line pointer to point to the line of the match.

    This function is used to find references to variable names and literal strings defined in a BASIC program:

    ```
    X=USR1("PAGE.COUNT") :LIST .
    ```

### CALL: Passing Multiple Arguments

Although the CALL statement can't be used with the same flexibility as the USR command (all arguments must be held in variables), it does provide a way to pass more than one value to a routine, and it may return multiple-values back to the caller. The format is:

```
CALL addr_var [(variable,[,variable]...)]
```

The *addr_var* is an address within the current DEFault SEGment to which the interpreter will pass control. The arguments to the CALL must be variable names; you cannot use an expression. Also, notice that all variable arguments are optional. It is quite legal to call a program with no parameters.

At last, we see an example of the standard parameter-passing convention in use. Listing 7.5a is named QPRINT because it Quickly PRINTs strings of characters. One of the big disappointments of the IBM PC is the sluggish speed at which BASIC prints on the screen. It takes nearly four seconds to fill the 80 by 25 screen with characters. You can almost see the delay between the printing of individual characters. Word processing and many other BASIC applications often require the entire screen to be rewritten, and the response time with the PRINT statement is intolerably slow. The difference between PRINT and QPRINT is astonishing.

QPRINT will display an 80-character line in the blink of an eye and fill the screen in one-tenth the time required by BASIC. The program avoids the character-by-character processing that typifies the BASIC PRINT command. It displays the entire string in a tight loop. Also, since QPRINT ignores the attribute byte that normally accompanies a printed character, it makes half as many screen memory accesses. Functionally, QPRINT combines the LOCATE command with PRINT, thereby saving even more BASIC overhead.

A call to QPRINT displays characters of an argument string starting at the horizontal and vertical screen coordinates specified in two integer arguments. It does not update the cursor position, nor does it specify any color for the characters printed. The characters take on the color, blink, and underline attributes of whatever characters were previously there. If a string will not fit on one screen line, it will wrap around to the next one.

The routine includes the logic for determining which type of display card is being used (color graphics or monochrome), and the horizontal and vertical coordinates that are passed to it are valid for either 40- or 80-column modes. However, it does not work when the color graphics card is in any of the graphics modes.

Read the comments at the start of Listing 7.5a to see the format of the CALL command. QPRINT expects one string argument (VAR$) and two integer arguments (ROW% and CLM%) *in that order*. The argument values that BASIC passes are always pointers, or references to the values of the variables; BASIC never passes the values themselves. As BASIC processes the call, it first encounters the VAR$ reference; thus, the pointer to the string descriptor block is the first value that is PUSHed onto the stack. Both ROW% and CLM% are integer arguments (the percent sign is optional if you have used a DEF INT command). BASIC PUSHes the addresses where QPRINT will be able to find these 16-bit values.

## Listing 7.5a
## QPRINT Subroutine CALLED from BASIC

```
;-------------------------------------------------------------------------
; Listing 7.5a  QPRINT subroutine called from BASIC.
;
; This routine prints a string to the video display at 10 times the speed of
;  BASIC.  It works for color or monochrome in 80 or 40 column TEXT modes.
; Characters are displayed with the existing color, blink, and underline
;  attributes.
; Called from BASIC via:
;
;          CALL QPRINT(VAR$,ROW%,CLM%)
; Where:
;          VAR$ is a string variable name.
;          ROW% is an integer variable name: 1 to 25
;          CLM% is an integer variable name: 1 to 80 (or 1 to 40)
;
; Action:  VAR$ is displayed beginning at position CLM% of line ROW%.
;                If it's too long, it will wrap around to the next line.
; Note: Color card pages 1-7 may be accessed by setting ROW% above 25.
;
; Implementation:  Set the equate in the first line to a 1 to make
;  QPRINT compatible with Compiler BASIC.  For interpretive BASIC, process
;  the OBJ file with EXE2BIN and BIN2BLD.

BASCOM_VER equ    0         ;default setting is for interpretive BASIC

          public qprint     ;needed when using the compiler; otherwise harmless
code_seg segment 'code'
          assume CS:code_seg, DS:nothing, ES:nothing
qprint    proc   far
          push   bp         ;save the frame pointer
          mov    bp,sp      ;point to arguments on the stack
          push   es         ;always save and restore altered segment registers

          mov    bx,[bp+6]  ;get address of CLM% storage
          mov    di,[bx]    ; get the column value
          dec    di         ; adjust from LOCATE format (make it 0 to 79)

          mov    bx,[bp+8]  ;get address of ROW% storage
          mov    dx,[bx]    ; get the screen line value into DL
          dec    dx         ; adjust (make it 0 to 24)

          mov    bx,[bp+10] ;get pointer to string descriptor

     if bascom_ver
          mov    cx,[bx]    ;BASCOM string length is 2 bytes long
          mov    si,[bx+2]  ;point to the characters of the string
          %out BASCOM version
     else
          mov    ch,0       ;Interpretive BASIC string length is 1 byte
          mov    cl,[bx]    ;fetch the length
          mov    si,[bx+1]  ; and point SI to first character of VAR$
          %out BASIC interpreter version
     endif

          cmp    cx,0       ;null string?
          je     exit       ; if so, do nothing. Else,
```

**Listing 7.5a
(continued)**

```
;--- get the current number of columns and the display type to ---
;--- calculate the physical memory address to write the string ---

        mov     ah,0FH
        int     10H             ;fetch the number of columns in current mode
        mov     al,ah
        mul     dl              ;AX = ROW% * characters per screen line
        add     di,ax           ;DI = words from start of screen
        shl     di,1            ; times 2 for attribute bytes

        mov     bx,0b800H       ;assume color/graphics card
        int     11H             ;EQUIPMENT_DETERMINATION service
        and     ax,30H
        cmp     ax,30H          ;is it the B/W card?
        jne     card_ok         ; no, go
        mov     bx,0B000H       ; yes, set for monochrome
card_ok:
        mov     es,bx           ; point ES to video

        push    ds
        mov     dx,40H          ;temporarily point to BIOS data area
        mov     ds,dx
        mov     dx,ds:[0063H]   ;get BIOS address of CRT controller base port
        add     dx,6            ;point to status port
        pop     ds              ;restore BASIC data segment

; DS points to BASIC variables area
; ES points to video card memory
; SI is the offset of the characters of the string to be printed
; DI is the offset of the screen memory to receive the characters
; CX is the length of the string
; DX points to the video card status port to test for video retrace period
; Now display VAR$ on the screen.

;-------------- wait for horizontal retrace
test_low:
        in      al,dx           ;get status
        test    al,1            ; is it low?
        jnz     test_low        ; no, keep checking
        cli                     ;turn off interrupts
test_hi:
        in      al,dx           ;get status
        test    al,1            ; is it high?
        jz      test_hi         ; no, keep checking
; -------------- okay to write to screen now (no 'snow')
        movsb                   ;DS:[SI] -> ES:[DI], DI++, SI++, CX--
        inc     di              ;skip the attribute byte
        loop    test_low        ;do until the end of the string is reached
exit:
        sti                     ;turn interrupts back on
        pop     es
        pop     bp
        ret     6               ;discard the 3 arguments
qprint  endp

code_seg ends
        end     qprint          ;start address needed for .BIN file conversion
```

Note how the assembler's IF/ELSE/ENDIF structure is used in this program. It tests the value of the BASCOM_VER flag and assembles a slightly different code sequence when it is nonzero. The differences between the interpreter and compiler versions are discussed in Section 7.4.

Once the values of the arguments are read into the registers, the program has to go through the additional overhead of finding which display adapter is active and whether it is in 40- or 80-column mode. These lines are instructional because this type of test is often needed to make sure that your software is compatible with the full range of standard IBM PC equipment.

Finally, the routine copies each of the bytes in the string into video memory, skipping the attribute bytes as it goes. The program checks to make sure that the monitor is in its retrace period before it moves each byte into the display area. This procedure avoids the irritating "snow" that may appear when characters are rapidly written into video memory. (Chapter 8 contains more detailed information on the way that text characters are displayed.)

As with UPSHIFT, this program is written to reside in a single physical segment, and is thus eligible to be converted into a BIN file by EXE2BIN. After the conversion, use BIN2BLD.BAS (the program in Listing 7.3) to create a BLOAD module. Finally, type in and run Listing 7.5b to test the QPRINT code. You may find that it is the only possible way to throw characters onto the screen fast enough for some applications.

**Listing 7.5b**
**QPTEST.BAS**

```
1 '** Listing 7.5b    QPTEST.BAS
3 '** Loads and tests the call to the QPRINT subroutine
4 '** Delete lines 10-30 for compiler BASIC.
5 '**
10 CLEAR,60000                    '** protect memory above 60000
20 QPRINT=60000                   '** define load, call address
30 BLOAD"B:QPRINT.BLD",QPRINT     '** load routine into memory
997  '**
998 '** Repeatedly fill the screen.
999 '**
1000 CLM%=1                        '** start output at left edge
1010 FOR J%=0 TO 255               '** loop through entire character set
1020   A$=STRING$(80,J%)           '** define one line of 80 characters
1030   FOR ROW%=1 TO 24            '** loop through the 25 screen lines
1040     CALL QPRINT(A$,ROW%,CLM%) '** invoke the procedure
1050   NEXT
1060 NEXT
1070 END
```

**Debugging the Hybrid Program**

As with any assembler program, there are an almost infinite number of ways to wipe out a hybrid program. Besides the obvious worry about calling the wrong address, you can chew your nails over mismatched variable types; you can get heartburn over misplaced data; you can scratch your head about messing up BASIC's data and code area; you can stare hatefully at incorrectly addressed screen memory; you can sob in frustration over disabled interrupts . . . After repeated lockups, you will begin to wonder what you can do about the problem(s).

How do you spell relief? D-E-B-U-G. When any other assembler program goes wrong, just whip out DEBUG and trace through the code, looking for the error, but interpretive BASIC seems incompatible with DEBUG. The trick is to make DEBUG active when your assembly language subroutine takes control. This turns out to be a relatively simple operation.

First, you must get DEBUG into memory *below* BASIC. The sequence

```
A>DEBUG BASIC.COM

-G
```

will install DEBUG below BASIC. This procedure allows you to create and run BASIC programs just as if DEBUG were still out on the diskette. But as soon as you type SYSTEM, you will see the reassuring message "Program terminated normally," and you are back at the DEBUG prompt. How can you activate DEBUG at the critical moment when your assembly language subroutine begins executing? Just modify your BASIC test routine so that it sets a DEBUG breakpoint into the assembler code. The modification for Listing 7.5b is as follows:

```
40 PRINT HEX$(PEEK(QPRINT))

50 POKE QPRINT,&HCC
```

Line 50 changes the first byte of the assembler code to 0CCH, the 1-byte INT 3 that DEBUG uses to place breakpoints into a program. Line 40 displays the original value of that byte so that you can change the byte back after you're in DEBUG. As soon as execution reaches the CALL QPRINT in line 1040, you will suddenly be looking at the DEBUG register display.

When DEBUG encounters a 0CCH breakpoint, it will attempt to replace that byte with a value from its breakpoint address table. In this case, there will be no entries in that table so you must manually change the byte back to what it was before the 0CCH was poked into that address. It's no coincidence that the original value of that address has been displayed by line 40 above.

To make the whole sequence more clear, let's go over the steps that will help you to debug assembler code that is interfaced with interpreted BASIC:

1. At the DOS prompt, enter: DEBUG BASIC.COM (execute DEBUG and load BASIC).

2. At the DEBUG prompt, enter: G         (execute BASIC).

3. Type in (or load) and run the BASIC testing program.

4. At the DEBUG prompt, enter: E CS:*nnnn*   (*nnnn* is the IP value—EA60H here).

5. In the DEBUG editor, enter: *nn*        (*nn* is the number printed by line 40).

6. Use U, T, D, G, or any DEBUG command.

After you have changed the first byte back to its original value, you may run the gamut of DEBUG commands, including disassembling the code, executing the code with breakpoints, single-step tracing the program, displaying parts of BASIC's data area, and looking at the stack. Now that you are back in control, you can throw out the antacid—your problem is all but solved.

Notes: Pay special attention to the stack pointer and the way your parameters are handled. If everything looks good, check through your code to find the RETF that sends execution back to BASIC. Execute your routine, placing a breakpoint at the address of the RETF opcode, then use the T command to single-step the return. Your routine should return to F600:5DE9 (ROM BASIC code area). If it doesn't (i.e., you "returned" to outer space), you can either try using the G command to transfer control to F600:5DE9 (G=F600:5DE9) or use Ctrl-Alt-Del to reboot the system. Don't use DEBUG's Q command here because DEBUG is nested beneath BASIC.

Other things to watch for: Make sure that all segment registers are restored to their original values before exiting back to BASIC. If you changed the direction flag with STD, your program should be sure to change it back. If you disable interrupts with CLI, be sure to turn them back on with STI.

Incidentally, you needn't stop tracing when your program is finished. You may single-step right through ROM BASIC and glean interesting information about how BASIC works.

**THINGS TO DO**

1. Try removing the part of the code in Listing 7.5a (QPRINT) that keeps the snow from forming on the screen. See if this procedure makes it any faster. Try slipping two or more characters onto the screen during a single retrace period. Does this speed up the program significantly?

2. Change QPRINT to make it accept a screen attribute parameter, so that the characters of VAR$ will be printed with a given color, blink, or underline attribute.

3. Write a program that makes QPRINT into an interpretive BASIC USR function. It should interpret the first two characters of the string as being the desired cursor location:

```
UU=USR0(CHR$(ROW%)+CHR$(CLM%)+"PRINT THESE CHARACTERS")
```

4. (*) Go one step further and give this USR (or called) procedure the ability to draw text-character "shapes." For example, if QPRINT encounters a Ctrl-U, CHR$(21), the cursor should move up after each character rather than left. Have it change the "vector" of the cursor motion when it encounters a Ctrl-L, Ctrl-R, or Ctrl-D. You could even add special color codes to change the screen attributes of the text characters that are being displayed.

## 7.4 LINKING TO COMPILED BASIC PROGRAMS

Application programs compiled by the IBM-PC Compiler BASIC (BASCOM) often run more than twice as fast as interpretive BASIC programs. One area where this is not true is the PRINT command. A BASCOM program that prints 2000 characters to fill the screen takes nearly as long as its interpretive counterpart. Obviously, a program such as QPRINT is needed whether the code is compiled or not.

The general format of the BASCOM CALL statement may, at first glance, look identical to that used in interpretive BASIC:

```
CALL subrtn_name [(variable[,variable]...)]
```

The difference in format is only one of nomenclature (*addr_var* is replaced with *subrtn_name*), but there is a major difference in the way the assembler subroutine interfaces with the BASCOM program. Instead of being loaded with POKEs or BLOAD, the subroutine is brought into the program when the BASCOM object file is linked into an .EXE program. In fact, this is the real purpose of the linker—to connect a series of modules (whether BASCOM, Pascal, or assembler) into a single executable program. Note: It is still possible to BLOAD a binary file into memory, but it cannot be accessed with this form of the CALL command.

The *subrtn_name* is the label of a procedure that has been declared PUBLIC in the source code. The BASCOM command: CALL MYPROG actually generates an external reference identical to those created by using the EXTRN pseudo-op in an assembler source file. The external reference must be satisfied by a PUBLIC symbol from another module or else the linker will indicate an "Unresolved External Reference" error.

The CALL statement passes parameters the same way in BASCOM programs as it does with interpretive BASIC; the first argument in the argument list is PUSHed first, followed by the second, and so on. Numeric arguments are passed *by reference* in an identical manner. For integers, the address that is on the stack points to the 16-bit, two's complement value. For single- and double-precision numbers, the parameter on the stack points to a 4-byte or 8-byte floating point value.

String arguments are passed by a reference to a string descriptor; however, BASCOM stores string data in a slightly different format. BASCOM strings may be as long as 32,767 bytes, and their length is specified by a 2-byte value in the string descriptor block. Thus, the assembly language module must be coded slightly differently when it is to be interfaced with a compiled BASIC program.

Looking back to Listing 7.5a, notice that the program includes an IF/ELSE/ENDIF conditional pseudo-op construct. It is set to mask the differences between the two separate ways that strings must be handled. When the BASCOM_VER symbol has been set to a nonzero value, the string length is taken to be a 16-bit value and the string's address is assumed to start at the third byte of the string descriptor block. When BASCOM_VER is set to 0, the program is to be used with the BASIC interpreter, the string length is described by a 1-byte value, and the address starts at the second byte of the string descriptor. Also notice that the %OUT command will let you know which version is being assembled.

Notice that the CODE_SEG segment has been given a class name of 'code.' This name ensures that it will be grouped next to the other BASCOM code. This detail is only critical in the compiler version. When BASCOM initializes its variables, it zeros out memory segments that don't have a class name of 'code.'

As you can see, this difference is slight but critical. In order to get the best service from the BASIC compiler, you should use the interpreter during the testing and debugging phase of program development and then switch over to the compiler when you are ready for production. By using this technique to mask the differences in the assembly module, you can avoid writing two separate assembly language programs.

You will, however, need two slightly different versions of the BASIC program. The BASCOM version must not use the DEF SEG and BLOAD commands to load the program, and you should not CLEAR memory for the assembler code. The segment and address of the code are automatically set up by the linker according to the group, segment, and procedure definitions in the assembler source text.

To make the QPRINT procedure work from a BASCOM program, you must first set the equate in the first program line to 1. Then assemble the code. Next, use BASCOM to compile Listing 7.5b (QPTEST.BAS). Be sure to delete lines 10 through 30; they are needed only for the interpretive BASIC version. To interface the two object modules, invoke the linker with this line:

```
LINK QPTEST+QPRINT;
```

If you tell the linker to generate a list file, you will see that CODE_SEG is listed along with the segments created by BASCOM. If you select the /MAP option, you will see an extensive list of compiler procedure and variable names.

It is instructive to select the /A and /O options when you compile Listing 7.5b. They will let you see the opcode mnemonics that BASCOM generates. Listing 7.5c is the file created when these options are selected. The CALL $531 is the call to the BASCOM.LIB routine that initializes for BASCOM version 5.31. The calls to $ST$ and $SASA are to library string-handling procedures. Pay special attention to how line 1040 PUSHes the parameters onto the stack before making the external call to the QPRINT procedure. It is also interesting to examine the code that BASCOM generates to implement the nested FOR/NEXT loops in the program. You can learn a lot about the BASIC compiler by using the following batch file:

```
REM -FUN.BAT-batch file for learning about BASCOM
BASCOM CON:,,CON:/A/O;
```

```
PAUSE

FUN
```

## Listing 7.5c
## BASCOM Output of QPTEST.BAS After Deleting Lines 10-30

```
                                                           PAGE   1
                                                           08-23-83
                                                           22:48:47
Offset  Data    Source Line          IBM Personal Computer BASIC Compiler V1.00

001A    0002    1000 CLM%=1                   '** start output at left edge
0026    **           I00001: CALL   $531
002B    **           L01000: MOV    CLM%,0001H
0031    0004    1010 FOR J%=0 TO 255          '** loop through character set
0031    **           L01010: XOR    AX,AX
0033    **                   JMP    I00002
0036    0004    1020 A$=STRING$(80,J%)        '** define one 80-character line
0036    **           I00003:
0036    **           L01020: MOV    BX,0050H
0039    **                   MOV    DX,J%
003D    **                   CALL   $ST$
0042    **                   MOV    DX,OFFSET A$
0045    **                   CALL   $SASA
004A    000A    1030 FOR ROW%=1 TO 24         '** loop through 25 lines
004A    **           L01030: MOV    AX,0001H
004D    **                   JMP    I00004
0050    000A    1040 CALL QPRINT(A$,ROW%,CLM%) '** invoke the procedure
0050    **           I00005:
0050    **           L01040: MOV    AX,OFFSET A$
0053    **                   PUSH   AX
0054    **                   MOV    AX,OFFSET ROW%
0057    **                   PUSH   AX
0058    **                   MOV    AX,OFFSET CLM%
005B    **                   PUSH   AX
005C    **                   CALL   QPRINT
0061    **                   PUSH   DS
0062    **                   POP    ES
0063    **                   CLD
0064    000C    1050 NEXT
0064    **           L01050: MOV    AX,ROW%
0067    **                   INC    AX
0068    **           I00004: MOV    ROW%,AX
006B    **                   CMP    WORD PTR ROW%,18H
0070    **                   JNG    $-22H
0072    000C    1060 NEXT
0072    **           L01060: MOV    AX,J%
0075    **                   INC    AX
0076    **           I00002: MOV    J%,AX
0079    **                   CMP    J%,00FFH
007F    **                   JNG    $-4BH
0081    000C    1070 END
0081    **           L01070: CALL   $END
0086    000C
0086    **                   CALL   $ENP
008B    000C

22151 Bytes Available
21863 Bytes Free

    0 Warning Error(s)
    0 Severe  Error(s)
```

This batch file allows you to enter BASIC statements to the compiler from the keyboard. Just enter a series of BASIC lines and press the F6 (or Ctrl-Z) key. This action forces the compiler to display the machine language mnemonics that your lines generate.

## BASCOM USR and CALL ABSOLUTE

The BASCOM version of the USR function is all but useless because it does not pass an argument. Its only use is to transfer control to some code that is in a predefined location in memory. As with its interpretive counterpart, the transfer address is specified by using the DEF SEG and DEF USR*n* statements.

The CALL ABSOLUTE command is much more useful for transferring control. The syntax is:

```
CALL ABSOLUTE ([variable[,variable] . . . ,]int_var)
```

This command pushes the addresses of each variable argument onto the stack and then calls the address specified by the current DEF SEG at an offset named by *int_var*. The primary purpose of CALL ABSOLUTE is to invoke code that has been brought into memory with a BLOAD command. It is also the only way to pass parameters to a procedure that was fixed in memory before the BASIC program began executing. Let's look at these two options separately.

## BLOADing Into an Array

The normal CALL command transfers control to an external subroutine that must be brought into the program by the linker. If you prefer to BLOAD or POKE a small routine into memory, you may still do so, but you must use this ABSOLUTE variation of the CALL command to transfer control to the code. The major difference is that you must include the address of the routine as an additional argument to the call. This final argument is *not* passed to your routine. You retrieve the arguments just as if *int_var* had not been included in the CALL statement.

If you choose to BLOAD or POKE your subroutine into memory, you must be sure to select suitable addresses. The CLEAR command does not work the same way in BASCOM as it does in interpretive BASIC. Here one of the exotic techniques might be needed to load the code. One way to BLOAD code into a protected area is to place it into an integer array as follows:

```
10 DIM CODE%(100)             '** set up a 200-byte area for the code
20 MY.PROG%=VARPTR(CODE%(0))  '** find the address of the first byte
30 BLOAD ''MYPROG.BLD'',MY.PROG%   '** load the code into the array
40 CALL ABSOLUTE(A1,A2,A3,MY.PROG%)  '** invoke the code with three arguments
```

## Placing Code in Low Memory

If you have written several interlocking BASCOM programs, you have already discovered the value of using the BASCOM run-time package. This set of commonly called procedures is made resident before any program begins running. It is especially valuable when the CHAIN command is used to transfer control between BASCOM modules. The real savings is in diskette space. If you select the BASCOM/O option (to avoid IBM's licensing fee), you will find that every program module takes at least 18K of diskette space because a large part of the library must be included with each module. The run-time package contains all of this common code—keeping it in a single file.

You can use a similar technique to avoid duplication of assembly language code in your programs. When you write a set of compiled programs that all call the same assembly language subroutines, you would normally link the code into each program. When you have several such subroutines, it is convenient to write your own run-time package to avoid having to include the code in each EXE file. This procedure will shorten each module.

There are other advantages of writing a set of procedures and fixing them in low memory. For example, you can set aside a large area to contain "screens" that could be copied directly into video memory—avoiding a laborious sequence of PRINT commands. You could use this area to "page" arrays of data rapidly into and out of memory, thus getting around BASCOM's 64K data limit. You could pass information from module to module (the CHAIN command with COMMON variables has some bugs in BASCOM version 1.0, and it doesn't work at all without the run-time package).

The problem is to find a way to let each BASCOM module know where the assembly language code resides. One way is to pass that information via the interprocess communication area at address 0000:04F0. Listing 7.6 shows what your own run-time package would look like and how you would access the code that it contains.

## COMMON Variables

BASCOM's COMMON statement forces the compiler to store some variables in an area apart from other variables. The syntax is:

```
COMMON variable[,variable . . .]
```

where the variable is the name of a numeric variable of any precision or a string variable or an array of variables. COMMON forces the compiler to set aside a special "logical" segment for the variables named in the statement. It is primarily used to pass data from module to module via the CHAIN command, but it may be used as a mechanism for passing data from the BASCOM program to an assembler module.

This use of COMMON gives your assembly language code an alternative to the stack-oriented argument-passing techniques that we have used throughout this chapter. The BASCOM manual is rather sketchy on the subject, so let's see how this very convenient feature is used.

## Listing 7.6
## Partial Listing

```
;----------------------------------------------------------------------
; Listing 7.6  partial listing
;
; Outline of a user-supplied "run-time package" to be used with BASCOM
; The code uses the DOS FIX_IN_MEMORY service to reserve an area
;    that is below any BASCOM program.

max_pages equ  4       ;increase equate for more video paging area
rtp_seg  segment       ;run-time package segment
         assume cs:rtp_seg, ds:nothing, es:nothing
init     proc    far
         mov    ax,0
         mov    ds,ax           ;point to segment 0
         mov    si,4F0H        ;point to interprocess comunication address
         mov    word ptr [si],offset router  ;save the offset
         mov    [si+2],cs                  ;and segment of your code
         mov    dx,offset CS:last_byte+1    ;DX pionts to end of storage
         int    27H                       ;fix it in memory and exit to DOS
init     endp
router:
         jmp    save_scrn   ;jumps to reach the several procedures
         jmp    get_scrn
         .
         .
         .
save_scrn proc far          ;saves screen number named by the argument

         .(code copies the screen to a page of video storage)

         ret    2           ;discard the argument and return to BASIC
save_scrn endp
get_scrn  proc far          ;restores the screen number named by the argument

         .(code copies a page of storage to the screen)

         ret    2           ;discard the argument and return to BASIC
get_scrn  endp

data_area dw 2000 * max_page dup(?)     ;storage area for the screens
last_byte equ $
rtp_seg  ends

1 '** ----------------------------------------------------------------
2 '** Example of how to invoke the routines
3 '**
10 DEF SEG=0                             '** fetch the address
20 ROUTER.OFF%=PEEK(&H4F0)+PEEK(&H4F1)*256  '** saved by the INIT procedure
30 ROUTER.SEG%=PEEK(&H4F2)+PEEK(&H4F3)*256
40 SAVE.SCRN%=ROUTER.OFF%      '** absolute address of first procedure
50 GET.SCRN%=ROUTER.OFF%+3     '** absolute address of second procedure
60 DEF SEG=ROUTER.SEG%
70 CUR.PAGE%=1
80 CALL ABSOLUTE(CUR.PAGE%, SAVE.SCRN%)  ;save the screen
90 CALL ABSOLUTE(CUR.PAGE%, GET.SCRN%)   ;restore the screen
```

```
7   '**------------------------------
8   '** in the BASCOM source file
9   '**
10  DIM A%(5)         '** 12 bytes of storage (elements 0-5 with two bytes each)
20  COMMON VAR1%.A$.A%()                    '** 18 bytes: var%=2, A$=4, a%()=12
30  VAR1%=1 :A$="THIS IS A$" :A%(3)=3
40  CALL MYPROC

;-------------------------------------

; in the assembler module

DGROUP     GROUP    COMMON                      ;physical segment is named DGROUP

COMMON     SEGMENT COMMON 'BLANK'               ;logical segment is named COMMON

VAR1       DW      ?                               ;set up the template

A$_LEN     DW      ?                            ;  to access BASCOM's data

A$_ADDR    DW      ?

A_ARRAY    DW      6 DUP (?)

COMMON     ENDS

           PUBLIC  MYPROC

CODE_SEG SEGMENT PARA PUBLIC 'CODE'

           ASSUME  CS:CODE_SEG, DS:DGROUP

MYPROC     PROC    FAR

           MOV     VAR1,1234H                   ;change the value of VAR1%

           MOV     BX,OFFSET DGROUP:A_ARRAY        ;BX points to A%(0)

           MOV     CX,A$_LEN                    ;fetch the length of A$

           LEA     SI,A$_ADDR                  ;SI points to the first character

           .

           .
```

Notice that the COMMON segment physically contains the values of VAR1% and the 12 bytes of the A%() array. But it only contains the string descriptor of A$.

As you can see in the example, this method makes it somewhat easier to access the variables. Instead of looking in the stack for a pointer to VAR1%, we simply move a new value to it. The length and address of A$ are also available directly. In time-critical applications, this method will save all of the time that BASCOM programs usually spend PUSHing data on the stack before the call, and its speeds up the code that examines or modifies the data. Imagine how quickly a machine language procedure can sort an array!

You should be familiar with the mechanism that makes this possible; it was explained in Chapter 4. In brief, any segment that has a combine type of COMMON will overlay all other segments with that attribute. In this case, the DW commands within the segment *do not add data to the module.* They are just a convenient way to create a template for the data that BASCOM will place in that segment. The GROUP pseudo-op tells the linker that the COMMON segment is only a small chunk of a larger group of segments. It says that COMMON is one of the logical segments that make up the DGROUP physical memory segment. Thus, the COMMON segment is actually a template that is laid over a fraction of the 64K segment that BASCOM uses to contain and manipulate its data.

If you examine the link map that is created whenever you link a compiled program, you will see the names of all of the segments that BASCOM creates. It's perfectly possible to define segments that will be concatenated with or laid over any of the segments defined by BASCOM. However, it is advisable to keep your code and data in your own segments to avoid the possibility of stepping on BASCOM's toes.

One final note on COMMON: I thought I could define an entire array of values in an assembly module and bring it in at link time, thereby avoiding a long series of READ and DATA lines. After struggling for a while, it occurred to me that BASCOM clears all arrays to 0 before it begins to execute a program. It also sets all string variables to the null string. Thus, any values defined in your own COMMON segment will be lost as soon as BASCOM starts. However, it is possible to move a block of data into an array from an external segment. You can even BLOAD data from a previously prepared disk file into BASCOM's work area (hint: use the VARPTR function to find the destination for the BLOAD).

### THINGS TO DO

1. Flesh out Listing 7.6 so that it performs the outlined procedures (i.e., saving and restoring screen data). (*) Add modules that perform other needed functions such as parsing an input field to check for valid alphabetic or numeric data.

2. Experiment with COMMON variables to gain some understanding of the speed and power of this technique. (*) Write a machine language routine that sorts an array in the COMMON segment.

## 7.5 LINKING TO PASCAL PROGRAMS

The power and flexibility of Pascal are proven by the large number of major application programs that are written in this language. Perhaps its most outstanding feature is its modularity. Pascal programs are composed of procedures, which are composed of blocks, which are composed of statements. If your primary experience is with Pascal, you will find it much easier to learn assembly language than a programmer with only BASIC experience. To typify the difference between BASIC and Pascal, consider this: BASIC has three separate commands to interface with machine language and Pascal has none—because it doesn't need any!

There is no Pascal equivalent to the BASIC CALL or USR commands because Pascal treats assembly language modules the same way it treats its own procedures. Interfacing with Pascal is simply a matter of knowing the argument-passing protocol that we covered at the beginning of this chapter. Just define the procedure (or function) as being EXTERN or EXTERNAL and specify the types and sequence of the arguments that will be passed to it. What's more, there is no need for BASIC's clumsy COMMON interface. Pascal variables that are declared PUBLIC may be accessed directly by an assembly language program.

First, let's look at Pascal variable types to find out just what parameters will be passed to your assembly language module.

INTEGER values are 16-bit two's complement values (-32768 through 32767).

WORD values are 16-bit unsigned values (0 through 65535).

CHAR values are eight bits.

BOOLEAN values are eight bits. 0 is FALSE; 1 is TRUE.

POINTER values are 16-bit addresses offset from DS (in the DATA segment).

REAL values are 32-bit, single-precision, floating point values in this format:

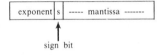

This format is laid out in the reverse order of the actual memory storage. In other words, if you have a REAL value at offset address 1000H, the bytes are laid out as follows:

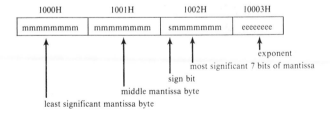

## Pascal Procedures

External procedures use the same calling conventions as do the internal procedures generated from the high-level Pascal statements. Your assembly language code may alter any registers except BP, SS, and DS. However, you must restore the Pascal stack before returning control to the caller.

Upon entry into a procedure, the SS register points to Pascal's stack segment, the CS register points to the segment in which the procedure resides, and the DS register points to Pascal's data segment. The BP register points to the frame of the calling procedure or program. SP points to the called procedure's frame: the 32-bit return address and any data that are to be referenced by the procedure—the procedure's parameters.

Each parameter that is passed to your assembly language procedure (in fact, to any Pascal procedure or function) may be either a value or a reference. Simple arguments are passed by value:

```
PROCEDURE MYPROC(A,B:INTEGER; C:REAL); EXTERNAL;
```

PUSHes two 16-bit values and one 32-bit value onto the stack before the call. When an argument is passed by value, the procedure is working with a copy of the value. If you alter it, there will be no effect on the Pascal program.

Complex data types and all VAR parameters are passed by reference:

```
PROCEDURE MYPROC(A:ARRAY_REC; VAR B:INTEGER); EXTERNAL;
```

PUSHes two 16-bit pointers onto the stack. The first reference points to a superarray type variable created with a RECORD statement. The next reference points to a 16-bit variable. Both values are offsets within the memory segment pointed to by DS. When an argument is passed by reference, it is possible to modify its value; the rest of the Pascal program will be aware of the modification.

This second-guessing about how Pascal is going to pass the parameters can become complex. It is helpful to diagram the frame of data with which the external routines will be working. For instance, the procedure

```
PROCEDURE MYPROC(A:REAL; B:WORD; C:LSTRING; D:CHAR); EXTERNAL;
```

begins with a frame that contains 10 bytes of data and a 4-byte return address. After PUSH BP and MOV BP,SP the frame will look like this:

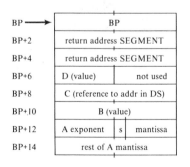

| | | |
|---|---|---|
| BP → | BP | |
| BP+2 | return address SEGMENT | |
| BP+4 | return address SEGMENT | |
| BP+6 | D (value) | not used | value of the CHAR |
| BP+8 | C (reference to addr in DS) | pointer to the LSTRING |
| BP+10 | B (value) | value of the WORD (low byte first) |
| BP+12 | A exponent | s | mantissa | first 16 bits of value of the REAL |
| BP+14 | rest of A mantissa | last 16 bits of the REAL |

The code of MYPROC must end with:

```
POP      BP
RET      10     ; 4 (for A) + 2 (for B) + 2 (for C) + 2 (for D)
```

Of course, it's legal to have procedures and functions that have no arguments at all. In that case, you needn't worry about the frame; just finish your task and return to Pascal.

These different types of parameters can be confusing, even alarming. Pay attention to the types of parameters as they are specified in the PROCEDURE declaration. The best way to make sure that your external procedure is receiving arguments of the expected type and in the expected order is to take a careful look at the code file (MYPROG.COD) that is created during compilation. Alternatively, use DEBUG to examine both parts of a hybrid program. Place a breakpoint at the call to your code and single-step through it to make sure that everything works as expected.

## Pascal Functions

Functions start with the same environment as do procedures. But functions, by their very nature, must return a value. If the return value is eight bits, it is returned in the AL register; 16-bit values are returned in AX, and 32-bit values are returned in ES and BX. Of course, a function may also return values by modifying any memory addresses that are passed to it as variables.

Arguments for Pascal functions are PUSHed just as with procedures; the leftmost argument is farthest from SP, and the rightmost argument is closest to it. After your external procedure PUSHes BP and copies SP into it, the rightmost value in the argument list will be at [BP+6]; the preceding argument will be at either [BP+8] or [BP+10], depending on the size of the rightmost argument.

As with procedures, assembly language functions don't need to preserve any registers except BP, SS, and DS. However, you must be careful to return the right type of value in the correct register(s). For instance, a function declared

```
FUNCTION MYFUNC(A,B:INTEGER):INTEGER; EXTERNAL;
```

must return an INTEGER value in AX. But the function

```
FUNCTION MYFUNC(A,B:INTEGER):STR_ARRAY; EXTERNAL;
```

must return in AX a pointer to a user-defined data structure that matches STR_ARRAY.

Listing 7.7, SYSINT, is a useful assembly language addition to your Pascal toolbox. It provides the ability to invoke any of the ROM-BIOS and PC-DOS services from a Pascal program. It is really a building block for more powerful functions. The comments show how to use it with a procedure named LOCATE. This procedure sets the BIOS cursor position to provide some screen control for Pascal applications. You would generally invoke the LOCATE procedure right before a WRITE or WRITELN statement:

```
LOCATE(0,0); WRITELN('<- this is the upper left corner');
```

## Listing 7.7
## SYSINT External Pascal Procedure

```
;----------------------------
; Listing 7.7 SYSINT external Pascal procedure
;
; Forces a SYStem INTerrrupt from a Pascal program.
;
; Pascal global data declarations:
;   TYPE regs_type = RECORD
;     ax[0]:WORD; al[0]:BYTE; ah[1]:BYTE;
;     bx[2]:WORD; bl[2]:BYTE; bh[3]:BYTE;
;     cx[4]:WORD; cl[4]:BYTE; ch[5]:BYTE;
;     dx[6]:WORD; dl[6]:BYTE; dh[7]:BYTE;
;   END;
;   VAR regs:regs_type; flags:WORD; int_type:BYTE;
;
; Pascal function declaration:
;   FUNCTION sysint(int_type:WORD; VAR regs:regs_type):WORD; EXTERNAL;
;
; Example Usage:
;   PROCEDURE locate(row,clm:BYTE) [PUBLIC];
;   BEGIN
;     regs.ah := 2;                  {select SET_CURSOR_POS}
;     regs.bh := 0;                  {video page 0}
;     regs.dh := row ;regs.dl := clm; {screen row and column}
;     flags   := sysint(16#10,regs)  {force an INT 10H (VIDEO_IO service)}
;   END;
;
;-------------------- Assembler code begins ----------------------
regs_struc  STRUC          ;"template" for the RECORD passed from Pascal
ax_reg      dw      ?
bx_reg      dw      ?
cx_reg      dw      ?
dx_reg      dw      ?
regs_struc  ENDS
            public  sysint        ;SYSINT is passed to the linker

code_seg segment para public 'code'
            assume  cs:code_seg, ds:nothing

sysint      proc    far
            push    bp
            mov     bp,sp           ;point BP to the frame
            mov     ax,[bp+8]       ;AX is requested interrupt type
            mov     cs:int_opcode+1,al ;modify program for interrupt type

            mov     si,[bp+6]       ;point SI to the regs structure
            mov     ax,[si].ax_reg
            mov     bx,[si].bx_reg
            mov     cx,[si].cx_reg
            mov     dx,[si].dx_reg

int_opcode label byte
            INT     0               ;modified by previous opcodes

            mov     si,[bp+6]       ;just in case SI is modified
            mov     [si].ax_reg,ax  ;send the return register values back
            mov     [si].bx_reg,bx
            mov     [si].cx_reg,cx
            mov     [si].dx_reg,dx
            pushf
            pop     ax              ;flags returned as function value

            pop     bp              ;restore the outer frame pointer
            ret     4               ;dump the two 16-bit arguments
sysint      endp
code_seg ends
            end
```

The assembly language part is surprisingly simple. The program saves the frame pointer, interrogates the frame data to find the requested interrupt number (passed by value), and fetches the address of the REGS record (passed by reference). Notice how the assembler's STRUC pseudo-op is used to simplify accessing of the data. Assembly language structures are particularly useful for more complex data types such as LSTRING and structures with fields of varying length. Compare the STRUC definition in the program with the Pascal RECORD definition in the comments.

The interrupt itself is achieved by a bit of sleight-of-hand. The program modifies itself by overlaying one byte of the code with the interrupt type value (MOV CS:INT_OPCODE+1,AL). Thus, the opcode INT 0 is replaced with INT *n*, where *n* is the INT_TYPE value passed to the procedure from Pascal.

After SYSINT reprograms itself, it fetches values from the REGS array and places them into the corresponding CPU registers. The next instruction invokes the interrupt, and the rest of the program returns the resulting values of each register to their respective positions in the REGS array (so that the Pascal program can read any values returned by the interrupt). SYSINT then places the value of the FLAGS register into AX, making it the WORD value of the function (several of the ROM-BIOS and PC-DOS services return information in the FLAGS register).

To make this function available to your Pascal program, compile the program as you normally do and then include the SYSINT.OBJ filename in the object module list processed by the linker:

```
A> PAS1 MYPROG;

A> PAS2

A> LINK MYPROG+SYSINT;

A> MYPROG
```

### Speed with PUBLIC Variables

As mentioned earlier, it is possible to bypass the standard parameter-passing convention altogether. This action allows a machine language program to access Pascal variables directly instead of by reference. In other words, instead of scanning the stack to determine where a variable is stored and then examining or modifying that address, you "buy directly from the factory"—skipping the middleman. Thus, the sequence

```
PUSH     BP

MOV      BP,SP

MOV      SI,[BP+6] ;SI points to address of WORD_VAR

MOV      WORD PTR [SI],5       ;modify the variable

POP      BP

RET      2       ;exit, clearing stack of one argument
```

is replaced by

```
MOV       WORD_VAR,5    ;no indirect reference needed

RET                     ;simple FAR return
```

    This method involves creating Pascal variables with the PUBLIC attribute and letting the linker pass the addresses of those variables to your external assembly language module. The assembly module simply declares the names of those variables to be EXTRN. Thus, you use the same variable names in your external module as you do in the Pascal program. There is no need to fuss about frame pointers, the position in the stack, or the POP value of the RET.

    However, it's not quite that simple. Pascal STATIC variables (and thus PUBLIC variables and any variables declared at the PROGRAM level) are all stored in the physical segment named DS, but they are passed to the linker as offsets within one of Pascal's logical segments. The physical data segment includes the heap (variable program data) and all program constants. Even though variable A, for example, is offset from Pascal's logical data segment (named DATA in the linker map) by exactly 18 bytes, it may actually reside at 0FF20H in the segment pointed to by DS.

    The trick is to make sure that the linker relocates your external variable references with offsets from Pascal's DGROUP—the true physical data segment. Since we have already discussed the GROUP and EXTRN pseudo-ops in Chapter 4, it should come as no surprise to learn that there is a method to make the linker create the correct offsets.

    Recall that EXTRN symbols are assumed to reside in the segment within which the EXTRN declaration is made. For instance, external NEAR procedures should be declared within a program's code segment; the EXTRN declaration for FAR procedures should be placed either outside all segments or within a dummy segment.

    Look at the EXTRN declaration in Listing 7.8, the MYPROC procedure. Notice that it resides within the segment MY_DATA, which is otherwise empty. Thus, the program is saying that references to the Pascal PUBLIC variables will be linked as if they were offset from MY_DATA. Pascal produces no segment named MY_DATA. Are we asking for meaningless offsets? Not a chance! The key is the GROUP command that precedes the segment declaration. Because MY_DATA is named as a logical segment in the DGROUP physical segment, offsets of variables within that segment are treated as offsets from DGROUP. In effect, the MY_DATA segment is used as a bridge for accessing a *segment group* in an external module.

    Also note the align type and class name that are specified in the MY_DATA declaration. As a byte-aligned segment with a length of 0, it will not force the linker to pad with the NOP bytes needed with paragraph alignment. The class name of 'data' ensures that MY_DATA will be placed next to the other Pascal segments with that class name. So this 0-byte segment will be loaded next to the Pascal DGROUP segments.

    Listing 7.8 does very little, but that's part of its beauty. There is none of the BP shuffling and indirect addressing that are typical of assembly language modules that use the standard argument-passing convention. The program fetches the values of two global Pascal variables, VAR1 and VAR2, adds them, and places the sum into another PUBLIC variable, RESULT.

**Listing 7.8**
**MYPROC External Pascal Procedure**

```
;------------------------------
; Listing 7.8   MYPROC  external procedure for Pascal
;
; Performs an unsigned addition of VAR1 and VAR2, placing the sum in RESULT.
; Uses Pascal PUBLIC variables to avoid stack references.
;
; Sample Pascal Program:
;
; PROGRAM main(input,output);
; VAR [PUBLIC] var1, var2, result :WORD; {assembly code can access these}
;
; PROCEDURE myproc; EXTERNAL;          {declare the external module}
;                                      {no arguments passed--all are global}
; BEGIN
;   write('Enter two numbers: ');
;   readln(var1,var2);
;   myproc;                            {invoke the assembly language code}
;   writeln('The result is: ',result);
; END.
;
;---------------- assembler code begins --------------------

        public  myproc          ;pass the name to the linker
dgroup  group   my_data         ;enable addressing of Pascal's data

my_data segment byte 'data'      ;dummy segment in DGROUP for externals
        extrn   var1:word, var2:word, result:word
my_data ends

code_seg segment para public 'code'
        assume  cs:code_seg, ds:dgroup
myproc  proc    far
        mov     ax,var1        ;Just as if they were assembler data!
        add     ax,var2
        mov     result,ax
        ret
myproc  endp
code_seg ends
        end
```

There are disadvantages of using PUBLIC variables this way. For one thing, the procedure must always work with the same variables. Also, using global or public variables detracts from the Pascal concept of local, frame-oriented variables (PUBLIC variables aren't much good in recursive and reentrant procedures).

On the other hand, PUBLIC variables can always be accessed more quickly than local variables. If MYPROC were rewritten to use frame-oriented argument-passing techniques, it would take 215 clock cycles to complete (including Pascal's MOV-and-PUSH overhead before the call). As written, it requires only 78 clock cycles, making it nearly three times as fast. And the program itself occupies only ten bytes. Including savings on Pascal's overhead, this saves 20 or more bytes of code area. In a 64K machine, Pascal's code area steals space from its data area.

Finally, you can reverse the process described above: Have Pascal access data that have been declared PUBLIC in your assembler module. Just put those data in a segment that is part of the DGROUP group, a segment with the name DATA and the class name 'data.' Declare the Pascal variables to be EXTERNAL, and make sure that they match the type of storage created in your external module.

## Summary

These techniques for interfacing 8088 code with other languages can add flexibility, speed, and conciseness to code written in high-level languages. Although interpretive BASIC and BASCOM are in a class by themselves, the techniques described in this section are quite close to those used to interface with Fortran and Microsoft C. Just watch out for segments and groups, and make sure that the linker is passing the correct information.

If you have trouble with a hybrid program, turn to your trusty friend DEBUG. Use it to examine both modules of the hybrid program in order to ascertain the integrity of the connection. Make sure that the expected types of arguments are being passed in the expected order. The best bet is to test an assembler module by writing a short Pascal or BASIC "stub." By keeping the testing program small, you will easily be able to find the call that bridges the gap between the languages. From that lofty viewpoint, the insectoid gremlins don't stand a chance. DEBUG kills bugs dead!

The time and effort spent in developing a hybrid program yields a high payment on your investment. You can obtain the speed and extensibility of assembly language without giving up the power and flexibility of a high-level language. Thus, you can develop programs more quickly than is possible with pure assembly language, but with a much smaller cost in terms of updating and maintenance.

## THINGS TO DO

1. Convert Listing 7.5 (QPRINT) so that it works with Pascal. The ROW% and CLM% arguments may be BYTE- or INTEGER-type local variables, and the VAR$ should be replaced with an LSTRING variable or an array of CHAR plus a length argument.

2. Write a series of Pascal procedures that are built around the SYSINT module. Write one to change the size of the cursor, one to enter any graphics or text screen mode, and (*) one to read a selected sector from a diskette into a Pascal array.

3. Write versions of SYSINT that work from interpretive and compiled BASIC.

4. (*) Recode the slowest procedure of an existing Pascal program into assembly language. Use the .COD file to see how Pascal normally handles the call, and then look for ways to increase its efficiency. Use the LOOP command for high-speed iteration control, and use clever tricks such as look-up tables to avoid time-consuming calculations. Use the repeating string commands to initialize, copy, compare, and search through strings and arrays.

```
{$A-,B-,D-,E-,F-,I-,L-,N-,O-,R-,S-,V-}
program Hat; TBT.AB  V22/89

uses graph;

var grDriver : Integer;
    grMode   : Integer;
    ErrCode  : Integer;
    col      : integer;

begin
  grDriver := Detect;
  InitGraph(grDriver,grMode,'A:\');
  ErrCode := GraphResult;
  if ErrCode = grOk then begin
    setgraphmode(getgraphmode(CGAC3);
    col := getmaxcolor;
    setcolor(0);
    setwritemode(copyput);
    putpixel(16,32,col);
    line(2,4,6,8);
  end; (* if error *)
  CloseGraph;
end. (* Hat *)
```

# Chapter 8

# Text and Graphics

## 8.1 OVERVIEW

Perhaps the most often cited reason for learning IBM-PC assembly language is the need to gain control over the video display. Most business and scientific packages can be written completely in a high-level language; they can put up with the sluggish BIOS screen functions. But video-intensive programs such as arcade games and word processors must display their output quickly. No one will buy a word processor that scrolls the screen at the speed of BASIC and there is no market for games like "Space Snails" or "Molasses Man."

The ROM-BIOS has all of the routines needed to display any character in any color at any screen location. It also includes functions that handle other video-related requirements such as updating the current cursor position, changing the size of the cursor, and scrolling the screen. One ROM-BIOS service combines all of these primitive functions to handle the simplest form of video output—treating the screen as a glass teletype. The IBM technical reference manual and Appendix B of this book give the details of these services.

What all of the ROM-BIOS and PC-DOS video services have in common is that they are slow. Part of the problem is that these routines must be very general. They spend a lot of time deciding what type of monitor is active, what mode it is in, what page is being processed, and so on. When speed is of the essence, you will need to write video routines that duplicate these functions, but at a much faster pace. This involves knowing in advance what type of monitor will be used in your application and tailoring your code to it.

### Monochrome Versus Color/Graphics

In trying to satisfy everyone, IBM introduced two different types of video display cards for the IBM PC. The monochrome adapter (sometimes called the *B/W card*) displays only text characters and works only with the IBM monochrome display screen. Its hardware supports only one *page*, or screenful of characters, but its display is quite pleasing to the eye and is an excellent choice for systems that are used primarily for word processing.

The color/graphics adapter (hereafter called the *color card*) can display text in up to 16 different colors and in two different sizes (40 or 80 columns). It supports up to eight pages of text. It also supports dot or *pixel* (picture element) graphics at resolutions up to 640 across by 200 down. The color card may be connected to several different types of display screens. This adapter option is the more flexible of the two, but the characters that are displayed by the color card are not as crisp as those seen on the IBM monochrome monitor.

The color card may be used with a standard black-and-white or color television connected via a radio frequency (RF) converter. This combination is perhaps the least desirable because of the low resolution of television sets. Television sets are unable to display 80 legible columns of text.

The most attractive combination is the color card and a high-quality *RGB monitor*. The color card outputs four signals to the RGB monitor, so each dot on the screen is composed of three individually controlled components—Red, Green, and Blue. RGB monitors will easily display 80-column output and take advantage of all of the capabilities of the color card.

Somewhere in the middle ground (less expensive than an RGB monitor, but having better resolution than RF-modulated television output) is the combination of the color card and a low-cost *composite* monitor. These monitors can be either color or monochrome (often black and green). Because the composite output of the color card is less detailed than the RGB output, much of the color information is lost in transit. This combination works well with text applications because all 80 columns are legible (although not as detailed as those of the B/W card with the IBM monochrome monitor).

All of these display options involve more work for you, the programmer. Your program has to take into account which type of adapter is being used in the target machine. If it is the B/W card and the IBM monochrome display, you must avoid using any pixel graphics. If the target machine is using the color card, you must try to make your programming compatible with the most standard configurations. If you make extensive use of color, you must check to see that the display looks good on a composite monochrome monitor. Many of the IBM-PC-compatible machines use this type of display, so don't discount its significance. However, you can probably ignore the users who have the television/RF-modulator configuration because very few target machines rely exclusively on this combination.

Even though the color card is equipped with the hardware to support four or eight pages of text, the B/W card has only one page. Therefore, to make your programs compatible with both cards, you must disregard the color card's multipage capability. This following discussion on text mode focuses on the features common to both cards.

## 8.2 TEXT MODE VIDEO MEMORY

The B/W card is always in *text* mode (i.e., it displays only ASCII characters). The color card can be in either 40- or 80-column text mode or any of several graphics modes. First, let's discuss text mode and how to bypass the ROM-BIOS and PC-DOS procedures and display textual characters directly on the video screen.

The B/W and color cards have much in common; it is not difficult to write text-oriented applications that work perfectly well on both cards. The QPRINT program presented in Chapter 7 works with either card. That program uses only six lines of code to determine which card is active and to implement the decision. Both cards are *memory-mapped, DMA devices.* DMA, which stands for direct memory access, indicates that the characters seen on the video display correspond directly to ASCII bytes stored in memory. To print an *A,* we need only place the ASCII value for *A* (i.e., 41H or 65 decimal) into the correct memory location. For the B/W card, these memory locations begin at B000:0000; the color card video memory begins at B800:0000.

Video memory for both cards is mapped the same way. Each has a 4000-byte *regen* (video memory buffer) area that represents the first page of display memory (with the B/W card, this is the only page; the color card has four such pages). This memory is arranged in groups of 2-byte addresses. The even addresses contain the bytes that the hardware interprets and displays as characters. The odd addresses contain *attribute* bytes, bit-mapped codes that the hardware interprets to modify the way that the character is displayed. Thus, each character that you see on the screen, whether black and white or color, is composed of an ASCII character followed by an attribute:

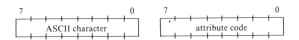

The ASCII character byte is any of the 256 characters that are defined in the video card's character generator. Appendix D has a complete listing of these codes. The attribute codes are mapped somewhat differently for each of the adapters (see Figure 8.1), but many of them are the same for both. For instance, an attribute of 07H is the normal attribute (i.e., a white character on a black background). An attribute of 70H is displayed in reverse video. An attribute code with the high bit set to a 1 (i.e., the byte is above 7FH) will cause its character to blink.

The RGB color bits of the attribute have little meaning when used on the B/W card. Only certain combinations are useful. The main thing to watch for is that when the lowest three bits of the foreground fields are 001, the B/W card displays the character as being underlined. Other combinations of these bits, except for 000, cause a character to be displayed with a white foreground. A 000 value indicates a black foreground, and unless the background is white, the character will not be visible.

Figure 8.2 diagrams the memory mapping of these character/attribute pairs for 80-column text mode on either card. Here's the formula for calculating a video memory offset address given a screen line and column coordinate pair:

```
character offset =(line*80+column)*2
```

**Figure 8.1**
**Attribute Bit Patterns for Monochrome and Color Adapters**

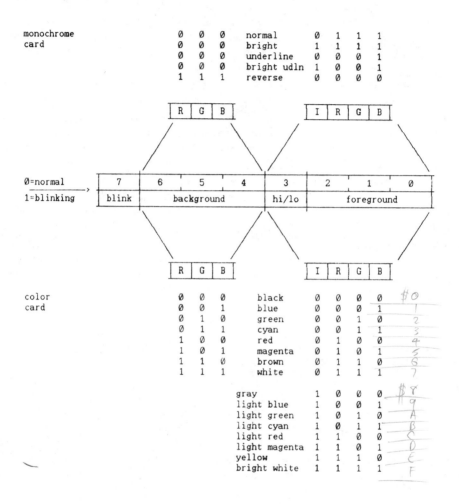

```
monochrome            0  0  0    normal       0  1  1  1
card                  0  0  0    bright       1  1  1  1
                      0  0  0    underline    0  0  0  1
                      0  0  0    bright udln  1  0  0  1
                      1  1  1    reverse      0  0  0  0
```

```
            ┌───┬───┬───┐              ┌───┬───┬───┬───┐
            │ R │ G │ B │              │ I │ R │ G │ B │
            └───┴───┴───┘              └───┴───┴───┴───┘

0=normal  ┌─────┬──────────────┬──────┬──────────────┐
   ──────>│  7  │   6     5    │  4   3│  2     1    0│
1=blinking│blink│  background  │hi/lo │  foreground  │
          └─────┴──────────────┴──────┴──────────────┘

            ┌───┬───┬───┐              ┌───┬───┬───┬───┐
            │ R │ G │ B │              │ I │ R │ G │ B │
            └───┴───┴───┘              └───┴───┴───┴───┘
```

```
color                 0  0  0    black        0  0  0  0    #0
card                  0  0  1    blue         0  0  0  1     1
                      0  1  0    green        0  0  1  0     2
                      0  1  1    cyan         0  0  1  1     3
                      1  0  0    red          0  1  0  0     4
                      1  0  1    magenta      0  1  0  1     5
                      1  1  0    brown        0  1  1  0     6
                      1  1  1    white        0  1  1  1     7

                                 gray         1  0  0  0    #8
                                 light blue   1  0  0  1     9
                                 light green  1  0  1  0     A
                                 light cyan   1  0  1  1     B
                                 light red    1  1  0  0     C
                                 light magenta 1 1  0  1     D
                                 yellow       1  1  1  0     E
                                 bright white 1  1  1  1     F
```

**Figure 8.2**
**Diagram of 80-Column Text Mode Memory**

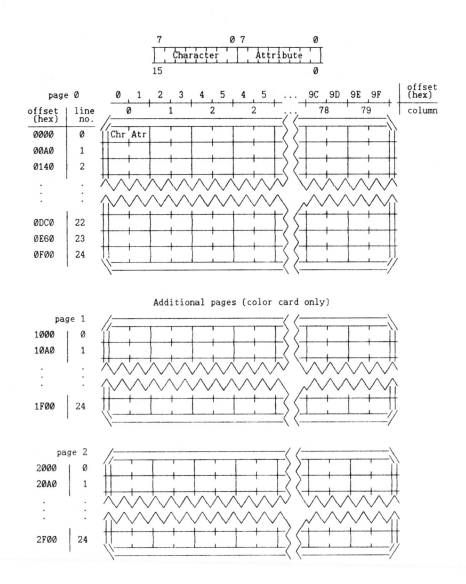

**Figure 8.2
(continued)**

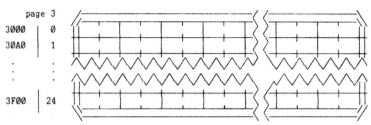

Note: color card addresses ØFAØH–ØFFFH, 1FAØH–1FFFH, 2FAØH–2FFFH, and 3FAØH–3FFFH
   are not used when in 80-column text mode.

```
                    address calculation
char.addr =: page*1000H + (line*80 + column)*2
attr.addr =: char.addr + 1
```

   This formula finds the offset from the base segment of the adapter card. If you can't be sure which type of adapter card is being used, you can use the ROM-BIOS EQUIPMENT_CHECK service (INT 11H). It returns a bit code that indicates the type of adapter that is currently active. Just check bits 4 and 5 of the value returned in AL. If both bits are 1s, the monochrome card is active. Here's a typical sequence used to determine the segment and offset that equate to a line and column:

```
          INT     11H          ;fetch the equipment bit flags

          AND     AL,00110000B     ;mask irrelevant bits

          CMP     AL,00110000B        ;is it B/W?

          MOV     AX,0B000H        ; (assume B/W card)

          JE      SEG_OK        ; yes, no change needed

          MOV     AX,0B800H     ; no, set up for graphics

  SEG_OK:

          MOV     ES,AX             ;ES points to video
                                    ;memory of correct card
```

```
;------- now calculate the offset address from DH and DL
        (line, column)
        MOV     AL,80
        MUL     DH                      ;AX = line number * 80
        MOV     DI,AX           ; save in pointer register
        XOR     AX,AX           ; (must use 16-bit register)
        MOV     AL,DL
        ADD     DI,AX                   ;add in the column offset
        SHL     DI,1        ;times 2 to account for attributes
                        ; ES:[DI] points to address to write
```

If speed is absolutely essential, there are several ways to speed up this routine. First, you could skip the EQUIPMENT_CHECK interrupt; there is no reason to make this call for every character that you place on the screen. Just make that call once, early in the program. When you determine the segment of the active card, store it in a variable. This procedure shaves scores of clock cycles from the calculation time.

The next step (used whenever you need to optimize for speed) is to try to avoid multiplication operations. The MUL DH in this listing requires 77 clock cycles. You can reduce this number considerably by using a series of left shifts. Listing 8.1, CAL_ADDR, is the same code as the one used in the previous example, but it is written as a complete procedure. It includes the changes that cut its execution time to a small fraction (less than one-tenth) of the previous example.

As you know, left shifts can be used only to multiply a number by a power of 2; yet I have claimed that Listing 8.1 uses them to multiply by 80. The trick is to use addition in conjunction with the multiplication. If you review your early math skills, you will recognize this as an example of the *associative property* of multiplication. The program uses this formula to find LINE * 80:

```
address=(LINE*64)+(LINE*16)
                        (both 16 and 64 are powers of 2)

address=LINE*(64+16)
                        (apply associative property)

address=LINE*80
                        (simplify)
```

which is exactly what we wanted. Because of the physical mapping of video memory, many screen operations are made more efficient by using this technique.

After calling the CALC_ADDR routine, you are ready to move data directly into video memory to begin displaying characters. If you move a byte into the calculated address, you will alter only the character at that position. For instance,

```
        MOV     ES:[DI],BL
```

**Listing 8.1**
**CALC_ADDR**

```
;-------------------------------------------------------------------
;Listing 8.1  CALC_ADDR
;This subroutine calculates an 80-column text-mode memory address
; from a pair of horizontal and vertical coordinates.
;
;expects: DH = line number (0-24)
;         DL = column number (0-79)
;         VIDEO_SEG variable contains either B000H or B800H
;returns: ES:DI points to address in regen buffer
;         AX is destroyed.

calc_addr proc    near
          mov     es,VIDEO_SEG   ;fetch the stored video segment pointer
          mov     ah,0
          mov     al,dh          ;AX = line number
          shl     ax,1           ; * 2
          shl     ax,1           ; * 4
          shl     ax,1           ; * 8
          shl     ax,1           ; * 16
          mov     di,ax          ;save partial value
          shl     ax,1           ; * 32
          shl     ax,1           ; * 64
          add     di,ax          ; DI = line * 80
          mov     ah,0
          mov     al,dl
          add     di,ax          ;add in the column
          shl     di,1           ;adjust for attribute bytes
          ret                    ;ready to display character
calc_addr endp
```

will place the character defined by the ASCII value in BL into the calculated position. However, it is not by chance that the address is returned in ES and DI; thus, the STOSB opcode is an ideal way to display a character that is in AL. If you want that character to be displayed with a certain attribute, you must also move an attribute code into the adjacent address in video memory. One way to do this is to put the characteer code in AL and the attribute code into AH, and then use the STOSW opcode.

Simply put, when the screen is in an 80-column text mode, you can bypass the ROM routines and send characters directly to video memory with this sequence:

1. Determine the correct segment (color card = B800H and B/W card = B000H).

2. Calculate an offset from that segment; use ((line*80)+column)*2.

3. Set a pointer or index register to that address.

4. Use indexed or string addressing to move data into that memory location.

The ASCII value that you store in video memory is displayed immediately. To display characters in a particular color or to make them blink or underline them (B/W card only), you must store an attribute byte in the sequentially adjacent address.

## Snow on the Screen

When you read from or write to any part of the color card's video memory while the display is in 80-column text mode, you may see some distracting flashes randomly scattered over the screen. This problem is discussed in detail in Chapter 9, but because it is relevant only to text mode, a rote solution is presented in this section.

The trick is to avoid accessing the video memory during certain parts of the display cycle. You can find out when it is safe to access video memory by reading color card input port 03DAH. If the lowest bit of the byte read from that port is a 1, you can go ahead with the read or write operation. If that bit is a 0, you should wait until it becomes a 1.

This safe period occurs when the CRT is in its *horizontal retrace interval,* that is, when the electron beam is not currently lighting up any part of the screen. The lowest bit in the video card's status register (color card port 3DAH) indicates when this is happening.

It is possible just to check that bit and, if it's a 0, to access the video memory. But occasionally, the retrace flag will toggle off during the interval between reading the port and writing the byte. When you are writing a significant number of characters to the screen (for instance, if your program is filling a page of video memory with characters from a buffer), you will see a few sparkles on the left side of the screen. Listing 8.2, WRITE_CHAR, avoids even this possibility by making sure that the input port is read at the start of the safe period. It first waits for an unsafe period and then immediately writes the character as soon as it is safe again.

## Listing 8.2
## WRITE_CHAR

```
;---------------------------------------------
; Listing 8.2  WRITE_CHAR
; Writes the character in BL into video address ES:[DI]
; Avoids all traces of "snow" on the screen by waiting for
;  a horizontal or vertical retrace interval.

write_char proc near
           push    dx
           mov     dx,03DAH    ;address the status port (B/W card use 03BAH)
           cli                 ; turn off interrupts for exact timing
await_snow:
           in      al,dx
           test    al,1        ;starting out in retrace period?
           jnz     await_snow ; no, wait until retrace begins

snow_fall:             ;------ now wait through one non-retrace period ---
           in      al,dx
           test    al,1        ;is it ok to write?
           jz      snow_fall  ; no, wait until it is
           mov     es:[di],bl ; yes, write the character
           sti                 ;turn interrupts back on
           pop     dx
           ret
write_char endp
```

It should be noted that all of this waiting for the hardware consumes a lot of time. Even so, the process is at least 10 times as fast as using the ROM-BIOS WRITE_CHAR routine. The horizontal retrace period is long enough to place both a character and an attribute byte into memory, but the interval is too short for writing two or more characters without causing at least a sprinkling of video snow.

### THINGS TO DO

1. Write a PRINT procedure that displays an ASCIIZ string (i.e., a string of ASCII characters terminated by a byte of 0). Pass the address of the string in the SI register and pass the screen location (line, column) in DH and DL. Make sure that each character is displayed with a normal (white-on-black) attribute.

2. Improve the routine so that it displays the string with a selected attribute passed in the AH register.

3. (*) Write a procedure that displays a box made up of the special ASCII characters C9H, CDH, BBH, BAH, and CAH—the double-line business graphics characters. Pass the coordinates of the upper left-hand corner in DH,DL and the lower right-hand corner in BH,BL.

4. (**) Generalize the above procedure so that it selects from among one of several box types—a single-line, double-line, block characters, double-line top and bottom with single-line sides, and so on.

### 8.3 GRAPHICS MODE VIDEO MEMORY

The ROM-BIOS supports essentially two graphics modes, a 320 by 200 *mid-resolution* mode and a 640 by 200 *high-resolution* mode. There are really two versions of the mid-resolution modes; the second works just like the first; the difference is that there is no color signal, so all of the dots appear to be either black or white. The color is also disabled in the high-resolution mode, but this mode offers the advantage of more detailed shapes and plots.

Graphics mode memory is mapped quite differently from that of the text modes. When the color card is initialized to a graphics mode, the adapter treats its 16K bytes of memory as a series of bit fields. You no longer move ASCII characters into memory. Instead, the memory is interpreted according to which bits are 1s and which are 0s.

### High-Resolution Graphics

In the 640 by 200 mode (BASIC calls this SCREEN 2), each bit is an on/off flag indicating if its corresponding pixel is lit or dark. Thus, a byte of high-resolution memory contains enough information to determine the state of eight adjacent pixels.

Graphics memory is laid out in two banks of 80-byte lines, 100 lines to a bank. The even-numbered lines begin at offset 0 and the odd-numbered lines at offset 2000H. Figure 8.3 shows how high-resolution graphics memory is mapped. The screen is laid out with 80 8-pixel bytes per screen line. Each byte is displayed with the most significant dot on the top line of the high-resolution screen. Bit 6 is just to its right, and so forth. The pixel represented by bit 7 of the byte at B800:0001 is just to the right of bit 0 of the byte at B800:0000.

**Figure 8.3**
**Map of Video Memory in High-Resolution Graphics Mode**

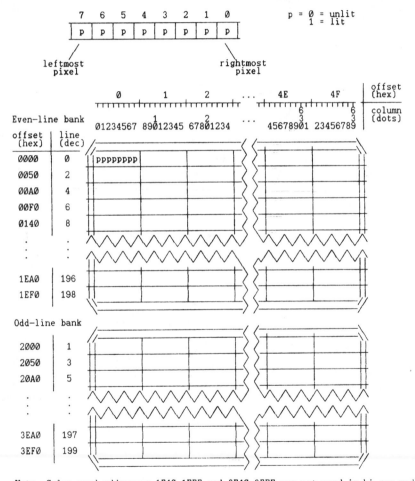

Note: Color card addresses 1F40–1FFF and 3F40–3FFF are not used in hi–res mode.

```
                    address calculation
     addr =: line*80 + INT(column/8)
              IF (line AND 1)=1 THEN addr =: addr + 2000H
     mask =: 10000000B SHR (column MOD 8)
```

The even-line/odd-line arrangement can be a trifle confusing. For instance, the dot directly below bit 0 of the byte at B800:0000 is located at bit 0 of the byte at B800:2000. The dot directly below that is represented by bit 0 of address B800:0050 (50H is 80 in decimal). In other words, the bytes of graphics memory do not have a direct correspondence to a 2-dimensional array, nor is there a simple arithmetic formula to determine the memory location of a particular pixel. However, the calculation is easy; the following pseudo-code yields a video memory address given the line (0-199) and column (0-639) of any high-resolution pixel:

```
ADDR=: (LINE/2)*80+INT(COLUMN/8)

IF (LINE AND 1)=1

  ADDR=: ADDR+2000H

ENDIF
```

Assuming that the LINE number is in DX and the COLUMN number is in CX, you could use the following code to calculate the address and place it in DI:

```
        MOV     DI,0               ;assume even line
        TEST    DX,1               ;need to adjust for odd-line
                                   ;graphics bank?
        JZ      EVEN               ; no, go
        ADD     DI,2000H   ; yes, use with odd-line address
EVEN:   SHR     DX,1               ;get LINE/2
        MOV     AX,80              ; and set up multiplier
        MUL     AX,DX              ;get AX=(LINE*80)
        ADD     DI,AX              ;add in offset of graphic line
        MOV     AX,CX              ;get COLUMN
        SHR     AX,1               ;divide by 2
        SHR     AX,1               ;divide by 4
        SHR     AX,1               ;AX=int(COLUMN/8)
        ADD     DI,AX              ;adjust pointer register
                           ;B800:[DI] is address of byte to access
```

Notice that because this sequence uses multiplication, it is not particularly fast. And because graphics programs are always in a hurry, you may want to use a "synthetic" multiplication by 80 such as that used in Listing 8.1.

Once we know the graphics memory address, we must still isolate an individual pixel. That is, we can't just change the whole byte; that change would alter the other seven pixels represented by the byte. In order to turn on an individual pixel, we must form a mask byte that has a 1 bit only in the desired position.

The position of the correct bit can be calculated by finding the remainder of the previous COLUMN/8 division (i.e., finding COLUMN MOD 8). This procedure yields an offset *from the left side of the byte.* For instance, if COLUMN is 0, COLUMN MOD 8 is 0, and we are working with leftmost bit (bit 7). The same is true when COLUMN is 8, 16, 24, and so on. When COLUMN is 1 (or 9, 17, 25, etc.), then we will set or reset bit 6 of the byte—the bit that is directly to the "right" of bit 7. In other words, we need a mask that has a 1 only in the bit that is COLUMN MOD 8 from the left side of the byte:

```
MASK = 10000000B SHIFTED_RIGHT (COLUMN MOD 8)
```

Perhaps the easiest way to form such a byte is to use a multi-shift operation. Just place that bit position value into CL, place a 1 bit in the highest position of an operand, and shift that operand to the right by the count in CL. For instance, assuming that the CX register starts out holding the COLUMN value, the sequence

```
MOV    AL,10000000B   ;start out with the high bit set in AL

AND    CX,7           ;get CL=column MOD 8

SHL    AL,CL          ;shift that bit into position
```

will create a byte in AL that has a 1 bit only in the position of interest. This arrangement yields a byte with one of the following values:

```
pixel   bit   hex   decimal   binary

left     7     80     128     10000000

 .       6     40      64     01000000

 .       5     20      32     00100000

 .       4     10      16     00010000

 .       3     08       8     00001000

 .       2     04       4     00000100

 .       1     02       2     00000010

right    0     01       1     00000001
```

To turn that bit on, we need only OR that value into screen memory. Assuming that ES has previously been set to point to the video segment at B800H, we could use the following command to turn an individual pixel on.

```
OR     ES:[DI],AL    ;turn the bit on (light up the pixel)
```

To determine whether that pixel is currently off or on (for example, to find out if a missile has collided with a space gremlin), we can use the TEST opcode:

```
    MOV       COLLISION_FLAG,0          ;assume no collision

    TEST      ES:[DI],AL     ;is the indicated bit already lit?

    JZ        EMPTY          ; no, go

    MOV       COLLISION_FLAG,1          ; yes, set the flag
EMPTY:

                                        ;program continues
```

To turn the pixel off, we need to extract the indicated bit, forcing it to become a 0. The simplest method is to use the NOT opcode to toggle all bits in the mask value, and then AND the memory location with the resulting mask. For instance, if the mask is 00100000B, a NOT operation will force the byte to become 11011111B. ANDing that value with any byte will result in a byte that is certain to have a 0 in the relevant bit position. In high-resolution graphics memory, this darkens a particular pixel.

```
    NOT       AL                  ;flip-flop all bits in the mask

    AND       ES:[DI],AL     ;turn the bit off (darken the pixel)
```

Many graphics applications need the ability to toggle the state of an individual pixel; that is, if it's on, to turn it off, and vice versa. This is called an XOR of the pixel. Remember that XOR toggles the bits of the destination operand that are 1s in the source operand. In high-resolution graphics, this toggling is accomplished by directly XORing the memory operand by the calculated mask value:

```
    XOR       ES:[DI],AL          ;flip-flop the state of the pixel
```

You can move a dot across the screen without altering any shapes or lines that are in the background by XORing the pixel twice in succession at every point along the trajectory.

## Medium-Resolution Color Graphics

In 320 by 200 mid-resolution graphics mode (BASIC's SCREEN 1), each byte of graphics memory is represented as a set of four 2-bit values. Each 2-bit value represents a single pixel, and each pixel can be in any of four different states (in contrast to the two states of the high-resolution pixels). The two bits are actually flags that indicate the red and green components of the RGB that make up the color signal that is seen on a color monitor.

When the color card is in mid-resolution mode, its physical memory is laid out similarly to that of high-resolution mode. The even-numbered lines start at B800:0000, and the odd-numbered lines start at B800:2000. Each line still contains 80 bytes of information, but since each byte represents only four pixels (instead of eight), each graphics line can contain only 320 pixels (see Figure 8.4).

**Figure 8.4**
**Map of Video Memory in Mid-Resolution Graphics Mode**

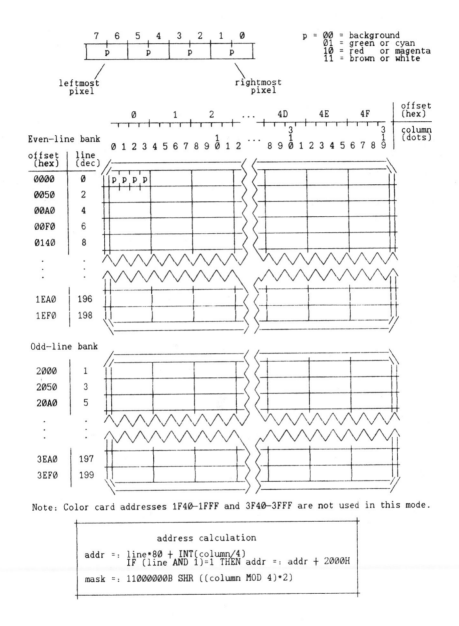

Note: Color card addresses 1F40–1FFF and 3F40–3FFF are not used in this mode.

```
                    address calculation
addr =: line*80 + INT(column/4)
        IF (line AND 1)=1 THEN addr =: addr + 2000H
mask =: 11000000B SHR ((column MOD 4)*2)
```

Thus, we can use the same formula to calculate the start of any particular line of graphics, but finding the full address and creating the mask are done somewhat differently. Compare the pseudo-code with that given in the previous section:

```
ADDR=(LINE/2)*80+INT(COLUMN/4)

IF (LINE AND 1)=1

    ADDR=ADDR+2000H

ENDIF

MASK=11000000B SHIFTED_RIGHT ((COLUMN MOD 4)*2)
```

The only differences are that the column number is divided by 4 and the shift count is a number from 0 to 3, so that it must be adjusted to account for the 2-bit pixels of medium-resolution graphics. The assembler source code used to implement these calculations is also similar. Assuming that DX contains a line number (0-199) and CX contains a column number (0-319), the following code will calculate the offset of the address of the pixel and format a mask to be used to query or alter the state of the pixel:

```
        MOV     DI,0            ;assume even line
        TEST    DX,1            ;odd-line graphics bank?
        JZ      EVEN            ;  no, go
        MOV     DI,2000H        ;  yes, set up for odd line
EVEN:
        SHR     DL,1            ;get LINE/2
        MOV     AL,80           ; and set up multiplier
        MUL     DL              ;get AX=(line*80)
        ADD     DI,AX           ;add in offset of graphics line
        MOV     AX,CX           ;fetch the column argument
        SHR     AX,1
        SHR     AX,1            ;get AX=int(COLUMN/4)
        ADD     DI,AX           ;adjust pointer register
        MOV     AL,11000000B    ;start out with the 2 low bits set in AL
        AND     CX,3            ;get CL=column MOD 3
        SHL     CL,1            ; times 2 for each 2-bit pixel
        SHR     AL,CL           ;shift mask bits into position
                                ;B800:[DI] is byte to examine or modify
                                ; and AL is the MASK to use
```

The big difference between high-resolution and mid-resolution now comes into play. In the high-resolution routine, the mask value was ORed to turn the pixel on, but in mid-resolution each pixel can be in any of four different states and we will want to alter it to any of four different colors. Thus, the final operations will require some extra processing.

Setting a medium-resolution pixel to a desired color requires five steps:

1. Fetch the current graphics memory byte.

2. Mask off the two bits of the target pixel.

3. Move the bits of the desired color into the 2-bit pixel position.

4. OR in the value of the desired color code.

5. Place the modified byte back into screen memory.

Assuming that the registers are set up with the values from the previous address calculation [i.e., ES points to graphics memory, the mask is in AL, CL has a shift count, and the desired color (0-3) is in the BL register], the process would be this:

```
MOV     BH,ES:[DI]  ;fetch the current byte

NOT     AL          ;set up the mask

AND     BH,AL       ;BH has a ''hole'' for the desired bits

ADD     CL,2        ; adjust shift count for rotation

ROR     BL,CL       ;move color code into position

OR      BH,BL       ;put the color bits into the byte

MOV     ES:[DI],BH  ;place the byte into video memory
```

This example moves the color code bits into position by rotating them from the lowest bit positions around through the highest positions and into the correct place in the byte. This procedure is less than efficient because if the pixel to be replaced is the rightmost one (bits 0 and 1), the bits are rotated eight times and brought full-circle back into their original position. However, the test-and-jump alternative is slightly slower.

When you test the state of a certain pixel, you probably want to know exactly what its current color is, not just whether the dot is lit or unlit. The following code places the value of the current dot into the AL register:

```
MOV     AL,ES:[DI]  ;fetch the relevant byte

SHR     AL,CL       ;move color bits to lowest positions

AND     AL,3        ;mask off the other bits (AL=0, 1, 2, or 3)
```

The graphic XOR operation is also simple because the graphics byte can be directly manipulated in memory. Once the bits in BL (the color code) have been moved into the target position, we need only XOR the register with the current value of the byte in video memory. The following code will flip-flop the bits of the current color code according to the bits of the color code in BL:

```
ADD        CL,2

ROR        BL,CL        ;move the color code into position

XOR        ES:[DI],BL   ;flip-flop only the relevant bits
```

This code still works like the high-resolution XOR, but because we are working with four possible colors, there is more to the story. If the current dot is blank (i.e., the background color), the effect will be the same as that of ORing the color into position. But if the current color is anything else, this operation will produce a somewhat puzzling side effect. For instance, if the current dot is brown (color 3) and the dot that you want to XOR is green (color 1), the XOR forces that dot to be displayed as red (color 2).

```
current color = 3 = 00000011  (brown)

XOR color     = 1 = 00000001  (green)

new color     = 2 = 00000010  (red)
```

next pass:

```
current color = 2 = 00000010  (red)

XOR color     = 1 = 00000001  (green)

new color     = 3 = 00000011  (brown)
```

Thus, the original purpose of the XOR operation is intact: Two such operations with the same color code will result in the restoration of the original color.

### Look-Up Tables for Fast Graphics

In many graphics applications, your pixel-handling routine is likely to be the bottleneck that slows execution. The calls to this routine are likely to be nested two or three deep within a shape-drawing routine, so that every clock cycle shaved off the execution time could save millions of clock cycles in the course of a graphics-intensive application. In the next section, we will look at a high-powered method that avoids repetitive calls to a dot-plotting routine by handling shapes in groups of four or eight pixels. But sometimes you must set or test the state of individual pixels.

Listing 8.3, PLOTDOT, is a very fast pixel manipulation routine. It works much like the ROM-BIOS WRITE_DOT service, but it is many times faster. It avoids the long-distance call that is inherent in any software interrupt, has no subfunction code that must be decoded, and makes certain assumptions about the call that the ROM-BIOS routine is unable to make. For one thing, it assumes that it will be working with medium-resolution dots (you will need to rewrite parts of it to manipulate high-resolution dots). In addition, it performs only the WRITE_DOT service. It does not include the code to test the value of a pixel to perform n XOR operation (when speed is the overriding priority, you must write separate subroutines for each function). Finally, a most significant speed advantage is gained by using a look-up table to avoid the most time-consuming calculations. Binary shifts are used to speed up the calculations that can't be avoided.

## Listing 8.3
## PLOTDOT NEAR Library Procedure

```
;----------------------------------------
;Listing 8.3  PLOTDOT  near library procedure
; This routine writes 1 dot in medium-resolution graphics mode.
; Avoids lengthy calculations for finding graphics addresses
;  and uses a look-up table to find the mask value.
;
; expects: DX = line number (0-199)
;          CX = column number (0-319)
;          BL = color (0-3)
; on exit: dot is plotted
;          All registers preserved.

        public  plotdot
code_grp group  lib_seg
lib_seg segment byte public 'code'
        assume cs:code_grp

plotdot proc    near
        push    ax
        push    bx
        push    di
        push    es

;------- this code determines the mask and color bits with a look-up table
                        ;table index =: ((pixel number * 4) + color) * 2
        mov     di,3
        and     di,cx           ;DI is pixel number (low 2 bits of column)
        shl     di,1
        shl     di,1            ;DI points to pixel number * 4

        and     bx,3            ;fetch color
        add     di,bx           ; add it in and ...
        shl     di,1            ; multiply it all by 2
        mov     bx,cs:mask_tbl[di] ;BL = mask, BH = bits of color

;------- following code multiplies ROW * 80 to get the address of a line

        mov     di,dx           ;copy the line number value
        and     di,0FFFEH       ; eliminate odd/even bit (& multiply * 2)
        shl     di,1            ; * 4
        shl     di,1            ; * 8
        shl     di,1            ; * 16
        mov     ax,di           ; save partial result
        shl     di,1            ; * 32
        shl     di,1            ; * 64
        add     di,ax           ; DI = line number * 80

        test    dx,1            ;is this an odd line?
        jz      pd1             ; no, go
        add     di,2000H        ; yes, point to the odd-line bank
pd1:
        mov     ax,cx           ;fetch the column number
        shr     ax,1            ;divide it by 4 to create
        shr     ax,1            ;  offset from start of line
        add     di,ax           ;DI is offset of byte to alter

;------- this code sets up the segment register and writes the dot

        mov     ax,0B800H
        mov     es,ax           ;ES:DI points to byte to alter
        and     es:[di],bl      ;set up a "hole" for the color
        or      es:[di],bh      ;put the color in that hole
```

**Listing 8.3
(continued)**

```
        pop     es
        pop     di
        pop     bx
        pop     ax
        ret
plotdot endp

mask_tbl label word

        db      00111111B, 00000000B    ;leftmost pixel, color 0
        db      00111111B, 01000000B    ;                color 1
        db      00111111B, 10000000B    ;                color 2
        db      00111111B, 11000000B    ;                color 3

        db      11001111B, 00000000B
        db      11001111B, 00010000B
        db      11001111B, 00100000B
        db      11001111B, 00110000B

        db      11110011B, 00000000B
        db      11110011B, 00000100B
        db      11110011B, 00001000B
        db      11110011B, 00001100B

        db      11111100B, 00000000B    ;rightmost pixel, color 0
        db      11111100B, 00000001B    ;                color 1
        db      11111100B, 00000010B    ;                color 2
        db      11111100B, 00000011B    ;                color 3
lib_seg ends
        end
```

The PLOTDOT routine is instructive as well as useful. It is a library procedure that we will use later in this chapter; it demonstrates how segments and public declarations are handled in this type of module. It also demonstrates how a little bit of preprocessing and some shifty alternatives to multiplication can speed up what is normally a time-consuming operation.

The first part of the routine calculates an offset into a table of mask and color values. The table is formatted in two dimensions—four rows with four columns per row. Each element contains two bytes of data. The listing contains the binary values of the table elements, making the structure less than obvious. Here it is laid out in columns and rows:

| table offset | | 0000 | 0002 | 0004 | 0006 |
|---|---|---|---|---|---|
| | | | color | | |
| | | 0 | 1 | 2 | 3 |
| 0000H | 0 | 3F 00 | 3F 40 | 3F 80 | 3F C0 |
| 0008H | 1 | CF 00 | CF 10 | CF 20 | CF 30 |
| 0010H | 2 | F3 00 | F3 04 | F3 08 | F3 0C |
| 0018H | 3 | FC 00 | FC 01 | FC 02 | FC 03 |

(pixel labels the rows 0–3)

mask  color

Instead of doing a series of variable shifts and rotates to position the bits of the mask and color value, the program does some quick calculations to determine where to find those values in the table. It uses the pixel number (the value of COLUMN MOD 3) and the color value to index into the table. All we need to know is (1) which of the four pixels we need to modify and (2) the color we need to make it. We know that the color is held in the BL register and that the pixel number is named by the lowest two bits of the column value in CX.

You find the physical address of an element in any 2-dimensional table by multiplying the desired row number by the count of elements per row, adding the desired column number, and multiplying the sum by the size of each element:

```
offset=((table_row*row_size)+table_column)*element_size
```

In this case, each row contains four elements and each element is two bytes long, so:

```
offset=((table_row*4)+table_column)*2
```

This table is arranged so that the rows identify the target pixel (0-3; i.e., COLUMN MOD 4) and the columns identify the color. So, in this application, the formula looks like this:

```
offset=((pixel*4)+color)*2
```

The program extracts the table offset by fetching the two low bits of the graphics column number in CX, multiplying this pixel number by 4, adding the color value in BL, and multiplying the sum by 2. Of course, all of the multiplications are performed with fast, efficient shift opcodes. Once this offset has been calculated and placed into the DI register, the program reaches into the table and extracts both the mask and the color value. The result is that BL contains a mask with which the program may isolate the pixel, and BH contains a byte that has the color bits in the right positions.

Take a good long look at this table look-up technique. It is useful in many phases of assembly language programming. In this case, it was used for speed; the look-up operation is more than twice as fast as the variable-shifting code presented earlier. But look-up tables come in handy whenever it is easier to preprocess some data in order to avoid a tricky bit of code. For instance, it is much faster (and easier) to look up a SINE or COSINE value than it is to calculate one.

When you use PLOTDOT, remember that it does not trap for invalid coordinates. If it receives, say, (-1,5000) as the X,Y coordinates, it will plot a dot—but it will be either at an indeterminate location or completely off of the screen. The code to trap input error is quite easy to write (just two comparisons and conditional jumps), but remember that the error trap would need to be executed *every time your program plots a dot.* It makes no sense to burden every program that calls PLOTDOT with even such a small surcharge.

**THINGS TO DO**

1. Write a generalized version of PLOTDOT that will also handle subfunctions of returning the current value of a pixel (READ_DOT) as well as XORing a dot value with the current dot.

2. Write a fast PLOTDOT subroutine that sets, resets, and tests high-resolution pixels.

## 8.4 DRAWING LINES

The dot-plotting routine is a primitive tool. A single dot does not an arcade game make. Its real value is as a library module that may be used in more sophisticated tools. By organizing the screen so that it is conceptually a 2-dimensional array, the PLOTDOT tool opens up many possibilities for creating new and more powerful tools. The first higher-level tool we will examine is a line-drawing procedure.

Remembering your geometry, recall that a line is defined by any two points along that line. Each point is defined by an X and Y coordinate pair, and the two points that define a line are X1,Y1 and X2,Y2. Call these the *endpoints* of the line.

To draw a line, we must find all of the X,Y pairs that connect the two endpoints. This procedure normally involves determining which axis of the line is longer and making that ordinate an independent variable that increments steadily as we draw the line. The other ordinate is calculated using a floating point equation. The following discussion leads, in several steps, to an *incremental line-drawing algorithm* that eliminates the floating point operations, making it suitable for implementation in assembly language.

Let's start by examining one type of line—a line that starts somewhere in the upper left-hand corner of the screen and ends up closer to the lower right-hand corner. This type of line always has an X1 that is less than or equal to X2 and a Y1 that is less than or equal to Y2. Let's further assume that the line is longer along the X axis than it is along the Y axis (i.e., it is closer to being horizontal than vertical). The following BASIC code allows us to plot all of the dots of the line X1,Y1 to X2,Y2:

```
10 X.DELTA=X2-X1          '** horizontal distance to travel
20 Y.DELTA=Y2-Y1          '** vertical travel
30 SLOPE=Y.DELTA/X.DELTA  '** the fractional step size
                          'for the short axis
40 PSET(X1,INT(Y1))
50   X1=X1+1              '** increment long axis
60   Y1=Y1+SLOPE         '** fractionally adjust short axis
70 IF X1<X2 THEN GOTO 40
```

Each horizontal step also moves a partial step downward. If the slope of the line is 1/1, every horizontal step will be accompanied by one vertical step. If the slope is 5/8, every eight horizontal steps will force five vertical steps, and so forth.

Thus, knowing the ratio of horizontal to vertical steps, we could use a cycling variable and just keep checking it until it says that the vertical ordinate should be increased:

```
10 X.DELTA=X2-X1                '** horizontal distance to travel
20 Y.DELTA=Y2-Y1                '** vertical travel
30 SLOPE=Y.DELTA/X.DELTA
35 CYCLE=0.5                    '** start in the middle of a cycle
40 PSET (X1,INT(Y1))
50    X1=X1+1                   '** increment long axis pointer
60    CYCLE=CYCLE+SLOPE         '** bump the cycling value
65    IF CYCLE<1.0 THEN 70      '** if not at threshold, skip
67       Y1=Y1+1 :CYCLE=CYCLE-1.0 '** else make adjustment
70 IF X1<X2 THEN GOTO 40        '** loop back till finished
```

This algorithm appears to be no better than the previous one. It still uses floating point addition, and it now contains a floating point comparison as well as a floating point subtraction. This is only an intermediate step toward our final algorithm. The next step is to eliminate all the floating point operations by multiplying each floating point value by a constant that makes it an integer.

The only floating point values are CYCLE, SLOPE, and the constant 1.0. If we multiply them all by X.DELTA, we obtain the following variation of the above algorithm:

```
10 X.DELTA=X2-X1                '** horizontal distance to travel
20 Y.DELTA=Y2-Y1                '** vertical travel
30 SLOPE=Y.DELTA               '** was Y.DELTA/X.DELTA
35 CYCLE=INT(X.DELTA/2)        '** was 0.5
40 PSET(X1,Y1)
50    X1=X1+1
60    CYCLE=CYCLE+SLOPE         '** now uses integer addition
65    IF CYCLE<X.DELTA THEN 70  '** integer comparison
67       Y1=Y1+1               '** integer adjustment
68       CYCLE=CYCLE-X.DELTA
70 IF X1<X2 THEN GOTO 40
```

The only division operation is a division by 2, which can be accomplished by shifting the value to the right by one bit position. This algorithm works only for lines that move downward and toward the right side of the screen, but with only a couple of minor changes, it can be generalized for all possible lines. There are four main variations of the relationships between X1,X2 and Y1,Y2:

| relationship | example (X1,Y1)    (X2,Y2) | description |
|---|---|---|
| X1<X2, Y1<Y2 | (0,0) to (1,1) | drawn from upper left to lower right |
| X1>X2, Y1>Y2 | (1,1) to (0,0) | drawn from lower right to upper left |
| X1>X2, Y1<Y2 | (1,0) to (0,1) | drawn from upper right to lower left |
| X1<X2, Y1>Y2 | (0,1) to (1,0) | drawn from lower left to upper right |

The cases in which X1 = X2 and Y1 = Y2 can be considered special cases of any of these relationships; the line will be exactly horizontal or vertical, making the SLOPE value equal to 0. Thus, the CYCLE variable will never cross the threshold that forces the relevant axis pointer to change.

We have been working with the first case in which X1 < X2 and Y1 < Y2, but it's easy to see that the second relationship can be handled with similar logic. The only difference is that the pointers get smaller instead of larger. The long axis is decremented at each step, and the short axis is decremented at cyclical intervals. The other two cases are also similar, except that one ordinate is decremented while the other is incremented. To generalize for all four relationships, we need only set up two variables, X.STEP and Y.STEP, and assign them values of 1 or -1. Then, instead of incrementing or decrementing pointers, we just add this step-size variable to the pointer. The following code does this:

```
10 X.DELTA=X2-X1              '** horizontal distance to travel
20 Y.DELTA=Y2-Y1              '** vertical travel
25                           '** set up stepping directions
30 IF X.DELTA<0 THEN X.STEP=-1 ELSE X.STEP=1
32 IF Y.DELTA<0 THEN Y.STEP=-1 ELSE Y.STEP=1
35 CYCLE=INT(X.DELTA/2)       '** cycle starts in the middle
40 PSET(X1,Y1)
50   X1=X1+X.STEP             '** adjust the long axis pointer
60   CYCLE=CYCLE+Y.DELTA      '** adjust the cycling value
65   IF CYCLE<X.DELTA THEN 70 '** if not ready, don't adjust
67      Y1=Y2+Y.STEP          '** else, adjust the Y axis
68      CYCLE=CYCLE-X.DELTA    '** reset the cycling pointer
70 IF X1<>X2 THEN 40          '** loop back until done
```

We must account for two variations of each of the four possible directions. We have been discussing lines that have a slope between 0 and 1; that is, they are closer to the horizontal than the vertical, and the X axis is always longer than the Y axis. For each of the four main variations of the relationships of the endpoints, there are two minor variations that depend on whether the X axis is longer or shorter than the Y axis. Remember that the algorithm adjusts the long axis by 1 at each pass, but adjusts the short axis only when the CYCLE variable reaches a threshold. Up to now, we have assumed that the X axis is longer, making the Y axis the one that is adjusted occasionally.

In practice, we can't make that assumption. In order to generalize the line-drawing algorithm further to handle lines that have a steeper slope, we transpose the axes. That may sound complicated, but it just involves pretending that the X axis is the Y axis, and vice versa. In other words, where we normally adjust X1, we adjust Y1; where we normally adjust Y1, we adjust X1. The easiest way to implement this is to write code for two separate branches—one to handle the normal case and one to handle the situation in which axes must be swapped. BASIC Listing 8.4 calls the axes SH (short) and LG (long) instead of X and Y to show that either may be a horizontal or a vertical reference. This BASIC subroutine will plot a line between any two points (X1,Y1) and (X2,Y2).

## Listing 8.4
## BASIC Subroutine Plots and Dots of a Line

```
996 '** Listing 8.4
997 '** BASIC subroutine plots the dots of a line.
998 '** Expects: X1,Y1 and X2,Y2 are endpoints
999 '**
1000 LG.DELTA = (X2-X1)              '** assume "normal" case (X-axis is long axis)
1010 SH.DELTA = (Y2-Y1)
1020 IF LG.DELTA < 0 THEN LG.DELTA = -LG.DELTA :LG.STEP = -1 ELSE LG.STEP = 1
1030 IF SH.DELTA < 0 THEN SH.DELTA = -SH.DELTA :SH.STEP = -1 ELSE SH.STEP =  1
1040 IF SH.DELTA > LG.DELTA THEN 1200 '** skip to "alternate" case
1100 CYCLE = INT(LG.DELTA/2)          '** else begin "normal" case
1110 PSET(X1,Y1)
1120   X1 = X1 + LG.STEP             '** always adjust X (the long axis)
1130   CYCLE = CYCLE + SH.DELTA      '** adjust the cycling value
1140   IF CYCLE < LG.DELTA THEN 1170 '** adjust yet? No, skip
1150     Y1 = Y1 + SH.STEP          '**   Yes, bump Y (the short axis)
1160     CYCLE = CYCLE - LG.DELTA    '**      and reset the cycling value
1170 IF X1 <> X2 THEN 1110           '** loop back till done
1180 RETURN                          '** then return to caller
1190 '** --------- branch taken when Y-axis is longer than X-axis -----------
1200 CYCLE = INT(SH.DELTA / 2)       '** calculate cycling threshold
1210 SWAP LG.DELTA, SH.DELTA         '** exchange the variables for the axes
1220 SWAP LG.STEP, SH.STEP
1230 PSET(X1,Y1)
1240   Y1 = Y1 + LG.STEP            '** always adjust Y (the long axis)
1250   CYCLE = CYCLE + SH.DELTA      '** adjust cycling pointer
1260   IF CYCLE < LG.DELTA THEN 1290 '** adjust yet? No, skip
1270     CYCLE = CYCLE - LG.DELTA    '**   Yes, bump the cycle pointer
1280     X1 = X1 + SH.STEP          '**      and bump X (the short axis)
1290 IF Y1 <> Y2 THEN 1230           '** loop back to complete the line
1300 RETURN
```

Listing 8.5, PLOTLINE, is the assembly language translation of the BASIC code with one additional feature. Besides drawing a line that connects two points, this code gives you the option of plotting a *subset* or *superset* of the points that connect (X1,Y1) to (X2,Y2). Thus, you can draw a partial line starting at (X1,Y1) that *ends before* (X2,Y2), and you can draw a line that *extends beyond* (X2,Y2). What's more, you can plot any contiguous subset of the line. That is, although the line originates at (X1,Y1), the routine doesn't necessarily begin plotting dots at that location. You can specify a skip-count that makes the first part of the line invisible.

I created this feature when I needed to draw a laser beam in an arcade-style game. By repeatedly calling the routine, specifying the same endpoints but with a longer length, and a greater skip-count at each call, I was able to make the beam appear to move across the screen.

## Listing 8.5
## PLOTLINE NEAR Library Procedure

```
;---------------------------------------------------------------
; Listing 8.5   PLOTLINE  near library procedure
; Plots a line on the color/graphics adapter screen.
; Calls external PLOTDOT procedure
;
; On entry: DS:SI has address of a data packet in this format:
;    si+0   = X1    starting column (0-319)
;    si+2   = Y1    starting row (0-159)
;    si+4   = X2    ending column
;    si+6   = Y2    ending row
;    si+8   = color  (0, 1, 2, or 3)
;    si+10  = line length
;             0     = plot entire line
;             else = plot subset or superset of this vector
;    si+12  = skip length
;             0     = plot entire line
;             else = number of dots to skip before starting to plot
;
;On exit: line is plotted.
;         all registers and values in data packet are preserved

            public  plotline
code_grp group   lib_seg
lib_seg  segment byte public 'code'
            extrn   plotdot:near       ;<--- external library module
            assume  cs:code_grp        ;set up for correct addressing of
                                       ; variables stored in code segment
X1       equ     word ptr [si]      ; === DATA PACKET passed by caller ===
Y1       equ     word ptr [si+2]    ;give names to variables
X2       equ     word ptr [si+4]    ; and arguments to simplify
Y2       equ     word ptr [si+6]    ; programming
COLOR    equ     byte ptr [si+8]
LEN      equ     word ptr [si+10]
SKIP     equ     word ptr [si+12]

;Register usage during plotting loops:
;    CX = X1  starting (current) X ordinate to plot
;    DX = Y1  starting (current) Y ordinate to plot
;    BL = color code
;    AX = SHORT_DELTA (length of short axis)
;    BP = LONG_DELTA (length of long axis)
;    DI = CYCLE (keeps track of when to move along short axis)
;variables:
;    CS:[SHORT_STEP] (-1 or 1; step size for short axis)
;    CS:[LONG_STEP] (-1 or 1; step size for long axis)
;    CS:[LINE_START] (first dot to plot; i.e., skip length)
;    CS:[LINE_STOP] (last dot to plot or length of full line)

plotline proc    near
            push    ax              ;all registers are used
            push    bx              ; so they must be saved
            push    cx
            push    dx
            push    bp
            push    si
            push    di
            push    es

            mov     cs:long_step,1  ;assume motion down or right
            mov     bp,X2
            sub     bp,X1           ;get BP = LONG_DELTA
            jge     pl1             ;if X1 <= X2 then no change
            neg     cs:long_step    ; else, LONG_STEP = -1 (motion up or left)
            neg     bp              ;          LONG_DELTA = abs(LONG_DELTA)
```

**Listing 8.5
(continued)**

```
pl1:
        mov     cs:short_step,1 ;assume motion down or right
        mov     ax,Y2
        sub     ax,Y1           ;get AX = SHORT_DELTA
        jge     pl2             ;if Y1 <= Y2 then no change
        neg     cs:short_step   ; else, SHORT_STEP = -1 (motion up or left)
        neg     ax              ;          SHORT_DELTA = abs(SHORT_DELTA)
pl2:
        mov     cs:line_start,0 ;assume no skip length
        mov     di,SKIP         ;check data packet
        cmp     di,0            ;is skip count specified?
        je      pl3             ; no, leave it as assumed
        mov     cs:line_start,di ; yes, use it
pl3:
        mov     bl,COLOR        ;set up for PLOTDOT procedure.  COLOR in BL
        mov     cx,X1           ; X ordinate in CX
        mov     dx,Y1           ; Y ordinate in DX

        cmp     ax,bp           ;is SHORT_DELTA longer than LONG_DELTA?
        ja      alt_code        ; yes, use alternate line drawing code

;------- "normal" setup for when line has slope between 0 and 1

        mov     cs:line_stop,bp ;assume length = LONG_DELTA
        mov     di,LEN          ;read from the data packet
        cmp     di,0            ;user want subset or superset?
        je      pl4             ; no, leave as assumed
        mov     cs:line_stop,di ; yes, store the desired length
pl4:
        mov     di,bp           ;set up the cycle pointer
        shr     di,1            ;CYCLE = LONG_DELTA / 2
        mov     si,0            ;initialize loop counter
norm_loop:
        cmp     si,cs:line_start ;start to plot yet?
        jl      pl5             ; no, skip
        call    plotdot         ; yes, plot (CX,DX) with color BL
pl5:
        add     cx,cs:long_step ;always move along X axis
        add     di,ax           ;CYCLE = CYCLE + SHORT_DELTA
        cmp     di,bp           ;is CYCLE >= LONG_DELTA?
        jl      pl6             ; no, skip (don't move along Y axis yet)
        sub     di,bp           ; yes, reset CYCLE pointer
        add     dx,cs:short_step ;    and bump the Y ordinate
pl6:
        inc     si              ;bump dot counter
        cmp     si,cs:line_stop ;done?
        jbe     norm_loop       ; no, plot next dot
        jmp     pl_exit         ; yes, go to common exit code
;------- "alternate" branch is taken when the slope has an absolute value > 1
alt_code:
        xchg    ax,bp           ;swap LONG_DELTA,SHORT_DELTA
        mov     di,cs:long_step
        xchg    cs:short_step,di
        mov     cs:long_step,di ;swap LONG_STEP,SHORT_STEP

        mov     cs:line_stop,bp ;assume length = LONG_DELTA
        mov     di,LEN          ;read from the data packet
        cmp     di,0            ;user want subset or superset?
        je      pl7             ; no, leave as assumed
        mov     cs:line_stop,di ; yes, store the desired length
```

**Listing 8.5
(continued)**

```
p17:
        mov     di,bp           ;set up the cycle pointer
        shr     di,1            ;CYCLE = LONG_DELTA / 2
        mov     si,0            ;initialize loop counter
alt_loop:
        cmp     si,cs:line_start ;start to plot yet?
        jl      p18             ; no, skip
        call    plotdot         ; yes, plot (CX,DX) with color BL
p18:
        add     dx,cs:long_step ;always move along Y axis
        add     di,ax           ;CYCLE = CYCLE + SHORT_DELTA
        cmp     di,bp           ;is CYCLE >= LONG_DELTA?
        jl      p19             ; no, skip (don't move along X axis yet)
        sub     di,bp           ; yes, reset CYCLE pointer
        add     cx,cs:short_step ;      and bump the X ordinate
p19:
        inc     si              ;bump dot counter
        cmp     si,cs:line_stop ;done?
        jbe     alt_loop        ; no, plot next dot
                                ; yes, fall through to common exit
pl_exit:
        pop     es              ;common exit
        pop     di
        pop     si
        pop     bp
        pop     dx
        pop     cx
        pop     bx
        pop     ax
        ret                     ;NEAR return to caller <----- EXIT -----
plotline endp

;----------- local variables for this procedure ---------
short_step   dw      ?
long_step    dw      ?
line_start   dw      ?
line_stop    dw      ?

lib_seg  ends
         end
```

A not so obvious advantage of this feature is that you can draw lines at a desired angle without needing to calculate the endpoints of a line with that angle. For instance, if $X1 = X2$ and $Y2 = Y1 - 1$, if you draw a superset of the vector of that 1-pixel line, it will lie 90 degrees from horizontal (i.e., it will be a vertical line). If $X2 = X1 + 1$ and $Y2 = Y1 + 1$, the line you draw will be at a 45-degree angle from horizontal. Figure 8.5 shows variations on this possibility.

Listing 8.6, TESTLINE, is a routine that you can use to test the PLOTLINE library module. This is a good example of how a program that calls a library routine should look. Notice how the segments are set up. Study the code to find the EXTRN statement that is the vital link between a program and a library module. After you assemble the TESTLINE program, you must link it with both the PLOTLINE and PLOTDOT modules:

```
LINK TESTLINE+PLOTLINE+PLOTDOT;
```

**Figure 8.5**
**Angles of Lines Plotted with PLOTLINE**

| angle (degrees) | values for (X2,Y2) | Compass point |
|---|---|---|
| 0 | X1+1, Y1+0 | West |
| 1 | X1+60,Y1+1 | |
| 3.75 | X1+16,Y1+1 | |
| 5 | X1+12,Y1+1 | |
| 7.5 | X1+8, Y1+1 | |
| 15 | X1+4, Y1+1 | |
| 30 | X1+2, Y1+1 | West by Northwest |
| 45 | X1+1, Y1+1 | Northwest |
| 60 | X1+1, Y1+2 | North by Northwest |
| 90 | X1+0, Y1-1 | North |
| 180 | X1-1, Y1+0 | East |
| 270 | X1+0, Y1+1 | South |

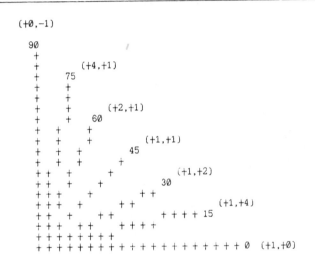

## Listing 8.6
## TESTLINE Program

```
;----------------------------------------
; Listing 8.6    TESTLINE  program
; Tests the the PLOTLINE and PLOTDOT library routines by drawing
;  a mosaic of medium resolution lines.
; External calls: PLOTLINE and (indirectly) PLOTDOT
;
stack_seg segment para stack
          db        256 dup(?)
stack_seg ends

data_seg segment para public 'data'
line_packet label word

X1       dw       159         ;starting X,Y in the center of the screen
Y1       dw       99
X2       dw       ?           ;ending X,Y calculated by program
Y2       dw       ?
color    dw       3
len      dw       0           ;change these to test the variable-length
skip     dw       0           ; line size options

data_seg ends

code_grp group    code_seg
code_seg segment para public 'code'
         assume  cs:code_grp, ds:data_seg
         extrn   plotline:near            ;<--- external module ----

testline proc    far
         push    ds
         mov     ax,0
         push    ax
         mov     ax,data_seg
         mov     ds,ax

         mov     ah,0
         mov     al,4
         int     10H
         mov     si,offset line_packet ;DS:SI points to line data-packet
         mov     X2,0
         mov     Y2,0            ;start with the upper left corner
top_side:
         call    plotline
         inc     color
         and     color,3     ;cycle through the colors
         inc     X2          ;point one dot the the right
         cmp     X2,320      ;at the right side yet?
         jb      top_side    ; no, plot another line
         dec     X2          ; yes, point back to valid X-ordinate
right_side:
         call    plotline
         inc     color
         and     color,3     ;cycle through the colors
         inc     Y2          ;point one dot downward
         cmp     Y2,200      ; at the bottom?
         jb      right_side
         dec     Y2
```

**Listing 8.6
(continued)**

```
bot_side:
          call      plotline
          inc       color
          and       color,3     ;cycle through the colors
          dec       X2          ;point one dot to the left
          cmp       X2,0        ; at the left side?
          jg        bot_side
          inc       X2

left_side:
          call      plotline
          inc       color
          and       color,3     ;cycle through the colors
          dec       Y2          ;point one dot up
          cmp       Y2,0        ; at the top?
          jg        left_side

          ret
testline  endp
code_seg  ends
          end
```

Notice how easily the TESTLINE procedure modifies its parameters between calls to PLOTLINE. The modules communicate by passing the address of a data packet structure. This is a convenient technique when a subroutine needs several parameters. It offers flexibility and ease of use to both the calling program and the called routine. The calling program can set up several parameter packets in advance and then just point SI to the desired one before the call to the library module. Changing and querying parameters at either end is a snap. The indirect addressing mode makes it as easy to change a packet parameter as it is to manipulate a register, and the parameters can be given meaningful names such as COLOR and START_X so that you can avoid needing to keep track of which register holds which value.

Using a data packet avoids the time-consuming series of PUSHes that typify the frame-oriented parameter-passing system. And you can use a packet in conjunction with high-level language parameter-passing conventions. Just set up an integer array (BASIC) or a record (Pascal) and pass the address of that array to the module.

Because PLOTLINE requires no multiplication and holds most of its data in registers, it is a very fast routine. However, it could still be improved upon. The BASCOM line-drawing routine is about 20 percent faster. Even though PLOTDOT has been optimized for speed, it is the bottleneck that slows execution of PLOTLINE. It's not hard to see the reason. Every call to PLOTDOT requires a conversion of an X,Y coordinate pair into a screen memory address. Consider that after the first dot is plotted, each subsequent dot is either adjacent to or actually in the *same byte as the dot that was just plotted.* BASCOM's speed is possible because it takes advantage of this fact. It uses an algorithm that is very similar to the one we have been discussing; that is, it keeps track of a cycle pointer that indicates when the short axis must be adjusted. However, instead of adjusting an X,Y pointer and making calls to a general-purpose dot-plotting routine, it simply adjusts its current position in a byte and its current screen address.

**THINGS TO DO**

1. Write a companion module for PLOTLINE that draws a box. Use the X1,Y1 and X2,Y2 parameters as opposite corners of the box. The routine should make four calls to PLOTLINE. (*) Provide an option to fill the box.

2. Write a version of PLOTDOT that works with the monochrome card of the text mode of the color card. Of course, you won't be plotting graphics dots, but you could make good use of the 80 by 25 resolution by moving the block character 0DBH (or a character passed as a parameter) into appropriate places in video memory.

3. (*) Use the text characters ASCII 0DCH and 0DFH (upper half and lower half filled) to expand the text mode resolution of 80 by 50. Interface this character-plotting routine to the PLOTLINE subroutine.

4. (*) Modify the incremental line-drawing algorithm so that you can use it to plot the path of projectiles without actually drawing a line. In other words, write a subroutine that returns the next X,Y coordinate pair along a previously defined vector.

5. (**) Optimize PLOTLINE so that it does not need to recalculate a screen address from an X,Y coordinate pair for each dot. If you have BASCOM and its library, you may want to give yourself a head start by disassembling its line-drawing routines.

## 8.5 DRAWING CIRCLES

Another useful procedure for your graphics toolbox is a circle-drawing subroutine. You will find this procedure handy for making eye-catching displays for the "attract" mode of your arcade-style game. Or, used in conjunction with the line-drawing procedure, it can be the face of a clock or a simulated depth meter in a submarine or an altimeter in an aircraft.

A circle is pretty complex. You may have drawn one in BASIC by using a series of transcendental functions such as this:

```
10 SCREEN 1                      '** mid-resolution graphics
20 CX=159 :CY=99                 '** define centerpoint
30 INPUT ''RADIUS'';R
40 FOR J=.001 to 2*3.14159 STEP 1/R '** step in tiny increments
50   A=SIN(J)*R :B=COS(J)*R       '** calculate each point
60   PSET(CX+A,CY+B)              '** light it up
70 NEXT
```

This program calculates points on a perfect circle but draws an elliptical shape. The circle is elongated because of the size differential between the screen's horizontal and vertical axes. By changing line 60 to read

```
60   PSET(CX+A,CY+B*200/320)     '** adjust for asymmetrical
                                    screen (5/6 aspect)
```

you can make the circle appear to be perfectly round. This is called the *aspect* of the circle. By using a ratio other than 5/6, you can make the circle into an ellipse.

As you can see, this method is short and sweet, but it has little value for the average 8088 programmer. True, if you have access to an 8087 coprocessor, this BASIC program could be converted to assembly language in minutes. However, because the 8087 is not yet part of the standard IBM-PC configuration, we shall examine the options available to the majority of users. As with the line-drawing program, we need a way to avoid the floating point arithmetic that is at the heart of this circle-drawing algorithm.

One way to eliminate the need for SINE and COSINE functions is to fall back on the tried-and-true equation of a circle:

$$R^2 = B^2 + A^2$$

A circle with radius $R$ is composed of points defined by all of the $A$s and $B$s that satisfy this equation. Here's the equation again, solved for $B$:

$$B = \sqrt{R^2 - A^2}$$

By iteratively substituting for $A$ all of the integer values from 0 to $R$, we can specify a collection of points that are on the circumference of the circle with radius $R$. For example:

```
10 SCREEN 1            '** mid-resolution graphics
20 CX=159 :CY=99       '** define centerpoint
30 INPUT "RADIUS";R
40 FOR A=0 to R
50  B=SQR(R*R-A*A)     '** derive B from A and R
60  PSET(CX+A,CY+B)    '** light it up
70 NEXT
```

This lights up dots in only the lower right quadrant of the circle. And many of the dots are separated by one or more blank spaces (see Figure 8.6a). We could cover more of the circle just by echoing the points in that quadrant symmetrically around the rest of the circle:

```
62 PSET(CX-A,CY+B)    '** plot the lower left quadrant
64 PSET(CX-A,CY-B)    '**  and the lower right
66 PSET(CX+A,CY-B)    '**  and the upper left
```

This procedure plots points all around the circle, but there would still be gaps. By swapping the $A$ offset with the $B$ offset and plotting the circle again, we could close those gaps. Figure 8.6b shows how reversing the $A$ and $B$ values would plot dots in the "unconnected" parts of the circle. Thus, we could add the following lines to the BASIC program and obtain a completely connected circle:

```
61 PSET(CX+B,CY+A)    '** plot the inverted lower right quadrant
63 PSET(CX-B,CY+A)    '**  and the inverted lower left
65 PSET(CX-B,CY-A)    '**  and the inverted upper right
67 PSET(CX+B,CY-A)    '**  and the inverted upper left
```

**Figure 8.6a**
**Points of the Circle Plotted with PLOT (CX+A,CY+B)**

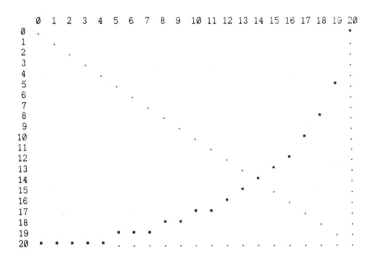

**Figure 8.6b**
**Points of a Circle Plotted with PLOT (CX+B,CY+A)**

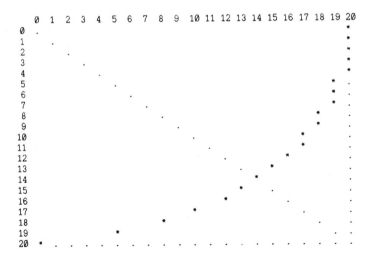

However, this procedure is inefficient because many of the points would be plotted twice. By inspecting Figures 8.6a and 8.6b, you should be able to see a simple method to eliminate this redundancy. At some point in the plotting loop, *A* and *B* reach the same value. After that point, all of the rest of the dots are just repetitions of previously plotted points. Therefore, we can modify our BASIC program as follows so that it plots the circle without skipping or overlaying any dots:

```
10 SCREEN 1              '** mid-resolution graphics
20 CX=159 :CY=99         '** define centerpoint
30 INPUT "RADIUS";R
40 A=0 :B=R
45 WHILE A<B
50    B=SQR(R*R-A*A)     '** derive B from A and R
55                       '**Plot in all four quadrants
60    PSET(CX+A,CY+B)  :PSET(CX+B,CY+A)
62    PSET(CX-A,CY+B)  :PSET(CX-B,CY+A)
64    PSET(CX-A,CY-B)  :PSET(CX-B,CY-A)
66    PSET(CX+A,CY-B)  :PSET(CX+B,CY-A)
70    A=A+1
80 WEND
```

This program works as is, but we'll make one more logic change before we convert it to assembly language. Each pass through the loop between lines 50 and 70 squares two numbers and extracts the square root of the difference. The *R* * *R* can be removed and performed outside of the loop, but even so, the remaining calculations take time.

Fortunately, there is a simple way to eliminate most of the arithmetic. The trick is to iterate the *A* value backward from *R*. This iteration generates the X,Y coordinates for the unconnected portion of each quadrant. Then the program need only connect successively generated points. We could whip out our handy line-drawing program, but this is no time for brute strength. Each pair of points can be connected by a straight horizontal or vertical line. After calculating a new pair of *A* and *B* values, we just plot a set of points along the *A* vector, increasing *B* until it matches the new value. Here's the outline:

```
35 TARGET=0
40 A=R :B=0              '** start at R and work down
45 WHILE A>B             '** until A and B converge
50    B=SQR(R*R-A*A)     '**derive B from A and R
52    SWAP TARGET,B      '** use the new B as the target
53    WHILE B<TARGET
60       '** --- plot the eight points ---
68       B=B+1
69    WEND
70    A=A-1
80 WEND
```

## A Square Root to Make a Circle

Finally, we need to do something about that square root function. You can look through the 8088 instruction set until you are blue (Big Blue) in the face, and you won't come across a SQRT operation. There is more than one way to extract the square root of a number, but we won't go into the complexities of successive approximation. We'll use an ancient method that is well suited to assembly language. It is based on the unusual fact that the integer square root of a number is a count of the successively higher odd integers that can be subtracted from it.

In other words, if you subtract 1, then 3, then 5, and so on from a number, and you count the number of times that you can do this without forcing the number to go negative, then you will have found the square root. For example:

```
25 - 1 = 24        (one time)

24 - 3 = 21        (two times)

21 - 5 = 16        (three times)

16 - 7 = 9         (four times)

 9 - 9 = 0         (five times)
```

Since five successively higher odd numbers can be subtracted from 25, the integer square root is 5.

Another way to look at it is this: After increasing the subtrahend through the odd integers until the subtraction results in a negative difference, the last number that is subtracted is twice the value of the square root. Examine the SQRT procedure in Listing 8.7 to see it in action. This subroutine also makes an extra adjustment to the return value to make sure that it is as near as possible to the desired root. Without this adjustment, the routine would return 9 as the square root of 99 even though 10 is a better approximation. This algorithm is very fast for calculating the small square roots needed for generating circles that fit on the screen, but it becomes inefficient with larger numbers.

Listing 8.7, CIRCLE, provides added flexibility to our circle-drawing algorithm by including an *aspect* parameter. This parameter allows the caller to request a circle that is stretched on either axis. As we saw earlier, this can be accomplished by multiplying the Y axis offset by an X/Y ratio. Another floating point value is the last thing we need, but this one is easily circumvented. Instead of bothering with floating point math, the program simply scales the Y offset up by a factor of 1000, multiplies the ratio, and scales it back down with a division by 1000. This operation results in a number with plenty of accuracy for the medium-resolution screen. Examine the PLOT_8 procedure to see how this is done.

Another notable feature is the PLOT_OK procedure. This is a "filter" for the PLOTDOT library module. Its input is exactly the same: DX = row, CX = column, and BL = color. The only difference is that it checks to see if valid medium-resolution coordinates have been passed to it. This code could have been included in the PLOTDOT module, but that would have meant extra overhead that would seldom be needed. Included in this CIRCLE procedure, it allows a calling program to draw circles that are partially off the screen.

**Listing 8.7**
**CIRCLE NEAR Library Procedure**

```
;-------------------------------------------------------------
; Listing 8.7   CIRCLE     NEAR library procedure
; Plots a full circle on the color/graphics adapter screen.
; Calls PLOTDOT
; On entry: DS:SI has address of a data packet in this format:
;
;   si+0 = X_CENTER  horizontal centerpoint (0-319)
;   si+2 = Y_CENTER  vertical centerpoint (0-199)
;   si+4 = RADIUS
;   si+6 = COLOR  (0, 1, 2, or 3)
;   si+8 = ASPECT X/Y ratio * 1000
;          833  = round circle (5/6 or .833*1000)
;          else = oblique circle (1000 = 1/1)
;
;On exit: circle is plotted (may be partially off the screen)
;         all registers and data packet values are preserved

          public  circle
code_grp  group   lib_seg
lib_seg   segment byte public 'code'
          extrn   plotdot:near      ;<--- external library module
          assume  cs:code_grp

;get a handle on the data packet structure
X_CENTER  equ     word ptr [si]
Y_CENTER  equ     word ptr [si+2]
RADIUS    equ     word ptr [si+4]
COLOR     equ     byte ptr [si+6]
ASPECT    equ     word ptr [si+8]

circle    proc    near
          push    ax            ;all registers but SI are lost,
          push    bx            ; so they must be saved
          push    cx
          push    dx
          push    bp
          push    di
          push    es

          mov     ax,RADIUS
          mul     ax
          mov     di,ax         ;DI = RADIUS * RADIUS
          mov     ax,RADIUS
          dec     ax            ;AX = ALPHA (initially RADIUS-1)
          mov     bx,0          ;BX = BETA
          mov     cx,0          ;CX = target BETA
cir1:
          push    ax            ;save ALPHA
          mul     ax            ;get AX = ALPHA squared
          mov     dx,di
          sub     dx,ax         ;DX = RADIUS*RADIUS - ALPHA*ALPHA
          mov     ax,dx         ;set up for square root call
          call    SQRT          ;get BX (i.e., BETA) = sqrt(AX)
          pop     ax            ;retrieve ALPHA
          xchg    bx,cx         ;old TARGET is new BETA
```

**Listing 8.7
(continued)**

```
cir2:
          call    plot_8          ;plot the ALPHA and BETA offsets
          inc     bx              ;adjust BETA for next dots
          cmp     bx,cx           ;has BETA reached TARGET?
          jl      cir2            ; no, continue connecting

          cmp     ax,bx           ; yes, is circle complete?
          jl      cir_exit        ;    yes, exit
          dec     ax              ;    no, get new ALPHA
          jmp     cir1            ;        and go back for next group
cir_exit:
          pop     es              ;restore registers for exit
          pop     di
          pop     bp
          pop     dx
          pop     cx
          pop     bx
          pop     ax
          ret                     ;<---- CIRCLE procedure exit ----
circle    endp
;----------
; SQRT
; Extracts square root by subtraction of successive odd integers.
; expects: AX = radicand
; returns: BX = square root, rounded up or down to the nearest integer

sqrt      proc    near
          push    ax
          mov     bx,-1           ;starts as first odd integer -2
sqrt_1:
          add     bx,2            ;get next odd integer
          sub     ax,bx           ;subtract it from radicand
          jg      sqrt_1          ; until it goes below 0

          shr     bx,1            ;divided by 2 = rounded square root
          add     ax,bx           ;is result closer to next higher?
          jnc     sqrt_exit       ; no, exit
          inc     bx              ; yes, adjust the answer
sqrt_exit:
          pop     ax
          ret
sqrt      endp

;-------------
; PLOT_8
; plots points in the eight octants of a circle
; expects: AX and BX are ALPHA and BETA offsets from centerpoint
;          variable ASPECT = X/Y ratio * 1000

plot_8    proc    near
          push    ax              ;save ALPHA
          push    bx              ; and BETA
          push    cx
          push    dx
          push    bp
```

**Listing 8.7
(continued)**

```
        push    ax              ;will need this later
        mul     ASPECT          ;ALPHA = (ALPHA*ASPECT)/1000
        mov     cx,1000
        div     cx              ;now AX is ALPHA for first four points
        mov     bp,bx           ; and BP is BETA
        call    plot_4

        mov     ax,bp           ;get BETA
        mul     ASPECT
        mov     cx,1000
        div     cx              ;AX is now alternate BETA for last four points
        pop     bp              ; and BP = alternate ALPHA
        call    plot_4

        pop     bp
        pop     dx
        pop     cx
        pop     bx
        pop     ax
        ret                     ;<<<--- PLOT 8 procedure EXIT -----
;------- following code plots 1 point in each of four octants of the circle.
;        expects BP = ALPHA (or BETA), AX = alternate ALPHA (or alternate BETA)

plot_4:
        mov     cx,X_CENTER
        mov     dx,Y_CENTER
        mov     bl,COLOR

        add     cx,bp
        add     dx,ax
        call    plot_ok         ;PLOT(X+n,Y+alt_m)
        sub     dx,ax
        sub     dx,ax
        call    plot_ok         ;plot(X+n,Y-alt_m)
        sub     cx,bp
        sub     cx,bp
        call    plot_ok         ;plot(X-n,Y-alt_m)
        add     dx,ax
        add     dx,ax
        call    plot_ok         ;plot(X-n,Y+alt_m)
        ret
plot_8  endp

;------------
; PLOT_OK
; Calls PLOTDOT, but makes sure that screen coordinates are valid.
;
plot_ok proc    near
        cmp     cx,319
        ja      pok_exit
        cmp     dx,199
        ja      pok_exit
        call    plotdot
pok_exit:
        ret
plot_ok endp

lib_seg ends
        end
```

As with PLOTLINE, all of the CIRCLE parameters are passed in a data packet. This avoids the work of PUSHing a group of parameters onto the stack or trying to squeeze them all into registers. Listing 8.8, TESTCIR, is a simple example of how to use the CIRCLE module. It draws a series of concentric circles centered in the middle of the screen.

**Listing 8.8**
**TESTCIR Program**

```
;----------------------------------------
; Listing 8.8   TESTCIR   program
; Tests the the CIRCLE library routine.
; Plots a series of concentric circles with centerpoints in the
;  middle of the mid-resolution screen.
; External calls: CIRCLE and (indirectly) PLOTDOT

stack_seg segment para stack
          db        256 dup(?)
stack_seg ends

data_seg segment para public 'data'

cir_packet label word
X_CENTER   dw     159         ;put centerpoint in center of screen
Y_CENTER   dw     99
RADIUS     dw     90
COLOR      dw     3           ;use brown (or white)
ASPECT     dw     5000/6      ;this ratio makes the circle round
                             ; (note: assembler won't accept 5/6*1000)
data_seg ends

code_grp group    code_seg
code_seg segment para public 'code'
         assume   cs:code_grp, ds:data_seg
         extrn    circle:near
testcir  proc     far
         push     ds                  ;set up FAR return to DOS
         mov      ax,0
         push     ax
         mov      ax,data_seg         ;establish data segment addressing
         mov      ds,ax

         mov      ah,0
         mov      al,4                ;enter mid-resolution color graphics mode
         int      10H

         mov      si,offset cir_packet ;point to data for CIRCLE procedure
         mov      radius,200          ;just catches the corners at first
again:
         call     circle
         sub      radius,3            ;move inward
         jg       again
         ret                          ;back to DOS
testcir  endp
code_seg ends
         end
```

I urge you to experiment with this circle-drawing tool in order to get some ideas of the spectacular, eye-catching displays that it can create. When you link CIRCLE to your own code, be sure that you use the (by now familiar) library module linkage conventions. Use the GROUP pseudo-op to connect LIB_SEG to CODE_SEG (or whatever you call the code segment of your main program). And be sure to place the EXTRN declaration inside that code segment. When you link it, be sure to include PLOTDOT in your response to the linker's "Object Modules" prompt because CIRCLE calls it as a subfunction.

### THINGS TO DO

1. Use the STRUC pseudo-op to set up the parameter packet for the CIRCLE procedure. If you place the structure definition in an INCLUDE file, it can easily be brought into any program that calls CIRCLE.
2. Write a routine that moves a small circle around the screen. That is, draw the circle in the background color, adjust the centerpoint, draw it with white pixels, and repeat the process.
3. Change the SQRT procedure of the CIRCLE module so that it uses a look-up table to find the square root of a number.

## 8.6 INSTALLING A CUSTOM GRAPHICS CHARACTER SET

When you invoke the WRITE_CHAR service (INT 10, subfunction 90H or 0AH), the ROM-BIOS normally just stores an ASCII value somewhere in video memory. But when the card is in graphics mode, the BIOS "paints" an 8 by 8 block of pixels from a graphics character table. This section discusses how the ROM-BIOS does this and explains how to install your own extensions to that table. This operation leads to more sophisticated shape-drawing procedures that can be used to draw and animate small objects in arcade-style games.

Let's start by considering the situation in which the color card is in high-resolution mode. You will recall that each dot in this mode is controlled by a single bit in graphics memory. A byte of graphics memory defines eight consecutive pixels. By writing a single byte into any graphics memory address, we can define the on/off values of a horizontal line of eight dots. Figure 8.7 shows how a series of eight bytes (64 bits) can define all of the dots needed to draw the ASCII character A.

**Figure 8.7**
**The Graphic Definition of the ASCII Character "A"**

bit positions

| | 7 | 6 | 5 | 4 | 3 | 2 | 1 | Ø |
|---|---|---|---|---|---|---|---|---|
| byte Ø | | | + | + | | | | |
| byte 1 | | + | + | + | + | | | |
| byte 2 | + | + | | | + | + | | |
| byte 3 | + | + | | | + | + | | |
| byte 4 | + | + | + | + | + | + | | |
| byte 5 | + | + | | | + | + | | |
| byte 6 | + | + | | | + | + | | |
| byte 7 | | | | | | | | |

| | binary | hex |
|---|---|---|
| byte Ø | ØØ11ØØØØ | 3Ø |
| byte 1 | Ø1111ØØØ | 78 |
| byte 2 | 11ØØ11ØØ | CC |
| byte 3 | 11ØØ11ØØ | CC |
| byte 4 | 111111ØØ | FC |
| byte 5 | 11ØØ11ØØ | CC |
| byte 6 | 11ØØ11ØØ | CC |
| byte 7 | ØØØØØØØØ | ØØ |

The ROM-BIOS WRITE_CHAR service accesses a look-up table in ROM that contains each of the 8-byte definitions of ASCII characters 0-127. In order to print a particular character, it first calculates the address in the look-up table of that character. The 8-byte element starts at the byte that is offset from the start of the table by eight times the ASCII value of the character. Then it calculates a screen address from the line and column coordinates that are passed to it by the caller. Finally, it begins transferring bytes from the table into video memory.

Remember that the graphics lines are not consecutive. Each odd line is in the second bank of graphics memory, 2000H bytes beyond the even row that is physically above it. So, assuming that DS:SI points to the first byte of the 8-byte element in the character table and ES:DI points to the relevant address in video memory, the following sequence would move the entire eight bytes into adjacent lines of graphics memory:

```
LODSB                               ;fetch the first byte

MOV       ES:[DI],AL                ;move it into even bank

LODSB                               ;fetch the second byte of the character

MOV       ES:[DI+2000H],AL          ;move into odd bank (row+1)

LODSB

MOV       ES:[DI+80*1],AL           ;next byte into even bank (row+2)

LODSB

MOV       ES:[DI+2000H+80*1],AL     ;odd bank (row+3)

LODSB

MOV       ES:[DI+80*2],AL           ;even bank (row+4)

LODSB

MOV       ES:[DI+2000H+80*2],AL     ;odd bank (row+5)

LODSB

MOV       ES:[DI+80*3],AL           ;even bank (row+6)

LODSB

MOV       ES:[DI+2000H+80*3],AL     ;odd bank (row+7)
```

This code could be made more concise by setting up a loop, but this technique of hard-coding the offsets and using the indexed direct addressing mode is faster.

The ROM-BIOS has a separate routine to handle medium-resolution characters because there is no one-to-one relationship between the bits of the character table and mid-resolution graphics memory. It must interpret each bit in the table element as a lit/dark flag and then move the two bits of the requested foreground color into position for each such flag. It is instructive to see how the ROM-BIOS accomplishes this task, and I recommend that you look through the BIOS listing in the technical reference manual to examine the technique used there. That code also contains some sophisticated pattern recognition routines for reading characters from the graphics screen.

In both high- and mid-resolution modes, the ROM-BIOS interprets the same data, but its look-up table contains definitions of only the first 128 ASCII characters. However, there is a provision for adding a user-defined table for the upper 128 characters (ASCII 128-255). If the ROM-BIOS has been instructed to print a character that has an ASCII value above 127, it fetches the low-memory vector for interrupt 1FH (absolute address 0000:007C) and uses it as the start of the look-up table.

Try entering this short BASIC program to display the default character set for characters above 127:

```
10 SCREEN 1           '** mid-resolution color
20 FOR J=0 TO 255     '** cycle through all characters
30   PRINT CHR$(J);" ";
40 NEXT
```

The characters above CHR$(127) are displayed as a series of meaningless random patterns. That's because the vector at 0000:007C is not pointing at a graphics character table. We can change that situation with a few POKEs. Add these lines and run the program again:

```
4  DEF SEG=0
5  POKE &H7C,&H6E ;POKE &H7D,&HFA    'set up the offset
8  POKE &H7E,&H00 :POKE &H7F,&HF0    'set up the segment
```

These lines move the address F000:FA6E into the graphics character set vector in low memory. That's the address of the ROM table for the *first* 128 characters. This gives you an alternative way to specify any character. PRINTing either CHR$(n) or CHR$(n+128) will display the same character. This duplication can be useful because BASIC will not allow you to display certain characters by PRINTing their normal value; CHR$(7) and CHR$(13) are examples. However, the reason for this exercise is to demonstrate how easy it is to set up a secondary graphics character set. The next step is to install your own, customized character table.

Listing 8.9, CHARS, is a COM format file that loads a 1K look-up table into memory and changes the character table vector to point to the data it contains. The character set that it defines is a graphics representation of the upper 128 characters that are normally displayed when the color card is in text mode. This operation allows you to access the entire IBM-PC character set, regardless of the screen mode. Most importantly, it makes the business graphics characters such as CHR$(189), the block characters such as CHR$ (219), and the dot patterns such as CHR$(176) available from graphics mode. This feature is most useful when you want to mix graphics lines and circles with some of the extended character set, and especially when you want to make a graphics screen dump with the DOS 2.0 GRAPHICS.COM program.

## Listing 8.9
## CHARS.COM

```
;-------------------------
; Listing 8.9  CHARS.COM
; Installs extended ASCII graphics character set.
; The new set makes characters 128-255 the same for graphics and text modes.
; This is a COM-format file.  It requires processing by EXE2BIN.
; Executing this program adds 1400 bytes to the resident size of DOS.

code_seg segment
        assume cs:code_seg
        org     100H                    ;must have for COM-format program
install proc    far
        mov     ax,0                    ;change the BIOS character set vector
        mov     ds,ax
        mov     ds:[1FH*4],offset char_table ;alter INT 1FH offset
        mov     ds:[1FH*4+2],cs         ;   "    "   "  segment

        push    cs
        pop     ds                      ;point back to this segment
        mov     dx,offset ok_msg
        mov     ah,9
        int     21H                     ;print reassuring message

        mov     dx,offset last_byte+1   ;point to end of this program
        int     27H                     ;fix program & data in memory
                                        ; and exit to DOS
install endp

ok_msg  db      'Extended graphics character set is installed',0DH,0AH,'$'

char_table label byte

DB 078h,0CCh,0C0h,0CCh,078h,01Ch,00Eh,07Ch ; ASCII 128
DB  0,0CCh,  0,0CCh,0CCh,0CCh,07Eh,  0 ; ASCII 129
DB 00Eh,   0,078h,0CCh,0FCh,0C0h,078h,  0 ; ASCII 130
DB 07Eh,081h,07Ch,006h,03Eh,066h,03Fh,  0 ; ASCII 131
DB 0CCh,   0,078h,00Ch,07Ch,0CCh,07Eh,  0 ; ASCII 132
DB 0E0h,   0,078h,00Ch,07Ch,0CCh,07Eh,  0 ; ASCII 133
DB 030h,030h,078h, 00Ch,07Ch,0CCh,07Eh,  0 ; ASCII 134
DB    0,   0,078h,0C0h,0C0h,078h,00Ch,038h ; ASCII 135
DB 07Eh,081h,03Ch,066h,07Eh,060h,03Ch,  0 ; ASCII 136
DB 0CCh,   0,078h,0CCh,0FCh,0C0h,078h,  0 ; ASCII 137
DB 0E0h,   0,078h,0CCh,0FCh,0C0h,078h,  0 ; ASCII 138
DB 0D8h,   0,070h,030h,030h,030h,078h,  0 ; ASCII 139
DB 07Ch,082h,038h,018h,018h,018h,03Ch,  0 ; ASCII 140
DB 0E0h,   0,070h,030h,030h,030h,078h,  0 ; ASCII 141
DB 0C6h,038h,06Ch,0C6h,0FEh,0C6h,0C6h,  0 ; ASCII 142
DB 030h,030h,   0,078h,0CCh,0FCh,0C0h,  0 ; ASCII 143
DB 01Ch,   0,0FCh,060h,078h,060h,0FCh,  0 ; ASCII 144
DB    0,   0,07Fh,006h,07Fh,0C6h,07Fh,  0 ; ASCII 145
DB 03Eh,06Ch,0CCh,0FEh,0CCh,0CCh,0CEh,  0 ; ASCII 146
DB 078h,0CCh,   0,078h,0CCh,0CCh,078h,  0 ; ASCII 147
DB    0,0CCh,   0,078h,0CCh,0CCh,078h,  0 ; ASCII 148
DB    0,0E0h,   0,078h,0CCh,0CCh,078h,  0 ; ASCII 149
DB 078h,0CCh,   0,0CCh,0CCh,0CCh,07Eh,  0 ; ASCII 150
DB    0,0E0h,   0,0CCh,0CCh,0CCh,07Eh,  0 ; ASCII 151
DB    0,0CCh,   0,0CCh,0CCh,07Ch,00Ch,0F8h ; ASCII 152
DB 0C3h,018h,03Ch,066h,066h,03Ch,018h,  0 ; ASCII 153
DB 0CCh,   0,0CCh,0CCh,0CCh,0CCh,078h,  0 ; ASCII 154
DB 018h,018h,07Eh,0C0h,0C0h,07Eh,018h,018h ; ASCII 155
DB 038h,06Ch,064h,0F0h,060h,0E6h,0FCh,  0 ; ASCII 156
DB 0CCh,0CCh,078h,0FCh,030h,0FCh,030h,030h ; ASCII 157
DB 0F8h,0CCh,0CCh,0FAh,0C6h,0CFh,0C6h,0C7h ; ASCII 158
DB 00Eh,01Bh,018h,03Ch,018h,018h,0D8h,070h ; ASCII 159
DB 01Ch,   0,078h,00Ch,07Ch,0CCh,07Eh,  0 ; ASCII 160
DB 038h,   0,070h,030h,030h,030h,078h,  0 ; ASCII 161
```

**Listing 8.9
(continued)**

```
DB    0,00Ch,    0,078h,0CCh,0CCh,078h,    0 ;  ASCII 162
DB    0,01Ch,    0,0CCh,0CCh,0CCh,07Eh,    0 ;  ASCII 163
DB    0,0F8h,    0,0F8h,0CCh,0CCh,0CCh,    0 ;  ASCII 164
DB 0FCh,    0,0CCh,0ECh,0DCh,0DCh,0CCh,    0 ;  ASCII 165
DB 03Ch,06Ch,06Ch,03Fh,    0,07Eh,    0,    0 ;  ASCII 166
DB 03Ch,066h,066h,03Ch,    0,07Eh,    0,    0 ;  ASCII 167
DB 030h,    0,030h,060h,0C0h,0CCh,078h,    0 ;  ASCII 168
DB    0,    0,    0,0FCh,0C0h,0C0h,    0,    0 ;  ASCII 169
DB    0,    0,    0,0FCh,00Ch,00Ch,    0,    0 ;  ASCII 170
DB 0C3h,0C6h,0CCh,0DEh,033h,066h,0CCh,00Fh ;  ASCII 171
DB 0C3h,0C6h,0CDh,0DBh,037h,06Dh,0CFh,003h ;  ASCII 172
DB 018h,018h,    0,018h,018h,018h,018h,    0 ;  ASCII 173
DB    0,033h,066h,0CCh,066h,033h,    0,    0 ;  ASCII 174
DB    0,0CCh,066h,033h,066h,0CCh,    0,    0 ;  ASCII 175
DB 022h,088h,022h,088h,022h,088h,022h,088h ;  ASCII 176
DB 055h,0AAh,055h,0AAh,055h,0AAh,055h,0AAh ;  ASCII 177
DB 0DDh,077h,0DDh,077h,0DDh,077h,0DDh,077h ;  ASCII 178
DB 018h,018h,018h,018h,018h,018h,018h,018h ;  ASCII 179
DB 018h,018h,018h,018h,0F8h,018h,018h,018h ;  ASCII 180
DB 018h,018h,0F8h,018h,0F8h,018h,018h,018h ;  ASCII 181
DB 036h,036h,036h,036h,0F6h,036h,036h,036h ;  ASCII 182
DB    0,    0,    0,0FEh,036h,036h,036h,036h ;  ASCII 183
DB    0,    0,0F8h,018h,0F8h,018h,018h,018h ;  ASCII 184
DB 036h,036h,0F6h,006h,0F6h,036h,036h,036h ;  ASCII 185
DB 036h,036h,036h,036h,036h,036h,036h,036h ;  ASCII 186
DB    0,    0,0FEh,006h,0F6h,036h,036h,036h ;  ASCII 187
DB 036h,036h,0F6h,006h,0FEh,    0,    0,    0 ;  ASCII 188
DB 036h,036h,036h,036h,0FEh,    0,    0,    0 ;  ASCII 189
DB 018h,018h,0F8h,018h,0F8h,    0,    0,    0 ;  ASCII 190
DB    0,    0,    0,0F8h,018h,018h,018h,018h ;  ASCII 191
DB 018h,018h,018h,018h,01Fh,    0,    0,    0 ;  ASCII 192
DB 018h,018h,018h,018h,0FFh,    0,    0,    0 ;  ASCII 193
DB    0,    0,    0,0FFh,018h,018h,018h,018h ;  ASCII 194
DB 018h,018h,018h,018h,01Fh,018h,018h,018h ;  ASCII 195
DB    0,    0,    0,0FFh,    0,    0,    0,    0 ;  ASCII 196
DB 018h,018h,018h,018h,0FFh,018h,018h,018h ;  ASCII 197
DB 018h,018h,01Fh,018h,01Fh,018h,018h,018h ;  ASCII 198
DB 036h,036h,036h,036h,037h,036h,036h,036h ;  ASCII 199
DB 036h,036h,037h,030h,03Fh,    0,    0,    0 ;  ASCII 200
DB    0,    0,03Fh,030h,037h,036h,036h,036h ;  ASCII 201
DB 036h,036h,0F7h,    0,0FFh,    0,    0,    0 ;  ASCII 202
DB    0,    0,0FFh,    0,0F7h,036h,036h,036h ;  ASCII 203
DB 036h,036h,037h,030h,037h,036h,036h,036h ;  ASCII 204
DB    0,0FFh,    0,0FFh,    0,    0,    0,    0 ;  ASCII 205
DB 036h,036h,0F7h,    0,0F7h,036h,036h,036h ;  ASCII 206
DB 018h,018h,0FFh,    0,0FFh,    0,    0,    0 ;  ASCII 207
DB 036h,036h,036h,036h,0FFh,    0,    0,    0 ;  ASCII 208
DB    0,    0,0FFh,    0,0FFh,018h,018h,018h ;  ASCII 209
DB    0,    0,    0,0FFh,036h,036h,036h,036h ;  ASCII 210
DB 036h,036h,036h,036h,03Fh,    0,    0,    0 ;  ASCII 211
DB 018h,018h,01Fh,018h,01Fh,    0,    0,    0 ;  ASCII 212
DB    0,    0,    0,01Fh,018h,01Fh,018h,018h ;  ASCII 213
DB    0,    0,    0,    0,03Fh,036h,036h,036h ;  ASCII 214
DB 036h,036h,036h,036h,0FFh,036h,036h,036h ;  ASCII 215
DB 018h,018h,0FFh,018h,0FFh,018h,018h,018h ;  ASCII 216
DB 018h,018h,018h,018h,0F8h,    0,    0,    0 ;  ASCII 217
DB    0,    0,    0,    0,01Fh,018h,018h,018h ;  ASCII 218
DB 0FFh,0FFh,0FFh,0FFh,0FFh,0FFh,0FFh,0FFh ;  ASCII 219
DB    0,    0,    0,    0,0FFh,0FFh,0FFh,0FFh ;  ASCII 220
DB 0F0h,0F0h,0F0h,0F0h,0F0h,0F0h,0F0h,0F0h ;  ASCII 221
DB 00Fh,00Fh,00Fh,00Fh,00Fh,00Fh,00Fh,00Fh ;  ASCII 222
DB 0FFh,0FFh,0FFh,0FFh,    0,    0,    0,    0 ;  ASCII 223
```

**Listing 8.9
(continued)**

```
DB    0,    0,076h,0DCh,0C8h,0DCh,076h,    0 ;  ASCII 224
DB    0,078h,0CCh,0F8h,0CCh,0F8h,0C0h,0C0h ;  ASCII 225
DB    0,0FCh,0CCh,0C0h,0C0h,0C0h,0C0h,    0 ;  ASCII 226
DB    0,0FEh,06Ch,06Ch,06Ch,06Ch,06Ch,    0 ;  ASCII 227
DB 0FCh,0CCh,060h,030h,060h,0CCh,0FCh,    0 ;  ASCII 228
DB    0,    0,07Ch,0D8h,0D8h,0D8h,070h,    0 ;  ASCII 229
DB    0,066h,066h,066h,066h,07Ch,060h,0C0h ;  ASCII 230
DB    0,076h,0DCh,018h,018h,018h,018h,    0 ;  ASCII 231
DB 0FCh,030h,078h,0CCh,0CCh,078h,030h,0FCh ;  ASCII 232
DB 038h,06Ch,0C6h,0FEh,0C6h,06Ch,038h,    0 ;  ASCII 233
DB 038h,06Ch,0C6h,0C6h,06Ch,06Ch,0EEh,    0 ;  ASCII 234
DB 01Ch,030h,018h,07Ch,0CCh,0CCh,078h,    0 ;  ASCII 235
DB    0,    0,07Eh,0DBh,0DBh,07Eh,    0,    0 ;  ASCII 236
DB 006h,00Ch,07Eh,0DBh,0DBh,07Eh,060h,0C0h ;  ASCII 237
DB 038h,060h,0C0h,0F8h,0C0h,060h,038h,    0 ;  ASCII 238
DB 078h,0CCh,0CCh,0CCh,0CCh,0CCh,0CCh,    0 ;  ASCII 239
DB    0,0FCh,    0,0FCh,    0,0FCh,    0,    0 ;  ASCII 240
DB 030h,030h,0FCh,030h,030h,    0,0FCh,    0 ;  ASCII 241
DB 060h,030h,018h,030h,060h,    0,0FCh,    0 ;  ASCII 242
DB 018h,030h,060h,030h,018h,    0,0FCh,    0 ;  ASCII 243
DB 00Eh,01Bh,01Bh,018h,018h,018h,018h,018h ;  ASCII 244
DB 018h,018h,018h,018h,018h,0D8h,0D8h,070h ;  ASCII 245
DB 030h,030h,    0,0FCh,    0,030h,030h,    0 ;  ASCII 246
DB    0,076h,0DCh,    0,076h,0DCh,    0,    0 ;  ASCII 247
DB 038h,06Ch,06Ch,038h,    0,    0,    0,    0 ;  ASCII 248
DB    0,    0,    0,018h,018h,    0,    0,    0 ;  ASCII 249
DB    0,    0,    0,    0,    0,018h,    0,    0 ;  ASCII 250
DB 00Fh,00Ch,00Ch,00Ch,0ECh,06Ch,03Ch,01Ch ;  ASCII 251
DB 070h,06Ch,06Ch,06Ch,06Ch,    0,    0,    0 ;  ASCII 252
DB 070h,018h,030h,060h,078h,    0,    0,    0 ;  ASCII 253
DB    0,    0,03Ch,03Ch,03Ch,03Ch,    0,    0 ;  ASCII 254
DB    0,    0,    0,    0,    0,    0,    0,    0 ;  ASCII 255

last_byte label byte
code_seg  ends
          end install
```

Perhaps more importantly, the CHARS program provides an outline to define your own special characters. Just take a sheet of graph paper and fill in an 8 by 8 pattern with the dots that make up your new character. Convert the dots to a binary number (each lit dot is a 1 and each dark dot is a 0), convert that binary value to hexadecimal, and substitute the resulting eight hex bytes into any line of CHAR_TABLE. Assemble, link, and process the program with EXE2BIN, and then install the new character set by issuing the CHARS command from the DOS prompt. You can also make temporary changes in any character by altering the relevant 8-byte table element after the table has been made resident. Any program can find the address of the table by checking the doubleword value at 0000:007C.

It is instructive to note that I did not painstakingly define each of these 128 characters on graph paper, convert dots to binary, convert binary to hex, and then type in each line of the CHAR_TABLE. I wrote a short BASIC program (fewer than 100 lines) that allowed me to use the cursor control keys to edit the 8 by 8 matrix that defines a character. When I was satisfied that the dot pattern looked like its text mode equivalent, I stored the eight bytes of the character as hexadecimal ASCII digits in a text file. Then I used a text editor to rearrange that file into lines of eight bytes separated by commas, with each line preceded by "DB." That operation provided me with a text file that could be merged into the assembler source text of the CHARS program.

In effect, I wrote a BASIC program that writes assembly language program lines. This is an idea with which you should become comfortable. In the next section when we discuss graphics shapes and shape tables, we will be talking about massive amounts of data. Some readers will prefer to define shapes on graph paper and transfer them by hand into an assembler source file. But my experience is that writing a quick and dirty program to aid in creating that data will save many hours, avoid many errors, and make it easy to change a shape table as a graphics program evolves.

**THINGS TO DO**

1.  Define a double-height and double-width character set; that is, design a series of characters (or shapes) that fill a 16 by 16 dot matrix. To print any such character, four 8-byte elements of the character set must be printed—two side by side on top and two side by side beneath.

2.  Experiment with this set in BASIC, using the PRINT command while in graphics mode. For instance:

    ```
    100 LOCATE 10,10 :PRINT CHR$(&H80);CHR$(&H81); '**display top half
    110 LOCATE 11,10 :PRINT CHR$(&H82);CHR$(&H83); '**bottom half
    ```

3.  (*) Include as part of the character set installation procedure the logic to capture INT 10H, subfunction 9. Reroute control to your own code for displaying these special characters.

## 8.7 FAST SHAPE TABLE GRAPHICS

The ROM-BIOS routine that displays elements of the graphics character set table is actually a specialized version of a broader category of *shape-drawing* tools. In this section, we will examine techniques used to draw objects on the graphics screen very rapidly.

In the PLOTDOT procedure, we worked hard to isolate individual pixels on the graphics display. As we have seen, this procedure is necessary for drawing elemental shapes such as dots, lines, and circles where the X,Y coordinates of each pixel are calculated separately. But all of these calculations take time—and time is a critical element of arcade-style games.

Most arcade-style games contain a series of small shapes that are moved around the screen. *Pac-persons* gobble tiny *dots* and *power-pellets* as they are chased by small *monsters*. Space *invaders* slither across the screen and descend upon a mobile *gun* that shoots *missiles*. *Submarines* fire *torpedoes* and avoid *depth charges* and chain-tethered *underwater mines*. All of the items in italics are elemental shapes that are at the heart of an arcade-style game.

We could draw any shape by calling the mid-resolution PLOTDOT many times, varying the X,Y coordinates and the color as needed for each dot. But you will recall that each call to PLOTDOT requires a series of calculations to convert an X,Y coordinate pair into a screen address and a pixel bit value. The color bits must be moved into position and ORed with the current graphics byte.

We can speed up this process by working with bytes of screen memory rather than the individual pixels. That is, we can convert sets of four 2-bit pixels into bytes and then move those values directly into video memory. For instance, consider a simple shape of four brown dots side by side. We could display them with four calls to PLOTDOT via:

```
MOV     DX,Y_ORDINATE
MOV     CX,X_ORDINATE
MOV     BL,COLOR
CALL    PLOTDOT         ;plot(X,Y)
INC     CX
CALL    PLOTDOT         ;plot(X+1,Y)
INC     CX
CALL    PLOTDOT         ;plot(X+2,Y)
INC     CX
CALL    PLOTDOT         ;plot(X+3,Y)
```

But the same four brown pixels could be painted just by calculating a screen address, placing it in ES:DI, and then moving a 4-pixel byte into that address:

```
MOV     ES:[DI],0FFH    ;paint four dots at once
```

The value 0FFH is a binary 11111111B, which is four 2-bit fields that each have a value of 3 (binary 11) (i.e., the value of an individual brown dot). If this 4-dot shape needed to be all red (four fields of binary 10), the byte placed into video memory would be 0AAH (binary 10101010). A combination of two red dots followed by two brown dots would be 0AFH (binary 10101111).

Moving a whole byte of data into video memory is orders of magnitude faster than four individual calls to PLOTDOT. It does have the drawback that a shape can only be moved horizontally in 4-dot increments (making the motion seem jerky in some cases), but we'll discuss a solution to that problem later. First, let's construct a general-purpose algorithm for displaying complex shapes.

## A Shape-Drawing Routine

Any arcade game will have a number of objects that must be moved around on the screen. To avoid being overwhelmed by the complexity of the overall task (writing an arcade-style game), we break it into subtasks. Among the major subtasks will be displaying a title page or "attract mode," initializing program variables, accepting keyboard and/or joystick input, and moving shapes around the screen.

The last subtask can be further simplified if we separate the logic (when to move the object, how far to move it, what direction, etc.) of the motion from the actual drawing of the shape. Going back to the toolbox approach, it obviously makes sense to write a routine that draws shapes.

Keeping in mind that the shape must be drawn in many different screen locations, we see that we need a way to specify a screen position. We can simplify the logic of the subtask if we set up the shape-drawing tool to accept an X,Y coordinate pair. That way, we can move the shape up or down by manipulating the Y ordinate, and we can move the shape left or right by manipulating the X ordinate. Thus, part of the shape-drawing function will be to determine a screen address from an X,Y coordinate. As we will be working with bytes of screen data (instead of pixels), the X ordinate will range from 0 to 79 and the Y ordinate will range from 0 to 199.

Since we want to make the routine general enough to be able to draw a variety of shapes (missiles, aliens, power pellets, etc.), all with different sizes and color combinations, we'll write the routine so that it works with a data set that defines the shape. These data must include not only the bytes that define the colors of the pixels, but also some values to define the size of the shape. For example, a bullet may be only four dots wide by two dots high, but an alien spacecraft is likely to be 20 or more dots wide and perhaps 10 dots tall.

Thus, we must define a flexible format for the shape table data. It is simplest to think of a shape as being enclosed by a rectangular frame. That way, we will be able to move a series of adjacent horizontal bytes into position, then drop down to the next lower screen line and draw the next series of bytes, and so forth. If one horizontal line is shorter than the others, we can just pad it with graphics blanks (pixels in the background color). Assuming that each shape will be enclosed by a rectangular area, we can use the following format for our shape table data:

byte 0 = horizontal size in bytes (i.e., dots/4)

byte 1 = vertical size in dots

byte 2 = data for upper left corner

.

.

.

byte *n* = data for lower right-hand corner

This gives us the option of defining a shape of any size, and it is relatively easy to process the shape table data. Figures 8.8a through 8.8d show the steps used to convert the shape of a flying saucer into the hexadecimal values of the bytes that are needed to define it. Figure 8.8e is the assembler source code that will be interpreted by the shape-drawing subroutine.

**Figure 8.8a**
**The Flying Saucer Shape Defined as Colored Pixels**

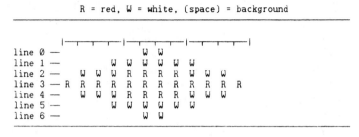

```
                          R = red, W = white, (space) = background

          |——————|——————|——————|
line 0 —                W  W
line 1 —          W  W  W  W  W  W
line 2 —    W  W  W  R  R  R  R  W  W  W
line 3 — R  R  R  R  R  R  R  R  R  R  R  R
line 4 —    W  W  W  R  R  R  R  W  W  W
line 5 —          W  W  W  W  W  W
line 6 —                W  W
```

**Figure 8.8b**
**The Pixels Converted to Color-Code Bits**

```
line 0 — 00 00 00 00 00 11 11 00 00 00 00 00
line 1 — 00 00 00 11 11 11 11 11 11 00 00 00
line 2 — 00 11 11 11 10 10 10 10 11 11 11 00
line 3 — 10 10 10 10 10 10 10 10 10 10 10 10
line 4 — 00 11 11 11 10 10 10 10 11 11 11 00
line 5 — 00 00 00 11 11 11 11 11 11 00 00 00
line 6 — 00 00 00 00 00 11 11 00 00 00 00 00
```

**Figure 8.8c**
**Color Bits Grouped into Nibbles and Bytes**

```
line 0 —  0000 0000   0011 1100   0000 0000
line 1 —  0000 0011   1111 1111   1100 0000
line 2 —  0011 1111   1010 1010   1111 1100
line 3 —  1010 1010   1010 1010   1010 1010
line 4 —  0011 1111   1010 1010   1111 1100
line 5 —  0000 0011   1111 1111   1100 0000
line 6 —  0000 0000   0011 1100   0000 0000
```

**Figure 8.8d**
**Binary Converted into Hexadecimal Bytes**

```
line 0 —   000H, 03CH, 000H
line 1 —   003H, 0FFH, 0C0H
line 2 —   03FH, 0AAH, 0FCH
line 3 —   0AAH, 0AAH, 0AAH
line 4 —   03FH, 0AAH, 0FCH
line 5 —   003H, 0FFH, 0C0H
line 6 —   000H, 03CH, 000H
```

**Figure 8.8e**
**Assembler Source Code for Flying Saucer Shape Data**

```
saucer    db   3                      ;width in bytes
          db   7                      ;height in lines
          db   000H, 03CH, 000H
          db   003H, 0FFH, 0C0H
          db   03FH, 0AAH, 0FCH
          db   0AAH, 0AAH, 0AAH
          db   03FH, 0AAH, 0FCH
          db   003H, 0FFH, 0C0H
          db   000H, 03CH, 000H
```

Listing 8.10, SHAPE, is the tool that will be used to draw the shape defined by the data in Figure 8.8e. As always, this program is written as a library module so that we can link it with a main program. The module expects DS:SI to point to a shape table entry in the previously described format. The DX register must contain the horizontal and vertical coordinates that define where the shape should be drawn. Also, the AH register is used to select one of two subfunctions.

Depending on the parameter passed in the AH register, the shape will either be transferred directly to the screen or XORed into screen memory. Transferring is straightforward; the data bytes are moved from the shape table directly into screen memory. Because this option does not require any checking of the screen data, it is very fast. When SHAPE is entered with AH = 1, the shape is simply drawn at the indicated coordinates.

The second option is not quite as fast, but it's more flexible. For one thing, it returns a collision flag indicating if the object was drawn over the top of anything. Also, it provides a mechanism for both drawing and erasing an object. When an object is XORed in the same position twice, the first time will make it appear and the second time will make it disappear. Thus, an object can be quickly moved around the screen by XORing it once to erase it, calculating a new position, and then XORing it at the new position.

With the shape-drawing tool in hand, we can begin to work on a more ambitious project. Listing 8.11, SAUCER, uses the SHAPE module to move a flying saucer around the screen. Before we discuss the logic of the program (how it controls the saucer), let's take a look at the data.

The first data variable is a DELAY_COUNT. The SAUCER program moves the shape around so quickly that it looks like a crazed moth trapped in a lampshade. By changing this variable, you can speed up or slow down the action. The smaller the value of DELAY_COUNT, the faster the program goes (except that a value of 0 is the slowest speed).

## Listing 8.10
## SHAPE NEAR Library Procedure

```
;------------------------------------------------------------
; Listing 8.10  SHAPE  near library procedure
; Fast shape-drawing routine.  XORs or draws the shape.
; On entry: AH   = function code.  0 = XOR, 1 = draw (fastest)
;           DH   = line to draw shape (0-199)
;           DL   = column (0-79)
;           DS:SI = address of a shape-table entry in this format:
;                   si+0 = count of horizontal bytes
;                   si+1 = count of vertical lines
;       si+2 through si+n = data to be transferred to video memory
;
;On exit: shape is displayed.
;         if function is XOR (AH = 0) then
;           AH returns collision flag: 0 = no collision
;         AX destroyed.  All other registers preserved.

          public  shape             ;standard
code_grp group   lib_seg           ; opening for
lib_seg  segment byte public 'code'  ;  library
          assume  cs:code_grp       ;   modules

shape     proc    near
          push    bx                ;all registers are used,
          push    cx                ; so they must be saved, except
          push    dx                ;  AX which returns a value
          push    bp
          push    di
          push    si
          push    es

;------- calculate address in video memory from DH,DL (line,column reference)
          push    ax                ;save function code

          mov     al,dh
          sub     ah,ah             ;AX = requested line number
          and     ax,0FFFEH         ;mask off even/odd bit (mult * 2)
          shl     ax,1              ; * 4
          shl     ax,1              ; * 8
          shl     ax,1              ; * 16
          mov     di,ax             ; save partial result
          shl     ax,1              ; * 32
          shl     ax,1              ; * 64
          add     di,ax             ; DI = line number * 80
          test    dl,1              ;line in odd bank?
          jz      line_ok           ; no, skip
          add     di,2000H          ; yes, add odd-bank offset
line_ok:
          sub     ah,ah
          mov     al,dl
          add     di,ax             ;add in the horizontal offset
          mov     ax,0B800H         ;DI = screen address to alter
          mov     es,ax             ;ES:[DI] is destination

;------- set up horizontal and vertical loop counters
          lodsb                     ;fetch the count of horizontal bytes
          sub     ah,ah
          mov     cx,ax             ; and place it in CX

          lodsb                     ;fetch the count of vertical lines
          mov     dx,ax             ; and place it in DX
          inc     dx                ;prime for first pass
```

**Listing 8.10
(continued)**

```
        pop     ax              ;fetch function code
        cmp     ah,0            ;is XOR function requested?
        je      xor_1           ; yes, select the XOR loop
                                ; else, just move the bytes directly

;------- transfer the bytes of the shape directly to the screen (fastest)
draw_1:
        dec     dx              ;done?
        jz      shape_exit      ; yes, exit to caller
        mov     bx,cx           ; no, continue.  Save counter
        mov     bp,di           ; save destination
      rep movsb                 ;transfer the data directly to screen
        mov     di,bp
        mov     cx,bx           ;restore count, destination
        cmp     di,2000H        ;was this an odd line?
        jae     draw_2          ; yes, make odd adjustment
        add     di,2000H        ; no, point to odd line, below current
        jmp     draw_1          ;     and loop back for next line
draw_2:
        sub     di,2000H-80     ;point to even line, below current
        jmp     draw_1          ; and loop back for next

;------- XOR the bytes and test for collision (slower than direct draw)
xor_1:
        dec     dx              ;done?
        jz      shape_exit      ; yes, exit to caller
        mov     bx,cx
        mov     bp,di           ;save count, destination
xor_2:
        lodsb
        test    es:[di],al      ;did it hit anything?
        jz      xor_3           ; no, skip
        mov     ah,-1           ; yes, set collision flag to true
xor_3:
        xor     es:[di],al      ;XOR (display or erase the dots)
        inc     di              ;point to next screen location
        loop    xor_2           ;and repeat for each horizontal byte

        mov     di,bp
        mov     cx,bx           ;restore count, destination
        cmp     di,2000H        ;was this an odd line?
        jae     xor_4           ; yes, make odd adjustment
        add     di,2000H        ; no, point to odd line below current
        jmp     xor_1           ;     and loop back for next line
xor_4:
        sub     di,2000H-80     ;point to even line below current
        jmp     xor_1           ; and loop back for next

shape_exit:
        pop     es              ;restore regs for exit
        pop     si
        pop     di
        pop     bp
        pop     dx
        pop     cx
        pop     bx
        ret                     ;<---- SHAPE procedure exit --------
shape   endp

lib_seg ends
        end
```

**Listing 8.11**
**SAUCER Program**

```
;----------------------------------------
; Listing 8.11  SAUCER  program
; Illustrates how to use the SHAPE library module.
; Animates a flying saucer, bouncing it off of the
;  edges of the screen.  Exit to DOS by pressing any key.
; External calls: SHAPE

stack_seg segment para stack
          db      256 dup(?)
stack_seg ends

data_seg segment para public 'data'
delay_count dw   20000        ;variable delay between frames
shape_data label byte
saucer_0 db  3                       ;data for when cycle = 0
         db  7
         db  000H, 03CH, 000H  ;           W W
         db  003H, 0FFH, 0C0H  ;         W W W W W W
         db  03FH, 00AH, 0FCH  ;      W W W     r r W W W
         db  0A0H, 0A0H, 0A0H  ;  r r      r r      r r
         db  03FH, 00AH, 0FCH  ;      W W W     r r W W W
         db  003H, 0FFH, 0C0H  ;         W W W W W W
         db  000H, 03CH, 000H  ;           W W

saucer_1 db  3                       ;data for when cycle = 1
         db  7
         db  000H, 03CH, 000H  ;           W W
         db  003H, 0FFH, 0C0H  ;         W W W W W W
         db  03FH, 082H, 0FCH  ;      W W W r       r W W W
         db  028H, 028H, 028H  ;    r r      rr       r r
         db  03FH, 082H, 0FCH  ;      W W W r       r W W W
         db  003H, 0FFH, 0C0H  ;         W W W W W W
         db  000H, 03CH, 000H  ;           W W

saucer_2 db  3                       ;data for when cycle = 2
         db  7
         db  000H, 03CH, 000H  ;           W W
         db  003H, 0FFH, 0C0H  ;         W W W W W W
         db  03FH, 0A0H, 0FCH  ;      W W W r r      W W W
         db  00AH, 00AH, 00AH  ;        r r      r r      r r
         db  03FH, 0A0H, 0FCH  ;      W W W r r      W W W
         db  003H, 0FFH, 0C0H  ;         W W W W W W
         db  000H, 03CH, 000H  ;           W W

saucer_3 db  3                       ;data for when cycle = 3
         db  7
         db  000H, 03CH, 000H  ;           W W
         db  003H, 0FFH, 0C0H  ;         W W W W W W
         db  03FH, 028H, 0FCH  ;      W W W   r r    W W W
         db  082H, 082H, 082H  ;  r       r r       r r      r
         db  03FH, 028H, 0FCH  ;      W W W   r r    W W W
         db  003H, 0FFH, 0C0H  ;         W W W W W W
         db  000H, 03CH, 000H  ;           W W

;------- variables control position and motion of saucer
cur_xy   label  word          ;get a handle on the following two bytes
cur_x    db     39            ;start in center of screen
cur_y    db     99            ;
cycle    db     0             ;start with shape 0
x_vect   db     -1            ;start by moving left by 1 byte (4-dots)
y_vect   db     4             ;          and down by 4-lines
```

**Listing 8.11
(continued)**

```
s_ptrs     dw       saucer_0     ;mini-table for quick access to
           dw       saucer_1     ; the four different saucer shapes
           dw       saucer_2
           dw       saucer_3
data_seg ends

code_grp group  code_seg         ;linkage for library modules
code_seg segment para public 'code'
           assume  cs:code_grp, ds:data_seg

           extrn   shape:near
saucer     proc    far
           push    ds               ;set up FAR return to DOS
           mov     ax,0
           push    ax
           mov     ax,data_seg      ;establish data segment addressing
           mov     ds,ax
           mov     ah,0
           mov     al,4             ;enter mid-res color graphics mode
           int     10H

           call    draw_saucer      ;draw the saucer before starting
main:                               ; (so that the first XOR erases it)
           mov     ah,1
           int     16H              ;see if a key has been pressed
           jnz     s_exit           ;  if so, exit to DOS
           call    draw_saucer      ;erase it
           call    move_saucer      ;move it
           call    draw_saucer      ;re-draw at new position
           call    delay            ;let it stay there a while
           jmp     main
s_exit:
           mov     ah,0
           mov     al,3             ;return to 80x25 text mode
           int     10H
           ret                      ;far return back to DOS
saucer     endp

;----------------------
; DRAW_SAUCER
; Draws the the saucer shape as indexed by the CYCLE value
; at the coordinates named by CUR_X and CUR_Y
; All registers preserved.

draw_saucer proc near
           push    ax
           push    bx
           push    dx
           push    si

           mov     si,offset s_ptrs ;point to start of 4-element table
           mov     bl,cycle         ;fetch the current state
           mov     bh,0
           shl     bx,1             ;BX indexes into 4-element S_PTRS table
           mov     si,[si+bx]       ;now DS:SI points to data of shape

           mov     dx,cur_xy        ;fetch both the coordinates
           mov     ah,0             ;select XOR sub-function
           call    shape            ;<--- external call draws shape

           pop     si
           pop     dx
           pop     bx
           pop     ax
           ret
draw_saucer endp
```

**Listing 8.11**
**(continued)**

```
;----------------------
; MOVE_SAUCER
; Updates the X,Y, and cycle of the saucer by moving it in
;   the current direction.
; If it touches the edge of the screen, its direction is reversed.
; All registers preserved
; Alters the saucer's X,Y and (sometimes) its X and Y vectors

move_saucer proc near

;------- first update current position
        push    dx
        mov     dx,cur_xy           ;fetch current X,Y
        cmp     dl,76               ;at right side of screen?
        jae     ms_1                ; yes, change the vector
        cmp     dl,2                ; no, at left side?
        jae     ms_2                ;   no, don't change vector
ms_1:
        neg     x_vect              ;   yes, reverse horiz. direction
ms_2:
        cmp     dh,191              ;at bottom of screen?
        jae     ms_3                ; yes, reverse the vector
        cmp     dh,6                ; no, at top of screen?
        jae     ms_4                ;   no, don't change
ms_3:
        neg     y_vect              ;   yes, reverse vert. direction
ms_4:
        add     dl,x_vect           ;update X
        add     dh,y_vect           ;update Y
        mov     cur_xy,dx           ;save new X and Y

;------- now update cycle pointer
        inc     cycle               ;adjust cycle ptr
        and     cycle,3             ;cycle 4 back to 0
        pop     dx
        ret
move_saucer endp

;------------
; DELAY
; pauses the action for the count named in variable DELAY_COUNT.
; preserves all registers

delay   proc near
        push    cx
        mov     cx,delay_count
delay_1: loop   delay_1             ;empty loop
        pop     cx
        ret
delay   endp

code_seg ends
        end     saucer
```

The next lines in the DATA_SEG define four shape table entries that you'll recognize as being in the format that the SHAPE module expects. The comments on each line of shape data describe how the colors are arranged. Notice that the shapes are essentially the same, except that the center part of each saucer is different. These are the different "states" of the saucer. When the program changes the position of the saucer, it also cycles a variable that is used as an index to point to one of the four saucer shape table entries. In other words, as the saucer moves around the screen, its middle part also changes. The four shapes are set up so that when displayed sequentially, the saucer seems to have a moving band of red around its center.

After the normal prelude of setting up a return to DOS and setting the screen into mid-resolution mode, the program draws the saucer and then enters its main loop. The main loop checks the keyboard to see if you want to exit; then it draws (XORs) the saucer to erase it, moves it, and draws it again to display it at its new position. The saucer must be drawn once *outside of the loop* to make this strategy work; the first XOR in the loop must erase the shape.

The DRAW_SAUCER subroutine determines which of the four saucer shapes to draw, loads SI with the address of the correct data, and then calls the external SHAPE module. In order to determine the address of the shape table element, it uses the CYCLE variable as an index into the 4-element table, S_PTRS. That table has been set up with pointers to each of the four 23-byte elements of the actual shape data table. Notice that the base-relative indexed addressing mode is used to access the shape data pointers. Strictly speaking, this routine could function very well using direct indexed addressing. But by avoiding the use of a hard-coded reference to the start of the pointer table, this routine provides a pathway toward a more flexible routine, one that chooses from among many different pointer tables.

The MOVE_SAUCER procedure changes the data parameters that are accessed by the DRAW_SAUCER procedure. Its main job is to update the current horizontal and vertical coordinates of the saucer. It performs this operation by adding the current horizontal and vertical vectors (step values) to the current X and Y. It also checks to see if the saucer is about to fly off the edge of the screen. If it is, MOVE_SAUCER reverses the direction of motion along the axis that is about to be violated. In other words, if the saucer is moving up and to the right when it hits the right side of the screen, negating the value of X_VECT will force the saucer to continue to move up and to the left. It appears to bounce off the edge of the screen.

The other job of MOVE_SAUCER is to update the CYCLE pointer so that DRAW_SAUCER can determine which set of shape data should be displayed. Notice how simple it is to cycle a quad-state pointer. The CYCLE value is first incremented and then ANDed with 3. This operation is much faster than a compare and jump sequence.

As written, the SAUCER program just moves a single object around the screen. But imagine what would happen if the DRAW_SAUCER routine were named DRAW_OBJ. Instead of starting the routine by loading SI with the offset of S_PTRS, suppose that the calling routine passes a pointer to an *object control block*. That block would be composed of a series of data items that describe the object's current position, vector, cycle, and so on, as well as a list of pointers to its various shape table elements. Can you see how easily this program could be converted to handle a large number of objects—not only multiple saucers, but multiple types of objects, each type with its own logic routine? This indexing through object control blocks is the nucleus of many arcade-style games.

In a complete arcade-style game, you will end up with a large table of object control blocks and a large block of shape data. As the number of objects and the amount of shape data grows, you will probably want to put parts of your data segment in an external module. The shape table is a prime candidate because once you have decided how an object should look, there is no reason to reassemble the data bytes that define it. (Note: Be sure to declare your data within a segment named DATA_SEG and use the PUBLIC and EXTRN pseudo-ops to pass addresses of variables and procedures between modules.) Your final program will be massive in any case. But if you can keep the data out of the main module, your development time will decrease considerably. You may also choose to write separate external modules for each of the object logic routines. Again, once a module has been debugged, there is no reason to reassemble it. Let the linker do its job.

### Taking Smaller Steps

When we animated the objects in the SAUCER program, we specified an X and a Y vector for each object. These values were added to the current horizontal and vertical coordinates before each shape was drawn, making the shape appear to move. Since we are working with the 4-dot bytes displayed by the SHAPE module, the horizontal vector is actually specified in increments of four dots. When we want to send something shooting quickly across the screen, this is not a problem; the player's eye will follow the object without noticing the blank area between the positions where the object is actually drawn. However, when we need fine control of an object—when it must be moved in small increments with a very smooth motion—we need a way to specify intermediate steps between bytes.

Since the data in a shape table are actually just a sequence of bits, we could use a logical shift operation to transform the data before moving them to the screen. However, this procedure would cost cycles for every shape that is drawn. The alternative is to set up a series of *preshifted* shapes. Then, without changing the current X ordinate, we can select the shape data that define the same object only slightly displaced. In some cases, we'll need to define four different versions of an object, providing a horizontal increment of a single dot. But most often, two versions (and a 2-dot step size) are enough.

Figure 8.9 should help to clarify this idea. To move the saucer to the right, we would first draw and erase version A, then draw and erase version B, then add 1 to the X ordinate, and draw version A again. One way to keep track of the position is to expand the conceptual size of the screen from 80 by 200 to 160 by 200. Then, whenever the X ordinate is even, draw version A. When the X ordinate is odd, use version B. This operation adds a second level of complexity to animating a shape, but sometimes the technique is necessary to keep the motions of an object from appearing too choppy. Some programmers keep track of a "big X" to indicate the byte column and a "little X" to track the position within that byte and the corresponding shape that must be drawn.

**Figure 8.9**
**Shape A Is Shifted Within Its Frame to Create Shape B, Allowing**
**the Saucer to Be Moved Horizontally in Increments of Two Dots**

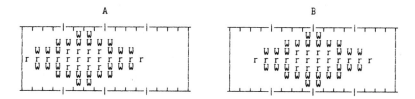

## THINGS TO DO

1.  Using the COLORS macro (Listing 6.4) as a starting point, write a macro that defines a shape table entry, including the horizontal and vertical size bytes.

2.  Add logic to that macro so that it produces two versions of a shape, the second version being shifted to the right by two pixels.

### Specialized Shapes

The SHAPE routine is flexible enough to be used as the backbone of an arcade-style game. However, because it is so general, it is not as fast as a specialized shape-drawing routine. Every time it is called, it must convert an X,Y coordinate pair into a screen memory address. Then it does extra work as it scans line by line, placing the shape in memory. What's more, it works entirely with bytes, and it is 44 percent faster to transfer a 16-bit word than it is to transfer two bytes.

Let's say that your program has an aircraft that spews air-to-air missiles whenever the player presses the joystick button. At any given time, there may be zero to 20 air-to-air missiles flying across the screen. To handle this action, you could define the shape of a missile and pass it through the SHAPE procedure 20 times. A more clever idea is to write a special routine that draws a missile very rapidly.

Using graph paper, you come up with this shape for your missile:

```
       colors                    binary             bytes    words

  r r r                  = 1010 1000 0000 0000 = A8 00 = 00A8

      r r r    r         = 0010 1010 0010 0000 = 2A 20 = 202A

  W W W W W r            = 0011 1111 1111 1000 = 3F F8 = F83F

      W W W r r r        = 0000 1111 1110 1010 = 0F EA = EA0F

  W W W W W r            = 0011 1111 1111 1000 = 3F F8 = F83F

      r r r    r         = 0010 1010 0010 0000 = 2A 20 = 202A

  r r r                  = 1010 1000 0000 0000 = A8 00 = 00A8
```

This shape can be displayed very rapidly by hard-coding the shape data as immediate operands. The following code assumes that an X,Y coordinate pair has been converted into a screen offset address held in ES:DI. It also assumes that the missile will always travel along an even-numbered screen line:

```
     MOV     WORD PTR ES:[DI]            , 00A8H
     MOV     WORD PTR ES:[DI+2000H]      , 202AH
     MOV     WORD PTR ES:[DI+80]         ,0F83FH
     MOV     WORD PTR ES:[DI+2000H+80]   ,0EA0FH
     MOV     WORD PTR ES:[DI+160]        ,0F83FH
     MOV     WORD PTR ES:[DI+2000H+160], 202AH
     MOV     WORD PTR ES:[DI+240]        , 00A8H
```

Compare the speed of this code to the time required to loop through a shape-drawing procedure. A similar routine could be used to erase the missile. The following variation could be used to determine if a missile collides with anything that has already been drawn:

```
     MOV     AX,0
     OR      AX,WORD PTR ES:[DI]
     OR      AX,WORD PTR ES:[DI+2000H]
     OR      AX,WORD PTR ES:[DI+80]
     OR      AX,WORD PTR ES:[DI+2000H+80]
     OR      AX,WORD PTR ES:[DI+160]
     OR      AX,WORD PTR ES:[DI+2000H+160]
     OR      AX,WORD PTR ES:[DI+240]
```

If AX ends up as 0, then there was no collision.

At some point, you would probably need to convert an X,Y coordinate pair into a screen offset, but you wouldn't need to do it each time. You could optimize the missile motion logic by just keeping track of a screen address. For example, to move the missile to the right, just add 1 (or more) to the current address. To move it upward by two dots, subtract 80 from that address.

By analyzing the specific needs of your graphics applications, you can avoid much of the overhead that slows programs down. Creating special tools to handle particularly time-critical applications trades code space for execution speed—at bargain basement prices.

### THINGS TO DO

1. Using the clock rates listed in Appendix A, determine how long it takes to draw the torpedo. Calculate the time needed to draw the same shape with the SHAPE program.

2. Is it any faster to set BX to 2000H and use the base-relative indexed addressing mode for moving the data to the screen?

3. Find a simple way to shave 14 cycles from the torpedo-drawing sequence.

### Paging the Graphics Screen

When a program becomes so complex that it is moving dozens of objects around the screen and erasing each object before redrawing any of them, you will begin to notice a flickering effect. Some programs can be written to erase and redraw each object separately. But this procedure can cause a simultaneity problem. For example, if you update the position of your ship before moving your torpedoes, the ship might collapse with its own torpedo—even if the torpedo would have moved out of the way in a couple of microseconds.

An alternative is to draw each object on an invisible secondary page of memory and then, after updating the position of each object, to transfer the whole page into video memory.

One immediate advantage of this screen paging is that you can eliminate the part of each cycle where an object is erased. Instead, just erase all of the secondary page and start fresh with each frame of the cycle. Depending on the game, this can be the simplest procedure, and it may even be the fastest.

A secondary video page can simplify the complexities of the graphics screen layout. Your own internal screen does not need to have the even-line/odd-line format of the physical screen memory. Eliminating it could also simplify the design of your shape-drawing and pixel-manipulation routines.

Finally, creating a secondary video page allows you to create a *logical* screen that is larger or smaller than the *physical* screen. In many games, only part of the video display contains the constantly changing graphics images. The rest contains information that needs to be updated only occasionally—such as the score and the remaining number of ships, frogs, or what have you. The occasional changes can be made directly on the screen, and the smaller "game board" can be swapped into the screen. If you create a secondary page that is larger than the video screen, you can simplify some of your logic because an object could be gracefully moved off the screen. The entire object can be drawn, but only part of it will be within the area that is displayed.

Figure 8.10 illustrates a logical screen that is both larger and smaller than the physical screen. It has a border area so that objects can be drawn partially off the screen, and it leaves the lower part of the screen available for text messages that can be printed using the ROM-BIOS services.

**Figure 8.10**
**Physical and Logical Graphics Screens**

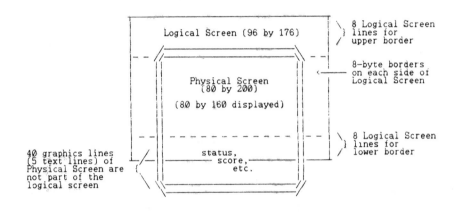

This logical screen uses 16K bytes, but since every IBM PC has at least 64K and probably more than 128K available, memory is usually not a limitation. The logical screen can be cleared by the repeated STOSW opcode, and a MOVSW sequence can be used to transfer its visible parts to the physical screen.

For instance, to clear the logical screen, you would use a sequence such as this:

```
MOV     AX,SCREEN_SEG      ;point to the logical screen memory
MOV     ES,AX
MOV     DI,0               ;point to the upper left-hand corner
MOV     CX,96*176/2        ;working with words
MOV     AX,0               ;set up a graphics blank
REP STOSW
```

Transferring data from the logical screen to the physical screen is slightly more complex, but it could be handled with this sequence:

```
        MOV     AX,SCREEN_SEG       ;point to the logical screen
        MOV     DS,AX
        MOV     SI,96*8+8           ;source is first visible byte
        MOV     AX,0B800H
        MOV     ES,AX
        MOV     DI,0                ;destination is upper left-hand
                                    ;corner of screen
        MOV     BX,160/2            ;counter: 160 lines,
                                    ;two lines per loop
AGAIN:
        MOV     CX,40               ;words per physical line
        REP MOVSW
        ADD     DI,2000H-80         ;odd bank of the physical screen
        ADD     SI,16               ;point past the left and right borders
        MOV     CX,40               ;set up count of words to transfer
        REP MOVSW
        SUB     DI,2000H            ;the physical screen's even bank
        ADD     SI,16               ;skip borders of the logical screen
        DEC     BX                  ;check for last line
        JNZ     AGAIN               ; and loop back if not done
```

To use this particular logical page format, you would need to rewrite your PLOTDOT and SHAPE modules. The address calculations are very similar, but the lines are 96 bytes wide instead of 80 (you can still use a rapid shift-multiply to determine the address of a line), and there need be no adjustment for odd lines. Also, any dots plotted in the border area will not be visible unless they have an X ordinate between 32 and 231; visible Y ordinates range between 8 and 167.

The logical screen concept opens up several other possibilities. If you are satisfied with a coarser vertical resolution, you can set up your logical screen with only 100 lines. Then when you page it into the screen, just copy each logical line to both the even and odd physical lines. You could create your own custom "macro-pixels" represented in your logical screen by one format, but interpreted differently when they are copied to the physical screen. You can even create several pages and implement an overlay system or a way to flick back and forth from page to page.

Although memory limitations can probably be ignored, the time needed to copy a logical screen to the physical screen can be significant. You will need to balance this time constraint against the needs of your program. If your program is continuously scrolling new scenes in from the sides of the screen, you might find that building a logical page "offstage" is most convenient. But if your game board is fairly constant, you will probably be better off writing directly to the physical memory of the color card.

### THINGS TO DO

1. (*) Write a set of modules for manipulating a logical screen as described in this section. It should contain a procedure for clearing the screen, a module for displaying the screen, and modules for plotting dots, lines, shapes, and circles.

# Chapter 9

# The 6845 CRT Controller

In this chapter, we look at the Motorola 6845 CRT controller chip—the heart of both the IBM monochrome and color/graphics display adapters. As we gain insight into this complex chip, we will discuss some advanced video techniques, including hardware paging and scrolling and the "secret" 16-color low-resolution graphics modes.

## 9.1 INs AND OUTs OF THE COLOR/GRAPHICS CARD

The B/W card is set up to work specifically with the IBM monochrome display and has essentially only one display mode. There is very little that can be done to squeeze any special functions from this adapter.

The color card, on the other hand, is capable of many different display modes. There are two basic modes of operation, text and graphics, but there can be many variations on these modes. The ROM-BIOS supports six color card modes, including 40- and 80-column versions of both color and black-and-white text displays as well as three graphics modes. The technical reference manual tantalizingly suggests that with "clever programming" many different modes are available.

All of this flexibility is tied to the Motorola 6845 CRT controller chip. The 6845 is a programmable device set up as a bridge between the 8088 and your raster-scan video display. It is initialized and monitored by outputs to and inputs from a series of CPU ports. During operation, it takes information from a block of memory (up to 16K) and translates it into either text characters or graphics pixels.

The 6845 controls the beam of light that scans across the CRT of your black and white or color monitor. It generates the signals that guide that beam as it traverses your CRT—left to right and top to bottom. It tells the display device what color to display at every point in the display cycle. Finally, it determines the timing that makes the beam sweep invisibly to the right side of the screen after completing a horizontal pass and back up to the top of the screen after it makes a vertical pass.

You communicate with the color card (and thus control the 6845) by using IN and OUT opcodes to read from and write to certain ports mapped into the IBM PC's port address space. Figure 9.1 summarizes the port mapping for the color card.

| port | name | access |
|------|------|--------|
| 3D4H | 6845 register pointer | Write only |
| 3D5H | 6845 data registers | Read/Write |
| 3D8H | Mode Select register | Write only |
| 3D9H | Color Select register | Write only |
| 3DAH | Status register | Read only |
| 3DBH | Light Pen Latch Reset | Read/Write |
| 3DCH | Light Pen Latch Set | Read/Write |

**Figure 9.1**
**The Color Graphics Card Control Ports**

Mode Select Register (3D8H)

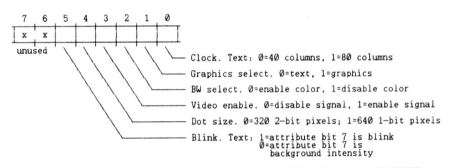

Color Select Register (3D9H)

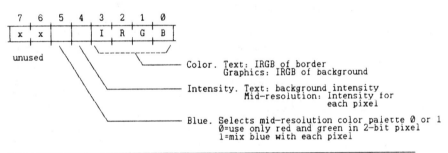

Status Register (3DAH)

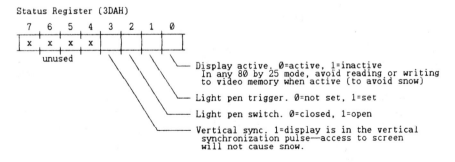

### 6845 Address Register (Port 3D4H)

Port 3D4H is used to select one of the 6845's 18 internal registers. The register is selected by outputting the register number to this port. The selected register is then read or written to via the 6845 Data Register.

### 6845 Data Register (Port 3D5H)

After selecting one of the 6845's internal registers (via the 6845 Address Register), an output to port 3D5H will return the current value of that register. Certain of the 6845's internal registers may also be read through this port with an input command.

### Mode Select Register (Port 3D8H)

Port 3D8H, a 6-bit write-only port, controls various aspects of color card function. The bit pattern that is written to this port determines the basic operating mode of the color card. Figure 9.2a summarizes the patterns that the ROM-BIOS uses to initialize this register for the various screen modes. Each bit is relevant, so let's look at them individually:

Bit 0: high-resolution dot clock. This bit determines the frequency of the color card's dot clock. A 0 selects the 7.15909-MHz clock that is used in the 40-column text mode. A 1 selects the 14.31818-MHz clock used in the 80-column text mode.

Bit 1: graphics select. When this bit is 0, the card is in text mode and the regen buffer is interpreted as alternating character and attribute bytes. Characters are generated from a ROM chip on the color card. When this bit is 1, the card is in graphics mode and the bytes in the regen buffer are interpreted as graphic bit patterns.

Bit 2: black and white select. When this bit is 1, the color burst signal is disabled for composite monitors and TVs connected via an RF modulator. Notice that the 80 by 25 color mode is identical to the 80 by 25 black and white mode except for the state of this bit.

Bit 3: video enable. Resetting this bit to 0 causes all characters and attributes or pixel bit patterns to be displayed as blanks—in effect disabling the video signal. When you move a screenful of text data directly into the regen buffer, you can avoid the snow effect by resetting this bit to 0 just before the move, and then setting it back to 1 right after the move.

Bit 4: dot size. When this bit is 1 and bit 1 is 0, the 640-dot graphics mode is in effect. Setting this bit to 0 selects the 320-dot lines of the mid-resolution graphics mode.

Bit 5: blink enable. When in text mode (bit 1=1), this bit enables or disables the character-blink bit of the next attribute byte. When set to 1, setting bit 7 of an attribute byte forces its character to blink. This also limits the background of the character to one of eight colors (the intensity for the background of all characters may be set in the Color Select Register). When this bit is 0, all 16 background colors are available for each text mode character.

**Figure 9.2a**
**ROM-BIOS Initialization of the Mode Select Port**

```
        mode           Mode Select port

0   40x25 bw           2CH = 1 0 1 1 0 0   \
1   40x25 color        28H = 1 0 1 0 0 0   |
2   80x25 bw           2DH = 1 0 1 1 0 1   |
3   80x25 color        29H = 1 0 1 0 0 1   } Color/graphics card: port 3D8H
4   320x200 bw         2AH = 1 0 1 0 1 0   |
5   320x200 color      2EH = 1 0 1 1 1 0   |
6   640x200            1EH = 0 1 1 1 1 0   /

7 80x25 bw             29H = 1 0 1 0 0 1   } B/W card: port 3B8H
```

Note: ROM–BIOS stores the most recently used value at 0040:0065.

**Color Select Register (Port 3D9H)**

The Color Select Register, a 6-bit write-only register, determines certain constant color values for the various screen modes, including the border shades for text mode and the background color for graphics modes. Notice that bits 4 and 5 constitute the intensity and blue of the IRGB of each 2-bit dot; the green and red components are defined by the two bits of each mid-resolution pixel in graphics-mapped memory. Figure 9.2b shows the values that the ROM-BIOS uses to initialize this port for the various BIOS-supported display modes.

Bit 0-3: text border, mid-resolution background, high-resolution foreground. In text modes (i.e., bit 1 of the Mode Select Register is 0), these bits define the IRGB color of the border. In 320 by 200 graphics mode, these bits select the color for the background pixels—those with a value of 00. In 640 by 200 graphics mode, they select the foreground color (the background and border are always black).

**Figure 9.2b**
**ROM-BIOS Initialization of the Color Select Port**

```
        mode           Color Select port

0   40x25 bw           30H = 1 1 0000   \
1   40x25 color        30H = 1 1 0000   |
2   80x25 bw           30H = 1 1 0000   |
3   80x25 color        30H = 1 1 0000   } Color/Graphics card: port 3D9H
4   320x200 bw         30H = 1 1 0000   |
5   320x200 color      30H = 1 1 0000   |
6   640x200            3FH = 1 1 1111   /

7 80x25 bw             30H = 1 1 0000   } B/W card: port 3B9H
```

Note: ROM–BIOS stores the most recently used value at 0040:0066.

Bit 4: intensity. In text modes with blink enabled (Mode Select Register bits 1 and 5 are both 0), this bit determines the intensity of the background—replacing bit 7 from each attribute byte. When in mid-resolution color graphics mode, this bit determines the intensity of each 2-bit pixel.

Bit 5: blue. This bit is also called the *palette select bit.* It determines whether the blue component will be mixed with the red and green of each mid-resolution pixel. When this bit is 0, each 2-bit pixel is displayed as either brown, red, green, or the background. When this bit is 1, the pixels are either white, magenta, cyan, or the background (i.e., the same red and green components, but with blue mixed in).

### Status Register (Port 3DAH)

The Status Register port is a 4-bit read-only port. It allows a program to monitor the timing of the video signal and read the status of a light pen.

Bit 0: display active. When this bit is 1, the CRT is in its horizontal or vertical blanking interval. That is, the electron beam sweeping across the monitor has been temporarily turned off as the beam traces back to the left side or the top of the screen.

When in 80-column text mode, accessing screen memory when this bit is not set will cause snow or random flecks of white. You can eliminate the problem by checking this bit before writing to or reading from the video regen area. The horizontal retrace period is very short, lasting for approximately 80 clock cycles (about 16.8 milliseconds).

Bit 1: light pen trigger. When this bit is 1, the light pen trigger has been set and the screen memory address where the trigger was set can be read from the 6845 light pen registers (R16 and R17).

Bit 2: light pen switch. When this bit is 1, the light pen switch is open. A 0 indicates that the switch is closed.

Bit 3: vertical sync. This bit flags the vertical retrace period. When it changes from 0 to 1, the CRT's electron beam has just begun its 60-times-per-second cycle of refreshing the display. While this bit is 1, it is possible to update the video memory area without causing snow. The vertical retrace period lasts about 3,400 clock cycles (about 408 milliseconds). This is enough time to copy a line of 80 characters and attributes from a storage area to video memory.

### Light Pen Latch Reset (Port 3DBH)

Any output to port 3DBH resets (clears) the light pen latch, preparing for a new light pen input.

**Light Pen Latch Set (Port 3DCH)**

Any output to port 3DCH sets the light pen latch. It is used for diagnostic testing.

## 9.2 THE 6845 INTERNAL REGISTERS

The 6845 has a set of 18 internal registers that you may initialize from your program to determine various aspects of the video display. The 6845 constantly refers to the current values in these registers to determine the timing of the signal that controls the electron beam sweeping across the CRT. Certain registers establish which part of the 16K regen buffer is to be displayed; others establish the current cursor location. Two registers are used in conjunction with the 6845's light pen logic.

Only by manipulating the values of these internal registers can you realize the full potential of the 6845. The ROM-BIOS is set up for six different color card display modes, but with proper programming of the 6845, many other variations are available. The internal registers are not accessed directly, as are the color card's external registers (Mode Select, Color Select, etc.). Each access is a 2-step process. First, you tell the 6845 which register you want to access by outputting a number to the 6845 Address Register (port 03D4H). Then you read from or write to the 6845 Data Register (port 03D5H).

Only six (three pairs) of the internal registers can be read. Registers R12 and R13 can be read to determine the address of the currently displayed video page; R14 and R15 can be read to determine the current location of the cursor; R16 and R17 are read to find the address where the light pen trigger was set. The following code reads the value of R14 into AL:

```
MOV     DX,3D4H   ;point to 6845 address port
MOV     AL,14     ;prepare to make selection
OUT     DX,AL     ;select R14
MOV     DX,3D5H   ;point to the 6845 data port
IN      AL,DX     ;read the data
```

More often, you will need to write data to a register. This is done by first selecting the register and then outputting a byte through the 6845 Data port. Both of the following sequences write the value 59H to register R2:

```
MOV     DX,3D4H   ;point to 6845 address port
MOV     AL,2      ;prepare to select
OUT     DX,AL     ;R2 is selected
MOV     DX,3D5H   ;point to 6845 data port
MOV     AL,59H    ;prepare the new data
OUT     DX,AL     ;write it to register R2
```

or

```
MOV     DX,3D4H   ;point to 6845 address port

MOV     AX,5902H  ;specify both the register and the data

OUT     DX,AX     ;select and initialize
```

The latter method uses the 8088's ability to output two bytes with one opcode. You may recall that when a word of data is outputted to a port, the action is very similar to a 16-bit register to memory MOV operation. First, the LSB is sent to the named address, and then the MSB is sent to the next higher address (remember the mnemonic phrase: The high part of the operand goes to the higher address). Thus, the 02H part of 5902H is sent to the port named in DX (the 6845 Address Register port), and almost simultaneously the 59H part of 5902H is sent to the port at DX+1 (the 6845 Data Register port).

Now that we know how to read and program the 6845's internal registers, let's take a look at selected registers. Figure 9.3 shows the names of each register and gives the values that the ROM-BIOS uses when it initializes each of the standard display modes.

**Figure 9.3**
**ROM-BIOS Initialization of the 6845 Internal Registers**

| | 6845 Register | Units | BW card 80x25 | Color/graphics card 40x25 | 80x25 | 320x200 | 640x200 |
|---|---|---|---|---|---|---|---|
| R0 | Horizontal Total | Characters | 61H | 38H | 71H | 38H | 38H |
| R1 | Horizontal Displayed | Characters | 50H | 28H | 50H | 28H | 28H |
| R2 | Horiz. Sync. Position | Characters | 52H | 2DH | 5AH | 2DH | 2DH |
| R3 | Horizontal Sync. Width | Characters | 0FH | 0AH | 0AH | 0AH | 0AH |
| R4 | Vertical Total | Char. Lines | 19H | 1FH | 1FH | 7FH | 7FH |
| R5 | Vertical Total Adjust | Scan Lines | 06H | 06H | 06H | 06H | 06H |
| R6 | Vertical Displayed | Char. Rows | 19H | 19H | 19H | 64H | 64H |
| R7 | Vert. Sync. Position | Char. Rows | 19H | 1CH | 1CH | 70H | 70H |
| R8 | Interlace Mode | 0,1,2 or 3 | 02H | 02H | 02H | 02H | 02H |
| R9 | Max Scan Line Address | Scan lines | 0DH | 07H | 07H | 01H | 01H |
| R10 | Cursor Start | Scan lines | 0BH | 06H | 06H | 06H | 06H |
| R11 | Cursor End | Scan lines | 0CH | 07H | 07H | 07H | 07H |
| R12 | Start Address (high) | Words | 00H | 00H | 00H | 00H | 00H |
| R13 | Start Address (low) | Words | 00H | 00H | 00H | 00H | 00H |
| R14 | Cursor Address (high) | Words | 00H | 00H | 00H | 00H | 00H |
| R15 | Cursor Address (low) | Words | 00H | 00H | 00H | 00H | 00H |
| R16 | Light Pen (high) | Words | | | | | |
| R17 | Light Pen (low) | Words | | | | | |

## Centering the Screen

R0 through R3 are the horizontal timing group. These registers determine the length of each scan line and the physical position on the CRT where each line starts.

R0 defines the horizontal synchronization frequency. It is the total number of characters, displayed and nondisplayed (border), on each line.

R1 specifies the number of characters to be displayed on a line.

R2 determines the point in each horizontal scan where the display actually begins. If you program smaller values into this register, the display is shifted closer to the left side of the screen. Larger values shift the display to the right. This register is changed by the DOS MODE ,R and the MODE ,L commands.

R3 determines the width of the horizontal synchronization pulse.

R4 through R9 are the vertical timing group. These registers set the height of the display and, when properly programmed, eliminate vertical rolling of the screen.

R4 and R5 together determine the vertical synchronization pulse. R4 is the total number of character lines -1, displayed and nondisplayed (retrace). R5 is an adjustment to the timing—a fraction of a character line— that keeps the screen from rolling.

R6 defines the number of lines of characters that are normally displayed.

R7 determines the point in the display cycle where the CRT beam is activated after a vertical retrace. Programming smaller values into this register lowers the displayed image; larger values raise it.

R8 determines whether or not the scan lines are interlaced. The BIOS always uses a value of 2, selecting the noninterlace mode. This setting causes each scan line to be refreshed twice per display cycle. A value of 1 or 3 tells the 6845 to alternate its scans between the even and odd lines. Unless you have a monitor with high-persistence phosphors, this interlace mode will make the scan lines flicker and jiggle because each line is refreshed only half as often.

R9 is the number of scan lines (including blank lines) per character line -1.

## Cursor Control

R10 and R11 control the way that the cursor is displayed. R10 is a number between 0 and 7 (0-15 on the B/W card) that names the starting scan line for the cursor. R11 names the ending scan line. Placing new values in these registers makes the cursor larger or smaller. The typical color card values of 6 and 7 create a 2-line cursor. Values of 4 and 7 create an enlarged cursor (usually used by word processing programs to indicate the insert mode). Values of 0 and 7 (0 and 15 of the B/W card) create a block cursor as large as a full character. If you program a larger value into R11 than that in R10, the cursor will appear in two pieces or will hang above the character.

Bits 5 and 6 of R10 are intended to change the cursor blink rate. The 6845 is capable of displaying a nonblinking cursor, but the color card hardware overrides this possibility with external blink logic. You can turn the cursor off by setting bit 5 of R10 to 1 and setting bit 1 to 0; in other words, when R10 is set to 20H, the cursor is invisible.

R14 and R15 define the regen buffer address of the cursor. To position the cursor, you calculate the desired address as the number of character/attribute pairs from the start of video memory, and then program the low eight bits of that value into R15 and the high six bits into R14. For instance, to place the cursor at the start of line 20 of 80-column video page 0, you calculate that it is the 1000th character (20*80). The value 1000 decimal converts to 03E8H; therefore, you set R15 to 0E8H and R14 to 03H. These registers can also be read to determine the current position of the cursor.

### Light Pen Interface

R16 and R17 can be read to find the address in the color card's regen buffer at which the light pen was pointing when its input signal went high. When bit 1 of the color card's Status Register (input port 03DAH) is found to be 1, the light pen trigger has been set. The next step is to read these registers to determine the character (or graphics byte) at which the user was pointing the light pen when the trigger was set.

These registers are in the same format at R14 and R15. R17 contains the low-order eight bits and R16 holds the high-order six bits. The resulting address is the number of byte pairs from the start of video memory. For instance, if R17 contains 0E8H and R16 contains 03H (character address 03E8H), the light pen was pointing to the leftmost character in line 20 of page 0 of the video screen (i.e., 1,000 bytes above B800:0000).

### Hardware Paging and Scrolling

Registers R12 and R13 are the key to a powerful display action. These two registers together form a 14-bit register that selects the first character to be displayed. R13 holds the lower eight bits and R12 holds the upper six bits. By changing the values in these registers, you can display different parts of the color card's 16K regen buffer. The address is normally initialized to 0, so that writing to B800:0000 will normally alter the character (or graphics pixels) in the upper left-hand corner of the screen. Programming larger values into these registers causes the 6845 to ignore the bytes starting at B800:0000 and to display characters (or pixels) that start at a higher offset in the video memory segment.

These registers may also be *read* to determine the address the 6845 is currently using as the start of video memory.

This feature is usually associated with the four or eight pages of text mode video memory. For instance, in 80-column text mode, 2,000 character/attribute pairs are constantly being displayed; so the screen is 7D0H words long. The first page begins at B800:0000 and ends at B800:0F9F. To display the second page, which (for programming convenience) begins at B800:1000, we would program the 6845 to begin displaying at the 800H-th word of the regen buffer. This is done by setting R13=0 and setting R12=8. Thereafter, writing to addresses between B800:1000 and B800:1F9H would change the image on the display. Writing to the normal screen addresses starting at B800:0000 would have no apparent effect on the screen. However, if after doing so you reprogrammed R12 and R13 to point back to the first page of the regen buffer, those changes would become visible.

The value in R12 and R13 indicates the number of character/attribute pairs (i.e., the number of 16-bit memory words) to be skipped. Figure 9.4 is a chart indicating the starting address of the standard video pages and the values to be programmed into R12 and R13 to make those pages visible.

**Figure 9.4**
**6845 Start Address Page Boundaries**

| | 40 x 25 text modes | | | 80 x 25 text modes | | |
|---|---|---|---|---|---|---|
| page | buffer addresses | 6845 programming R12 | R13 | buffer addresses | 6845 programming R12 | R13 |
| 0 | 0000H - 07CFH | 00H | 00H | 0000H - 0F9FH | 00H | 00H |
| 1 | 0800H - 0F9FH | 04H | 00H | 1000H - 1F9FH | 08H | 00H |
| 2 | 1000H - 17CFH | 08H | 00H | 2000H - 2F9FH | 10H | 00H |
| 3 | 1800H - 1F9FH | 0AH | 00H | 3000H - 3F9FH | 18H | 00H |
| 4 | 2000H - 27CFH | 10H | 00H | | | |
| 5 | 2800H - 2F9FH | 14H | 00H | | | |
| 6 | 3000H - 37CFH | 18H | 00H | | | |
| 7 | 3800H - 3F9FH | 1AH | 00H | | | |

The most obvious use of this multiple-page potential is to build screens offstage by writing to an undisplayed page of video memory, and then, with a single command to the 6845, making that page visible. In business applications, this technique could be used to store several data input forms and make them active as needed. Word processing applications could take advantage of this capability by writing a new screenful of words on an invisible page (say, when the user presses PgDn), and then displaying it all at once.

Perhaps the most exciting potential use is in arcade-style games. A program could make all of the between-frame changes on an invisible page, and could make them visible very quickly. Alas, the color card only has 16K of memory on board, and the graphics modes need all of this memory for page 0; there is no extra memory available for paging in graphics mode. However, there is a lot that can be done with color text-mode quasi-graphics, and there are four hardware pages while in 80-column text mode.

Even though a particular page of video memory is not currently visible, you must be careful to avoid the snow that results from unsynchronized screen access. A page of video memory can be made visible all at once, but preparing that page must be done piecemeal—with frequent delays while waiting for the blanking interval.

Video paging is only a special case of a more general property of the color card. There is no rule that says that you may change the 6845 Start Address registers only to point to a complete new page. You can use this feature to implement a function called *hardware scrolling.*

First, consider the normal way that the screen is scrolled. A software loop physically copies all the text from display line 1 into line 0. Then line 2 is copied to line 1 and so forth, until line 24 is copied to line 23. After all of the lines have been moved up, the lowest line is filled with blank spaces. You can see this procedure in action by using the DOS TYPE command to read a large file. As the screen is scrolling, press the Ctrl-NumLock key. If you do this at just the right moment (try it several times), you will find a line duplicated somewhere on the screen. That's because you caused the computer to pause when the software loop had only partially completed the scroll.

After the lowest line is blanked out, it becomes available for new text. The result is that the top line of the display is seemingly scrolled out of the display and a new line is scrolled into the bottom. The software scroll can also be done in reverse by copying lines 0-23 into lines 1-24 and blanking out line 0. The result would appear as a reverse scroll.

You'll recall that in order to prevent snow on the screen, each time a program reads from or writes to video memory, it must always wait for the blanking interval. Thus, a complete scroll of the 80-column screen will require 2,000 such waiting periods. This wait causes a discernible delay in the scrolling action, a delay just long enough to make word processing programs appear to be sluggish.

Hardware scrolling avoids these delays because the characters in video memory are not physically moved. Instead, the 6845 registers R12 and R13 are given new address values. If the new start address is 80 greater than the old one, all of the lines appear to move up one notch and a new line becomes visible at the bottom of the screen. Presto! Your screen becomes a moving window into the entire 16K of video memory.

Aside from the obvious advantage of speed, in hardware scrolling *characters scrolled off the screen are not lost.* They can be brought back into view just by changing R12 and R13 back to their former values. Scrolling backward from the start of the regen buffer displays lines from the end of the buffer; likewise, scrolling beyond the end of the buffer wraps around to the start.

Another interesting possibility: If you add only 1 to the start address, the screen seems to scroll to the left by one column. Well, almost. The leftmost character on each line suddenly appears on the rightmost column of the line directly above it. However, if you were to blank out the rightmost column or move new data into those positions, you would have the rudiments of a horizontal scrolling facility.

Why haven't we seen these innovative features used in most of the software for the IBM PC? It's because most programs are written to be compatible with both the color/graphics and the monochrome display adapters. This compatibility involves sinking to the lowest common denominator—and the monochrome card has only enough memory to contain one page of text. It is impossible to implement hardware paging and scrolling on the B/W card.

## 9.3 16-COLOR GRAPHICS

The technical reference manual hints at the possibility of a 160 by 100, 16-color low-resolution graphics mode. But it states that this mode is not supported in the ROM-BIOS. In this section, we will discuss two different ways to initiate and use this "secret" graphics mode. Both require programming of the 6845 CRT controller chip and special software to access the individual pixels. One method is a true graphics mode, but it makes artificial colors. The other method makes true colors, but it's really a text mode.

## Artifact Colors

You may have already seen some popular graphics games and simulations that can display 16 different colors at the same time. You may also know that these games work correctly only when used with TV sets and composite color monitors; the display is a coarse black-and-white image on even the highest-quality RGB monitors. The reason for this unlikely situation is that composite monitors tend to blur or misinterpret the signals they receive.

Even mid-resolution graphics are affected by this lack of clarity on composite monitors. For instance, some composite color monitors will correctly display a vertical white line only when it is next to another white line. If the line stands alone, it may appear blue or red; on the worst monitors, a vertical red line is totally invisible if it stands by itself. These low-cost composite monitors perform reasonably well in 640 by 200 high-resolution mode because there is no color signal to misinterpret. You may recall that when the ROM-BIOS enters this mode, it disables the color burst signal by writing a 1 to bit 2 of the Mode Select register (port 3D8H). Enabling the color signal while in high-resolution mode causes the composite monitor to become very confused. Dots on the same scan line are blurred together.

This pandemonium can be turned to our advantage. The monitor blurs the dots together, but it does so in a uniform manner. The resolution of the composite signal tends to blur the colors in groups of four high-resolution pixels. Recall from Chapter 8 that high-resolution graphics bits are normally mapped one-to-one with the pixels. When we enable the color signal, a composite monitor will interpret these in groups of four. By selecting from among the 16 possible combinations of four bits and placing these into video memory, we create artifact or false colors. These are not the same 16 colors that are available in text mode, but they are nevertheless 16 distinct colors, and they look quite good (on a bad enough monitor!).

Thus, low-resolution color graphics mode is really just high-resolution graphics with the color burst enabled and special bit mapping. Each of these artificial pixels is colored according to four adjacent bits (i.e., each nibble of screen memory defines a color). To provide a clear definition to each pixel, we will color a pixel by writing four bits to the even scan line and the same four bits to the odd scan line directly below it.

Figure 9.5 is the video memory map for low-resolution graphics mode. Each graphics line contains 80 bytes, and each byte defines two pixels. The odd-numbered scan lines are all identical to the even-numbered scan lines. This layout gives us an effective resolution of 160 across by 100 down, which is fine for most applications. Now that we know how to access this mode, and we've settled on a pixel format, it's time to try to implement it in code. If you're in a hurry, you can enter this short BASIC program, which displays your new 16-color graphics "palette."

**Figure 9.5**
**Map of Video Memory in Low-Resolution, 16-Color Graphics Mode**

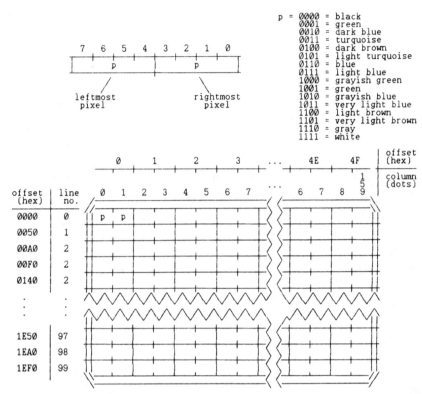

```
                                        p = 0000 = black
                                            0001 = green
                                            0010 = dark blue
                                            0011 = turquoise
        7  6  5  4  3  2  1  0              0100 = dark brown
                                            0101 = light turquoise
                                            0110 = blue
             p           p                  0111 = light blue
                                            1000 = grayish green
                                            1001 = green
          /               \                 1010 = grayish blue
      leftmost         rightmost            1011 = very light blue
       pixel             pixel              1100 = light brown
                                            1101 = very light brown
                                            1110 = gray
                                            1111 = white
```

Note: Each pixel is written both at the indicated address and at the
      address 2000H above it.

      Addresses 1F40–1FFF and 3F40–3FFF are not used in this mode.

```
                     address calculation

      addr =: line*80 + INT(column/2)
         IF (column AND 1)=1 THEN mask =: 00001111B
         ELSE mask =: 11110000B
```

```
10  SCREEN  2                         '** hi-resolution mode
20  OUT  &H3D8,&H1A                   '** enable color signal
30  DEF  SEG=&HB800                   '** point to video memory
50  FOR  C=0  TO  15                  '** display each color
60    BYTE=C+C*16              '** set both nibbles to the same color
70    GOSUB 100
80    X=X+10  :IF  C=7  THEN  Y=40  :X=0  '** new position for block
90  NEXT
99  GOTO  99                          '** press Ctrl-Break to exit
100 FOR J=X  TO  X+7                  '** fill a rectangle with color C
110   FOR K=Y TO Y+30
120     POKE  K*80+J,BYTE             '** the even line
130     POKE  &H2000+K*80+J,BYTE      '** the odd line
140 NEXT  :NEXT  :RETURN
```

Listing 9.1 is a low-resolution graphics tool. It's actually two separate library procedures. The first procedure, LOW_RES, initiates the 160 by 100 graphics mode. The second procedure, LRPLOT, is a modification of the PLOTDOT procedure (Listing 8.3) tailored especially for low-resolution graphics. As the comments indicate, you enter it with the coordinate values in the DH and DL registers and the color code in BL. You can change the background color for the display by outputting the desired IRGB value to the Color Select Register (port 03D9H). Minor modifications to the PLOTLINE and the CIRCLE modules (Listings 8.4 and 8.6) will make them work with this new pixel format.

### Listing 9.1
### LOW_RES and LRPLOT (NEAR Library Routines)

```
;------------------------------------------
;Listing 9.1  LOW_RES and LRPLOT  (NEAR library routines)
; These routines support the low-resolution graphics capability of
; the color card.   Writes "artifact" colors on COMPOSITE monitors.
;
;LOW_RES initiates 160 by 100, 16-color graphics mode.
; Requires no argument, saves all registers
;
;LRPLOT plots a single pixel with an artifact color.
; expects: DH = line number (0-99)
;          DL = column number (0-159)
;          BL = color (0-15)
;
; on exit: low resolution dot is plotted
;          All registers preserved.

          public  lrplot, low_res
code_grp  group   lib_seg
lib_seg   segment byte public 'code'
          assume cs:code_grp

low_res   proc    near
          push    ds
          push    dx
          push    ax
          mov     ah,0        ;set mode
          mov     al,6        ; to 640 by 200
          int     10H
```

**Listing 9.1
(continued)**

```
            mov     dx,03D8H            ;point to Mode Select port
            mov     al,1AH
            out     dx,al              ;enable color burst

            mov     ax,40H
            mov     ds,ax
            mov     byte ptr ds:[0065H],1AH  ;let ROM know the new mode value
            pop     ax
            pop     dx
            pop     ds
            ret
low_res     endp
;----------------------------------------------------------------------
lrplot      proc    near               ;expects DH=row, DL=clm, BL=color
            push    ax
            push    bx
            push    di
            push    es

;------- following code multiplies ROW * 80 to get the address of a line

            mov     al,dh
            mov     ah,0               ;AX = line number
            shl     ax,1               ; fast multiply   *2
            shl     ax,1               ;  *4
            shl     ax,1               ;  *8
            shl     ax,1               ;  *16
            mov     di,ax              ;  save partial result
            shl     ax,1               ;  *32
            shl     ax,1               ;  *64
            add     di,ax              ;  DI = line number*80

            mov     al,dl
            mov     ah,0               ;AX = column number
            shr     ax,1               ;divide it by 2 (2 pixels per byte)
            add     di,ax              ;DI is offset of byte to alter

            mov     bh,0F0H            ;BH is mask
            and     bl,0FH             ;BL is color code
            test    dl,1               ;is pixel on the left side of the byte?
            jnz     ok_plot            ; yes, no change
            mov     bh,0FH             ; no, put mask on other side
            shl     bl,1
            shl     bl,1
            shl     bl,1
            shl     bl,1               ;     and color bits are in high nibble

;------- this code sets up the segment register and writes the dot
ok_plot:
            mov     ax,0B800H
            mov     es,ax              ;ES:DI points to byte to alter
            and     es:[di],bh         ;set up a hole for the color
            or      es:[di],bl         ;put the color in that hole
            and     es:[di+2000H],bh   ;and repeat for odd line beneath
            or      es:[di+2000H],bl

            pop     es
            pop     di
            pop     bx
            pop     ax
            ret
lrplot      endp
lib_seg     ends
            end
```

A big advantage to this mode is that the ROM-BIOS character-handling routines work just as they do with the high-resolution mode. Characters are written from a table of bit patterns in ROM, and you can extend that set by using the CHARS program (Listing 8.9). The characters are a bit harder to read, but perfectly acceptable for displaying player scores and short messages.

Keep in mind that this graphics mode looks good only on composite monitors and televisions connected via an RF modulator. Anyone who pays $1,000 for a high-quality RGB monitor might be a bit miffed if your software displays only in black and white.

## Text-Mode Graphics

You may never have thought about it, but when your color card is in 80-column text mode, it is already configured for 160 by 25, 8-color graphics. The secret is to fill the screen with 2,000 character codes of 222 (0DEH), and then modify the bits in the attribute bytes to change the color. The 0DEH byte is a block graphics character that is half foreground and half background. The right side is the foreground part, so it is controlled by the low-order nibble of the attribute byte. Since the left side of the character is blank, the background part of the attribute byte (high-order nibble) defines its color.

Thus, after setting each character to the same value and initializing each attribute to 0, we can plot any of 160 horizontal characters on any of 25 lines by calculating the address of the relevant attribute byte and modifying its value. This is somewhat cumbersome to do in BASIC, but when we package it into an assembly language module, it is quite quick and easy to use. What's more, it will work with RGB as well as composite monitors.

Of course, 160 by 25 is hardly high enough resolution for sophisticated game programs. Also, the normal 80-column color text mode interprets bit 7 of each attribute byte as a blink indicator, so we would effectively have only an 8-color palette. However, by reprogramming the 6845 internal registers, we can easily set up a 160 by 100 quasi-graphics screen. With a single output to the Mode Select port, we can disable the blink bit and enable a palette of 16 colors for each text "pixel."

This mode is achieved by programming the 6845 to display each character as only one-fourth its normal height and then specifying that four times the usual number of character lines are to be displayed. That can be accomplished by programming four of the 6845 internal registers. The horizontal control registers (R0-R3) are already set up by the 80-column color mode, but several of the vertical control registers need to be altered. R4, the Vertical Total register, must be increased from 31 to 127; R6, the Vertical Displayed register, must be increased from 25 to 100; R7, the Vertical Sync register, must be increased from 28 to 112; and R9, the Max Scan Line register, must be decreased from 9 to 1 to reflect the foreshortened height of each character.

Once the internal registers are programmed, we need to tell the external registers to disable the blink bit so that both the foreground and background sides of each attribute byte may indicate any of 16 colors. Finally, each character byte in the entire 16K display buffer must be initialized to a byte of 0DEH and the attribute bytes must be cleared to 0. The following BASIC subroutine initializes the color card as described.

```
1000 SCREEN 0,1              '** start with 80-column color text mode
1010 OUT &H3D4,4 :OUT &H3D5,&H7F '** vertical total register
1020 OUT &H3D4,6 :OUT &H3D5,&H64 '** vertical displayed
1030 OUT &H3D4,7 :OUT &H3D5,&H70 '** vertical sync
1040 OUT &H3D4,9 :OUT &H3D5,1    '** max scan line
1050 OUT &H3D8,9                 '** change Mode Select: video on,
                                    fast clock, no blink, text
1060 DEF SEG=&HB800
1070 FOR J=0 TO &H4000 STEP 2    '** fill memory with
                                    half-and-half character
1080    POKE J &HDE :POKE J+1,0  '**  and set each attribute = 0
1090 NEXT :RETURN                '** screen is ready
```

The next BASIC subroutine paints any of the 16,000 text pixels, specified by variables X and Y, with the color named by C:

```
1999 '** plot the text pixel at (X,Y) with color C
2000 ADDR=(Y*80+X\2)*2+1
2010 TC=C :M=&HF0 :IF (X AND 1)=0 THEN TC=C*16 :M=&HF
2020 ATTR=PEEK(ADDR) :POKE ADDR,(ATTR AND M) OR TC
2030 RETURN
```

If you type this program in and execute it, you will probably be disgusted by how slowly it runs. You will also see a veritable blizzard of snow. All 80-column text modes have this problem, and the only way to overcome it is to check the Status Register (port 3DAH) and read or write to the screen only during the blanking interval. (You can also disable the video signal while writing by resetting bit 3 of the Mode Select register, but this procedure causes a slight flicker; it should be used only when you are moving a whole screenful of data into video memory.) Even compiled BASIC and Pascal programs are too slow to synchronize with the retrace interval.

The solution, of course, is to return to the cloistered paths of assembly language. Listing 9.2 provides the fundamental procedures you'll need for accessing this quasi-graphics video mode. It performs the same actions as the preceding BASIC subroutines, but it's fast enough to make text mode graphics a viable tool.

The advantage of this quasi-graphics mode is that all 16 colors will be visible on both composite and RGB color monitors. One disadvantage is that there is no direct way to display text; you would need to write your own shape table handler to display the "shapes" of each ASCII character. Perhaps the biggest disadvantage is the amount of time a program must spend avoiding the snow that is inherent with all 80-column text modes.

The IBM color/graphics adapter is a powerful and flexible device. By experimenting with the programming of the Motorola 6845, you can find innovative and attractive new display modes and access the special features that will give your program a competitive edge. And after all, there's no better reason for learning assembly language.

## Listing 9.2
## TEXT_RES and TEXTPLOT (NEAR Library Routines)

```
;-----------------------------------------
;Listing 9.2  TEXT_RES and TEXTPLOT  (NEAR library routines)
; These routines support low-resolution text-mode quasi-graphics.
; Uses the character ØDEH for all character positions, and
;  modifies attribute bytes to select from among 16 colors.
;
;TEXT_RES initiates 160 by 100, 16-color text graphics mode.
; Requires no argument, saves all registers.
;
;TEXTPLOT plots a single text-pixel by modifying its attribute byte.
; expects: DH = line number (0-99)
;          DL = column number (0-159)
;          BL = color (0-15)
;
; on exit: low resolution text-pixel is plotted
;          All registers preserved.

          public  textplot, text_res
code_grp group   lib_seg
lib_seg  segment byte public 'code'
          assume cs:code_grp

text_res proc    near
          push    es
          push    di
          push    dx
          push    cx
          push    ax
          mov     ah,0              ;start with 80 by 25 color text mode
          mov     al,2
          int     10H

          mov     dx,03D8H          ;point to Mode Select port
          mov     al,0
          out     dx,al             ;disable video during initialization

          mov     dx,03D4H          ;point to 6845 Address Register port
          mov     ax,7F04H          ;Vertical Total = 127
          out     dx,ax
          mov     ax,6406H          ;Vertical Displayed = 100
          out     dx,ax
          mov     ax,7007H          ;Vertical Sync = 112
          out     dx,ax
          mov     ax,0109H          ;Max Scan Line = 1
          out     dx,ax
          mov     ax,0B800H         ;point to video memory
          mov     es,ax
          mov     di,0              ;destination is B800:0000
          mov     ax,00DEH          ;fill byte is ØDEH character, blank attribute
          mov     cx,4000H          ;for all 16K of memory
          rep stosw

          mov     dx,03D8H          ;point to Mode Select port
          mov     al,9H             ;enable video, color burst, fast clock
          out     dx,al             ; no blink, not graphics

          mov     ax,40H
          mov     es,ax
          mov     byte ptr es:[0065H],9H  ;let ROM know the new mode value
```

# Listing 9.2
# (continued)

```
        pop     ax
        pop     cx
        pop     dx
        pop     di
        pop     es
        ret
text_res endp

;-----------------------------------------------------------------

textplot proc   near            ;expects DH=row, DL=column, BL=color (0-15)
        push    ax
        push    bx
        push    dx
        push    di
        push    es

;------- calculate DI = ((ROW*80)+CLM/2)*2+1 = regen address

        mov     al,dh
        mov     ah,0            ;AX = line number
        shl     ax,1            ; fast multiply   *2
        shl     ax,1            ; *4
        shl     ax,1            ; *8
        shl     ax,1            ; *16
        mov     di,ax           ; save partial result
        shl     ax,1            ; *32
        shl     ax,1            ; *64
        add     di,ax           ; DI = line number *80

        mov     al,dl
        mov     ah,0            ;AX = column number
        shr     ax,1            ; divide by 2 (2 dots per byte)
        add     di,ax           ;DI is character number
        shl     di,1            ; adjust for attributes
        inc     di              ;DI points to attribute of character to alter
;------- set up mask and color bits
        mov     bh,0F0H         ;BH is mask (assume pixel is on left side)
        and     bl,0FH          ;BL is color code (assume left side)
        test    dl,1            ;is pixel on the left side of the byte?
        jnz     ok_plot         ; yes, use the assumed value
        mov     bh,0FH          ; no, put mask on other side
        shl     bl,1
        shl     bl,1
        shl     bl,1
        shl     bl,1            ;     and color bits go in high nibble

;------- set up the segment register and paint the dot (attribute)
ok_plot:
        mov     ax,0B800H
        mov     es,ax           ;ES:DI points to byte to alter

;------- wait for retrace to avoid video snow
        mov     dx,03DAH        ;address the Status port
        cli                     ;interrupts off for exact timing
snow_1:
        in      al,dx
        test    al,1            ;in retrace period?
        jnz     snow_1          ; no, wait until retrace begins
snow_2:
        in      al,dx
        test    al,1            ;is it ok to read?
        jz      snow_2          ; no, wait until it is
        mov     al,es:[di]      ; yes, fetch the current attribute
```

**Listing 9.2
(continued)**

```
          and     al,bh           ;mask off old color bits
          or      al,bl           ;overlay with new color
          mov     bl,al           ;save in BL because must use AL below
snow_3:
          in      al,dx
          test    al,1            ;in retrace period?
          jnz     snow_3          ;  no, wait until retrace begins
snow_4:
          in      al,dx
          test    al,1            ;is it ok to write?
          jz      snow_4          ;  no, wait until it is

          mov     es:[di],bl      ;  yes, store the new attribute
          sti                     ;turn interrupts back on

          pop     es
          pop     di
          pop     dx
          pop     bx
          pop     ax
          ret
textplot endp

lib_seg  ends
         end
```

## THINGS TO DO

1.  Interface the LINE and CIRCLE modules from Chapter 8 with either the LRPLOT or TEXTPLOT procedures. The main difference is in the way the X,Y coordinate arguments are passed.

2.  Write a program to provide a fast shape-drawing capability for either of the low-resolution graphics modes discussed in this chapter.

3.  Implement a software paging tool to swap a page of text mode graphics into screen memory. During the transfer, disable the video signal with an output to the Mode Select register.

4.  (*) Program the 6845 for 160 by 50, 16-color text mode graphics. This operation will make available a secondary page of screen memory.

5.  (**) Write a DOS version 2.00 device driver to replace CON as the standard output device. Use hardware scrolling and paging techniques so that the user is able to look back at the four most recently scrolled pages of text.

# Appendix A

# The 8088 Instruction Set

### Reference

This appendix alphabetically lists each of the 8088 opcodes, including the mnemonic name, the syntax of the instruction, the CPU flags that it affects, and its execution time in clock cycles. Many of the opcodes may be referred to by more than one mnemonic. In that case, both mnemonics are listed together but separated by a slash (/). Each valid combination of operand parameters is listed beneath the mnemonic with a self-explanatory symbol.

The execution time of many opcodes varies, depending on several factors. When the number of clock cycles is displayed as two values with the second in parentheses, the operation can be performed as either an 8-bit (byte) or a 16-bit (word) operation. The second number is the execution time for the 16-bit version. The timing of the conditional jumps is listed as two values. The first is the execution time when the condition is met and the jump must be performed. Repeated string operations are shown with a notation indicating a minimum number of overhead cycles plus the number of clock cycles per repetition.

When an opcode accesses memory, there is often additional timing overhead as the CPU calculates the effective address (EA) of the memory operand. When the clocks are listed with a "+EA," the total execution time depends on which addressing mode is being used. Refer to Figure A.2 for the timing overhead needed for the EA calculation.

The actual amount of time that an opcode executes is based on the clock speed of the 8088. In the IBM PC, the clock runs at 4.77 MHz, so each clock cycle takes 1/4.77 MHz, or 210 nanoseconds. To find the total execution time for an individual opcode, add the opcode clock cycles to the amount of time of the EA calculation (including the 2-clock segment override, if used) and multiply the sum by 210E-9. For example, let's calculate the execution time for the opcode

```
MOV BX,ES:MY_ARRAY[SI]
```

This transfer is listed as taking "8(12)+EA" clocks. Select the 12 because this variation is a 16-bit operation. The EA includes both a displacement and an index register (nine clocks) with a segment override (two clocks). Thus, the total execution time is 12+9+2=23 clocks times 0.00000021 seconds per clock. This comes to 4.83 milliseconds or 0.00000483 of a second.

Clock cycles for Effective Address (EA) calculation

| EA Components | | Clocks * |
|---|---|---|
| Displacement only | disp | 6 |
| Base or Index only | BX, SI, DI | 5 |
| Base + Displacement<br>Index + Displacement | BX+disp, BP+disp<br>SI+disp, DI+disp | 9 |
| Base + Index | BP+DI, BX+SI<br>BP+SI, BX+DI | 7<br>8 |
| Base + Index + Displacement | BP+DI+disp, BX+SI+disp<br>BP+SI+disp, BX+DI+disp | 11<br>12 |

* Add two clock cycles when segment override is used.

Key to CPU flag codes

| | |
|---|---|
| * | affected by the instruction |
| ? | undefined after the instruction |
| 0 | always cleared to 0 |
| 1 | always set to 1 |
| − | not affected by the instruction |

| AAA | AAA (no operands) Adjust for ASCII addition | | | | Flags: O D I T S Z A P C  ? - - - ? ? * ? * |
|---|---|---|---|---|---|
| Operands | | Clocks | Transfers | Bytes | Coding Example |
| (no operands) | | 4 | — | 1 | AAA |

| AAD | AAD (no operands) Adjust for ASCII division | | | | Flags: O D I T S Z A P C  ? - - - * ? * ? ? |
|---|---|---|---|---|---|
| Operands | | Clocks | Transfers | Bytes | Coding Example |
| (no operands) | | 60 | — | 2 | AAD |

| AAM | AAM (no operands) Adjust for ASCII multiplication | | | | Flags: O D I T S Z A P C  ? - - - * ? * ? ? |
|---|---|---|---|---|---|
| Operands | | Clocks | Transfers | Bytes | Coding Example |
| (no operands) | | 83 | — | 2 | AAM |

| AAS | AAS (no operands) Adjust for ASCII subtraction | | | | Flags: O D I T S Z A P C  ? - - - ? ? * ? * |
|---|---|---|---|---|---|
| Operands | | Clocks | Transfers | Bytes | Coding Example |
| (no operands) | | 4 | — | 1 | AAS |

| ADC | ADC destination,source Add with carry (9-bit or 17-bit addition) | | | | Flags: O D I T S Z A P C  * - - - * * * * * |
|---|---|---|---|---|---|
| Operands | | Clocks | Transfers | Bytes | Coding Example |
| register,register | | 3 | — | 2 | ADC di,bx |
| register,memory | | 9(13)+EA | 1 | 2-4 | ADC bl,byte_table[di] |
| memory,register | | 16(24)+EA | 2 | 2-4 | ADC counter,al |
| register,immediate | | 4 | — | 3-4 | ADC bx,1234H |
| memory,immediate | | 17(25)+EA | 2 | 3-6 | ADC table[bx+di],5 |
| accumulator,immediate | | 4 | — | 2-3 | ADC ax,1234H |

| ADD | ADD destination,source Addition | | | | Flags: O D I T S Z A P C  * - - - * * * * * |
|---|---|---|---|---|---|
| Operands | | Clocks | Transfers | Bytes | Coding Example |
| register,register | | 3 | — | 2 | ADD ax,bx |
| register,memory | | 9(13)+EA | 1 | 2-4 | ADD bl,byte_table[di] |
| memory,register | | 16(24)+EA | 2 | 2-4 | ADD counter,al |
| register,immediate | | 4 | — | 3-4 | ADD bx,1234H |
| memory,immediate | | 17(25)+EA | 2 | 3-6 | ADD table[bx+di],5 |
| accumulator,immediate | | 4 | — | 2-3 | ADD ax,1234H |

| AND | AND destination,source Logical AND (mask bits from destination) | | | | Flags: O D I T S Z A P C  0 - - - * * ? * 0 |
|---|---|---|---|---|---|
| Operands | | Clocks | Transfers | Bytes | Coding Example |
| register,register | | 3 | — | 2 | AND bx,cx |
| register,memory | | 9(13)+EA | 1 | 2-4 | AND bl,byte_table[di] |
| memory,register | | 16(24)+EA | 2 | 2-4 | AND counter,al |
| register,immediate | | 4 | — | 3-4 | AND bl,11000000B |
| memory,immediate | | 17(25)+EA | 2 | 3-6 | AND table[bx+di],5 |
| accumulator,immediate | | 4 | — | 2-3 | AND ax,0F000H |

| CALL | CALL target Call a procedure | | | Flags: O D I T S Z A P C <br> - - - - - - - - - | |
|---|---|---|---|---|---|
| Operands | Clocks | Transfers | Bytes | Coding Example | |
| near_procedure | 23 | 1 | 3 | CALL near_proc | |
| far_procedure | 36 | 2 | 5 | CALL far_proc | |
| mem_ptr16 (near) | 29+EA | 2 | 2-4 | CALL near_proc_tbl[si] | |
| reg_ptr16 (near) | 24 | 1 | 2 | CALL ax | |
| mem_ptr32 (far) | 57+EA | 4 | 2-4 | CALL far_task_tbl[si] | |

| CBW | CBW (no operands) Convert byte to word (sign-extend AL through AX) | | | Flags: O D I T S Z A P C <br> - - - - - - - - - | |
|---|---|---|---|---|---|
| Operands | Clocks | Transfers | Bytes | Coding Example | |
| (no operands) | 2 | —— | 1 | CBW | |

| CLC | CLC (no operands) Clear carry flag (force CF = NC = 0) | | | Flags: O D I T S Z A P C <br> - - - - - - - - 0 | |
|---|---|---|---|---|---|
| Operands | Clocks | Transfers | Bytes | Coding Example | |
| (no operands) | 2 | —— | 1 | CLC | |

| CLD | CLD (no operands) Clear direction flag (make string operations auto-increment) | | | Flags: O D I T S Z A P C <br> - 0 - - - - - - - | |
|---|---|---|---|---|---|
| Operands | Clocks | Transfers | Bytes | Coding Example | |
| (no operands) | 2 | —— | 1 | CLD | |

| CLI | CLD (no operands) Clear interrupt flag (disable maskable interrupts) | | | Flags: O D I T S Z A P C <br> - - 0 - - - - - - | |
|---|---|---|---|---|---|
| Operands | Clocks | Transfers | Bytes | Coding Example | |
| (no operands) | 2 | —— | 1 | CLI | |

| CMC | CMC (no operands) Complement cary flag (toggle the state of CF) | | | Flags: O D I T S Z A P C <br> - - - - - - - - * | |
|---|---|---|---|---|---|
| Operands | Clocks | Transfers | Bytes | Coding Example | |
| (no operands) | 2 | —— | 1 | CMC | |

| CMP | CMP destination,source Compare destination to source (non-destructive subtraction) | | | Flags: O D I T S Z A P C <br> * - - - * * * * | |
|---|---|---|---|---|---|
| Operands | Clocks | Transfers | Bytes | Coding Example | |
| register,register | 3 | —— | 2 | CMP ax,bx | |
| register,memory | 9(13)+EA | 1 | 2-4 | CMP bl,byte_table[si] | |
| memory,register | 9(13)+EA | 1 | 2-4 | CMP counter,al | |
| register,immediate | 4 | —— | 3-4 | CMP bx,1234H | |
| memory,immediate | 10(14)+EA | 1 | 3-6 | CMP table[si],5 | |
| accumulator,immediate | 4 | —— | 2-3 | CMP al,30H | |

| CMPS | CMPS dest string,source string Compare ES:[DI] to DS:[SI] and adjust DI and SI according to DF | | | Flags: O D I T S Z A P C <br> * - - - * * * * | |
|---|---|---|---|---|---|
| Operands | Clocks | Transfers | Bytes | Coding Example | |
| string_1,string_2 | 22(30) | 2 | 1 | CMPS buff_1,buff_2 | |
| (repeated) | 9+22(30) /rep | 2/rep | 1 | REP CMPS test$,buffer | |

| CMPSB<br>CMPSW | CMPSB (no operands)<br>CMPSW (no operands)<br>(alternate forms of CMPS) | | | Flags: O D I T S Z A P C<br>* - - - * * * * * |
|---|---|---|---|---|
| Operands | Clocks | Transfers | Bytes | Coding Example |
| (no operand 8-bit)<br>(no operand 16-bit)<br>(repeated) | 22<br>30<br>9+22(30)<br>/rep | 2<br>2<br>2/rep | 1<br>1<br>1 | CMPSB<br>CMPSW<br>REP CMPSB |

| CWD | CWD (no operands)<br>Convert word to doubleword<br>(sign-extend AX through DX) | | | Flags: O D I T S Z A P C<br>- - - - - - - - - |
|---|---|---|---|---|
| Operands | Clocks | Transfers | Bytes | Coding Example |
| (no operands) | 2 | —— | 1 | CWD |

| DAA | DAA (no operands)<br>Decimal adjust for addition<br>(adjust AL after BCD addition) | | | Flags: O D I T S Z A P C<br>? - - - * * * * * |
|---|---|---|---|---|
| Operands | Clocks | Transfers | Bytes | Coding Example |
| (no operands) | 4 | —— | 1 | DAA |

| DAS | DAA (no operands)<br>Decimal adjust for subtraction<br>(adjust AL after BCD subtraction) | | | Flags: O D I T S Z A P C<br>? - - - * * * * * |
|---|---|---|---|---|
| Operands | Clocks | Transfers | Bytes | Coding Example |
| (no operands) | 4 | —— | 1 | DAA |

| DEC | DEC destination<br>Decrement<br>(subtract 1 from destination) | | | Flags: O D I T S Z A P C<br>* - - - * * * * - |
|---|---|---|---|---|
| Operands | Clocks | Transfers | Bytes | Coding Example |
| reg16<br>reg8<br>memory | 2<br>3<br>15(23)+EA | ——<br>——<br>2 | 1<br>2<br>2-4 | DEC ax<br>DEC bl<br>DEC line_counter |

| DIV | DIV source<br>Division of unsigned operands<br>(divide source into AX or DX:AX) | | | Flags: O D I T S Z A P C<br>? - - - ? ? ? ? ? |
|---|---|---|---|---|
| Operands | Clocks | Transfers | Bytes | Coding Example |
| reg8<br>reg16<br>mem8<br>mem16 | 80-90<br>144-162<br>(90-100)+EA<br>(154-172)<br>+EA | ——<br>——<br>1<br>1 | 2<br>2<br>2-4<br>2-4 | DIV bl<br>DIV cx<br>DIV seventeen<br>DIV scale_factor[si] |

| ESC | ESC external_opcode,source<br>Escape (indicate action for<br>coprocessor) | | | Flags: O D I T S Z A P C<br>- - - - - - - - - |
|---|---|---|---|---|
| Operands | Clocks | Transfers | Bytes | Coding Example |
| immediate,memory<br>immediate,register | 8(12)+EA<br>2 | 1<br>—— | 2-4<br>2 | ESC 6,array[di+3]<br>ESC 20,al |

| HLT | HLT (no operands)<br>Halt (await external interrupt<br>or reset) | | | Flags: O D I T S Z A P C<br>- - - - - - - - - |
|---|---|---|---|---|
| Operands | Clocks | Transfers | Bytes | Coding Example |
| (no operands) | 2 | —— | 1 | HLT |

| IDIV | IDIV source<br>Division of signed integers<br>(divide source into AX or DX:AX) | | | Flags: O D I T S Z A P C<br>? - - - ? ? ? ? ? |
|------|-------------------------------------------------------------------------------|---|---|------------------------------------------|
| Operands | Clocks | Transfers | Bytes | Coding Example |
| reg8 | 101-112 | — | 2 | IDIV bl |
| reg16 | 165-184 | — | 2 | IDIV cx |
| mem8 | (111-122)<br>+EA | 1 | 2-4 | IDIV neg_seventeen |
| mem16 | (175-194)<br>+EA | 1 | 2-4 | IDIV scale_factor[si] |

| IMUL | IMUL source<br>Multiply integers (signed)<br>(multiply AL or AX by source) | | | Flags: O D I T S Z A P C<br>* - - - ? ? ? ? * |
|------|---------------------------------------------------------------------------|---|---|------------------------------------------|
| Operands | Clocks | Transfers | Bytes | Coding Example |
| reg8 | 80-98 | * — | 2 | IMUL cl |
| reg16 | 128-154 | — | 2 | IMUL di |
| mem8 | (90-108)+EA | 1 | 2-4 | IMUL rate_table[bx] |
| mem16 | (138-164)<br>+EA | 1 | 2-4 | IMUL neg_1000 |

| IN | IN accumulator,port<br>Input byte to AL from [port] or<br>input port to AL, port+1 to AH | | | Flags: O D I T S Z A P C<br>- - - - - - - - - |
|----|---------------------------------------------------------------------------------------|---|---|------------------------------------------|
| Operands | Clocks | Transfers | Bytes | Coding Example |
| accumulator,immed8 | 10(14) | 1 | 2 | IN al,0ffH |
| accumulator,DX | 8(12) | 1 | 1 | IN ax,dx |

| INC | INC destination<br>Increment<br>(add 1 to destination) | | | Flags: O D I T S Z A P C<br>* - - - * * * * - |
|-----|-------------------------------------------------------|---|---|------------------------------------------|
| Operands | Clocks | Transfers | Bytes | Coding Example |
| reg16 | 2 | — | 1 | INC di |
| reg8 | 3 | — | 2 | INC al |
| memory | 15(23)+EA | 2 | 2-4 | INC line_counter |

| INT | INT type<br>Interrupt (execute interrupt-<br>handling procedure number type | | | Flags: O D I T S Z A P C<br>- - - - - - - - - |
|-----|-----------------------------------------------------------------------------|---|---|------------------------------------------|
| Operands | Clocks | Transfers | Bytes | Coding Example |
| immed8 (not type 3) | 72 | 5 | 2 | INT 21H |
| 3 | 71 | 5 | 1 | INT 3 |

| INTO | INTO (no operands)<br>Execute type 4 interrupt if<br>overflow flag is set (OF=OV=1) | | | Flags: O D I T S Z A P C<br>- - - - - - - - - |
|------|-----------------------------------------------------------------------------------|---|---|------------------------------------------|
| Operands | Clocks | Transfers | Bytes | Coding Example |
| (no operands) | 73 or 4 | 5 or 0 | 1 | INTO |

| IRET | IRET (no operands)<br>Return from an interrupt<br>(intersegment RET and POP flags) | | | Flags: O D I T S Z A P C<br>* * * * * * * * * |
|------|----------------------------------------------------------------------------------|---|---|------------------------------------------|
| Operands | Clocks | Transfers | Bytes | Coding Example |
| (no operands) | 32 | 3 | 1 | IRET |

| JA/JNBE | JA/JNBE short_label<br>Jump if above/Jump if not below<br>or equal (unsigned compare) | | | Flags: O D I T S Z A P C<br>- - - - - - - - - |
|---------|--------------------------------------------------------------------------------------|---|---|------------------------------------------|
| Operands | Clocks | Transfers | Bytes | Coding Example |
| short_label | 16 or 4 | — | 2 | JA skip_tag |

| JAE/JNB | JAE/JNB short_label<br>Jump if above or equal/Jump if<br>not below (unsigned compare) | | Flags: | O D I T S Z A P C |
|---|---|---|---|---|
| Operands | Clocks | Transfers | Bytes | Coding Example |
| short_label | 16 or 4 | —— | 2 | JAE skip_tag |

| JC | JC short_label<br>Jump if carry flag is set<br>(CF=CY=1, same opcode as JB) | | Flags: | O D I T S Z A P C |
|---|---|---|---|---|
| Operands | Clocks | Transfers | Bytes | Coding Example |
| short_label | 16 or 4 | —— | 2 | JC carry_is_set |

| JCXZ | JCXZ short_label<br>Jump if CX is zero | | Flags: | O D I T S Z A P C |
|---|---|---|---|---|
| Operands | Clocks | Transfers | Bytes | Coding Example |
| short_label | 18 or 6 | —— | 2 | JCXZ cx_is_0 |

| JE/JZ | JE/JZ short_label<br>Jump if equal/Jump is Zero flag<br>is set (ZF=ZR=1) | | Flags: | O D I T S Z A P C |
|---|---|---|---|---|
| Operands | Clocks | Transfers | Bytes | Coding Example |
| short_label | 16 or 4 | —— | 2 | JE both_the_same |

| JG/JNLE | JG/JNLE short_label<br>Jump if greater/Jump if not less<br>or equal (signed compare) | | Flags: | O D I T S Z A P C |
|---|---|---|---|---|
| Operands | Clocks | Transfers | Bytes | Coding Example |
| short_lablel | 16 or 4 | —— | 2 | JG greater_branch |

| JGE/JNL | JGE/JNL near_label<br>Jump if greater or equal/Jump if<br>not less (signed compare) | | Flags: | O D I T S Z A P C |
|---|---|---|---|---|
| Operands | Clocks | Transfers | Bytes | Coding Example |
| short_label | 16 or 4 | —— | 2 | JGE skip_tag |

| JL/JNGE | JL/JNGE short_label<br>Jump if less/Jump if not greater<br>or equal (signed compare) | | Flags: | O D I T S Z A P C |
|---|---|---|---|---|
| Operands | Clocks | Transfers | Bytes | Coding Example |
| short_lablel | 16 or 4 | —— | 2 | JL less_branch |

| JLE/JNG | JLE/JNG near_label<br>Jump if less or equal/Jump if<br>not greater (signed compare) | | Flags: | O D I T S Z A P C |
|---|---|---|---|---|
| Operands | Clocks | Transfers | Bytes | Coding Example |
| short_label | 16 or 4 | —— | 2 | JLE skip_tag |

| JMP | JMP target<br>Jump (unconditionally) | | Flags: | O D I T S Z A P C |
|---|---|---|---|---|
| Operands | Clocks | Transfers | Bytes | Coding Example |
| short_label | 15 | —— | 2 | JMP SHORT skip_tag |
| near_label | 15 | —— | 3 | JMP error_handler |
| far_label | 15 | —— | 5 | JMP rom_program |
| mem_ptr16 | 22+EA | 1 | 2-4 | JMP near_vect_tbl[bx] |
| reg_ptr16 | 11 | — | 2 | JMP CX |
| mem_ptr32 | 30+EA | 2 | 2-4 | JMP back_to_dos |

| JNC | JNC short_label<br>Jump if carry flag is reset<br>(CF=NC=0, same opcode as JAE) | | Flags: O D I T S Z A P C<br>– – – – – – – – – |
|---|---|---|---|

| Operands | Clocks | Transfers | Bytes | Coding Example |
|---|---|---|---|---|
| short_label | 16 or 4 | —— | 2 | JNC nc_branch |

| JNE/JNZ | JNE/JNZ short_label<br>Jump if not equal/Jump if Zero<br>flag is reset (ZF=NZ=0) | | Flags: O D I T S Z A P C<br>– – – – – – – – – |
|---|---|---|---|

| Operands | Clocks | Transfers | Bytes | Coding Example |
|---|---|---|---|---|
| short_label | 16 or 4 | —— | 2 | JNE not_same_branch |

| JNO | JNO short_label<br>Jump if Overflow flag is 0<br>(OF=NV=0) | | Flags: O D I T S Z A P C<br>– – – – – – – – – |
|---|---|---|---|

| Operands | Clocks | Transfers | Bytes | Coding Example |
|---|---|---|---|---|
| short_label | 16 or 4 | —— | 2 | JNO in_bounds |

| JNS | JNS short_label<br>Jump if Sign flag is reset to 0<br>(SF=NG=0) | | Flags: O D I T S Z A P C<br>– – – – – – – – – |
|---|---|---|---|

| Operands | Clocks | Transfers | Bytes | Coding Example |
|---|---|---|---|---|
| short_label | 16 or 4 | —— | 2 | JNS sign_positive |

| JNP/JPO | JNP/JPO short_label<br>Jump if no parity/Jump if parity<br>is odd (PF=PO=0) | | Flags: O D I T S Z A P C<br>– – – – – – – – – |
|---|---|---|---|

| Operands | Clocks | Transfers | Bytes | Coding Example |
|---|---|---|---|---|
| short_label | 16 or 4 | —— | 2 | JNP parity_odd_branch |

| JO | JO short_label<br>Jump if Overflow flag is set<br>(OF=OV=1) | | Flags: O D I T S Z A P C<br>– – – – – – – – – |
|---|---|---|---|

| Operands | Clocks | Transfers | Bytes | Coding Example |
|---|---|---|---|---|
| short_label | 16 or 4 | —— | 2 | JO overflow_occurred |

| JP/JPE | JP/JPE short_label<br>Jump if Parity/Jump if parity is<br>even (PF=PE=1) | | Flags: O D I T S Z A P C<br>– – – – – – – – – |
|---|---|---|---|

| Operands | Clocks | Transfers | Bytes | Coding Example |
|---|---|---|---|---|
| short_label | 16 or 4 | —— | 2 | JP even_parity_branch |

| JS | JS short_label<br>Jump if Sign flag is set to 1<br>(SF=PL=1) | | Flags: O D I T S Z A P C<br>– – – – – – – – – |
|---|---|---|---|

| Operands | Clocks | Transfers | Bytes | Coding Example |
|---|---|---|---|---|
| short_label | 16 or 4 | —— | 2 | JS negative |

| LAHF | LAHF (no operands)<br>Load AH from the flags register | | Flags: O D I T S Z A P C |
|---|---|---|---|

| Operands | Clocks | Transfers | Bytes | Coding Example |
|---|---|---|---|---|
| (no operands) | 4 | —— | 1 | LAHF |

| LDS | LDS destination,source<br>Load DS and destination from<br>source memory address | | | | Flags: O D I T S Z A P C |
|---|---|---|---|---|---|
| Operands | | Clocks | Transfers | Bytes | Coding Example |
| reg16,mem32 | | 24+EA | 2 | 2-4 | LDS si,buffer_ptr |

| LEA | LEA destination,source<br>Load Effective Address of source<br>operand into destination | | | | Flags: O D I T S Z A P C |
|---|---|---|---|---|---|
| Operands | | Clocks | Transfers | Bytes | Coding Example |
| reg16,mem16 | | 2+EA | — | 2-4 | LEA bx,[BP+DI+3] |

| LES | LES destination,source<br>Load ES and destination from<br>source memory address | | | | Flags: O D I T S Z A P C |
|---|---|---|---|---|---|
| Operands | | Clocks | Transfers | Bytes | Coding Example |
| reg16,mem32 | | 24+EA | 2 | 2-4 | LES di,buffer_ptr |

| LOCK | LOCK (no operands)<br>Prefix locks the system bus from<br>being accessed by coprocessor | | | | Flags: O D I T S Z A P C |
|---|---|---|---|---|---|
| Operands | | Clocks | Transfers | Bytes | Coding Example |
| (no operands) | | 2 | — | 1 | LOCK XCHG semaphore,al |

| LODS | LODS source_string<br>Load AX from DS:[SI] and adjust<br>SI according to Direction Flag | | | | Flags: O D I T S Z A P C |
|---|---|---|---|---|---|
| Operands | | Clocks | Transfers | Bytes | Coding Example |
| source_string<br>(repeated) | | 12(16)<br>9+13(17)<br>/rep | 1<br>1/rep | 1<br>1 | LODS input_buffer<br>REP LODS dummy_string |

| LODSB<br>LODSW | LODSB (no operands)<br>LODSW (no operands)<br>(alternate forms of LODS) | | | | Flags: O D I T S Z A P C |
|---|---|---|---|---|---|
| Operands | | Clocks | Transfers | Bytes | Coding Example |
| (no operand 8-bit)<br>(no operand 16-bit)<br>(repeated) | | 12<br>16<br>9+22(30)<br>/rep | 1<br>1<br>1/rep | 1<br>1<br>1 | LODSB<br>LODSW<br>REP LODSB |

| LOOP | LOOP short_label<br>Decrement CX and if CX does not<br>become 0, then jump to label | | | | Flags: O D I T S Z A P C |
|---|---|---|---|---|---|
| Operands | | Clocks | Transfers | Bytes | Coding Example |
| short_label | | 17 or 5 | — | 2 | LOOP get_next_char |

| LOOPE/<br>LOOPZ | LOOPE/LOOPZ short_label<br>Loop if equal<br>(jump if ZF=ZR=1 and CX>0) | | | | Flags: O D I T S Z A P C |
|---|---|---|---|---|---|
| Operands | | Clocks | Transfers | Bytes | Coding Example |
| short_label | | 18 or 6 | — | 2 | LOOPE again |

| LOOPNE/<br>LOOPNZ | LOOPE/LOOPZ short_label<br>Loop if not equal<br>(jump if ZF=NZ=0 and CX>0) | | | | Flags: O D I T S Z A P C |
|---|---|---|---|---|---|
| Operands | | Clocks | Transfers | Bytes | Coding Example |
| short_label | | 19 or 5 | — | 2 | LOOPNE again |

| MOV | MOV destination,source<br>Move (copy) data from source<br>to destination | | | Flags: O D I T S Z A P C<br>- - - - - - - - - |
|---|---|---|---|---|
| Operands | Clocks | Transfers | Bytes | Coding Example |
| memory,accumulator | 10(14) | 1 | 3 | MOV counter,al |
| accumulator,memory | 10(14) | 1 | 3 | MOV ax,result |
| register,register | 2 | — | 2 | MOV si,dx |
| register,memory | 8(12)+EA | 1 | 2-4 | MOV bl,byte_array[bx] |
| memory,register | 9(13)+EA | 1 | 2-4 | MOV current_line,cx |
| register,immediate | 4 | — | 2-3 | MOV dx,1234H |
| memory,immediate | 10(14)+EA | 1 | 3-6 | MOV BYTE PTR [si+3],20 |
| seg_reg,reg16 | 2 | — | 2 | MOV ds,ax |
| seg_reg,mem16 | 12+EA | 1 | 2-4 | MOV ds,segment_store |
| reg16,seg_reg | 2 | — | 2 | MOV bx,es |
| memory,seg_reg | 13+EA | 1 | 2-4 | MOV stack_save[bx],ss |

| MOVS | MOVS dest_string,source_string<br>Move DS:[SI] to ES:[DI] and<br>adjust DI and SI according to DF | | | Flags: O D I T S Z A P C<br>- - - - - - - - - |
|---|---|---|---|---|
| Operands | Clocks | Transfers | Bytes | Coding Example |
| dest_str,source_str | 18(26) | 2 | 1 | MOVS buff_1,buff_2 |
| (repeated) | 9+17(25)<br>/rep | 2/rep | 1 | REP MOVS text,buffer |

| MOVSB<br>MOVSW | MOVSB (no operands)<br>MOVSW (no operands)<br>(alternate forms of MOVS) | | | Flags: O D I T S Z A P C<br>- - - - - - - - - |
|---|---|---|---|---|
| Operands | Clocks | Transfers | Bytes | Coding Example |
| (no operand 8-bit) | 18 | 2 | 1 | MOVSB |
| (no operand 16-bit) | 26 | 2 | 1 | MOVSW |
| (repeated) | 9+17(25)<br>/rep | 2/rep | 1 | REP MOVSB |

| MUL | MUL source<br>Multiply unsigned values<br>(multiply AL or AX by source) | | | Flags: O D I T S Z A P C<br>* - - - ? ? ? ? * |
|---|---|---|---|---|
| Operands | Clocks | Transfers | Bytes | Coding Example |
| reg8 | 70-77 | — | 2 | MUL cl |
| reg16 | 118-113 | — | 2 | MUL di |
| mem8 | (80-87)+EA | 1 | 2-4 | MUL rate_table[bx] |
| mem16 | (128-143) | 1 | 2-4 | MUL rate_factor |
| mem16 | +EA | | | |

| NEG | NEG destination<br>Negate<br>(subtract from 0) | | | Flags: O D I T S Z A P C<br>* - - - * * * * * |
|---|---|---|---|---|
| Operands | Clocks | Transfers | Bytes | Coding Example |
| register | 3 | — | 2 | NEG al |
| memory | 16(24)+EA | 2 | 2-4 | NEG factor_1 |

| NOP | NOP (no operands)<br>No Operation.<br>(do nothing) | | | Flags: O D I T S Z A P C<br>- - - - - - - - - |
|---|---|---|---|---|
| Operands | Clocks | Transfers | Bytes | Coding Example |
| (no operands) | 3 | — | 1 | NOP |

| NOT | NOT destination<br>Invert all bits in destination<br>(form 1's complement) | | | Flags: O D I T S Z A P C<br>- - - - - - - - - |
|---|---|---|---|---|
| Operands | Clocks | Transfers | Bytes | Coding Example |
| register | 3 | — | 2 | NOT al |
| memory | 16(24)+EA | 2 | 2-4 | NOT graphics_byte |

| OR | OR destination,source<br>Logical inclusive OR<br>(set bits in destination) | | Flags: | O D I T S Z A P C<br>0 - - - * * ? * 0 | |
|---|---|---|---|---|---|
| Operands | Clocks | Transfers | Bytes | Coding Example | |
| register,register | 3 | — | 2 | OR bx,cx | |
| register,memory | 9(13)+EA | 1 | 2-4 | OR bl,byte_table[di] | |
| memory,register | 16(24)+EA | 2 | 2-4 | OR flag_byte,cl | |
| accumulator,immediate | 4 | — | 2-3 | OR al,10000000B | |
| register,immediate | 4 | — | 3-4 | OR bl,0F0H | |
| memory,immediate | 17(25)+EA | 2 | 3-6 | OR table[bx+di],3 | |

| OUT | OUT accumulator,port<br>output byte in AL to port or<br>output AL to port, AH to port+1 | | Flags: | O D I T S Z A P C<br>- - - - - - - - - | |
|---|---|---|---|---|---|
| Operands | Clocks | Transfers | Bytes | Coding Example | |
| immed8,accumulator | 10(14) | 1 | 2 | OUT 0ffH,ax | |
| DX,accumulator | 8(12) | 1 | 1 | OUT dx,al | |

| POP | POP destination<br>Transfer 16-bit stack data to<br>destination | | Flags: | O D I T S Z A P C<br>- - - - - - - - - | |
|---|---|---|---|---|---|
| Operands | Clocks | Transfers | Bytes | Coding Example | |
| register | 12 | 1 | 1 | POP ax | |
| seg_reg (CS illegal) | 12 | 1 | 1 | POP ds | |
| memory | 25+EA | 2 | 2-4 | POP save_parm | |

| POPF | POPF (no operands)<br>POP from stack into flags<br>register | | Flags: | O D I T S Z A P C<br>* * * * * * * * * | |
|---|---|---|---|---|---|
| Operands | Clocks | Transfers | Bytes | Coding Example | |
| (no operands) | 12 | 1 | 1 | POPF | |

| PUSH | PUSH source<br>Transfer 16-bit source to stack | | Flags: | O D I T S Z A P C<br>- - - - - - - - - | |
|---|---|---|---|---|---|
| Operands | Clocks | Transfers | Bytes | Coding Example | |
| register | 15 | 1 | 1 | PUSH ax | |
| seg_reg | 14 | 1 | 1 | PUSH es | |
| memory | 24+EA | 2 | 2-4 | PUSH return_code[di] | |

| PUSHF | PUSHF (no operands)<br>PUSH flags register onto stack | | Flags: | O D I T S Z A P C<br>- - - - - - - - - | |
|---|---|---|---|---|---|
| Operands | Clocks | Transfers | Bytes | Coding Example | |
| (no operands) | 14 | 1 | 1 | PUSHF | |

| RCL | RCL destination,count<br>Rotate left through carry<br>(9-bit or 17-bit rotation) | | Flags: | O D I T S Z A P C<br>* - - - - - - - * | |
|---|---|---|---|---|---|
| Operands | Clocks | Transfers | Bytes | Coding Example | |
| register,1 | 2 | — | 2 | RCL ax,1 | |
| register,CL | 8+4/bit | — | 2 | RCL al,cl | |
| memory,1 | 15(23)+EA | 2 | 2-4 | RCL date_field,1 | |
| memory,CL | 20(28)+EA<br>+ 4/bit | 2 | 2-4 | RCL colors[si],cl | |

| RCR | RCR destination,count<br>Rotate right through carry<br>(9-bit or 17-bit rotation) | | | Flags: O D I T S Z A P C<br>* - - - - - - - * |
|---|---|---|---|---|
| Operands | Clocks | Transfers | Bytes | Coding Example |
| register,1<br>register,CL<br>memory,1<br>memory,CL | 2<br>8+4/bit<br>15(23)+EA<br>20(28)+EA<br>+ 4/bit | ——<br><br>2<br>2 | 2<br>2<br>2-4<br>2-4 | RCR ax,1<br>RCR al,cl<br>RCR date_field,1<br>RCR colors[si],cl |

| REP/<br>REPE/<br>REPZ | REP/REPE/REPZ (no operands)<br>Repeat string operation until<br>ZF = ZR = 1, or CX = 0 | | | Flags: O D I T S Z A P C<br>- - - - - - - - - |
|---|---|---|---|---|
| Operands | Clocks | Transfers | Bytes | Coding Example |
| (no operands) | 2 | —— | 1 | REP MOVS page1,screen |

| REPNE/<br>REPNZ | REPNE/REPNZ (no operands)<br>Repeat string operation until<br>ZF = NZ = 0 or CX = 0 | | | Flags: O D I T S Z A P C<br>- - - - - - - - - |
|---|---|---|---|---|
| Operands | Clocks | Transfers | Bytes | Coding Example |
| (no operands) | 2 | —— | 1 | REPNE SCAS input_line |

| RET | RET<br>Return from procedure | | | Flags: O D I T S Z A P C<br>- - - - - - - - - |
|---|---|---|---|---|
| Operands | Clocks | Transfers | Bytes | Coding Example |
| (intrasegment)<br>(intersegment) | 20<br>32 | 1<br>2 | 1<br>1 | RET<br>RET |

| RET nnnn | RET pop_value<br>Return from procedure and<br>adjust stack pointer | | | Flags: O D I T S Z A P C<br>- - - - - - - - - |
|---|---|---|---|---|
| Operands | Clocks | Transfers | Bytes | Coding Example |
| immed16 (intrasegment)<br>immed16 (intersegment) | 24<br>31 | 2<br>2 | 3<br>3 | RET 4<br>RET 4 |

| ROL | ROL destination,count<br>Rotate left<br>(8-bit or 16-bit rotation) | | | Flags: O D I T S Z A P C<br>* - - - - - - - * |
|---|---|---|---|---|
| Operands | Clocks | Transfers | Bytes | Coding Example |
| register,1<br>register,CL<br>memory,1<br>memory,CL | 2<br>8+4/bit<br>15(23)+EA<br>20(28)+EA<br>+4/bit | ——<br><br>2<br>2 | 2<br>2<br>2-4<br>2-4 | ROL dx,1<br>ROL al,cl<br>ROL status_port,1<br>ROL colors[si],cl |

| ROR | ROR destination,count<br>Rotate right<br>(8-bit or 16-bit rotation) | | | Flags: O D I T S Z A P C<br>* - - - - - - - * |
|---|---|---|---|---|
| Operands | Clocks | Transfers | Bytes | Coding Example |
| register,1<br>register,CL<br>memory,1<br>memory,CL | 2<br>8+4/bit<br>15(23)+EA<br>20(28)+EA<br>+4/bit | ——<br><br>2<br>2 | 2<br>2<br>2-4<br>2-4 | ROR dx,1<br>ROR al,cl<br>ROR status_byte,1<br>ROR cmd_word[di+1],cl |

| SAHF | SAHF (no operands)<br>Store AH into flags register | | | Flags: O D I T S Z A P C<br>- - - - * * * * * |
|---|---|---|---|---|
| Operands | Clocks | Transfers | Bytes | Coding Example |
| (no operands) | 4 | —— | 1 | SAHF |

| SAL/SHL | SAL/SHL destination,count<br>Shift arithmetic left<br>Shift logical left | | | | Flags:  O D I T S Z A P C<br>        * — — — * * — * |
|---|---|---|---|---|---|
| **Operands** | **Clocks** | **Transfers** | **Bytes** | **Coding Example** | |
| register,1<br>register,CL<br>memory,1<br>memory,CL | 2<br>8+4/bit<br>15(23)+EA<br>20(28)+EA<br>+ 4/bit | —<br>—<br>2<br>2 | 2<br>2<br>2-4<br>2-4 | SAL dx,1<br>SHL al,cl<br>SHL factor,1<br>SAL [bx]word_var,cl | |

| SAR | SAR destination,count<br>Shift arithmetic right<br>(shift right retaining sign bit) | | | | Flags:  O D I T S Z A P C<br>        * — — — * * ? * * |
|---|---|---|---|---|---|
| **Operands** | **Clocks** | **Transfers** | **Bytes** | **Coding Example** | |
| register,1<br>register,CL<br>memory,1<br>memory,CL | 2<br>8+4/bit<br>15(23)+EA<br>20(28)+EA<br>+ 4/bit | —<br>—<br>2<br>2 | 2<br>2<br>2-4<br>2-4 | SAR dx,1<br>SAR al,cl<br>SAR dividend,1<br>SAR byte_count,cl | |

| SBB | SBB destination,source<br>Subtract with borrow<br>(9-bit or 17-bit subtraction) | | | | Flags:  O D I T S Z A P C<br>        * — — — * * * * * |
|---|---|---|---|---|---|
| **Operands** | **Clocks** | **Transfers** | **Bytes** | **Coding Example** | |
| register,register<br>register,memory<br>memory,register<br>accumulator,immediate<br>register,immediate<br>memory,immediate | 3<br>9(13)+EA<br>16(24)+EA<br>4<br>4<br>17(25)+EA | —<br>1<br>2<br>—<br>—<br>2 | 2<br>2-4<br>2-4<br>2-3<br>3-4<br>3-6 | SBB di,bx<br>SBB bl,byte_table[di]<br>SBB counter,bl<br>SBB ax,1234H<br>SBB bx,table[si],5<br>SBB counter,5 | |

| SCAS | SCAS dest_string<br>Compare ES:[SI] to AL or AX and<br>adjust DI according to DF | | | | Flags:  O D I T S Z A P C<br>        * — — — * * * * * |
|---|---|---|---|---|---|
| **Operands** | **Clocks** | **Transfers** | **Bytes** | **Coding Example** | |
| dest_string<br>(repeated) | 15(19)<br>9+15(19)<br>/rep | 1<br>1/rep | 1<br>1 | SCAS input_buffer<br>REPNE SCAS input_line | |

| SCASB<br>SCASW | SCASB (no operands)<br>SCASW (no operands)<br>(alternate forms of SCAS) | | | | Flags:  O D I T S Z A P C<br>        * — — — * * * * * |
|---|---|---|---|---|---|
| **Operands** | **Clocks** | **Transfers** | **Bytes** | **Coding Example** | |
| (no operand 8-bit)<br>(no operand 16-bit)<br>(repeated) | 15<br>19<br>9+15(19)<br>/rep | 1<br>1<br>1/rep | 1<br>1<br>1 | SCASB<br>SCASW<br>REP SCASB | |

| SEGMENT<br>CS:/DS:/<br>ES:/SS: | CS:/DS:/ES:/SS: (no operands)<br>Prefix overrides default segment<br>of addressing mode in next opcode | | | | Flags:  O D I T S Z A P C<br>        — — — — — — — — — |
|---|---|---|---|---|---|
| **Operands** | **Clocks** | **Transfers** | **Bytes** | **Coding Example** | |
| (no operands) | 2 | — | 1 | mov ax,ES:[bx] | |

| SHR | SHR destination,count<br>Shift logical right<br>(8-bit or 16-bit shift) | | | | Flags:  O D I T S Z A P C<br>        * — — — * * ? * * |
|---|---|---|---|---|---|
| **Operands** | **Clocks** | **Transfers** | **Bytes** | **Coding Example** | |
| register,1<br>register,CL<br>memory,1<br>memory,CL | 2<br>8+4/bit<br>15(23)+EA<br>20(28)+EA<br>+ 4/bit | —<br>—<br>2<br>2 | 2<br>2<br>2-4<br>2-4 | SHR dx,1<br>SHR al,cl<br>SHR port_value,1<br>SHR date_field,cl | |

| STC | STC (no operands)<br>Set carry flag<br>(set CF = CY = 1) | | Flags: | O D I T S Z A P C<br>– – – – – – – – 1 |
|---|---|---|---|---|
| Operands | Clocks | Transfers | Bytes | Coding Example |
| (no operands) | 2 | —— | 1 | STC |

| STD | STD (no operands)<br>Set direction flag (make string<br>operations auto–decrement) | | Flags: | O D I T S Z A P C<br>– 1 – – – – – – – |
|---|---|---|---|---|
| Operands | Clocks | Transfers | Bytes | Coding Example |
| (no operands) | 2 | —— | 1 | STD |

| STI | STI (no operands)<br>Set interrupt flag<br>(enable maskable interrupts) | | Flags: | O D I T S Z A P C<br>– – 1 – – – – – – |
|---|---|---|---|---|
| Operands | Clocks | Transfers | Bytes | Coding Example |
| (no operands) | 2 | —— | 1 | STD |

| STOS | STOS dest_string<br>Store AL or AX to ES:[DI] and<br>adjust DI according to DF | | Flags: | O D I T S Z A P C<br>– – – – – – – – – |
|---|---|---|---|---|
| Operands | Clocks | Transfers | Bytes | Coding Example |
| dest_string<br>(repeated) | 11(15)<br>9+10(14)<br>/rep | 1<br>1/rep | 1<br>1 | STOS cs:output_buffer<br>REP STOSB screen_page |

| STOSB<br>STOSW | STOSB (no operands)<br>STOSW (no operands)<br>Alternate forms of STOS) | | Flags: | O D I T S Z A P C<br>– – – – – – – – – |
|---|---|---|---|---|
| Operands | Clocks | Transfers | Bytes | Coding Example |
| (no operand, 8–bit)<br>(no operand, 16–bit)<br>(repeated) | 11<br>15<br>9+10(14)<br>/rep | 1<br>1<br>1/rep | 1<br>1<br>1 | STOSB<br>STOSW<br>REP STOSB |

| SUB | SUB destination,source<br>Subtraction<br>(8–bit or 16–bit subtraction) | | Flags: | O D I T S Z A P C<br>* – – – * * * * * |
|---|---|---|---|---|
| Operands | Clocks | Transfers | Bytes | Coding Example |
| register,register<br>register,memory<br>memory,register<br>accumulator,immediate<br>register,immediate<br>memory,immediate | 3<br>9(13)+EA<br>16(24)+EA<br>4<br>4<br>17(25)+EA | 1<br>2<br>——<br>——<br>2 | 2<br>2–4<br>2–4<br>2–3<br>3–4<br>3–6 | SBB di,bx<br>SBB bx,word_table[di]<br>SUB counter,al<br>SUB al,27H<br>SBB bl,5<br>SUB counter,64 |

| TEST | TEST destination,source<br>Test for bit pattern<br>(non–destuctive AND) | | Flags: | O D I T S Z A P C<br>0 – – – * * ? * 0 |
|---|---|---|---|---|
| Operands | Clocks | Transfers | Bytes | Coding Example |
| register,register<br>register,memory<br>accumulator,immediate<br>register,immediate<br>memory,immediate | 3<br>9(13)+EA<br>4<br>5<br>11+EA | ——<br>——<br>——<br>——<br>1 | 2<br>2–4<br>2–3<br>3–4<br>3–6 | TEST bx,cx<br>TEST bl,color[di+bx]<br>TEST ax,8000H<br>TEST bl,00100000B<br>TEST table[bx+di],3 |

| WAIT/<br>FWAIT | WAIT (no operands)<br>Wait until TEST line active<br>(synchronize with coprocessor) | | Flags: | O D I T S Z A P C<br>– – – – – – – – – |
|---|---|---|---|---|
| Operands | Clocks | Transfers | Bytes | Coding Example |
| (no operands) | 3+5/unsync | —— | 1 | WAIT |

| XCHG | XCHG destination,source<br>Exchange | | | | Flags: O D I T S Z A P C |
|------|------|------|------|------|------|
| Operands | Clocks | Transfers | Bytes | | Coding Example |
| accumulator,reg16<br>memory,register<br>register,register | 3<br>17(25)+EA<br>4 | —<br>2<br>— | 1<br>2-4<br>2 | | XCHG ax,cx<br>XCHG semaphore,al<br>XCHG al,bl |

| XLAT | XLAT source_table<br>Translate<br>(fetch AL = DS:[BX+value of AL]) | | | | Flags: O D I T S Z A P C<br>- - - - - - - - - |
|------|------|------|------|------|------|
| Operands | Clocks | Transfers | Bytes | | Coding Example |
| (no operand)<br>source_table | 11<br>11 | 1<br>1 | 1<br>1 | | XLAT<br>XLAT ascii_table |

| XOR | XOR destination,source<br>Logical exclusive OR<br>(toggle bits of destination) | | | | Flags: O D I T S Z A P C<br>0 - - - * * ? * 0 |
|------|------|------|------|------|------|
| Operands | Clocks | Transfers | Bytes | | Coding Example |
| register,register<br>register,memory<br>memory,register<br>accumulator,immediate<br>register,immediate<br>memory,immediate | 3<br>9(13)+EA<br>16(24)+EA<br>4<br>4<br>17(25)+EA | —<br>1<br>2<br>—<br>—<br>2 | 2<br>2-4<br>2-4<br>2-3<br>3-4<br>3-6 | | XOR di,bx<br>XOR bx,mask_table[si]<br>XOR bit_flag,ax<br>XOR al,00011000B<br>XOR bl,80H<br>XOR mask_byte,3 |

# *Appendix B.1*

# **Interrupt Summary**

| Interrupt type addr | AH: Sub-function | NAME/Description |
| ---- ---- | -------- | ------------------------------------------------------------ |
| Ø    Ø-3 | None | DIVIDE_BY_Ø/Automatically taken upon division overflow |
| 1    4-7 | None | SINGLE_STEP/taken after every instruction when CPU Trap Flag indicates single-step mode (bit 8 of FLAGS is 1) |
| 2    8-B | None | NON_MASKABLE/vector not disabled via CLI.  Taken when hard memory error occurs. Displays message, halts system |
| 3    C-F | None | BREAKPOINT/taken when CPU executes the breakpoint opcode (ØCCH) |
| 4    1Ø-13 | None | OVERFLOW/taken when OF=1 and INTO opcode is executed |
| 5    14-17 | None | PRINT_SCREEN/service dumps the screen to the printer Invoked by KBD_INT for shifted key 55 (PrtSc) |
| 6    18-1B | None | reserved |
| 7    1C-1F | None | reserved |
| 8    2Ø-23 | None | TIMER_INT/55ms timer "tick" taken 18.2 times per second Updates BIOS clock and turns off diskette drive motors after 2 seconds of inactivity. |
| 9    24-27 | None | KBD_INT/taken whenever a key is pressed or released Stores characters and scan-codes in buffer at ØØ4Ø:ØØ1E Updates shift key status at ØØ4Ø:ØØ17,18 |
| A    28-2B | None | reserved |
| B    2C-2F | None | reserved |
| C    3Ø-33 | None | reserved |
| D    34-37 | None | reserved |
| E    38-3B | None | DISKETTE_INT/indicates that a seek is in progress (sets bit Ø of ØØ4Ø:ØØ3F) |
| F    3C-3F | None | reserved |

```
Interrupt   AH: Sub-
type  addr  function                  NAME/Description
----  ----  --------  -------------------------------------------------------
10   40-43             VIDEO_IO/services handle video output
            0          SET_MODE/initialize for one of seven text or graphics modes
                       AL=0: 40x25 BW
                       AL=1: 40x25 color
                       AL=2: 80x25 BW
                       AL=3: 80x25 color graphics
                       AL=4: 320x200 color graphics
                       AL=5: 320x200 BW graphics
                       AL=6: 640x200 BW graphics
            1          SET_CUR_TYPE/set the size of the cursor or turn it off
                       CH=start line (bit 5=no cursor), CL=end line
            2          SET_CUR_POS/set the coordinates of the cursor
                       DH=row (0-24), DL=column (0-79 or 0-39), BH=video page
            3          READ_CUR_POS/return the position of the cursor
                       BH=video page
                       returns: DH=row, DL=column, CX=cursor size
            4          READ_LIGHT_PEN/fetch light pen information
                       returns: AH=0: light pen not triggered
                                AH=1: DH,DL=character row,column
                                      CH,CL=graphics row,column
            5          SELECT_ACTIVE_PAGE/set page number for services 6 and 7
                       AL=new page (0-7 for modes 0 and 1, 0-3 for modes 2 and 3)
            6          SCROLL_PAGE_UP/scroll up or clear a display window
                       AL=number of lines to scroll (0=blank entire window)
                       CH,CL=row,column of top left corner of window
                       DH,DL=row,column of lowest right corner of window
                       BH=video attribute for blanked lines
            7          SCROLL_PAGE_DOWN/scroll down or clear a display "window"
                       (see subfunction 6 for parameters)
            8          READ_CHAR_ATTR/fetch a character from the cursor position
                       BH=page
                       returns: AL=character, AH=attribute
            9          WRITE_CHAR_ATTR/display character(s) and attribute at cursor
                       BH=display page, CX=repeat count, AL=character to display
                       BL=attribute (graphics modes: BL=color (add 80H for XOR)
            A          WRITE_CHAR/display character(s) only (use current
                       attribute.  See subfunction 9 for parameters)
            B          SET_COLOR_PALETTE/set palette for graphics or border for text
                       BH=0: select border (text mode)
                             BL=color (0-31 [16-31 is high intensity])
                       BH=1: select graphics palette
                             BL=palette code
                             (0=green/red/yellow, 1=cyan/magenta/white)
            C          WRITE_DOT/plot 1 graphics pixel
                       DX=row, CX=column, AL=color (bit 7 to XOR the dot)
            D          READ_DOT/determine the color of 1 graphics pixel
                       DX=row, CX=column, returns: AL=color of dot
            E          WRITE_TTY/write one character and update cursor.  Also
                       handles CR (0DH), beep (07H), and scrolls screen if needed.
                       AL=char to write, BH=page, BL=foreground (in graphics mode)
            F          VIDEO_STATE/fetch the mode and width (columns) of the screen
                       returns: AL=mode (see subfunction 0), AH=width, BH=page

11   44-47   None      EQUIPMENT_CHECK/fetch a code describing active peripherals
                       returns: AX=equipment code bits:  PP-JSSS-DDVVRRNI
                       PP  = number of printers
                       J   = joystick
                       SSS = serial devices (RS-232 ports)
                       DD  = number of disk drives (00=1, 01=2, 10=3, 11=4)
                       VV  = video (11=BW card, 01 and 10 = color/graphics card)
                       RR  = RAM in mother-board (00=16K...11=64K),
                       N   = numeric coprocessor (8087 chip)
                       I   = disk-existence (0=no drives in system)

12   48-4B   None      MEMORY_SIZE/fetch AX=count of contiguous 1K RAM blocks
```

```
Interrupt  AH: Sub-
type addr  function                    NAME/Description
---- ----  --------   -------------------------------------------------------

13   4C-4F             DISKETTE_IO/access the diskette drives
            0          RESET/reset the disk controller chip
            1          GET_STATUS/fetch AL=status of most recent operation
            2          READ_SECTORS/read one or more sectors from diskette
                       DH=head    DL=drive (0=A, 1=B, etc.)
                       CH=track   CL=sector (1-8, 1-9 for DOS 2.0)
                       AL=sectors to read
                       ES:BX = address to store/fetch data
                       [0000:0078] = doubleword pointer to diskette parameters
                       returns: Carry Flag=NC (0) for successful
                                Carry Flag=CY (1) failure
                                AH=disk status (error reason)
                                 80H=timeout: disk failed to respond
                                 40H=seek operation failure
                                 20H=NEC disk drive controller failed
                                 10H=bad cyclical redundancy check (CRC error)
                                 09H=attempted access across 64K boundary
                                 08H=DMA overrun
                                 04H=record not found
                                 03H=write protect error
                                 02H=sector ID error (can't find address mark)
                                 01H=unknown command
            3          WRITE_SECTORS/write from memory to disk
                       (parameters as with subfunction 2)
            4          VERIFY/verify that a write operation was successful
                       (parameters as with subfunction 2, but ES:BX not needed)
            5          FORMAT_TRACK/write sector-ID bytes for one track
                       ES:BX points to 8 (or 9) 4-byte sector ID marks:
                          byte 0=track number
                          byte 1=head number
                          byte 2=sector number
                          byte 3=bytes in sector (0=128, 1=256, 2=512, 3=1024)

14   50-53             RS232_IO/initialize and access serial communications port
            0          INIT_COM/initialize port named by DX (0 or 1)
                       AL has initialization bit pattern: BBBPPSLL
                       BBB=baud rate:   110,150,300,600,1200,2400,4800,9600
                       PP =parity:      00=none, 01=odd, 11=even
                       S  =stop bits:   0=1, 1=2
                       LL =word length: 10=7 bits, 11=8 bits
            1          SEND_CHAR/send character to comm port DX (0 or 1)
                       AL=character
                       returns: bit 7 of AH=1 if error
            2          AWAIT_COMM_CHAR/wait for a character from comm port DX
                       returns: AL=character
                                AH=error code (0 for no error)
            3          COMM_STATUS/fetch the status of comm port DX (0 or 1)
                       returns: comm-line status in AH, modem status in AL
                         AH bit 7=timeout
                            bit 6=empty transmit shift register
                            bit 5=empty transmit holding register
                            bit 4=break detected ("long space")
                            bit 3=framing error
                            bit 2=parity error
                            bit 1=overrun error
                            bit 0=data ready
                         AL bit 7=received line signal detect
                            bit 6=ring indicator
                            bit 5=data set ready
                            bit 4=clear to send
                            bit 3=delta receive line signal detect
                            bit 2=trailing edge ring detector
                            bit 1=delta data set ready
                            bit 0=delta clear to send
```

```
Interrupt  AH: Sub-
type addr  function                    NAME/Description
---- ----  --------   -------------------------------------------------------

15   54-57            CASSETTE_IO/access cassette tape drive (NOP for IBM-XT)
           0           CASS_ON/start the motor
           1           CASS_OFF/turn the motor off
           2           CASS_READ/read CX bytes into buffer at ES:BX
           3           CASS_WRITE/write CX bytes to tape from buffer at ES:BX

16   58-5B            KBD_IO/access the keyboard buffer
           0           AWAIT_CHAR/read the next character in keyboard buffer,
                        If no key is ready, wait for one.
                        returns: AL=ASCII character, AH=scan code
           1           PREVIEW_KEY/see if key is ready
                        returns: ZF=ZR (1) if no key is ready, else
                                 ZF=NZ and AX=character and scan code
           2           SHIFT_STATUS/fetch bit flags indicating shift status
                        returns: AL=bit codes (same as 0040:0017)
                                bit 7=insert state
                                bit 6=CapsLock state
                                bit 5=NumLock state
                                bit 4=ScrollLock state
                                bit 3=alternate shift (Alt key)
                                bit 2=control shift (Ctrl key)
                                bit 1=left shift (left caps-shift key)
                                bit 0=right shift (right caps-shift key)
                         note: other codes found at 0040:0018
                                bit 7=insert shift (Ins key pressed)
                                bit 6=caps shift (CapsLock key pressed)
                                bit 5=num shift (NumLock key pressed)
                                bit 4=scroll shift (ScrollLock key pressed)
                                bit 3=hold state (Ctrl-NumLock is in effect)

17   5C-5F            PRINTER_IO/access the parallel printer(s)
           0           PRINT_CHAR/send AL to printer DX (0, 1, or 2)
                        returns: AH=1 if unable to print, else AH=status (as below)
           1           INIT_PRINTER/set init line low, send 0CH to printer DX
                        returns: status as below
           2           PRINTER_STATUS/read status of printer DX into AH
                        returns: bit flags:
                                 bit 7=printer is busy
                                 bit 6=acknowledge line state
                                 bit 5=out-of-paper line state
                                 bit 4=printer selected line state
                                 bit 3=I/O error
                                 bit 2=unused
                                 bit 1=unused
                                 bit 0=timeout error

18   60-63     None   ROM_BASIC/execute nondisk BASIC at F600:0000

19   64-67     None   BOOT_STRAP/read track 0, sector 1 into 0000:7C00,
                       then transfer control to that address.
                       If no diskette drive available, take INT 18H

1A   68-6B            TIME_OF_DAY/access the PC internal clock
           0           READ_CLOCK/fetch count of 55ms "ticks" since power up
                        returns: CX=high word of count
                                 DX=low word of count
                                 AL=0 when no 24-hour overflow since power up
           1            SET_CLOCK/set number of 55ms in clock variable
                         CX=high word of timer ticks
                         DX=low word of timer ticks
                        note: the clock ticks are incremented by TIMER_INT
                              at about 18.2 times per second.  Therefore:
                              counts per second =         18  (12H)
                              counts per minute =      1,092  (444H)
                              counts per hour   =     65,543  (10011H)   65,520
                              counts per day    =1,573,040    (1800B0H)  1,572,480
```

```
Interrupt  AH: Sub-
type addr  function                          NAME/Description
---- ----  --------   --------------------------------------------------------

1B   6C-6F  None      KEYBOARD_BREAK/routine taken when KBD_INT senses
                      Ctrl-Break

1C   70-73  None      USER_TIMER_INT/taken 18.2 times per second; invoked by
                      the TIMER_INT; normally vectors to dummy IRET

1D   74-77  None      VIDEO_PARMS_PTR/vector of video initialization parameters:
                      This doubleword address points to three sets of 16 bytes
                      cantaining data used to initialize for video modes.
                      Parameter table format corresponds to the Motorlla 6845 CRT
                      controller registers:
                        R0 =horizontal total (horizontal sync. in characters)
                        R1 =horizontal displayed (characters per line)
                        R2 =horizontal sync. position (move display left or right)
                        R3 =sync. width (vertical and horiz. pulse: 4 bits each)
                        R4 =vertical total (total character lines)
                        R5 =vertical adjust (adjust for 50 or 60 Hz refresh)
                        R6 =vertical displayed (lines of chars displayed)
                        R7 =vertical sync. position (lines shifted up or down)
                        R8 =interlace (bits 4 and 5) and skew (bits 6 and 7)
                        R9 =max scan line address (scan lines per character row)
                        R10=cursor start (starting scan line of cursor)
                        R11=cursor stop (ending scan line of cursor)
                        R12=display memory start address high byte (6 bits)
                        R13=display memory start address low byte (8 bits)
                        R14=cursor address high byte (6 bits)
                        R15=cursor address low byte (8 bits)

1E   78-7B  None      DISKETTE_PARMS_PTR/vector of diskette controller parameters:
                      This doubleword address points to a data table used by
                      DISKETTE_IO (INT 13H).  11-byte table format:
                        byte 0 =4-bit step rate, 4-bit head unload time
                        byte 1 =7-bit head load time, 1-bit DMA flag
                        byte 2 =55ms counts--delay until motor off
                        byte 3 =sector size (0=128, 1=256, 2=512, 3=1024)
                        byte 4 =last sector on track
                        byte 5 =gap between sectors
                        byte 6 =data length for DMA transfers
                        byte 7 =gap length for format
                        byte 8 =fill byte for format
                        byte 9 =head settle time (in milliseconds)
                        byte 10=motor start time (in 1/8-th second intervals)

1F   7C-7F  None      GRAPHICS_TBL_PTR/vector of data used by VIDEO_IO to
                      display characters above ASCII 127 in graphics modes.
                      This doubleword address points to a 1K table composed of 128
                      8-byte character definition bit patterns.  The first byte
                      of each entry is top row, last byte is bottom row.

20   80-83  None      TERMINATE/exit from the PC-DOS program that has a
                      PSP located at CS:0000.
                      DOS 2.0 EXIT (INT 21H, service 4CH) is similar but
                      provides a means to leave an exit code and does
                      not require CS to point to the PSP.

21   84-87            DOS_SERVICES/invoke DOS service named by AH
                      (see Appendix B-2)

22   88-8B            DOS_TERMINATE_ADDR/vector points to address of parent
                      process.  Jumped to by TERMINATE (INT 20H)

23   8C-8F            DOS_BREAK_ADDR/vector points to address of Ctrl-Break
                      handling routine for currently executing program

24   90-93            DOS_ERROR_ADDR/vector points to address of critical
                      error handling routine for currently executing program
```

```
Interrupt  AH: Sub-
type  addr   function              NAME/Description
----  ----   --------   --------------------------------------------------------

25    94-97             DOS_DISK_READ/transfers control to DOS disk driver logic
                        Expects:
                         AL=drive number (0=A, 1=B, etc.)
                         CX=count of sectors
                         DX=beginning logical sector number
                         DS:BX=address of data buffer
                        Returns: Carry Flag=CY (1) if error and AH=error code
                        warning: leaves 1 word (old flags) on stack

26    98-9B             DOS_DISK_WRITE/transfers control to DOS disk driver logic
                        (see DOS_DISK_READ, INT 25H, for parameters)

27    9C-9F    None     FIX_IN_MEMORY/exit to DOS, but leave program and/or data
                        resident.  Expects CS:DX to point to first byte available
                        for subsequent programs.  DOS 2.0 KEEP (service 31H) is
                        similar, but provides a means to leave an exit code.

28-3F A0-FF             Reserved by DOS

40    100-103           Reserved: XT fixed disk BIOS

41-5F 104-17F           Reserved

41-7F 104-1FF           Not used, available for applications

80-85 200-217           Reserved by BASIC

86-F0 218-3C3           Used by BASIC interpreter (BASIC exit/patch vectors)

F1-FF 3C4-3FF           Not used, available for applications
```

# Appendix B.2

# PC-DOS Function Summary

```
function
code in AH                        NAME/Description
----------  ------------------------------------------------------------------

    0       TERMINATE/terminate the program that has a PSP at CS:0000.
            Works exactly like INT 20H.

    1       KEYBOARD_INPUT/read (wait for) a character from the standard input
            and echo that character to the standard output.
              returns: AL=character read

    2       DISPLAY_OUTPUT/send a character to the standard output device.
              expects: DL=character to output

    3       AUX_INPUT/read (wait for) a character from the asynchronous
            communications adapter (COMn or AUX).
              returns: AL=character read

    4       AUX_OUTPUT/send a character to the asynchronous communications
            adapter (COMn or AUX).
              expects: DL=character to output

    5       PRINTER_OUTPUT/send a character to the printer (LPTn or PRN).
              expects: DL=character to output

    6       CONSOLE_IO/receive a character from standard input or send a
            character to the Standard Output.
              expects: DL=FFH to fetch waiting input character from input.
                       returns: ZF=ZR (1) if not ready, else AL=character
            if DL is not FFH, then the character in DL is output.

    7       CONSOLE_INPUT/read (wait for) a character from the standard input.
            The character is not displayed.
              returns: AL is input character.

    8       NO_ECHO_INPUT/identical to function 1, but the character is not output.

    9       PRINT_STRING/send a string of characters to the standard output.
              expects: DS:DX points to the string to print.
                       The string must be terminated by dollar sign ('$'=ASCII 24H).
```

```
function
code in AH                    NAME/Description
----------    -------------------------------------------------------------------
```

A      BUFFERED_INPUT/read a string of characters from the standard input.
       expects: DS:DX points to input buffer.  First byte is maximium
                number of characters desired.
       returns: second byte [DS:DX+1] is actual length of input--less the
                terminating carriage return (ASCII 0DH)--the rest of the
                buffer contains the characters read.

B      INPUT_STATUS/see if the standard input has a character ready.
       returns: AL=FFH if a  character ready, AL=00 if no character

Note: DOS 1.0 and DOS 1.1: the standard input device is always the keyboard and
      standard output device is always the screen.

C      CLEAR_AND_INPUT/clear the standard input device buffer of any
       pretyped keys and then invoke an input function.
       expects: AL=input function 1, 6, 7, 8, or 0AH

D      RESET_DISK/flush all file buffers.

E      SELECT_DISK/select new default disk drive, query valid drives.
       expects: DL=new default drive (0=A, 1=B, etc.)
       returns: AL=total number of drives (floppy and fixed disk drives)

F      OPEN_FILE/open a file with unopened FCB pointed to by DS:DX.
       returns: AL=FFH if file not found, AL=00 if file found.

10     CLOSE_FILE/close file with opened FCB pointed to by DS:DX.

11     SEARCH_FIRST/search the current directory for first file that
       matches the name in the unopened FCB pointed to by DS:DX.
       returns: AL=FFH if no match
                AL=0 if match found, and
                DTA is filled with a 32-byte directory entry

12     SEARCH_NEXT/after calling function 11H, this will search for other
       files that match the specified wildcard (global) filename.
       returns: same as SEARCH_FIRST (function 11H)

13     DELETE_FILE/delete file named by the FCB pointed to by DS:DX.

14     READ_SEQ/read sequential data from the file named by the opened FCB
       pointed to by DS:DX.  Count of bytes is in FCB RECORD_SIZE field.
       returns: one record is read into DTA (see DOS function 1AH)
                sets FCB CURRENT_RECORD field for the next read operation
                AL=0 if transfer was successful (no error)
                AL=1 if end of file and record is empty
                AL=2 if DTA segment was overrun (can't cross 64-K boundary)
                AL=3 if end of file and partial record is read.

15     WRITE_SEQ/write sequential data to the file named by the opened FCB
       pointed to by DS:DX.  One record is transferred from the DTA to
       the disk and the FCB CURRENT_RECORD field is updated.
       returns: AL=0 if transfer was successful (no error)
                AL=1 if diskette is full or access denied (read-only file)
                AL=2 if end of DTA segment was encountered (overrun error)

16     CREATE_FILE/like OPEN_FILE, except the file is truncated to length 0.

17     RENAME_FILE/special FCB format is used to change the name of a file
       returns: AL=FFH if file not found or new name already exists
                AL=0 if no error

18     Used internally by DOS

19     CURRENT_DISK/return the current default disk in AL (0=A, 1=B, etc.)

```
function
code in AH                       NAME/Description
----------  ------------------------------------------------------------------

  1A     SET_DTA/establish a Disk Transfer Address.  In DOS 1.0 and 1.1, all
         diskette data transfers pass through this area.
         expects: DS:DX points to the new buffer for diskette transfers (DTA).

  1B     FAT_DATA/in DOS 1.0 and 1.1, returns DS:BX=address of the file
         allocation table of the default disk.  DOS 2.0 returns address of
         the FAT identification byte for the default disk.

  1C     DISKETTE_FAT_DATA/like FAT_DATA (function 1BH), but will return
         information about a specific diskette drive. (DOS 2.xx only.)
         expects: DL = the number of the drive (0=default, 1=A, 2=B, etc.)

  1D     Used internally by DOS

  1E     Used internally by DOS

  1F     Used internally by DOS

  20     Used internally by DOS

  21     READ_RANDOM/read one disk record into the DTA.
         expects: RANDOM_RECORD field of FCB to identify the record.
                  DS:DX points to FCB of an opened file.

  22     WRITE_RANDOM/like subfunction 21H, but writes a record.

  23     FILE_SIZE/search the directory for file named in FCB pointed to
         by DS:DX, then set the FCB RANDOM_RECORD field to the number of
         records in the file; i.e., total bytes/(bytes per record field)
         returns: AL=FFH if file not found, AL=0 if file found

  24     SET_RANDOM_FIELD/sets the RANDOM_RECORD field of the FCB pointed to
         by DS:DX to agree with the CURRENT+BLOCK and CURRENT_RECORD fields.

  25     SET_INT_VECTOR/change doubleword address in interrupt vector table.
         expects: AL = interrupt type
                  DS:DX = new address to place in vector table.

  26     CREATE_PROG_SEGMENT/build a PSP at the paragraph named by DX.

  27     READ_BLOCK/read one or more records from an open FCB (at DS:DX)
         into the DTA.
         expects: CX = count of blocks to read.

  28     WRITE_BLOCK/write one or more records from the DTA to the open FCB
         pointed to by DS:DX.
         expects: CX = count of blocks to read.

  29     PARSE_FILENAME/scan a command line and create an unopened FCB.
         Note: this call is not useful for command lines with path names.
         expects: DS:SI points to the command line to parse
                  ES:DI points to an area to build an unopened FCB
                  AL=bit flags for special options

  2A     GET_DATE/fetch the date according to the DOS internal clock.
         returns: CX=year (1980-2099)
                  DH=month (1-12), DL = day (1-31)

  2B     SET_DATE/set the date for the DOS internal clock.
         expects: parameters as GET_DATE (function 2AH)
         returns: AL=FFH if invalid date, AL=0 if operation successful
```

```
function
code in AH                NAME/Description
----------  -----------------------------------------------------------------

   2C     GET_TIME/fetch the time of day according to the DOS internal clock.
          returns: CH=hours (0-23), CL=minutes (0-59)
                   DH=seconds (0-59), DL=hundredths of a second

   2D     SET_TIME/set the time of day for the DOS internal clock.
          expects: parameters as GET_TIME (function 2CH)
          returns: AL=FFH if invalid date, AL=0 if operation successful

   2E     VERIFY_SWITCH/sets or resets the flag that DOS checks to see if a
          diskette write operation should be followed by a verify operation.
          expects: DL=0, AL=1 (turn verify on)
                   DL=0, AL=0 (turn verify off)
```

The following DOS services are new to PC-DOS version 2.00. Error handling for these functions has been standardized. When a function returns with the Carry Flag set (CF=CY=1), an error has occurred and an error code has been placed into the AX register. The following table names the error condition that is associated with the error code:

```
error return
 code (hex)    meaning
----------   ------------------------------------------------
    1        Invalid function number
    2        File not found
    3        Path not found
    4        Too many open files (no handles available)
    5        Access denied
    6        Invalid handle
    7        Memory control blocks destroyed
    8        Insufficient memory
    9        Invalid memory block address
    A        Invalid environment
    B        Invalid format
    C        Invalid access code
    D        Invalid data
    E        (not used)
    F        Invalid drive specified
   10        Attempted to remove the current directory
   11        Not same device
   12        No more files

------------------------------------------------------------

function
code in AH                NAME/Description
----------  -----------------------------------------------------------------

   2F     GET_DTA/fetch the current DTA into ES:BX.

   30     GET_VERSION/fetch AL=DOS Version number, AH=subrelease.

   31     KEEP_PROCESS/terminate a program, leaving its code and data resident
          expects: DX = number of paragraphs to remain resident (starting at
                        the paragraph of the PSP)
                   AL = exit code (may be interrogated via ERRORLEVEL)

   32     Used internally by DOS.

   33     BREAK_CHECK/set or query the level of DOS Ctrl-Break checking.
          expects: AL=subfunction:
                       0=fetch switch into DL (0=OFF, 1=ON).
                       1=set switch to DL (0=OFF, 1=ON)
```

```
function
code in AH                    NAME/Description
---------- -----------------------------------------------------------------

   34    Used internally by DOS.

   35    GET_INT_VECTOR/fetche the doubleword value of an entry in the
         interrupt vector table. Vector of the interrupt type in AL is
         returned in ES:BX. Note: returns original values of vectors changed
         via SET_VECTOR (function 25H).

   36    GET_FREE_SPACE/determine the amount of free space on a disk.
         expects: DL=drive number (0=default, 1=A, 1=B, etc.)
         returns: AX=FFFFH if invalid drive number; otherwise,
                  AX=sectors per cluster
                  BX=free clusters
                  CX=bytes per sector
                  Note: total free bytes = BX*AX*CX

   37    SWITCHAR/set or query the current command-line parameter delimiter
         (usually slash ('/') ASCII 2FH)
         if AH=0, then set the switch character to the value of DL
         if AH=1, then return the current switch character in DL
         note: This is an undocumented DOS service

   38    COUNTRY_INFO/fetch country-dependent data (currency symbol, etc)

   39    MKDIR/create a subdirectory.
         expects: DS:DX points to ASCIIZ string with path name of directory.
         returns: error code in AX if CF=CY (codes: 3 or 5)

   3A    RMDIR/remove a sub-directory.
         expects: DS:DX points to ASCIIZ string with path name of directory.
         returns: error code in AX if CF=CY (codes: 3 or 5)

   3B    CHDIR/change current directory to that named by ASCIIZ string
         expects: DS:DX points to ASCIIZ string with path name of directory.
         returns: error code in AX if CF=CY (code: 3)

   3C    CREATE/create a file (supersedes CREATE_FILE, function 16H).  Open
         the file, truncating it to length 0.
         expects: DS:DX points to ASCIIZ string with drive, path, and name.
                  CX=file attribute:
                  01H=read-only
                  02H=hidden
                  04H=system
                  08H=entry contains VOLUME label
                  10H=entry is sub-directory
                  20H=archive bit (used by BACKUP utility)
         returns: AX=error code if CF=CY (codes: 3, 4, or 5); otherwise,
                  AX=file handle

   3D    OPEN/open a file (supersedes OPEN_FILE, function 0FH).
         expects: DS:DX points to ASCIIZ string of path and filespec.
                  AL=access code:
                  0=open for reading
                  1=open for writing
                  2=open for both reading and writing
         returns: AX=error code if CF=CY (codes: 3, 4, 5, or 12); otherwise
                  AX=file handle

   3E    CLOSE_HANDLE/close a file (supersedes CLOSE_FILE, function 10H)
         expects: BX is 16-bit file handle returned by OPEN or CREATE
         returns: AX=error code if CF=CY (code: 6)
```

```
function
code in AH                    NAME/Description
---------- ------------------------------------------------------------------

   3F      READ_HANDLE/read bytes from a file or device.
           expects: BX=16-bit file handle
                    CX=count of bytes to read
                    DS:DX points to buffer to receive data.
           returns: AX=error code if CF=CY (codes: 5 or 6); otherwise
                    AX=actual number of bytes read
                    note: AX=0 means end of file reached


   40      WRITE_HANDLE/write bytes to a file or device.
           expects: BX=16-bit file handle
                    CX=count of bytes to write
                    DS:DX points to buffer containing data to write.
           returns: AX=error code if CF = CY (codes: 5 or 6); otherwise
                    AX=actual number of bytes written
                    note: error occurred if AX not equal to CX after call

   41      UNLINK/delete a file from a specified directory.
           expects: DS:DX points to ASCIIZ string of path and filespec
           returns: AX=error code if CF=CY (codes: 2 or 5)

   42      LSEEK/move file read/write pointer according to method and offset
           expects: AL=method code:
                    0=pointer is moved to offset from start of file
                    1=pointer is increased by offset
                    2=pointer is moved to end of file +offset
                    CX:DX=offset value (CX is most significant word)
                    BX=16-bit file handle
           returns: AX=error code if CF=CY (codes: 1 or 6); otherwise,
                    DX:AX=new value of file pointer (DX is most significant)

   43      CHMOD/change or query file mode (alter the attribute of a file)
           expects: DS:DX points to ASCIIZ string of drive, path, and filename
                    AL=subfunction code:
                    0=return file attribute in CX
                    1=set file attribute to that named by CX
           returns: AX=error code if CF=CY (codes: 3 or 5)

   44      IOCTL/input and output device control.  Writes control information
           to or reads status from devices that support IOCTL requests.

   45      DUP_HANDLE/duplicate a file or device handle.  This function creates
           a new handle that may be used to refer to an existing file or device.
           expects: BX=handle of device or file to duplicate
           returns: AX=error code if CF=CY (codes: 4 or 6); otherwise,
                    AX=new handle for same device.

   46      REDIRECT/force an existing file or device to refer to the
           data stream defined by another file or device.
           expects: CX=handle of current file/device
                    BX=handle of file/device that will take over the data I/O.
           returns: AX=error code if CF=CY (code: 6)

   47      GET_DIR/fetch the pathspec of the current default directory.
           expects: DS:SI points to buffer to receive ASCIIZ string pathspec
                    DL=drive number (0=default, 1=A, etc.)
           returns: AX=error code if CF=CY (code: 15)

   48      ALLOCATE_MEM/request DOS to reserve bytes for a process.
           expects: BX=number of paragraphs requested
           returns: AX=error code if CF=CY (codes: 7 and 8)
                    and BX is number of free paragraphs; otherwise
                    AX:0000 is address of allocated block
```

```
function
code in AH                    NAME/Description
----------  -------------------------------------------------------------------

   49       FREE_MEM/return an allocated block of memory back to the common pool
            expects: ES is the segment of a block allocated by ALLOCATE_MEM
            returns: AX=error code if CF=CY (codes: 7 or 9)

   4A       SETBLOCK/change the size of an allocated block of memory.
            expects: ES is the segment of the block to change.
                     BX=the desired new size of the block (in paragraphs)
            returns: AX=error code if CF=CY (codes: 7, 8, or 9)
                     and BX is number of available paragraphs

   4B       EXEC/load and execute a program.  Create a "child" process.
            expects: DS:DX points to ASCIIZ string of path and filename
                     ES:BX points to a parameter block (see below)
                     AL=method code
                        0=create a PSP, load, and execute a program
                          ES:BX points to parameter block:
                          WORD  segment address of environment
                          DWORD points to command line for program
                          DWORD points to first FCB to be passed
                          DWORD points to second FCB to be passed
                        3=load only
                          ES:BX points to parameter block:
                          WORD segment address to load file
                          WORD relocation factor
            returns: AX=error code if CF=CY (codes: 1, 2, 5, 8, 10, or 11)
            note: this function may need to load the transient part of
                  COMMAND.COM.  Therefore, COMMAND.COM must be available
                  at the path of the COMSPEC defined in the environment.

   4C       EXIT/terminate the current process, transferring control to the
            parent process.  Supersedes TERMINATE (function 0).  CS need not
            point to the base segment of the terminating process.
            expects: AL=exit code (may be interrogated by WAIT (function 4DH)
                     or by ERRORLEVEL batch commands).

   4D       WAIT/fetch the exit code returned by a terminated process
            returns: AX=return code of most recently exited process
                          AH= 0=normal termination
                              1=terminated by Ctrl-Break
                              2=terminated by critical error handler
                              3=terminated by KEEP (function 31H)
                          AL=1-byte return code (ERRORLEVEL code)
            note: This works only once per termination.

   4E       FIND_FIRST/find a file that matches a path and filespec.
            Supersedes SEARCH_FIRST (function 11H)
            expects: DS:DX points to ASCIIZ string of drive, path, and filespec
                     CX is the attribute to be used to find the match.
                     (see function 3CH)
            returns: AX=error code if CF=CY (codes: 2 or 18); otherwise
                     DTA (set via function 1AH) is filled with 43 bytes:
                     21 bytes--used for subsequent searches
                      1 byte--attribute found
                      2 bytes--time stamp of file
                      2 bytes--date stamp of file
                      2 bytes--low word of file size
                      2 bytes--high word of file size
                     13 bytes--ASCIIZ string: "filename.ext",0

   4F       FIND_NEXT/after a call to FIND_FIRST, this function returns other
            directory entries that also match a global filespec. Supersedes
            SEARCH_NEXT (function 11H)
            expects: must be called after FIND_FIRST (parameters are the same)
            returns: AX=error code 18 and CF=CY when no match is found.

   50       Used internally by DOS.
```

```
function
code in AH                       NAME/Description
----------  ------------------------------------------------------------------

    51      Used internally by DOS.

    52      Used internally by DOS.

    53      Used internally by DOS.

    54      GET_VERIFY_STATE/find whether the write-verify switch is OFF or ON.
            returns: AL=0 if verify is OFF; AL=1 if verify is ON

    55      Used internally by DOS.

    56      RENAME/change a directory entry to give a file a new name and
            optionally, move a file to a different sub-directory (same drive).
            expects: DS:DX points to ASCIIZ string of existing path and file
                     ES:DI points to ASCIIZ string with new path and filename
            returns: AX=error code if CF=CY (codes: 3, 5, or 17)

    57      TIME_STAMP/fetch or change the date and time stamp of a file.
            expects: BX=the file handle
                     AL=subfunction code:
                        0=change date to DX, time to CX
                        1=fetch date into DX and get time into CX
            returns: AX=error code if CF=CY (codes: 1 or 6)
```

# Appendix C

# Program Templates

## Template C.1
## Simple EXE Program

```
;------------------------------------------------------------------
; Template C-1.  Simple EXE program
; This format makes a complete EXE program.
; It would be the only object module name given to the linker.

stack_seg  segment stack
           db      256 dup(?)      ;create a stack area (typical size)
stack_seg  ends

data_seg segment
           .
           . (insert DB, DW, etc. data defintions)
           .
data_seg ends

code_seg segment
           assume  cs:code_seg, ds:data_seg
program  proc    far
           push    ds            ;set up a FAR return (exit to DOS)
           mov     ax,0          ; to location DS:0000 to the INT 20
           push    ax            ; in the PSP.
                                 ; note: no needed with DOS 2.0
           mov     ax,data_seg
           mov     ds,ax         ;set up to address DATA_SEG variables
           .
           . (insert main program logic here
           .
           call    local_proc    ;example call to near procedure
           ret                   ;FAR return to DOS
                                 ;note: DOS 2.0 may use INT 21H, subfunction 4CH
program  endp

local_proc proc near
           .
           . (code of local procedure)
           .
           ret                   ;NEAR return to PROGRAM
local_proc endp

code_seg ends
           end     program     ;specify starting address in END statement
```

**Template C.2**
**EXE Program with External NEAR Calls and Data**

```
;-------------------------------------------------------------------
; Template C-2.  EXE program with external NEAR calls and data.
; This format uses an external NEAR library of preassembled modules.
; This program module must be linked with all external modules:
;  LINK PROGRAM +MODULE1 +MODULE2 +MY_DATA
;  where MODULE1, and MODULE2 are names of OBJ files containing PUBLIC
;  procedures with the names given in the EXTRN declaration herein.
; See Templates C-3 and C-4 for examples of library procedures and data.

stack_seg  segment stack
           db      256 dup(?)      ;create a 256-byte stack area
stack_seg  ends

data_seg segment para public 'data'
           extrn   var_16:word, message:byte ;external data from MY_DATA

              .  (insert local data defintions)
              .
data_seg ends

code_grp group   code_seg, lib_seg         ;for library code linkage
code_seg segment para public 'code'        ;notice name and class
           assume  cs:code_seg, ds:data_seg
           extrn   proc_1:near, proc_2:near ;external procedures
program  proc    far
           push    ds              ;set up a FAR return (exit to DOS)
           mov     ax,0            ; to location DS:0000 to the INT 20
           push    ax              ; in the PSP.
                                   ; note: these lines not needed with DOS 2.0
           mov     ax,data_seg
           mov     ds,ax           ;set up to address DATA_SEG variables

              .  (insert main program logic here)
              .
           call    proc_1          ;EXAMPLES:
           call    proc_2          ;calls to external NEAR procedures
           call    local_proc      ; and a call to a local procedure
           mov     ax,var_16             ;access external variable
           mov     dx,offset message    ; and data
              .
              .
              .
           ret                     ;FAR return to DOS
                                   ;note: DOS 2.0 may use INT 21H, subfunction 4CH
program  endp

local_proc proc near

              .  (code of local procedure)
              .
           ret                     ;NEAR return to PROGRAM procedure
local_proc endp

code_seg ends
           end     program         ;specify starting address in END statement
```

## Template C.3
## Library Module: Data

```
;-----------------------------------------------------------------------
; Template C-3.  Library module: data
; This is the format for external data modules.
; It must be linked with a main program as described in Template C-2.

        public  var_16, message
data_seg segment byte public 'data' ;notice same name and class name
                                    ; as in program module
var_16  dw      1234H               ;PUBLIC variables and data
message db      'This is printed by DOS service "9"',0DH, 0AH,'$'
        .
        . (insert other data and tables and declare each PUBLIC)
        .
data_seg ends
        end         ;no start label for library modules
```

## Template C.4
## Library Module: NEAR Procedure(s)

```
;-----------------------------------------------------------------------
; Template C-4.  Library module: NEAR procedure(s)
; This is the format for external NEAR code modules to be called by
;  programs in the format of Templates C-2 (EXE) and C-7 (COM).
; More than one procedure may be placed in a module.
; The OBJ file of this assembly must be linked with a main program
;  as described in Templates C-2 and C-7.

        public  proc_1
code_grp group   lib_seg            ;will reside in the same physical
                                    ; segment as calling program
lib_seg segment byte public 'code' ;different name, same class
        assume  cs:code_grp         ; notice use of group name
        assume  ds:data_seg ;optional linkage to external data
proc_1  proc    near        .
        .
        . (code of this procedure is called by external program module
        .   or external library module)
        .
        mov     ax,cs:code_var ;example of optional use of code segment data
        .
        ret                 ;NEAR return to caller
proc_1  endp
code_var dw     1234H        ;optional inclusion of code segment data
lib_seg ends
        end     ;no start label for library modules
```

## Template C.5
## EXE Program with FAR Library Code Modules

```
;-----------------------------------------------------------------------
; Template C-5.  EXE program with FAR library code modules
; This contains the main program template as well as the external
;  library module templates for interfacing a FAR library to an
;  EXE program.
; It is similar to Templates C-2 and C-3.  The difference is that all
;  calls to library procedures are 5-byte FAR calls, and all library
;  procedures are in a different physical segment than the main program.
; This must be linked with all OBJ files containing external procedures.

            . (define STACK_SEG and DATA_SEG as in Template C1)
            .
lib_seg  segment para public "'code'
         extrn   proc_1:far, proc_2:far     ;<--- the linkage
lib_seg  ends

code_seg segment para public 'code'
         assume  cs:code_seg, ds:data_seg
program  proc    far
         push    ds           ;set up a far return (for exit to DOS)
         mov     ax,0         ; to location DS:0000 to the INT 20
         push    ax           ; in the PSP
         mov     ax,data_seg
         mov     ds,ax        ;set up to address DATA_SEG variables

         call    proc_1       ;FAR calls into external LIB_SEG modules
         call    proc_2
         ret                  ;FAR return to DOS
program  endp
code_seg ends
         end     program      ;specify starting address in END statement

;------------------------
; External code library modules used with this template

         public  proc_1, proc_2      ;<--- the linkage
lib_seg  segment byte public 'code'  ;same name as in program module
                                     ;byte alignment avoids empty
                                     ; space between library modules
proc_1   proc    far
            .
            . (code of this PUBLIC procedure)
            .
         ret                  ;FAR return to caller
proc_1   endp

proc_2   proc    far
         call    local_proc   ;example intramodule NEAR call
            .
            . (other PUBLIC code)
            .
         ret                  ;FAR return to caller
proc_2   endp
local_proc proc near
            .
            . (code of this local procedure)
            .
         ret                  ;NEAR return to PROC_2
local_proc endp
         end
```

## Template C.6
## Simple COM Program

```
;---------------------------------------------------------------------
; Template C-6.  Simple COM program
; This format makes a complete COM program.
; This is the only object module name given to the linker.  Use:
;  LINK program;
;      (ignore the "no STACK segment" error message)
; Then convert program from EXE format to COM format with:
;  EXE2BIN program program.com
; Then delete the EXE format version (it should not be used)

code_seg segment
         assume  cs:code_seg, ds:code_seg, es:code_seg  ;<-- all the same
         org     100H                    ;<--------------- very important ---
program  proc    far
         jmp     start           ;jump around the data
         .
         . (DB, DW, etc. data fields)
         .
start:
         call    local_proc      ;sample call to local procedure
         .
         . (insert main program logic here)
         .
         int     20H             ;direct exit to DOS
program  endp

local_proc proc near
         .
         . (code of a local procedure)
         .
         ret                     ;NEAR return to PROGRAM
local_proc endp

code_seg ends
         end     program    ;specify starting address in END statement
```

**Template C.7**
**COM Program with External NEAR Library Calls**

```
;----------------------------------------------------------------------
; Template C-7.  COM program with external NEAR library calls
; This format uses an external NEAR library of previously assembled modules.
; The PROGRAM module must be linked with all external modules:
;  LINK program +module1 +module2;
;       (ignore the "no STACK segment" error message)
;  MODULE1 and MODULE2 are names of OBJ files containing PUBLIC
;  procedures with the names given in the EXTRN satement in this module.
; Then convert program from EXE format to COM format with:
;  EXE2BIN program program.com
; See Template C-4 for examples of NEAR library code modules.

code_grp group   code_seg, lib_seg  ;linkage to library modules
code_seg segment
         assume  cs:code_seg, ds:code_seg, es:code_seg
         extrn   proc_1:near, proc_2:near  ;EXTRN declared in CODE_SEG

         org     100H             ;<--------------- very important ---
program  proc    far
         jmp     start            ;jump around the data

         .  (DB, DW, etc. data fields)

start:
         ...                      ;insert main program logic here.
         call    local_proc
         call    proc_1           ;NEAR call to external procedure
         int     20H              ;direct exit to DOS
program  endp

local_proc proc near
         .
         .  (code of a local procedure)
         .
         call    proc_2     ;NEAR call to external procedure
         ret
local_proc endp

code_seg ends
         end     program    ;specify starting address in END statement
```

## Template C.8
## BLOAD Module for Interpretive BASIC

```
;-------------------------------------------------------------------
; Template C-8.  BLOAD module for interpretive BASIC
; This format builds the BLOAD header into the start of a program
;  so that after assembling, linking, and using EXE2BIN, it may
;  be loaded directly with the BASIC BLOAD command.
; Link with:              LINK program;   (ignore "No Stack" message)
; Convert with            EXE2BIN program
; From BASIC use:
;  10 CLEAR, 32000            '** or use "free bytes" - length of program
;  20 PROGRAM = 32000         '** set up calling address
;  30 BLOAD "program.bin",PROGRAM '** load into BASIC's DEFault SEGment
;  40 CALL PROGRAM            '** or CALL PROGRAM (ARG1,ARG2,etc)
;
; Warning: Do not define data in this program format.  If temporary
;          variables are needed, place them on the stack or in a safe
;          place with an absolute SEGMENT:OFFSET address (such as 0:04F0).

code_seg segment
         assume  cs:code_seg, ds:code_seg, es:code_seg
program  proc    far
         db      0FDH       ;BLOAD file ID byte
         dw      0B800H     ;default segment (video memory for safety)
         dw      0          ;default offset
         dw      prog_len   ;length of the program (less the header)
begin:                      ;Note: the bytes of the header are not
                            ; loaded into memory.
         push    bp
         mov     bp,sp      ;point to arguments on stack
         mov     si,[bp+6]  ; example: fetch rightmost argument of call
         .
         . (code of procedure)
         .
         pop     bp
         ret                ;FAR return to BASIC
                            ;note: use RET 2 for one argument,
                            ; RET 4 for two, etc.
program  endp
prog_len equ     $-begin    ;code length needed for the BLOAD header
code_seg ends
         end     program        ;must have address for conversion with EXE2BIN
```

**Template C.9**
**Routine to Be Called for Compiled BASIC (BASCOM)**

```
;------------------------------------------------------------------
; Template C-9.  Routine to be called from compiled BASIC
;
; Link with:   LINK program +module;
; From BASIC use:
;   10 CALL MODULE(STR.VAR$,INT.VAR%)  'pass expected number of variables
;                                       in the expected positions

          public  module
code_seg segment para public 'code'     ;<--- must use CLASS NAME of 'code'
          assume  cs:code_seg, ds:nothing, es:nothing ;DS and ES point
                                                ; to BASCOM variables
module    proc    far
          push    bp
          mov     bp,sp        ;point to arguments on stack
          mov     bx,[bp+6]    ; example: fetch address of rightmost argument
          mov     ax,[bx]      ;          fetch value of integer argument

          mov     bx,[BP+8]    ; example: get address of string descriptor block
          mov     cx,[BX]      ;          CX becomes length of string
          mov     si,[BX+2]    ;          DS:SI points to first byte
          .
          . (code of procedure)
          .
          pop     bp
          ret     4            ;FAR return to BASCOM, discarding two arguments
                               ;note: use RET for no argument,
                               ;  RET 2 for one argument, etc.
module   endp

some_data        db 'this and that'  ;data may be accessed with CS: override
screen_buf       db 4000 dup(?)

code_seg ends
          end                  ;no start address
```

## Template C.10
## FIX_IN_MEMORY Interrupt Handler

```
;-------------------------------------------------------------------
; Template C-10.  FIX_IN_MEMORY interrupt handler
; This is a specialized version of the COM-format file of Template C-6.
; It is used to install or "capture" an interrupt handler.
; As a COM-format program, it must be processed with EXE2BIN.
;
code_seg segment
         assume  cs:code_seg, ds:code_seg, es:code_seg

         org     100H             ;<--------------- very important
program  proc    far
         jmp     install          ;jump around the data
old_vect dd  0                    ;DWORD used to store original vector

         . (other DB, DW, etc. data used by program)
         .
INT_TYPE equ 10H                  ;or whatever interrupt desired
install:
         mov     ax,0
         mov     es,ax            ;point to vector table
         lds     ax,dword ptr es:[INT_TYPE*4] ;fetch the old vector
         mov     cs:old_vect,ax             ;save the offset
         mov     cs:old_vect+2,ds           ;save the segment

         . (other installation code)
         .
;------- now change the vector to point to this program
         cli                               ;stop hardware interrupts
         mov     word ptr es:[int_type*4],offset my_int ;set the offset
         mov     word ptr es:[int_type*4+2],cs ; and the segment
         sti                               ;restart hardware interrupts
         mov     dx,offset last_byte       ;set up for INT 27H
         int     27H              ;FIX_IN_MEMORY exit to DOS
program  endp

;------- following code is executed on every interrupt of type INT_TYPE
my_int   proc far
         . (save all registers used)
         . (code to process the interrrupt)
         . (restore resisters unless returning values)
         iret                     ;return from interrupt

; or use:
;        jmp     cs:[old_vect]    ;to exit to original handler

my_int   endp
last_byte label byte
code_seg ends
         end     program  ;specify starting address in END statement
```

# Appendix D.1

# Hex to Decimal Conversion Table

Hex to Decimal Conversion Table

| | d1 | | d2 | | d3 | | d4 | | d5 |
|---|---|---|---|---|---|---|---|---|---|
| hex | decimal | hex | decimal | hex | decimal | hex | decimal | hex | decimal |
| 0 | 0 | 00 | 0 | 000 | 0 | 0000 | 0 | 00000 | 0 |
| 1 | 1 | 10 | 16 | 100 | 256 | 1000 | 4,096 | 10000 | 65,536 |
| 2 | 2 | 20 | 32 | 200 | 512 | 2000 | 8,192 | 20000 | 131,072 |
| 3 | 3 | 30 | 48 | 300 | 768 | 3000 | 12,288 | 30000 | 196,608 |
| 4 | 4 | 40 | 64 | 400 | 1024 | 4000 | 16,384 | 40000 | 262,144 |
| 5 | 5 | 50 | 80 | 500 | 1280 | 5000 | 20,480 | 50000 | 327,680 |
| 6 | 6 | 60 | 96 | 600 | 1536 | 6000 | 24,576 | 60000 | 393,216 |
| 7 | 7 | 70 | 112 | 700 | 1792 | 7000 | 28,672 | 70000 | 458,752 |
| 8 | 8 | 80 | 128 | 800 | 2048 | 8000 | 32,768 | 80000 | 524,288 |
| 9 | 9 | 90 | 144 | 900 | 2304 | 9000 | 36,864 | 90000 | 589,824 |
| A | 10 | A0 | 160 | A00 | 2560 | A000 | 40,960 | A0000 | 655,360 |
| B | 11 | B0 | 176 | B00 | 2816 | B000 | 45,056 | B0000 | 720,896 |
| C | 12 | C0 | 192 | C00 | 3072 | C000 | 49,152 | C0000 | 786,432 |
| D | 13 | D0 | 208 | D00 | 3328 | D000 | 53,348 | D0000 | 851,968 |
| E | 14 | E0 | 224 | E00 | 3584 | E000 | 57,344 | E0000 | 917,504 |
| F | 15 | F0 | 240 | F00 | 3840 | F000 | 61,440 | F0000 | 983,040 |
| | d1 | | d2 | | d3 | | d4 | | d5 |

Convert hexadecimal to decimal

| format | calculation |
|--------|-------------|
| wxyzH | d4(w) + d3(x) + d2(y) + d1(z) |
| vwxyzH | d5(v) + d4(w) + d3(x) + d2(y) + d1(z) |
| stuv:wxyz | d5(s) + d4(t) + d3(u) + d2(v) + d4(w) + d3(x) + d2(y) + d1(z) |

Convert decimal to 16-bit hexadecimal

| step | instructions | result |
|------|-------------|--------|
| 1 | Subtract largest value in d4, write corresponding hex digit | w |
| 2 | From difference, subtract largest value in d3, write hex digit | wx |
| 3 | From difference, subtract largest value in d2, write hex digit | wxy |
| 4 | Write hex digit of difference, append "H" | wxyzH |

Powers of 2

| n | $2^n$ | n | $2^n$ | n | $2^n$ |
|---|-------|---|-------|---|-------|
| 0 | 1 | 8 | 256 | 16 | 65,536 |
| 1 | 2 | 9 | 512 | 17 | 131,072 |
| 2 | 4 | 10 | 1,024 | 18 | 262,144 |
| 3 | 8 | 11 | 2,048 | 19 | 524,288 |
| 4 | 16 | 12 | 4,096 | 20 | 1,048,576 |
| 5 | 32 | 13 | 8,192 | 21 | 2,097,152 |
| 6 | 64 | 14 | 16,384 | 22 | 4,194,304 |
| 7 | 128 | 15 | 32,768 | 23 | 8,388,608 |

# Appendix D.2
# Decimal/ASCII/Hex/ Binary Conversion Table

| Dec | ASCII | Hex | Binary |
|-----|-------|-----|----------|
| 0 | NUL | 00 | 00000000 |
| 1 | SOH | 01 | 00000001 |
| 2 | STX | 02 | 00000010 |
| 3 | ETX | 03 | 00000011 |
| 4 | EOT | 04 | 00000100 |
| 5 | ENQ | 05 | 00000101 |
| 6 | ACK | 06 | 00000110 |
| 7 | BEL | 07 | 00000111 |
| 8 | BS | 08 | 00001000 |
| 9 | HT | 09 | 00001001 |
| 10 | LF | 0A | 00001010 |
| 11 | VT | 0B | 00001011 |
| 12 | FF | 0C | 00001100 |
| 13 | CR | 0D | 00001101 |
| 14 | SO | 0E | 00001110 |
| 15 | SI | 0F | 00001111 |
| 16 | DLE | 10 | 00010000 |
| 17 | DC1 | 11 | 00010001 |
| 18 | DC2 | 12 | 00010010 |
| 19 | DC3 | 13 | 00010011 |
| 20 | DC4 | 14 | 00010100 |
| 21 | NAK | 15 | 00010101 |
| 22 | SYN | 16 | 00010110 |
| 23 | ETB | 17 | 00010111 |
| 24 | CAN | 18 | 00011000 |
| 25 | EM | 19 | 00011001 |
| 26 | SUB | 1A | 00011010 |
| 27 | ESC | 1B | 00011011 |
| 28 | FS | 1C | 00011100 |
| 29 | GS | 1D | 00011101 |
| 30 | RS | 1E | 00011110 |
| 31 | US | 1F | 00011111 |

| Dec | ASCII | Hex | Binary |
|-----|-------|-----|----------|
| 32 |   | 20 | 00100000 |
| 33 | ! | 21 | 00100001 |
| 34 | " | 22 | 00100010 |
| 35 | # | 23 | 00100011 |
| 36 | $ | 24 | 00100100 |
| 37 | % | 25 | 00100101 |
| 38 | & | 26 | 00100110 |
| 39 | ' | 27 | 00100111 |
| 40 | ( | 28 | 00101000 |
| 41 | ) | 29 | 00101001 |
| 42 | * | 2A | 00101010 |
| 43 | + | 2B | 00101011 |
| 44 | , | 2C | 00101100 |
| 45 | – | 2D | 00101101 |
| 46 | . | 2E | 00101110 |
| 47 | / | 2F | 00101111 |
| 48 | 0 | 30 | 00110000 |
| 49 | 1 | 31 | 00110001 |
| 50 | 2 | 32 | 00110010 |
| 51 | 3 | 33 | 00110011 |
| 52 | 4 | 34 | 00110100 |
| 53 | 5 | 35 | 00110101 |
| 54 | 6 | 36 | 00110110 |
| 55 | 7 | 37 | 00110111 |
| 56 | 8 | 38 | 00111000 |
| 57 | 9 | 39 | 00111001 |
| 58 | : | 3A | 00111010 |
| 59 | ; | 3B | 00111011 |
| 60 | < | 3C | 00111100 |
| 61 | = | 3D | 00111101 |
| 62 | > | 3E | 00111110 |
| 63 | ? | 3F | 00111111 |

| Dec | ASCII | Hex | Binary |
|-----|-------|-----|----------|
| 64 | @ | 40 | 01000000 |
| 65 | A | 41 | 01000001 |
| 66 | B | 42 | 01000010 |
| 67 | C | 43 | 01000011 |
| 68 | D | 44 | 01000100 |
| 69 | E | 45 | 01000101 |
| 70 | F | 46 | 01000110 |
| 71 | G | 47 | 01000111 |
| 72 | H | 48 | 01001000 |
| 73 | I | 49 | 01001001 |
| 74 | J | 4A | 01001010 |
| 75 | K | 4B | 01001011 |
| 76 | L | 4C | 01001100 |
| 77 | M | 4D | 01001101 |
| 78 | N | 4E | 01001110 |
| 79 | O | 4F | 01001111 |
| 80 | P | 50 | 01010000 |
| 81 | Q | 51 | 01010001 |
| 82 | R | 52 | 01010010 |
| 83 | S | 53 | 01010011 |
| 84 | T | 54 | 01010100 |
| 85 | U | 55 | 01010101 |
| 86 | V | 56 | 01010110 |
| 87 | W | 57 | 01010111 |
| 88 | X | 58 | 01011000 |
| 89 | Y | 59 | 01011001 |
| 90 | Z | 5A | 01011010 |
| 91 | [ | 5B | 01011011 |
| 92 | \ | 5C | 01011100 |
| 93 | ] | 5D | 01011101 |
| 94 | ^ | 5E | 01011110 |
| 95 | _ | 5F | 01011111 |

| Dec | ASCII | Hex | Binary |
|-----|-------|-----|----------|
| 96 | ` | 60 | 01100000 |
| 97 | a | 61 | 01100001 |
| 98 | b | 62 | 01100010 |
| 99 | c | 63 | 01100011 |
| 100 | d | 64 | 01100100 |
| 101 | e | 65 | 01100101 |
| 102 | f | 66 | 01100110 |
| 103 | g | 67 | 01100111 |
| 104 | h | 68 | 01101000 |
| 105 | i | 69 | 01101001 |
| 106 | j | 6A | 01101010 |
| 107 | k | 6B | 01101011 |
| 108 | l | 6C | 01101100 |
| 109 | m | 6D | 01101101 |
| 110 | n | 6E | 01101110 |
| 111 | o | 6F | 01101111 |
| 112 | p | 70 | 01110000 |
| 113 | q | 71 | 01110001 |
| 114 | r | 72 | 01110010 |
| 115 | s | 73 | 01110011 |
| 116 | t | 74 | 01110100 |
| 117 | u | 75 | 01110101 |
| 118 | v | 76 | 01110110 |
| 119 | w | 77 | 01110111 |
| 120 | x | 78 | 01111000 |
| 121 | y | 79 | 01111001 |
| 122 | z | 7A | 01111010 |
| 123 | { | 7B | 01111011 |
| 124 | ¦ | 7C | 01111100 |
| 125 | } | 7D | 01111101 |
| 126 | ~ | 7E | 01111110 |
| 127 | △ DEL | 7F | 01111111 |

| Dec | ASCII | Hex | Binary |
|-----|-------|-----|----------|
| 128 | Ç | 80 | 10000000 |
| 129 | ü | 81 | 10000001 |
| 130 | é | 82 | 10000010 |
| 131 | â | 83 | 10000011 |
| 132 | ä | 84 | 10000100 |
| 133 | à | 85 | 10000101 |
| 134 | å | 86 | 10000110 |
| 135 | ç | 87 | 10000111 |
| 136 | ê | 88 | 10001000 |
| 137 | ë | 89 | 10001001 |
| 138 | è | 8A | 10001010 |
| 139 | ï | 8B | 10001011 |
| 140 | î | 8C | 10001100 |
| 141 | ì | 8D | 10001101 |
| 142 | Ä | 8E | 10001110 |
| 143 | Å | 8F | 10001111 |
| 144 | É | 90 | 10010000 |
| 145 | æ | 91 | 10010001 |
| 146 | Æ | 92 | 10010010 |
| 147 | ô | 93 | 10010011 |
| 148 | ö | 94 | 10010100 |
| 149 | ò | 95 | 10010101 |
| 150 | û | 96 | 10010110 |
| 151 | ù | 97 | 10010111 |
| 152 | ÿ | 98 | 10011000 |
| 153 | Ö | 99 | 10011001 |
| 154 | Ü | 9A | 10011010 |
| 155 | ¢ | 9B | 10011011 |
| 156 | £ | 9C | 10011100 |
| 157 | ¥ | 9D | 10011101 |
| 158 | ₧ | 9E | 10011110 |
| 159 | ƒ | 9F | 10011111 |

| Dec | ASCII | Hex | Binary |
|-----|-------|-----|----------|
| 160 | á | A0 | 10100000 |
| 161 | í | A1 | 10100001 |
| 162 | ó | A2 | 10100010 |
| 163 | ú | A3 | 10100011 |
| 164 | ñ | A4 | 10100100 |
| 165 | Ñ | A5 | 10100101 |
| 166 | ª | A6 | 10100110 |
| 167 | º | A7 | 10100111 |
| 168 | ¿ | A8 | 10101000 |
| 169 | ⌐ | A9 | 10101001 |
| 170 | ¬ | AA | 10101010 |
| 171 | ½ | AB | 10101011 |
| 172 | ¼ | AC | 10101100 |
| 173 | ¡ | AD | 10101101 |
| 174 | « | AE | 10101110 |
| 175 | » | AF | 10101111 |
| 176 | ░ | B0 | 10110000 |
| 177 | ▒ | B1 | 10110001 |
| 178 | ▓ | B2 | 10110010 |
| 179 | │ | B3 | 10110011 |
| 180 | ┤ | B4 | 10110100 |
| 181 | ╡ | B5 | 10110101 |
| 182 | ╢ | B6 | 10110110 |
| 183 | ╖ | B7 | 10110111 |
| 184 | ╕ | B8 | 10111000 |
| 185 | ╣ | B9 | 10111001 |
| 186 | ║ | BA | 10111010 |
| 187 | ╗ | BB | 10111011 |
| 188 | ╝ | BC | 10111100 |
| 189 | ╜ | BD | 10111101 |
| 190 | ╛ | BE | 10111110 |
| 191 | ┐ | BF | 10111111 |

| Dec | ASCII | Hex | Binary |
|-----|-------|-----|----------|
| 192 | L | C0 | 11000000 |
| 193 | ⊥ | C1 | 11000001 |
| 194 | ⊤ | C2 | 11000010 |
| 195 | ⊢ | C3 | 11000011 |
| 196 | — | C4 | 11000100 |
| 197 | + | C5 | 11000101 |
| 198 | ⊨ | C6 | 11000110 |
| 199 | ⊩ | C7 | 11000111 |
| 200 | ⊫ | C8 | 11001000 |
| 201 | ⌐ | C9 | 11001001 |
| 202 | ⊥ | CA | 11001010 |
| 203 | ⊤ | CB | 11001011 |
| 204 | ⊩ | CC | 11001100 |
| 205 | = | CD | 11001101 |
| 206 | ⊹ | CE | 11001110 |
| 207 | ⊥ | CF | 11001111 |
| 208 | ⊥ | D0 | 11010000 |
| 209 | ⊤ | D1 | 11010001 |
| 210 | ⊤ | D2 | 11010010 |
| 211 | ⊔ | D3 | 11010011 |
| 212 | ⊢ | D4 | 11010100 |
| 213 | ⊏ | D5 | 11010101 |
| 214 | ⊓ | D6 | 11010110 |
| 215 | ⧺ | D7 | 11010111 |
| 216 | ⧻ | D8 | 11011000 |
| 217 | ⌐ | D9 | 11011001 |
| 218 | ⌐ | DA | 11011010 |
| 219 | ■ | DB | 11011011 |
| 220 | ▬ | DC | 11011100 |
| 221 | ▮ | DD | 11011101 |
| 222 | ▮ | DE | 11011110 |
| 223 | ▬ | DF | 11011111 |

| Dec | ASCII | Hex | Binary |
|-----|-------|-----|----------|
| 224 | $\alpha$ | E0 | 11100000 |
| 225 | $\beta$ | E1 | 11100001 |
| 226 | $\gamma$ | E2 | 11100010 |
| 227 | $\pi$ | E3 | 11100011 |
| 228 | $\Sigma$ | E4 | 11100100 |
| 229 | $\sigma$ | E5 | 11100101 |
| 230 | $\mu$ | E6 | 11100110 |
| 231 | $\tau$ | E7 | 11100111 |
| 232 | $\Phi$ | E8 | 11101000 |
| 233 | $\theta$ | E9 | 11101001 |
| 234 | $\Omega$ | EA | 11101010 |
| 235 | $\delta$ | EB | 11101011 |
| 236 | $\infty$ | EC | 11101100 |
| 237 | $\phi$ | ED | 11101101 |
| 238 | $\in$ | EE | 11101110 |
| 239 | $\cap$ | EF | 11101111 |
| 240 | $\equiv$ | F0 | 11110000 |
| 241 | $\pm$ | F1 | 11110001 |
| 242 | $\geq$ | F2 | 11110010 |
| 243 | $\leq$ | F3 | 11110011 |
| 244 | $\int$ | F4 | 11110100 |
| 245 | $\int$ | F5 | 11110101 |
| 246 | $\div$ | F6 | 11110110 |
| 247 | $\approx$ | F7 | 11110111 |
| 248 | $\bullet$ | F8 | 11111000 |
| 249 | $\circ$ | F9 | 11111001 |
| 250 | $\cdot$ | FA | 11111010 |
| 251 | $\sqrt{}$ | FB | 11111011 |
| 252 | $^{n}$ | FC | 11111100 |
| 253 | $^{2}$ | FD | 11111101 |
| 254 | ■ | FE | 11111110 |
| 255 |  | FF | 11111111 |

```
NUL  null
SOH  start of heading
STX  start of text
ETX  end of text
EOT  end of transmission
ENQ  enquiry
ACK  acknowledge
BEL  bell
```

```
BS   backspace
HT   horizontal tabulation
LF   line feed
VT   vertical tabulation
FF   form feed
CR   carriage return
SO   shift out
SI   shift in
```

```
DLE  data line escape
DC1  device control 1 (X-ON)
DC2  device control 2 (TAPE)
DC3  device control 3 (X-OFF)
DC4  device control 4 (TAPE)
NAK  negative acknowledge
SYN  synchronous idle
ETB  end transmission block
```

```
CAN  cancel
EM   end of medium
SUB  substitute
ESC  escape
FS   file separator
GS   group separator
RS   record separator
US   unit separator
DEL  delete
```

# Index